Public Administration

Power and Politics in the Fourth Branch of Government

Kevin B. Smith
University of Nebraska–Lincoln

Michael J. Licari
University of Northern Iowa

OXFORD
UNIVERSITY PRESS

OXFORD
UNIVERSITY PRESS

Oxford University Press, Inc., publishes works that further
Oxford University's objective of excellence in research, scholarship,
and education.

Oxford New York
Auckland Cape Town Dar es Salaam Hong Kong Karachi
Kuala Lumpur Madrid Melbourne Mexico City Nairobi
New Delhi Shanghai Taipei Toronto

With offices in
Argentina Austria Brazil Chile Czech Republic France Greece
Guatemala Hungary Italy Japan Poland Portugal Singapore
South Korea Switzerland Thailand Turkey Ukraine Vietnam

Copyright © 2006 by Roxbury Publishing Company

First published by Roxbury Publishing Company
Published by Oxford University Press,
198 Madison Avenue, New York, New York 10016
http://www.oup.com

Oxford is a registered trademark of Oxford University Press

Library of Congress Cataloging-in-Publication Data available

ISBN 978-0-19-533069-4

Contents

Chapter 10: Implementation 245

Chapter 11: The Future of Public Administration. . . 271

Acknowledgments

As with any book, a large number of people deserve credit for their help. Both authors are grateful to reviewers of early drafts of the manuscript, including the following: Regina Axelrod, Adelphi University; Thomas Barth, University of NC–Wilmington; John Bohte, University of Wisconsin; Ronald F. Brecke, Park University; Bernadette Costello, George Mason University; Daniel P. Gitterman, University of North Carolina–Chapel Hill; Neil Kraus, Valparaiso University; Myron "Mike" Mast, Grand Valley State University; David Patton, University of Utah; Saundra Schneider, Michigan State University; Christopher Simon, University of Nevada–Reno; and Larry Walker, University of West Florida. While all errors that follow are our responsibility, any credit is rightfully shared by the reviewers, whose feedback greatly improved the book. Both authors also would like to acknowledge the good folks at Roxbury Publishing, especially Claude Teweles for his faith and patience in bringing this project to fruition. We would also like to offer a joint thanks to Kenneth Meier for sparking our initial interest in public administration, and for all of his support throughout the years. Finally, Mike Licari more than anything thanks Kirsten Licari for her unwavering love and support. Kevin Smith thanks Kelly and the kids, who, for reasons best known to themselves, put up with him. ✦

Preface

Public Administration: Power and Politics in the Fourth Branch of Government is designed to offer a concise and comprehensive introduction to the field of public administration. It is written for undergraduate students taking a first survey course in this field, a course that typically is offered by political science departments. With that audience in mind, this book approaches public administration from a political science perspective.

Specifically, and in contrast to traditional undergraduate texts in public administration, the thematic focus of this book is centered on power and politics. In a nutshell, this book is designed to show students the central political role of the administrative branch of government, and how that role influences and shapes the daily lives of all citizens. The book does not ignore the traditional public management topics such as decision making, budgeting, personnel, and organizational theory. Rather, it places these topics in their political context and relates them to the broader policymaking role of the bureaucracy. We strongly believe that this focus on power and politics makes topics such as public management and personnel administration inherently more interesting and meaningful for students.

With power and politics as a general organizing theme, the text has several specific educational goals:

- Define and introduce administrative agencies as a fourth branch of government, i.e., as organizations that are important political and policy actors. These actors have different roles, responsibilities, and limitations compared to the three traditionally studied branches of government. Nonetheless, they play an important and central role in determining, not just executing, the will of the state.

- Examine and explain the influence of public agencies in public policy decisions. This includes examining the nature of that power, where it comes from, and how it might be controlled.

- Highlight the tension between democracy and bureaucracy. A central paradox at the heart of the political system is democracy's reliance on the very undemocratic bureaucratic institutions that characterize the administrative branch of government. Democracy seems to need bureaucracy to function. In this book we seek to explain why, and lay out the implications of that dependency.

- Detail the role and legitimacy of public administration in a democracy. There is an uneasy and fascinating relationship between the democratically elected leadership in government and the bureaucracies needed to carry out their decisions. This forms a running theme through the book.

In addition to these goals, the text is designed to cover all the basic issues and topics expected in an introductory course, everything from the formal organizational characteristics of bureaucracy, to ethical dilemmas in the public service, to the pros and cons of spoils- and merit-based personnel systems. We cover all these topics, and more, by putting them into a context that fits with the overarching theme of power and politics.

Finally, the book deliberately adopts a nonformal writing style—we use a magazine rather than an academic journal approach to language. Our writing style, examples, and sidebars are aimed at making this introduction to public administration an interesting and lively read. ✦

Chapter 1

The Government You Didn't Know You Had

Or, Why You Should Be Interested in Studying Public Administration

Rural Texans tend to be an independent bunch. The stereotypical image is a politically conservative business owner, farmer, or rancher, raised on the myth of rugged individualism and a strong supporter of property rights. Not the sort of people, in other words, who favor big government programs. Or even small ones. Surely such citizens are the least likely group to start agitating for more government bureaucracy.

So what does a conservative, small-government group like this do to help spur economic development and advocate for their issues? Well, it asks for a bureaucracy. And it gets one: the Office of Rural Community Affairs (ORCA).[1] Created in 2001 by the Texas legislature, ORCA annually spends tens of millions of dollars on a wide variety of programs ranging from health care initiatives to business development to disaster relief.[2] Rural Texas communities and their legislators are by all accounts pleased with ORCA. Now there is an agency full of bureaucrats whose job, as Texas State Representative Warren Chisum put it, is to get to work in the morning and ask themselves, "What are the people out in rural Texas doing, and how can we help them?"[3]

The irony in this story is bigger than Texas. A *lot* bigger than Texas. You see, it's not just conservative, "small-government" types in rural Texas that have contradictory and paradoxical attitudes towards bureaucracy. It's Americans in general. We berate bureaucracy and we bash it. Yet we don't seem to be able to get along without it. In fact, we keep asking for more of it. What gives?

What gives is the American political system itself. At the heart of the American political system is an often uncomfortable marriage between bureaucracy and democracy. This marriage is a necessary paradox. It is a paradox because bureaucracy and democracy are opposing systems; bureaucracy is hierarchical and authoritarian, while democracy is egalitarian and communal. It is a necessary paradox because the American system of democracy requires bureaucracy in order to function. Disparaged, despised, and denounced as often as it is, we Americans rely on bureaucracy for an astonishing array of tasks that make society as we know it possible—everything from picking up the trash, to educating children, to patrolling our borders, to regulating the markets. We don't like bureaucracy, or at least the idea of bureaucracy, but we want schools, garbage removal services, law and order, and our stock brokers to be kept on the up and up. Contradictory as democracy and bureaucracy are in theory, in practice democracy (and that means all of us in a we-the-people sense) needs bureaucracy to get things done. What makes this paradox work is the subject of this book: public administration.

The organizational paradox that defines the American political system—and creates the need for public administration to make it work—is generated by two forces: (1) the demands that citizens place on their government, and (2) the means the government uses to meet those demands. Citizens expect a lot from government: roads and utilities, clean air, income security for the elderly, not to mention peace, law and order, and subsidized college educations. Rural Texans wanted help in promoting rural economic development and making sure they had access to adequate health care services. Held accountable to these demands by polls, the media, and the ballot box, elected officials seek to satisfy them. Fulfilling these demands typically involves a policy or program implemented and managed by a public agency—a bureaucracy. ORCA is just one small example of a bureaucracy brought into being through the response of a legislature to the demands of a particular group of constituents. Duly authorized by laws produced by democratic means, bureaucracies, among other things, collect taxes, mail Social Security checks, direct traffic, regulate electricity grids, license people to drive, fish, hunt, and marry, and provide grants and programs to promote economic development and health care programs in rural Texas. The job of public administration is to carry out these myriad tasks while ensuring bureaucracy serves the public interest rather than its own interests.

This is a task of considerable scope and complexity. Public bureaucracies play such a large role in the lives of citizens that the American political and social system has been called an **administrative state**. This term is used to "describe the great influence governmental agencies have on political, economic, and social relations in the modern nation."[4] The public sector in the United States is large, multilayered, and heavily involved in a wide range of social and economic activities that, as we shall see, shape the everyday lives of virtually all those residing with the nation's borders.

Despite its scope and importance, public administration is the least understood dimension of government, and for good reason. Public administration covers such a broad variety of activities that it defies definition. Studying public administration means studying organization theory, management, personnel, budgeting, and a variety of other topics, while simultaneously applying them all to diverse policy and program areas and multiple layers of government. If that was not hard enough, to make the "public" in public administration meaningful, it also means trying to systematically understand how all this can be combined to ensure that bureaucracy serves democratic ends without entirely encroaching on democratic means. Setting out to understand public administration is not a task for the timid, or for those without an ample fund of intellectual curiosity.

So why bother? Given the complexities and difficulties involved, why try to come to some understanding of the administrative state and the paradox that makes it work? In other words, why would anyone take the trouble to study public administration? Those are reasonable questions. To begin the examination of our topic, let us try to find some reasonable answers.

Why Study Public Administration?

There is more than one justification for studying public administration. Three of the primary reasons people decide to study public administration are for the career opportunities, for a desire to understand more about government's purpose and role, and, perhaps most importantly, because of public administration's important role in shaping individual interests and ambitions.

Jobs and Careers

The public sector presents an astonishing array of job and career opportunities. These opportunities are available at every level of government in all geographic areas of the country. Public sector employment includes everything from serving the nation in the military to serving burgers in a school cafeteria.

Government jobs are not just for those with career ambitions specific to the public sector. Regardless of your individual job or career ambitions, chances are the government employs people with those skills and qualifications somewhere. Public agencies at all levels of government need the talents of accountants, microbiologists, carpenters, lawyers, musicians—even people with degrees in political science or public administration. Closely aligned with the public sector are a number of nongovernmental organizations (NGOs) such as the Red Cross or Habitat for Humanity, which offer rewarding volunteer as well as career opportunities. While NGOs are not technically government operations, they often receive at least some funding from the public sector, and frequently enter into contracts with government to provide public services. Knowing more about public administration makes it possible to better navigate the public- and nonprofit-sector world of job and career opportunities, and also provides a good grounding for the particular (and sometimes peculiar) responsibilities and expectations that go along with working for the taxpayer.

Curiosity About Government and Society

A second reason to be interested in public administration is intellectual curiosity, or simply to become a more knowledgeable and effective citizen. Most college students have an essential grasp of the nonadministrative elements of the political system, its institutions, and its primary mechanisms, and some idea of how they are supposed to operate. If nothing else, a high-school civics class or even just intermittent attention to the news media should convey the basics. This should include a rough understanding of the division of powers; i.e., in the United States power is divided between three branches of government (the legislature, the executive, and the judiciary) and between levels of government (federal, state, and, to a lesser extent, local). It also should include a general understanding of what authorizes these powers (state and federal constitutions), and the primary mechanism that links the exercise of that power to the will of the people (elections). Anyone who has been through an introductory course in American politics should know that Congress makes laws, that the president is chosen by the electoral college, and that the U.S. Supreme Court has the final say in interpreting the Constitution.

But what do most people know about the bureaucracy? As it turns out, not much. Though America is an administrative state, with public bureaucracies heavily involved in virtually every element of social and economic activity, most people are unaware of how bureaucracies get this regulatory and management power over our daily lives and are largely ignorant of how it is exercised. Given the large role of bureaucracy in our lives, public administration is in some ways the missing element of a typical civics education—it is the part of government that the average citizen will have the most contact with and yet be least knowledgeable about. If you do not have at least a basic grounding in public administration, you simply do not know and understand how government and the political system operates on a daily basis.

Self-Interest

Perhaps the most compelling reason to study public administration *is* the large role of public bureaucracies in your daily life. Whatever you did today, it almost certainly was affected by—perhaps even made entirely possible by—public agencies. Consider the morning routine of a typical American:

> Today's citizens awake in the morning to breakfasts of bacon and eggs, both certified as fit for consumption by the United States Department of Agriculture (although the Department of Health and Human Services would urge you to eat a breakfast lower in cholesterol). Breakfast is rudely interrupted by a phone call; the cost of phone service is determined by a state regulatory commission. When our citizens drive to work, their cars' emissions are controlled by a catalytic converter mandated by the Environmental Protection Agency. The cars have seat belts, padded dashboards, collapsible steering columns and air bags required by the National Highway Traffic Safety Administration. When our citizens stop for gasoline, they pay a price that is partly determined by the energy policies (or a lack thereof) administered by the Department of Energy. To take their minds off the bureaucracies regulating their lives, the bureaucratic citizens turn on their radios. Each radio station is licensed by the Federal Communications Commission, and all advertising is subject to the rules and regulations of the Federal Trade Commission.[5]

Within the first few hours of being awake, this typical citizen has been directly or indirectly touched by at least nine local, state, and federal bureaucracies. The typical citizen does not escape this regulation when he or she gets to work. In fact, a significant proportion of Americans work in or for public bureaucracies—there are more than 21 million government employees, representing roughly 20 percent of the entire labor force.[6] Those who work in the private sector depend on these public servants. Private-sector employees get to their jobs over publicly built and maintained roads, then use one publicly regulated utility to power up their computers and place their trust in another when they get a drink from the water fountain (government agencies not only assume responsibility for ensuring that the water is available, but also for making sure it is safe to drink).

Though it can have something of a Big Brother connotation when described in the abstract, in practice the administrative state consists of people doing jobs that are woven deeply into the fabric of virtually every community. The administrative state in person is not a faceless and vaguely threatening bureaucrat, it is more likely your high-school teacher, the mailman, the meter reader, and the people driving the snow plows or filling potholes in the street. The administrative state plays such a large and prominent role in our lives that we take it for granted; we only notice its role and its importance when it is absent. When the lights do not come on, when the school is closed, when the letter does not arrive on time—these tend to be when public bureaucracies intrude upon our conscious thoughts.

iStock.

We bash bureaucracy and we berate it, but we also expect a lot from it. In the aftermath of natural disasters like hurricanes, for example, people expect the Federal Emergency Management Agency, the National Guard, police, fire and road departments, and many other public bureaucracies to do everything from restoring order to clearing debris, from finding housing to getting the lights turned on.

Consider taking a shower, brushing your teeth, or getting a drink of water—utterly mundane and trivial daily activities for millions of Americans. They weren't so trivial in Milwaukee, Wisconsin, when the municipal water supply was contaminated with the cryptosporidium parasite in 1993. Hundreds of thousands became sick; more than a hundred died.[7] The agency in charge of the city's water supply was rarely praised (or even thought of) when water was taken for granted, even though the fact that citizens could take it for granted required a considerable administrative and logistical feat. It certainly came in for plenty of criticism when things went drastically wrong. We think of bureaucracies when they fail, but rarely when they succeed, which turns out to be most of the time. A better understanding of public administration brings with it a better understanding of daily life in the twenty-first century and what makes it possible.

This extends to your particular individual interests. Whatever these interests are, they are almost certainly intertwined deeply with the role of public bureaucracies. For example, if you are reading this textbook, you likely have an interest in getting a college degree. For most people, obtaining a college degree is an ambition heavily dependent upon public bureaucracies. The vast majority of college students attend public institutions of higher education. These systems of higher education were, for the most part, created at the behest of state legislatures and heavily subsidized by the taxpayer—tuition at the average public university covers only about 20 percent of the actual cost of providing educational services.[8] The educational systems themselves, both individual institutions and the broader educational network they belong to, are bureaucracies that are responsible for staffing, supplying, and maintaining the basic operations of higher education. There is a high probability that you are reading this textbook at the insistence of an employee of a public bureaucracy (your instructor) as part of the requirements set by a public bureaucracy (your college or university) in order for you to achieve one of your individual interests (a college degree).

Even if you attend a private university, chances are that you are still at least partially dependent upon a public bureaucracy to fulfill your ambitions of a higher education. Most students take out loans or receive grants to finance their educations. The vast majority of these are guaranteed or directly funded by public agencies (on average, private-school students receive more grant aid per capita than public-school students).[9] By determining whether you are qualified for a loan or grant, and, if so, for how much, and by offering this financial aid at reduced or no interest, public agencies make college educations possible for a large number of students in private colleges.[10]

So, as it turns out, one of the central reasons to study public administration is yourself and your life. It is not just your grade, your student loan, your course work, and your individual college. Whatever you are interested in, chances are public administration is heavily involved. This extends from going to a music concert (permits and regulations are required for public performances), to eating a hamburger (which involves everything from regulations on the pesticides sprayed on the wheat used to make the bun, to the municipal ordinance requiring servers to wash their hands after using the restroom), to simply going to bed (check your mattress—there should be a tag on it that says that by law it can only be removed by the consumer). Public bureaucracies are with us literally from the time we wake to the time we go to sleep.

What Is Public Administration?

Pointing out the important role of the administrative state in daily life may serve to help spark an interest in our topic, but it does little to define exactly what that topic is. It is a relatively easy matter to point out why people should be interested in public administration; simply put, above and beyond its critical role in the political, social, and economic system, people should be interested in public administration

because it involves their jobs, their ambitions, and the routines and expectations of their daily lives. It turns out to be frustratingly difficult to
describe with precision and clarity exactly what that interest should be
focused on.

Because it covers such a vast array of activities and purposes, there
is no universally agreed-upon definition of public administration. Public administration is a multidimensional concept, and simple one-
sentence definitions tend to be either so narrow that they leave out
some of the core elements of our topic or so broad that they convey
only a vague idea about what is actually being studied. Scholars of
public administration approach their topic from numerous perspectives, and it is perhaps best to convey a realistic notion of what public
administration is by borrowing from several of these. Though doing all
of these perspectives justice is a book unto itself, the basic concept of
public administration can be usefully conveyed by looking at it from
three basic viewpoints: public administration as process, public administration as organization, and public administration as politics.

Public Administration as Process

Administration is generically thought of as "the art of getting
things done."[11] In order for any organization or group to achieve a
given goal there must be some way to make decisions and to translate
these decisions into action. This process of translating decisions into
actions in order to effectively accomplish goals constitutes the "art" of
administration. In a general sense, this is a good way to think of *public*
administration, as the art of getting the public's business done. As a
process of "getting things done," **public administration** can be defined as the means used to translate the will of the state into the actions
of the state.

At its heart, the process of administration is centered on answering
a single question: how do you get a group of human beings to do what
you want them to do? In other words, given a task or a goal, administration is about making decisions on how to best achieve that task or
goal, and then following through on that decision by coordinating the
activities of the members of that organization so that they effectively
fulfill the desired objective. Administration is thus not a unique activity of the public sector, it is a necessary component of any organization
or goal-oriented collection of human beings. For both public and private sectors, administration consists of the process of coordinating
human behavior to achieve organizational goals.

One of the things that separates public administration from private
administration is its sheer scope. To get some idea of the enormity of
what "getting things done" means in the public sector, let us consider
the primary activities and responsibilities of the various levels of
government.

Table 1.1 shows a basic breakdown of government in the United States. As can be seen, there are three basic levels and tens of thousands of particular units of government, and combined they employ millions and spend billions. Those millions are hired and those billions spent so that the decisions made by federal, state, and local governments can be translated into action. When Congress passes a law to, say, promote clean water standards, the 535 members of the U.S. Senate and House of Representatives do not themselves troop down to inspect the Potomac or the Mississippi, nor do they start testing for impurities in municipal water wells. In passing such a law they provide a basic set of objectives and guidelines and turn the details of implementation over to a public bureaucracy (in the case of clean water, the Environmental Protection Agency). That bureaucracy is responsible for mapping out the specific actions that need to be taken in order to fulfill the objectives of the law while staying within its guidelines, is given the authority to hire the requisite specialists, and is appropriated a budget to accomplish these goals. These are the means used to translate the law into action, the tools used to "get things done."

Table 1.1 also makes clear that though the federal government tends to get the most attention, government in the United States is in many ways concentrated at the state and the local level. Combined, state and local governments spend roughly as much as the federal government, and they have more than six times as many employees. At the federal and state levels government is largely a general-purpose operation, but at the local level governments can have fairly narrow jurisdictions. The most common form of government in the United States is a special district, a government created for a single purpose. They include school, water, and sewer districts (there are more than 13,000 school districts, plus 35,000 other forms of special districts in the United States).[12] Just because some governments have smaller or narrower jurisdictions, however, does not mean they have an easier time in terms of connecting the decisions of the government to its actions.

Table 1.1   Government Levels, Numbers, Employees, and Expenditures

Level of Government	Number of Governments	Number of Employees (thousands)	Total Expenditures (billions)
Federal	1	2,690	2,318
State	50	5,072	1,073
Local	116,756	13,277	996

Source: Census Bureau. 2004. *Statistical Abstract of the United States.* http://www.census.gov/prod/www/statistical-abstract-04.html.

School districts, for example, are largely creatures of state constitutions and state law. State constitutions create an obligation to provide free and equitable education to all citizens. This obligation is fulfilled largely by creating separate governments—school districts—and giving them primary governance responsibility for public education. In practice, what this means is that school districts set educational standards, staff and supply schools, and make the capital investments necessary to create and maintain the physical infrastructure of education. Even for a modest-sized district this is an enormous administrative challenge and costs millions. Imagine trying to find, hire, and negotiate contracts with a hundred appropriately qualified teachers, getting them physically sound and well-equipped classrooms, setting up gifted and special-education programs, and on top of that, running a library, a cafeteria, a custodial service, a tax collection and business office, and a small construction/physical maintenance crew, all while paying attention to safety, security, and accessibility to parents, not to mention fielding a football team. Doing all this would account for a minuscule percentage of the employees and expenditures in Table 1.1, and it would have to be replicated 13,000 times just to account for one type of special district. This should give you some flavor of what the process of public administration is all about—translating a laudable but vague goal like a quality "free and equitable education" into action. It is a complicated, costly, and labor-intensive proposition.

If government spending and employment provides a basic picture of what governments do and what public administration needs to get done, then the information in Tables 1.2 and 1.3 provides additional information about the functional divisions in government. These tables show the top three areas of expenditure and the three primary areas of employment for federal, state, and local governments. As these tables indicate, the program areas where the federal government dominates are national defense, social security, and postal services. State government tends to play the lead role in public welfare, corrections, and higher education. Local government shoulders primary responsibility for elementary and secondary education and police protection.

Table 1.2   Primary Areas of Expenditure

Federal Government	State Government	Local Government
Social/Income Security	Public Welfare	Education
National Defense	Education	Utilities
Healthcare	Highways	Police Protection

Source: Census Bureau. 2004. *Statistical Abstract of the United States.* http://www.census.gov/prod/www/statistical-abstract-04.html.

Table 1.3 Primary Areas of Employment		
Federal Government	**State Government**	**Local Government**
Postal Service	Higher Education	Elementary and Secondary Education
National Defense	Corrections	Healthcare/Hospitals
National Resources	Healthcare/Hospitals	Police Protection

Source: Census Bureau. 2004. *Statistical Abstract of the United States.* http://www.census.gov/prod/www/statistical-abstract-04.html.

These tables also contain information that shows there is no clean functional division between governments. While there is a rough division of responsibilities between governments, these divisions are not clearly defined. Healthcare and hospitals, for example, show up as big areas of expenditure or employment for all three levels of government (this is not surprising; the United States is an aging society and its citizens increasingly demand more attention to the needs of the elderly, who tend to be greater consumers of healthcare services). Though education is typically thought of as a state and local government function, the federal government also plays an important role. It provides special education funds to school districts. It provides research grants to university faculty and makes grants and guarantees loans for college students. This process of connecting the various levels of government and braiding their decisions into action is also public administration.

Public Administration as Organization

Public administration consists of more than just a process connecting decisions to actions. The process of public administration takes place within the confines of a distinct institutional form: bureaucracy. Bureaucracy is so dominant in the public sector that it is sometimes difficult to separate the study of bureaucracy from the study of public administration. Indeed, some professional students of public administration spend their entire careers studying bureaucracy.

Because the term has such a disreputable public image, it is important to clarify what public administration scholars mean by bureaucracy. As one public administration scholar observes, ". . . governmental bureaucracy is pictured as over-staffed, inflexible, unresponsive, and dangerous, all at once. The cultural image of "bad bureaucracy" is sharply articulated, unhesitatingly advanced and endlessly reinforced."[13] *Bureaucratic* in our culture is a term used to disparage, typically employed as a synonym for waste, inefficiency, and incompetence. Students of administration, however, use bureaucracy in more neutral terms. A **bureaucracy** from this perspective is a description of a particular form of organization. These organizations can do good things or bad things, but they are not preordained to do either. Max Weber (pronounced *vay-ber*) is generally credited with articulating the best-known description of the bureaucratic model of organization. Among his many talents (he is considered one of the founding fathers of sociology and public administration), Weber was a gifted observer of the evolution of the administrative state. He argued that a natural product of the development and industrialization of democratic states was an increasing reliance on a particular form of organization to carry out the will of the state. According to Weber, this organizational form—bureaucracy—had the following basic characteristics.

Division of Labor. Bureaucracies tend to have defined jurisdictional areas, and divide labor according to areas of expertise. In other words, bureaucracies are organizations whose objectives relate to a particular policy or program area, and they achieve their objectives by organizing themselves into units of subdivisional expertise, and setting down clear expectations of what these experts are supposed to do.

Hierarchy. Bureaucracies are managed through a clear vertical chain of command. Authority flows from the top, and everyone in a bureaucracy knows his or her superiors and subordinates.

Formal Rules. Bureaucracies base their management practices upon written documents that set down clear expectations of duties and behavior.

Record Keeping. Bureaucracies preserve an "institutional memory" by keeping detailed records of their actions.

Professionalization. Bureaucrats are hired and promoted on the basis of professional qualifications and merit.[14]

These characteristics describe virtually all public agencies (and many private organizations), and thus also describe how the administrative state itself is organized. There is an intense debate about the role and nature of bureaucracy as a defining characteristic of public administration. As we shall see in later chapters, some suggest that bureaucracy is responsible for some of the better-known failures of the public sector, and that this particular form of organization represents an obstacle to greater efficiency and innovation. Such critics have repeatedly proposed alternate organizational forms for the public sector. Such reform attempts (which have been particularly strong in the past couple of decades) have met with very mixed success in replacing bureaucracy as the basic organizational feature of public administration. We will go into more detail on the reasons for bureaucracy's resilience in Chapter 3. For present purposes, we shall simply point out that the bureaucratic form of organization has a number of advantages that make it well-suited as the primary organizational element of the public sector. For example, bureaucracy's reliance on expertise and professionalization means employees in the public sector typically hold their jobs on the basis of merit, not because they have a particular set of partisan loyalties. Because they operate by formal rules and keep detailed records, bureaucracies can be held to account for their actions because their behavior and rules of action are well-documented and readily available. Because they are hierarchical, "top-down" organizations, they can be guided (at least in theory) from the people or institutions at the top of their chain of authority, which ultimately is an elected official or institution.

It is also important to point out that though bureaucracy is a particular form of organization, public administration itself does not consist of *a* bureaucracy or *the* bureaucracy. Public administration covers the operations of large numbers of bureaucracies. Each of the governments listed in Table 1.1 has at least one bureaucracy associated with it, and some (such as the federal government) have hundreds. There are literally tens of thousands of public agencies spread across all levels of government with multiple and overlapping jurisdictions. Though they are mostly associated with and housed in the executive branches of the various governments, there is little in the way of central direction or coordination of these administrative units. Bureaucracy is simply the all-purpose tool of government—whatever the program or policy, when it comes to implementation and management, bureaucracy offers a good mix of efficiency, effectiveness, accountability, and political responsiveness. Other organizational options may be superior in any one of these categories, but there are few alternatives that blend these attributes in how they organize and operate the means to connect government decisions to government action.

Public Administration as Politics

Public administration consists of more than a particular organizational form housing the means to connect government decisions to government action. As it turns out, public administration is not just a tool to execute the will of the state; it plays no small role in *determining* the will of the state. In essence, what this means is that public bureaucracies exercise political power. Public administration can thus be studied as the "fourth branch of government."[15]

Like bureaucracy, politics is a term carrying negative connotations. It is often used to suggest activities that are driven by suspect motives and are thus untrustworthy. Political scientists use the term more neutrally to describe a process common to all human groups. All groups must have some means to make collective decisions, i.e., decisions that are binding upon the whole group. These means can consist of everything from counting heads to breaking them. But regardless of those specifics, the process of making these collective decisions is what political scientists mean by politics. **Politics** is most famously defined as "the authoritative allocation of values," or the process that decides "who gets what," and both definitions attempt to succinctly capture the notion of collective decision making.[16]

For a good part of its intellectual history, students of public administration have tried to make a clear separation between politics and administration. Politics was viewed as the process that culminated in a collective decision, the decision that authoritatively decided "who would get what." Once that decision was made, the process of administration took over in order to translate it into action. So while politics was the process of formulating public policy, administration was the process of executing public policy. The so-called **politics-administration dichotomy** was theoretically convenient because it meant the decisions and actions of bureaucracies did not have to be squared with democratic values. As public agencies were not viewed as independent agents of political power, the organization and operations of public administration could be viewed as simply the means to a previously (and democratically defined) end. As some scholars quickly recognized, the problem with adopting this intellectual framework to study public administration is that it is obviously false.[17] Administrative decisions turn out to be political decisions, and public bureaucracies to be political institutions.

How can public bureaucracies be considered political institutions? Well, as the means to connect government decisions to government action they have little choice but to make decisions about who gets what. A number of respected public administration scholars have recognized that because they have **discretionary authority**, or the power to make choices about the actions they take in response to a given situation, bureaucracies make political decisions. In essence, being given the authority to enforce the law means being given the authority to determine the law.

As an example, consider the highway patrol officer given the job of enforcing the speed limit. The posted speed limit is determined by state law, a decision made by a state legislature and agreed to by a state governor. A bureaucracy (the state highway patrol) is given the job of translating that decision into action, which in this case means ticketing those who violate the speed limit. But who really makes the decision on how fast you can drive before being in violation of the law? The legislature, the governor, or the individual highway patrol officer? In one sense it is obviously the individual officer. If he or she decides not to stop anyone who is, say, doing less than 10 miles an hour above the speed limit on that stretch of highway at that particular time, the speed limit is in reality 10 miles an hour higher than that decided upon by the state legislature. In this case, the **street-level bureaucrat** is making a choice that, in practical terms, sets the maximum allowable speed limit for all the motorists traveling in his or her immediate jurisdiction.[18] In other words, the officer has made policy.

This is not to suggest that unelected bureaucrats scheme to accumulate and arbitrarily exercise political power. As public administration scholars have repeatedly observed, in many instances bureaucracies have no choice but to make political decisions. Getting a legislature to pass a law or getting a city council to approve an ordinance frequently requires compromise. This typically translates into language that describes a general goal, but is short on specifics about how that objective is to be obtained. If the devil is in the details, the first job of the public agency given responsibility for implementing or enforcing the law or ordinance is to deal with the devil. It is one thing to pass a law with a laudable goal

iStock.

Hot careers in public agencies involve more than paper shuffling. Public bureaucracies offer an enormous array of job opportunities and career paths, everything from fighting fires to teaching public administration classes.

such as ensuring water is safe for drinking, fishing, and swimming, but quite another to set the minimum standards for discharging toxins and impurities into the environment and force private businesses to take the necessary steps to meet those minimums. Regulatory agencies are routinely given jobs similar to the latter scenario—formulating rules and insuring that all who fall under their program jurisdiction abide by them. Public bureaucracies do this by using their discretionary authority, the power given to them by law to translate the decisions of elected officials or courts into action. This discretionary authority is used to make collective decisions that are backed by the coercive power of the state—for most practical purposes, these decisions *are* laws.[19] In other words, they get the job of authoritatively allocating values whether they like it or not.

The implications of having bureaucracy exercise political power, and how that power can be controlled and kept accountable to democratic values, will be dealt with in depth in Chapter 5. For now, accepting the notion of bureaucracy as a political actor is enough to help us fill in our picture of public administration. More than 70 years ago,

John Gaus, one of the most influential public administration scholars of his day, observed that because bureaucracies have discretionary authority and have little choice but to use it, students of public administration have no choice about what they ultimately study: public administration *is* the study of a particular form of politics.[20]

How to Study Public Administration

Though we have no clean, comprehensive, succinct single-sentence definition of public administration, by now we do have a clearer idea of our topic. Public administration is a process; it is about connecting the decisions of government to the actions of government. In the vast majority of cases, this process is shaped and determined within the confines of a distinct organizational form: bureaucracy. This process includes making political decisions—deciding "who gets what"—and public bureaucracies can be considered political institutions or a fourth branch of government.

Painting a clearer picture of public administration, however, does not necessarily include a road map of how to study our topic. If we are interested in public administration, if we have some reasonably sharp notions of what public administration is, how do we go about systematically studying it? This is not as trivial a question as it initially sounds. Public administration can be systematically studied in a variety of different ways, each with a set of advantages and disadvantages. For example, one way to study public administration is through the case-study approach. **Case studies** are in-depth explorations and explanations of a particular organization or problem. The advantages of approaching public administration using case studies is the rich contextual detail they provide—they convey the "real-world" challenges public agencies face and the actions public servants must undertake to meet those challenges. The big disadvantage of the case-study approach is that its width does not match its depth. Reading in detail about, say, the budget crisis faced by a particular state university and how it was creatively addressed by university administrators might convey important lessons; but those lessons do not necessarily translate well to other types of public agencies, or even to other budget crises at the same agency that arise in different times under different circumstances. Case studies are often bound by time and space—they are very revealing about the particular case, but are hit and miss in their potential to shed light on other issues for other agencies. For this reason, the systematic study of public administration tends to organize itself around one of the three dimensions we used to help define the concept of public administration: process, organization, and politics.

One way to study public administration with an eye to getting more universal applicability from the lessons learned is to take a **manage-**

ment/decision-theory approach. This is essentially the systematic study of public administration as process, and it tends to concentrate on **core functions** of public administration, such as decision making, personnel management, and budgeting. Staffing, coordinating actions and behavior, and accounting are indeed critical aspects of what public agencies do, and the management approach provides an excellent way to approach public administration from the perspective of the technical expertise required to actually run a public agency.

There are two basic drawbacks to taking the management approach to studying public administration. First, the topic of management is often approached universally in the same sense that administration is universal. Because it is something that occurs in both the public and private sectors, management techniques and approaches are sometimes thought of as equally applicable to business and to government. For a number of reasons covered in depth in Chapter 3, this turns out not to be the case. Second, because much of the thinking and innovation on management is driven by study of the private sector, the management approach can be overly technocratic; it tends to deemphasize the all-important political context of the public sector.[21] Politics are simply too fundamental to the topic of public administration to deemphasize.

Another approach to the systematic study of public administration is through **organization theory**. This seeks to explain why public agencies do what they do by looking at how institutional structure and culture shapes decisions and behavior. Institutional scholars and organization theorists who concentrate on the public sector are, unsurprisingly, greatly interested in bureaucracy and its reform. Given that bureaucracy is such a fundamental feature common to virtually all public agencies, the organization theory approach makes a good deal of sense. Understanding how particular organizational forms and reforms shape decisions and actions can provide broad insights into why public agencies do what they do and how they could do their jobs better. The organization theory approach shares at least one drawback with the management approach—it often downplays the differences between the public and private sector. Organizations in the public sector have different motivations, different purposes, and different legal obligations and constraints than do private-sector organizations.[22]

An alternate approach is to organize the study of public administration around the concept of politics. This means viewing public administration as the fourth branch of government. This is the general approach to studying public administration adopted in this book. We do so for a number of reasons:

- The political approach to studying public administration does not mean abandoning any of the other systematic approaches. Budgeting and organizational structure, for example, can be viewed as reflections of politics.

- The political approach focuses study on a context universal to all public agencies. A municipal library and the Department of Defense both exercise discretionary authority (albeit in different ways and directed towards different ends) and they are both dependent upon external political processes—the politics that surround mission and appropriation decisions.

- The political approach better conveys an understanding of the reality of the administrative state that is at the core of our economic and social systems. Most people intuitively recognize a political element to public bureaucracies, but it is usually a source of confusion and frustration (or disparagement) rather than enlightenment. The running theme in this book is that bureaucracies are political, but neither bureaucracy nor politics bears much resemblance to its popular image. Understand where, why, and how they intersect, and, we believe, you will have a firm grasp of public administration—what it is, what it does, how it does it, why it does it, and why you should be interested.

Conclusion

Despite its importance to the political, social, and economic systems—not to mention your own daily life—there are good reasons why public administration is frequently an understudied topic. Its sheer scope makes it hard to conceptualize in any meaningful or systematic fashion, and there is no universally agreed-upon definition of public administration. Yet there are good reasons to be interested in the study of public administration, it is possible to gain a clear grasp of the concept of public administration, and it is possible to study public administration systematically. The purpose of this chapter was to convince you of these possibilities and provide a basic road map for understanding how they can be realized.

Gaining some interest in public administration, getting a basic idea of what public administration is, and forming some systematic plan for attacking our topic, however, still leaves more questions than answers. Why do we have so much bureaucracy? Where did it come from? How do we control it and make sure it stays accountable to democratic values? How does it do its job? How do we know when it is doing a good job? Can we make it do a better job? The rest of this book is devoted to answering such questions.

Key Concepts

administration The art of getting things done.

administrative state A term used to describe the influence government agencies have on politics, economics, and other social activities.

bureaucracy A type of organization characterized by division of labor, hierarchy, formal rules, record keeping, and professionalization.

case studies In-depth explorations of a particular organization or problem.

core functions The primary tasks public agencies undertake, which include decision making, personnel management, and budgeting.

discretionary authority The power to make choices about what action to take.

management/decision-theory approach The systematic study of public administration as process. This approach focuses on the core functions of public administration, such as decision making and personnel management.

organization theory A theory that seeks to explain the behaviors of organizations.

politics The process of deciding who gets what.

politics-administration dichotomy The idea that politics and administration can be separated, with elected officials deciding who gets what, and bureaucrats implementing those decisions.

public administration The means used to translate the will of the state into the actions of the state.

street-level bureaucrat A public agency employee who actually performs the actions that implement laws. ✦

Chapter 2

The Administrative State

Or, Where Did All This Bureaucracy Come From?

As Chapter 1 shows, the administrative state plays such a large and constant role in our daily lives that we take it for granted. For many people it is unsettling to fully recognize the important role government bureaucracies play in how we live our lives. That role fuels visions of a Big Brother bureaucracy, a behemoth with a voracious appetite for tax dollars and power. Such visions seem to stand in stark contrast to the political ideals that the United States was founded on. The Founding Fathers believed in limited government: the notion that the government that governs the least, governs the best. Americans were so resistant to the notion of a powerful centralized government that the first national government in the United States, formed under the Articles of Confederation, had almost no power at all (it could not even levy taxes). Many opposed ratification of the United States Constitution on the grounds it created a central government with too much power. Given America's long suspicion of concentration of power in government, it is not surprising that the administrative state is usually seen in a negative light: "big government" means "oppressive government," it means bureaucracy meddling in the economy and our personal lives.[1] Yet if Americans are historically suspicious of big government and resist giving it too much power, where did all this bureaucracy come from? Why do we have the administrative state?

The short answer to such questions is simple: we need a large administrative branch of government and, moreover, we *want* a large administrative branch of government. While Americans have never fully relinquished the limited government philosophy that guided the Founding Fathers in constructing our system of government, the needs of that system as expressed through the democratic process have all but demanded an administrative state. The Texas Office of Rural Community Affairs (ORCA) discussed in the opening pages of Chapter 1 provides a perfect microcosm of how the administrative state is created and grows: even the most fervent small-government constituencies pressure the political system to respond to their interests. The result is laws and programs enforced and run by bureaucracy. This should seem to be perfectly reasonable to everyone in a democracy; a democratic government should listen to its citizens and should have the means to respond accordingly. The administrative state, in short, is a political project that has been under construction in the United States for more than two centuries, and there are few signs this building project is slowing.

In this chapter we are going to show why we need an administrative branch of government, why it is so big, and why the administrative state takes the form it does. Many of the answers boil down to politics. The demands we as citizens make on government, and the roles we assign our public organizations, create the administrative state and cause it to be organized in a very particular fashion.

The Need for Public Administration

Public administration and bureaucracy are not mentioned in the Constitution. This could be taken as proof that the Founding Fathers did not intend for our government to have a bureaucracy. If so, such intentions were quickly abandoned; one of the first acts of the new government formed under the Constitution was to create three major federal agencies. Though the Constitution says nothing about bureaucracy, the duties and responsibilities it assigns to the president and to Congress made an administrative arm of government a necessity. This need can be complicated to fully explain, but the underlying idea is simple enough: elected officials can't do it all themselves.

The Constitution gives rather broad policymaking powers to Congress, including the powers to levy taxes and spend government money (the so-called power of the purse). The president is assigned the positions of chief diplomat, commander-in-chief of the armed forces, and chief executive of government departments. Therefore, he is in charge of faithfully executing the laws of the land. The only time the Constitution directs our attention to an administrative state is in assigning the president the position of principal officer of the executive departments. Naturally, we cannot expect one individual, as president, to personally execute all of the laws of the land. We do not expect the occupant of the White House to micromanage all the programs and laws mandated by Congress. The authors of the Constitution did not expect this either, and they implied a set of administrative institutions was needed to actually carry out the decisions of the government. The base answer to the question of why we have an administrative state is simple: our system of government needs it for practical purposes, so that Congress and the president can carry out their constitutional duties.

This is illustrated by the creation of those first three executive departments: Treasury, State, and War. These perform what have been called the essential functions of government,[2] and are direct results of the particular powers reserved in the Constitution for the legislative and executive branches. Because the president is assigned the duties of chief diplomat and commander-in-chief of the armed forces, but cannot carry them out alone, the Departments of State and War were necessary to help him in these missions. It seems unreasonable, after all, to expect the president to raise, train, and equip an army all by himself, not to mention personally attend to every communication from a foreign government. The Department of Treasury was conceived to help Congress fulfill its roles of taxing and spending. While Congress might pass a law levying taxes, it was never believed that the legislators themselves would actually collect the money, keep the accounts, and write the checks.

Yet if constitutional necessity were the complete answer to why we have an administrative state, public administration would be a relatively brief topic, and our national government would have only three departments. It should be obvious, though, that there is more to this issue than constitutional duties. The federal government has more than three departments, and our government is not limited to performing the essential duties of diplomacy, national defense, and taxation. The administrative branches of state and local government also have more than "essential duty" agencies that are not mandated by their constitutions or charters. Examining constitutional powers can only explain (and partially at that) why an administrative arm of government is fundamentally necessary, not why we have such an extensive administrative state.

So the next questions become: why is our government's administrative arm so large, how did it get there, and why does it continue to grow? The answers to these questions have two parts. The first component is related to what we expect of our government. The second component is related to how the policy process works in the United States.

Understanding the Rise of the Administrative State

The federal government makes a good case study to answer these questions (similar developments occurred in most states, though the variation at the state and local levels is so large that accounting for it might detract from the central points). Our national government has obviously grown tremendously since its establishment. The number of departments has increased from three to 15. Alongside these 15

Sidebar 2.1   Just How Big Is Our Government?

It is true that the size of the federal government has increased dramatically since 1900. Many people even assume that the size of the federal bureaucracy is constantly expanding. Nothing could be further from the truth! While the number of federal employees does go up on occasion, it does not constantly do so. It also occasionally goes down. In 2001 federal civilian employment was just shy of 2.7 million people, excluding uniformed members of the military but including all civilian defense department workers and postal workers. This is 12 percent *fewer* than the federal government employed in 1985. Increases in federal employment on the figure below are due primarily to new government programs (the social programs and regulations started in the late 1960s, or the "war on drugs" in the 1980s). It is also interesting to note that most federal employees to not work in or near Washington, D.C. Only about 16 percent work in Washington D.C., Virginia, and Maryland.

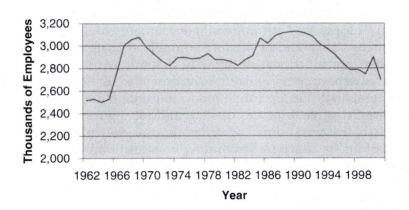

Federal Employment 1962–2001

So just how big is this, relative to our population and to other countries? As of 2001, total federal civilian employment represented just 1 percent of the population of the United States. In comparison, the total number of state and local bureaucrats was *over 6 times higher*. In fact, the number of state and local bureaucrats in California and Texas together outnumber the total number of federal civilian employees.[a] Compared to other similar countries, our bureaucracy is about average. In 1999, total civilian government employment in the United States (federal, state, and local) represented 14 percent of all employees. Figures for Canada, France, Australia, and Germany were 16 percent, 18.3 percent, 15.6 percent, and 11 percent, respectively.[b] So, it can not be said that our administrative state is "out of control" compared to other countries'.

[a]From the U.S. Census. http://www.census.gov/govs/www/index.html.
[b]OECD. 2002. *Highlights of the Public Sector Pay and Employment Trends, 2002 Update.*
   Paris: Organization for Economic Cooperation and Development.

cabinet departments is a host of independent agencies and even government-owned corporations[3] (see Figure 2.1).

The most familiar federal administrative organizations are **departments**. Each is headed by a cabinet secretary appointed by the president, and within each cabinet department is a host of bureaus, offices, administrations, and services. For example, in the Department of Agriculture, you will find the Farm Service Agency (which stabilizes commodity prices and provides income support to farmers), the Grain Inspectors, Packers, and Stockyards Administration (to facilitate the marketing of grain and meat), the Food Safety Inspection Service (to protect the public from food-borne illness), and the Food and Nutrition Service (which administers welfare programs aimed at providing adequate nutrition, such as food stamps) (see Figure 2.2).

Departments, though, are far from the only type of federal agency. **Independent regulatory boards and commissions** are also an important component of our administrative state. Chances are that you have heard of some of them, while you probably have not heard of others. You should be familiar with the Federal Reserve Board, chaired by Alan Greenspan, which is in charge of managing the supply of money (and thus the economy) in the country. Another familiar one is the National Transportation Safety Board, responsible for investigating and preventing airplane, highway, and other transportation accidents. All of these organizations are headed by a board or commission of many people, rather than just one person, as is the case in departments and their subunits. The members of these boards and commissions are appointed by the president, as are department and bureau leaders, but they enjoy protection from removal. They also serve longer terms, generally longer than the president's own term. All of these features were designed to make these organizations more independent of political control from either the president or Congress.

The administrative state even includes some **government corporations**. For the most part these look and act like private companies. Some of these try to make a profit (for example, Amtrak), while others do not (such as the Federal Deposit Insurance Corporation). Other examples of government corporations are the Postal Service and the Corporation for Public Broadcasting. Government corporations have more flexibility than normal government agencies, and can do things like buy property and real estate on their own. This flexibility and ability to make property purchases has obvious benefits for Amtrak and the Postal Service.

Where Did All of This Come From?

This huge collection of departments, agencies, commissions, and public corporations is no accident. They all exist because of a per-

The Government of the United States

Figure 2.1 Organization of the Federal Government

The Constitution

Legislative Branch

The Congress

Senate House

Architect of the Capitol
United States Botanic Garden
General Accounting Office*
Government Printing Office
Library of Congress
Congressional Budget Office

Executive Branch

The President

The Vice President

Executive Office of the President

White House Office
Office of the Vice President
Council of Economic Advisers
Council on Environmental Quality
National Security Council
Office of Administration

Office of Management and Budget
Office of National Drug Control Policy
Office of Policy Development
Office of Science and Technology Policy
Office of the U.S. Trade Representative

Judicial Branch

The Supreme Court of the United States

United States Courts of Appeals
United States District Courts
Territorial Courts
United States Court of International Trade
United States Court of Federal Claims
United States Court of Appeals for the Armed Forces

United States Tax Court
United States Court of Appeals for Veterans Claims
Administrative Office of the United States Courts
Federal Judicial Center
United States Sentencing Commission

Department of Agriculture
Department of Commerce
Department of Defense
Department of Education
Department of Energy
Department of Health and Human Services
Department of Homeland Security
Department of Housing and Urban Development

Department of the Interior
Department of Justice
Department of Labor
Department of State
Department of Transportation
Department of the Treasury
Department of Veterans Affairs

Independent Establishments and Government Corporations

African Development Foundation
Central Intelligence Agency
Commodity Futures Trading Commission
Consumer Product Safety Commission
Corporation for National and Community Service
Defense Nuclear Facilities Safety Board
Environmental Protection Agency
Equal Employment Opportunity Commission
Export-Import Bank of the U.S.
Farm Credit Administration
Federal Communications Commission
Federal Deposit Insurance Corporation
Federal Election Commission
Federal Housing Finance Board

Federal Labor Relations Authority
Federal Maritime Commission
Federal Mediation and Conciliation Service
Federal Mine Safety and Health Review Commission
Federal Reserve System
Federal Retirement Thrift Investment Board
Federal Trade Commission
General Services Administration
Inter-American Foundation
Merit Systems Protection Board
National Aeronautics and Space Administration
National Archives and Records Administration
National Capital Planning Commission
National Credit Union Administration

National Foundation on the Arts and the Humanities
National Labor Relations Board
National Mediation Board
National Railroad Passenger Corporation (Amtrak)
National Science Foundation
National Transportation Safety Board
Nuclear Regulatory Commission
Occupational Safety and Health Review Commission
Office of Government Ethics
Office of Personnel Management
Office of Special Counsel
Overseas Private Investment Corporation
Peace Corps
Pension Benefit Guaranty Corporation

Postal Rate Commission
Railroad Retirement Board
Securities and Exchange Commission
Selective Service System
Small Business Administration
Social Security Administration
Tennessee Valley Authority
Trade and Development Agency
U.S. Agency for International Development
U.S. Commission on Civil Rights
U.S. International Trade Commission
U.S. Postal Service

---

*Officially renamed Government Accountability Office, effective July 7, 2004.

Source: Office of the Federal Register, National Archives and Records Administration. 2005. *U.S. Government Manual, 2004–2005.* Washington, DC: U.S. Government Printing Office, 21. http://frwebgate.access.gpo.gov/cgi-bin/getdoc.cgi?dbname=2004_government_manual&docid=198805tx_xxx-2.pdf.

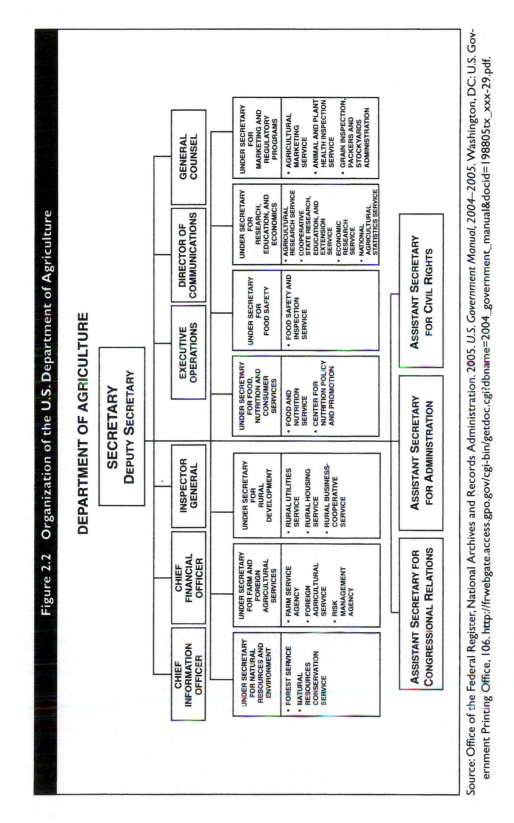

Figure 2.2   Organization of the U.S. Department of Agriculture

Source: Office of the Federal Register, National Archives and Records Administration. 2005. *U.S. Government Manual, 2004–2005.* Washington, DC: U.S. Government Printing Office, 106. http://frwebgate.access.gpo.gov/cgi-bin/getdoc.cgi?dbname=2004_government_manual&docid=198805tx_xxx-29.pdf.

ceived need or desire strong enough to prompt a response from the elected branches of government. A wide range of constituencies—we the people, in other words—asked for them. The notion of popular demand for big government may seem strange to those who believe in limited government and thought such principles were widely shared, even the bedrock on which the political system was founded. Although limited government may have been the guiding philosophy of the Founding Fathers, our expectations of government are very different from theirs. A more accurate way to describe what most Americans currently believe about government is the notion of **positive government**, not limited government. Positive government is the idea that the government is a useful and legitimate tool to fix and prevent social and economic problems. This philosophy is supported by liberals and conservatives alike, though often for different reasons. Liberals may want to increase government aid to poor families, or impose stricter controls on pollution and oil drilling. Conservatives may want to increase aid to small business owners, or impose stricter controls on the availability of pornography. The fact is that even though not all of us will agree on what to fix in society, most of us agree that we should use the government to do it.

Furthermore, as our country gets larger (both in terms of population and the size of our economy), our problems become more complicated. More complex problems often require more complex government responses, which require more resources, which means the administrative state will grow.[4] For example, larger communities require extensive planning and support—they require roads, schools, sewer and water facilities, and other programs and services on a large scale. The larger the scale, the more complex the problems, the greater the demands placed on government. Economic growth means we need more adjustments to manage booms and busts, to ensure fairness, to prevent fraud, and to foster the development of new markets. All of this requires more administrative resources to deliver what we want and need.

Some of the first uses of positive government were to solve economic problems in the late 1800s and early 1900s. Up until this time, the federal government did not regulate industries or economic activity. Based on a *laissez faire* philosophy of market competition (that is, the government should keep its hands off the market and allow it to function without controls), the federal government imposed almost no regulation at all on economic activity. As a result, some serious problems developed when companies became larger, more powerful, and more wealthy. As individual companies began to dominate their industries, these monopolistic trends represented a serious problem. Monopolies mean that competition disappears, and along with it, free markets. Prices and rates can be arbitrarily set (including extortionate pricing), consumers end up paying higher retail prices, the quality of products may diminish, and new competition is prevented.

As a response to the growth of monopolies in the late 1800s and early 1900s, several government agencies were created and policies passed to reduce the negative effects of the lack of competition. For example, the Interstate Commerce Commission (ICC) was created in 1887 to regulate railroads as a result of a Supreme Court decision. The Sherman Anti-Trust Act was passed in 1890 to ensure market competition by eliminating price fixing and monopolies. Organizations such as the Federal Reserve Board (FRB, created in 1913) and the Federal Trade Commission (FTC, created in 1914) were established to protect investors and consumers. Although the ICC has been disbanded, the rest of these organizations, along with the Sherman Anti-Trust Act, are still in use today. Some of the oldest portions of our bureaucracy were designed to manage the market to ensure competition and protect consumers against dangerous products and unfair trade. These obviously useful tasks are still being performed today by some of the same organizations (see Sidebar 2.2).

The idea of positive government remains strong. After the early 1900s, when we were creating agencies to solve problems in our economy, we did not dust off our hands and declare that we were finished. Instead, recognizing this tremendous power to fix social problems, we expanded our focus to include issues of consumer and worker protection. In fact, some of this shift began at the same time that we were designing policies and government agencies to deal with economic problems. When Upton Sinclair published *The Jungle* in 1906, it set off a wave of support for regulating the production process of food and other consumer goods. That same year the Pure Food and Drug Act was passed to regulate the safety of those products. As a result, the Food and Drug Administration (FDA, created in 1930) was eventually established to enforce food and drug safety laws, and to evaluate new drug proposals.

The Great Depression (which lasted from 1929 until America's entry into the Second World War in December of 1941) also spurred a number of new government programs, and new agencies were created to run them. Some of these programs and agencies, like the Federal Deposit Insurance Corporation (FDIC, created in 1933) and the Security Exchange Commission (SEC, created in 1934) were designed to fix the problems that led to the Great Depression, and to prevent them from recurring. The FDIC administers the government program that insures bank deposits so that people feel confident about saving money, because even if a bank fails, the money is safe. The SEC is supposed to oversee stock market transactions to prevent fraud. Both a run on the banks and improper stock market activity are considered causes of the Great Depression.

Other government agencies and programs, like the Tennessee Valley Authority (TVA, created in 1933) and the Civilian Conservation Corps (CCC, created in 1933 and terminated in 1942) were designed to put unemployed people to work and make social and economic improvements at the same time. In an important step to modernize much of the country, the TVA eventually provided electricity to large rural

---

Sidebar 2.2   Old But Not Irrelevant: The SEC's Activities and Corporate Fraud

One of the oldest regulatory organizations in the United States continues to be relevant today. By now, everyone is familiar with the corporate scandals that shocked the country and the national economy in 2001 and 2002. Ranging from price fixing to insider trading to fraudulent accounting, these illegal and unethical activities brought down several corporate giants, including the energy company Enron and the accounting firm Arthur Anderson. In charge of regulating these issues is the Securities Exchange Commission (SEC), which is supposed to oversee stock trading while regulating investment and holding companies. The SEC is headed by five presidentially appointed commissioners, who serve five-year terms. It has a staff of just 3,000 people, small in comparison to most federal agencies. It is organized into four divisions and 18 offices.

The main mission of the SEC is summarized in two points:

- Companies publicly offering securities for investment dollars must tell the public the truth about their businesses, the securities they are selling, and the risks involved in investing.

- People who sell and trade securities—brokers, dealers, and exchanges—must treat investors fairly and honestly, putting investors' interests first.[a]

As a result of these scandals, the SEC has been criticized by the public as well as by the president. In May of 2002, Common Cause, a group working to promote integrity in government and to monitor the influence of money in politics charged the SEC with operating in the interests of the companies it was supposed to be regulating. Specifically, they claimed that the Commission had a conflict of interests because the Chairman had such close ties to the securities industry.[b] In the fall of 2002 Harvey Pitt, the chair of the SEC, resigned under political pressure and the Commission is expected to watch more closely the activities it regulates.[c] Although some may doubt the current effectiveness of the SEC, it remains an example of the continued use of our original government organizations to regulate the economy.

[a]From the SEC website: http://www.sec.gov.

[b]Common Cause (2002), http://www.commoncause.org/publications/may02/051002.htm.

[c]Stephen Labaton, "S.E.C.'s Embattled Chief Resigns in Wake of Latest Political Storm," *New York Times*, November 6, 2002.

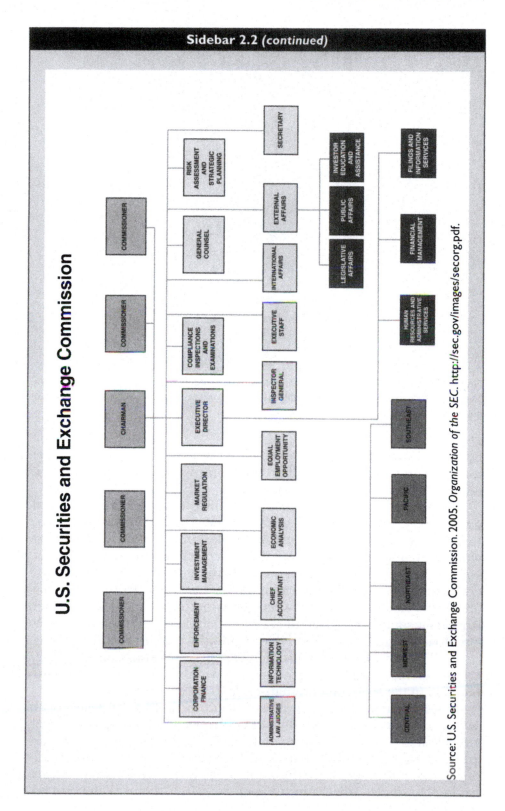

Source: U.S. Securities and Exchange Commission. 2005. *Organization of the SEC.* http://sec.gov/images/secorg.pdf.

One of the reasons for the development of food safety regulations was Upton Sinclair's book *The Jungle*. By exposing unsanitary conditions in meat packing plants, the book helped prompt the passage of the Pure Food and Drug Act in 1906.

areas in the central United States. The CCC used unemployed workers to plant millions of trees, build roads, improve agricultural and forest land usage, and string power lines.

Finally, agencies were created to administer programs that would help workers, both on the job and after they retire. The National Labor Relations Board (NLRB, created in 1934) enforces the laws that allow workers to organize into unions and use collective bargaining. This is a key component of maintaining peace between management and workers, something that was important during the Great Depression, which often saw violent clashes between the two groups. In 1935, President Roosevelt signed the Social Security Act, and created the Social Security Board (which in 1995 developed into the present-day Social Security Administration). Among other benefits, this program provides a small income to retirees and disabled workers, as well as survivors' benefits in the event of a premature death of a worker.

These agencies and programs created in the first 40 years of the twentieth century are generally not controversial. They all provide obvious benefits to the entire population. Parts of these certainly do create differences of opinion, particularly in terms of how they are funded or operated. But nobody really wants to go back to the bad old days of having to wonder what is in the food we eat, if the medicine we take

Library of Congress, Prints & Photographs Division, FSA/OWI Collection, LC-USF34-009098.

Widespread poverty during the Great Depression led to the creation of many government programs and agencies. Some were designed to regulate the marketplace to prevent future depressions, while others were aimed at providing income security for workers.

will actually work (or, even worse, seriously harm us), if the bank will run out of money, or if workers and employers will be battling in the streets.

Not all government agencies and programs have this much popular support. More recently, the government started to regulate social interactions and has tried to control personal risks.[5] As we noted previously, although we all want the government to do *something* for us, we don't always agree on what that something is. This more recent social regulation comprises everything from consumer and worker protection (via product safety and workplace safety regulations), to controls on personal choices (for example, restrictions on abortion or guns), to regulations that reduce risky behavior (like smoking in restaurants or not wearing a seatbelt).

The motivation for these government actions is that a decision has been made that society as a whole is worse off because of the choices made by individual people. What has not been concretely decided is exactly what those individual choices are. For example, some people feel that the moral character of society is damaged when abortions or gay marriages are freely available. Others feel that society unfairly pays the cost of those who get hurt or killed in traffic accidents when not wearing their seatbelts, or of those who smoke in the presence of nonsmokers. As a perfect example of how politically contentious social regulation can be, some people feel that society is better off with more restrictions on gun ownership, while others feel that society is safer with *fewer* restrictions. All of these are typically thought of as political issues, not administrative ones. Yet regardless of how these political issues are resolved, there are implications for the administrative side of government. If seatbelts are required, police officers have to enforce the law. If they are not, ambulance crews have to deal with the consequences.

Current notions of positive government have exacerbated these political battles, even as they sour public perceptions of bureaucracy and public administration. Ironically, as we make more demands on government to regulate society generally, we become increasingly upset with the specific policies and programs that we don't agree with. Unlike the government regulation and organizations established in the first half of the twentieth century, current regulations and programs rarely enjoy broad support.

Bureaucracy's Role in the Policy Process

The bottom line, though, is that the creation and the growth of the administrative state is in large part due to constituent demands and the needs created by the increasing complexity of social and economic life.[6] Once enough political support is mustered, our government responds to citizen demands by passing legislation. Congress will write and pass bills that are aimed at satisfying some need in society; once the president signs the bill into law, the policy process does not stop: somebody must actually carry out the policy. Technically our Constitution assigns the executive role (that is, the job of carrying out government decisions) to the president. Obviously, the job is too large to be done without help. To carry out (or implement) policy decisions, we need bureaucracy.

At a minimum, we need bureaucracy to enforce our laws. We rely on government agencies to actually put government decisions into practice. After all, what good is a speed limit if you know you'll never be fined for speeding? What good is an income tax code if you know that you'll never be audited? What good is a law prohibiting workplace discrimination if employers know they'll never be reviewed? Although there is some evidence that people will follow the law simply because it is "the right thing to do," most of us need to be at least threatened with the possibility of coercion before we change our behavior and slow down on the highway, or file our taxes on time, or act appropriately when making personnel decisions at work.

But while the need to enforce laws and regulations is an important reason why we have a bureaucracy, it is not enough for us to understand fully why we need it, and why it continues to play such an important role in public policy in the United States. In fact, the traditional focus on the bureaucracy as an institution engaged only in the roles of regulation (law enforcement, for example) and policy implementation (creating and managing public programs) is woefully incomplete. Public administration is much broader, and includes significant participation in agenda setting and policy formation. This is because, as you will see, government agencies have information, expertise, and resources that make them crucial to the policy process. Our bureaucracy is expected to make sure our programs run smoothly, but we also expect it to demonstrate why those programs are necessary in the first place.[7] We need government agencies to help us determine what problems are the most important. We then rely on government agencies to help us understand our policy options for addressing those problems. These functions of public administration are starkly political in nature, not in the sense of reacting to demands, but of being actively involved in the process of deciding who gets what. They involve questions about who will benefit from social resources, what problems are worth addressing, what goals our communities will have, and how those goals will be met. In short, public agencies are a fundamental component of our policy process. Without them, our ability to govern ourselves would be seriously damaged.[8] The bureaucracy's role in making policy, not just in implementing it, turns out to be another reason why the administrative state is so large and such an important feature of our social, political, and economic lives.

As you will see throughout this book, the bureaucracy has some very important features that allow it to play this key role in the policy process. In short, we depend upon the bureaucracy not only for law enforcement, but also because it brings information, expertise, and organizational resources to the policy process. All of these help us pass better legislation so that we are more likely to get what we want out of our government.

Information

Government agencies, by virtue of their being public, have a good view of American society, and the issues and problems it currently faces. This makes public bureaucracies centrally important warehouses of information and expertise, knowledge that helps us identify what problems need to be addressed and what solutions might best solve those problems. For example, a good way to learn about the problems of education is to talk to public school teachers and administrators. Welfare caseworkers have a great deal of information about the various needs of their clients. Police officers know what the current crime problems are, as well as what citizens fear. Government agencies have this information for two reasons.

First, they are in direct contact with citizens. Bureaucrats, when doing their job by implementing government policy, are the officials that talk to and work with citizens. Teachers know the problems in their classrooms and schools; they are the ones who deal with issues of overcrowded classrooms or lack of resources. Welfare workers know if their efforts to implement welfare programs are succeeding in moving people into decent jobs. Police officers understand what the public is concerned about, because they talk to ordinary people every day. We use government services daily, and we come into contact with bureaucrats frequently and regularly. Because bureaucrats are out in public all the time, it makes sense that they have firsthand knowledge of the current important issues or problems.[9]

Second, bureaucrats are typically the first government officials we complain to when government services are not as we want them to be. When the street in front of our house is full of potholes we call the public works department first, not the mayor's office. We complain to the police when we think they should be concentrating on violent criminals rather than speeders. We complain to the IRS about the complexities of the income tax. When professors at a public university are incompetent or acting inappropriately, students usually contact university administrators (department chairs, college deans, officials in student affairs) rather than elected officials such as state legislators or the governor. Much of this is due to accessibility. Bureaucrats are not hard to find, and, unlike elected officials (particularly those in Washington, DC), we frequently get the chance to speak to them in person. For example, parent-teacher conferences in public schools are as much for parents to report their concerns about the school as they are for the teacher to report about a student's progress. Bureaucrats also typically function under strict due-process rules; in effect, they know members of the public have a right to lodge a complaint and expect a fair hearing. In this way bureaucrats help insure that government is really "for the people, by the people." Government agencies are thus "public" in every sense of the word, and the interaction between bureaucrats and citizens should be taken seriously (by both parties!).

Thus, bureaucrats have a tremendous amount of information on the current status of society. Perhaps more than any other group of people in government, they know through their close relationships with citizens how well government policies are working, if new policies are needed, and what the general attitudes are about the various government services and programs.

The bureaucracy also enjoys an information advantage over other participants in the policy process. Each government agency performs a relatively narrow range of tasks in order to meet an established set of goals. For example, the Department of Agriculture has a goal of stabilizing the agricultural economy in the United States. Some of the tasks done to meet this goal involve keeping track of commodity markets and adjusting crop subsidies accordingly. This is done constantly throughout each year, by the same bureaus in the department. Thus, bureaucrats become familiar with the technical features of the policy issue because they repeatedly deal with them. No other participants in the policy process can devote all of their attention to one particular problem. Legislators must in fact deal with a wide variety of policy issues (whatever their constituents might demand, plus whatever is on the policy agenda at the moment). Bureaucrats, on the other hand, have the luxury of being able to get good at one thing. This is particularly important, since many policy problems in this country are highly technical. This affords them the opportunity to develop vast stores of information to help them meet their goals. What better place, for example, to learn about this country's agricultural economy than the U.S. Department of Agriculture?

This information is valuable to legislators who craft public policies.[10] In order to write policies that effectively deal with citizen demands, legislators must know exactly what those demands are and what problems society faces. They also need a great deal of technical information about the problems. In this way, government agencies play two related roles. First, they act to transmit the demands of the people they serve (their **clientele**). In this sense, some people have thought of them as interest groups acting on behalf of clients,[11] although it is certain that government agencies, for a variety of reasons, as you will find out, are not nearly the proponents of particular policies that they are sometimes made out to be.[12]

Second, they act as consultants for legislators.[13] Members of the House of Representatives and the Senate, while gaining important experience throughout their careers, must still be generalists. They must know a little bit about a lot of things in order to make themselves more appealing to the broad electorate within their constituencies. Consequently, they often do not know enough about a single issue to be able to craft high-quality public policy without outside help. Frequently, what happens is that broad policy goals are outlined by elected officials, and then bureaucrats are relied upon for professional advice and information on how to accomplish those goals.[14] Relevant government agencies are therefore frequently consulted, sometimes even by having agency leaders appear before a committee or subcommittee, to provide this help.

Beyond acting as consultants to legislators, bureaucrats use their information resources to shape *what* in fact will be done by government, rather than just *how* it will be done. That is, government agencies play an important role in advocating key social values and establishing the broad policy goals that we normally expect out of our legislatures.[15] In short, our bureaucracy is an integral part of our governing system in that it helps map out what our government will do. It is clear that with information that cannot be had anywhere else, the bureaucracy will continue to play an important role in the governance of the United States.

Expertise

Another reason why we rely on the bureaucracy is because of the expertise of individual bureaucrats. This expertise exists for many of the same reasons that the bureaucracy has its stores of information. Because they are able to devote their attention to a small set of issues and deal with them repeatedly, bureaucrats become experts on those issues. When faced with a task that needs to be done to achieve some agency goal, this experience saves time and other resources (money, perhaps most importantly), as the bureaucrat will have a good idea of what works, what does not, and what has been tried in the past. This experience is often reflected in **standard operating procedures (SOPs)** that save resources and speed up work because each new situation faced by the agency does not have to be treated as being unique. Imagine registering for classes next semester if the registrar's office had to establish new rules for every student!

Another important source of expertise is the professionals that work in each agency. By hiring professionals in their fields, agencies are able to tap into current research and expertise. This gives agencies important technical knowledge that is unavailable outside those professions on matters such as pollution, new advanced weapons, or medicine. By employing these experts, the bureaucracy's image is also enhanced, which improves its effectiveness. Popular perception being perhaps the key to all politics, it remains important that the bureaucracy's credibility be maintained. Professional expertise goes a long way to ensure this.

Hiring professionals has another benefit: **bureaucratic neutrality** is enhanced. As we will see later in this chapter, bureaucratic neutrality is desirable to ward off corruption, to increase fairness, and to increase effectiveness. For now, suffice it to say that while certainly passionate about their professional interests and certainly *not* completely apolitical, professionals are not hired for partisanship or personal loyalty. By having employees that should normally place professional interests before partisan interests, the technical issues of policy problems get the necessary attention. In the end, this eye toward practical problem solving, rather than politics, serves to increase the effectiveness of our public policies. In fact, one expert in the field of public health policy even argues that the public health challenges associated with industrialization and urbanization are so complex and highly technical that bureaucratic expertise is necessary because "solutions cannot be found within . . . representative assemblies or governors' offices."[16] This blunt statement serves as a reminder that the benefits we receive from public policies stem largely from the involvement of bureaucrats in the policy process.

Organizational Resources

As we have already stated, in order for policies to effectively make changes to society, they need to be implemented. This task is almost always given to existing agencies. This is because they already have established organizations (of workers, chains of commands, offices, equipment, and other resources). Sometimes, however, new organizations are created to deal with new or unique problems. For example, after the terrorist attacks of September 11, 2001, a new Office of Homeland Security was created (it was later enhanced and designated as a new Cabinet-level Department of Homeland Security). The point here is that organization matters. Rather than distributing authority to implement a new policy to individuals, we say that the authority rests within the agency. Because agencies are relatively permanent, they can store information and "learn," creating what is known as an "institutional memory."[17] This institutional memory is the collection of all past experiences that bureaucrats have had working in the organization. Over time, a set of standard operating procedures allows bureaucrats within the organization to ignore processes and options that did not work, and instead follow those that most efficiently addressed the issue at hand. So-called "red tape" therefore often has a beneficial effect of *speeding up* the activity of the bureaucracy, even if it is at the expense of individual client service.

Recap: Why We Need (And Want!) Bureaucracy

The administrative state exists for a very good reason: we could not possibly govern ourselves without it. We need and want bureaucracy precisely because we need and want government to do things for us. We want government to regulate the economy. We want it to protect us from dangers, both moral and physical. We want it to help solve social problems, ranging from poverty to public education. We want it so that we don't have to think about routine things in life, such as clean water to drink, safe food to eat, and roads to drive on. The idea of positive government is firmly established in the political philosophy of the United States.

We need and want bureaucracy, too, because without it our public policy process would grind to a halt. We rely upon our government agencies to implement our policies, since the three traditional branches of government (legislative, executive, and judicial) are unequipped to do so. Public policy is often meaningless unless put into practice by bureaucrats. Employees of the IRS must rewrite tax codes every time tax law changes. Police officers must patrol their communities. Occupational Safety and Health Administration (OSHA) inspectors make visits to factories to check for safety violations. Teachers change their lesson plans to abide by new state and federal standards.

By providing the necessary information, expertise, and other resources, government agencies help the policy process be more effective. This includes bureaucratic input to help determine overall policy goals as well as input about how to reach those goals. Due to the increasing population, the increases in complexity of society, and the increases in the technical nature of our social problems, we rely more and more on our administrative state to help us craft public policy. The bureaucracy provides technical guidance, and transmits the desires of citizens as well. Without this help, it is likely that our policies would be much less effective. The legislative branch is simply not able to adequately address our demands by itself.

The Structure of the Administrative State

Now that the need for, and importance of, the administrative state has been established, one question remains: why have we structured it in the way we have? Why do we rely upon bureaucracy, and not some other form of organization to structure public agencies? Indeed, why is the administrative state public at all, and not a set of private organizations?

Since our founding as an independent country, we have tried several forms of structures for our administrative state.[18] We first tried staffing our agencies with elites, on the idea that only the white, male, highly educated land-owner was capable of such a position. Certainly these elites would be wise, and considering that few outside this group even had political rights, this elitist method of staffing the bureaucracy perhaps was not all that outlandish for the era. Certainly, the elites not in government service benefited greatly. The responsiveness of the government to the demands of these people was greatly enhanced, since the elite network could work together for common goals. Of course, by today's standards, this method of staffing government agencies was grossly undemocratic, for obvious reasons: only the wealthy, the highly educated, or those with the right social connections qualified for government service.

By the early to mid-1800s, the populist movement swept away property requirements for political rights. This simultaneously did away with the elitist methods of staffing, and brought in a new method based on the average citizen. Moreover, the political parties were applying more pressure to institute a more patronage-based system, and Andrew Jackson made clear in his inaugural address after his 1828 electoral victory that administrative employees would be hired by a system of **patronage**. Patronage is a system of staffing positions based on applicants' personal and/or political loyalties. Jobs are won not by being competent, but by being loyal and politically valuable (in other words, "it's not what you know, but who you know"). Why would a patronage system be desirable for staffing the bureaucracy? From the perspective of a political party and those elected to office, patronage is desirable because it helps ensure that bureaucrats will do what the party and politicians want them to do. In short, it makes management a lot easier. It also helps elected officials achieve their policy goals. As you will see in Chapter 4, the bureaucracy is heavily engaged in politics and policymaking. If that bureaucracy is staffed with your political allies, it becomes much easier to get the policy results that you want.

Clearly, patronage is desirable from a certain perspective. It can speed up the processes of governance, and it makes personnel management easier by enhancing the powers of political leaders, especially the executive. However, these advantages come by sacrificing competence and fairness, and by increasing corruption. Competence is sacrificed by the overt rejection of professional or technical qualifications as the key criteria for employment. If the government is not hiring the most qualified applicants, then certainly its effectiveness will be reduced. We have already seen that today's problems are more complex and numerous than ever. It is unlikely that a personnel system based primarily on patronage would be able to adequately address them. Fairness is sacrificed, because bureaucrats will first work to serve their patrons rather than the public. Certainly some sections of the public will enjoy great benefits from a patronage system, as long as they belong to the "right" political party. However, those who do not belong will be unlikely to receive the same level of service. This of course is not fair, particularly because public policy is supposed to be uniformly implemented; getting a pothole filled or winning a government contract should not depend on campaign donations. This problem was perhaps most evident at the local level, in the form of the great political machines in cities like New York (from the mid-1850s to the early 1930s) and Chicago (from the early 1930s to essentially 1976, with the death of Richard J. Daley), and also at the federal level in the late 1800s.

Finally, corruption is, for many people, synonymous with patronage. Staffing organizations through patronage can indeed contribute to corruption. Corruption or unethical behavior can be defined as using one's own position in government to act selfishly rather than in the public interest.[19] In other words, patronage is assumed by many to be a breeding ground for people to make themselves better off at the expense of the broad public. This is because there are fewer "outsiders" watching over employees to monitor their behavior. Importantly, corruption due to patronage also is directly linked to electoral politics. By offering jobs if victorious, political parties could easily mobilize support and raise money. Voter turnout was very high, but only because those votes were being "bought" by candidates with promises of good jobs if elected.[20]

By the late 1800s, one important feature of the patronage system instituted by Jackson became so problematic that something had to be done: every time a new president took office, huge proportions of the bureaucracy turned over as the incoming president came in with his own set of personally loyal bureaucrats. To end this wholesale turnover and implement a more merit-based system, the Pendleton Act was passed in 1883. With the passage of the Act, most administrative positions were filled through competitive methods, based on competence and competition.

The Merit System

The Pendleton Act introduced the **merit system**, which is still in use today in the national government (with modifications, such as the introduction of collective bargaining and affirmative action). The merit system will be discussed later, in Chapter 9, but it is important to note here that besides stabilizing the workforce in the bureaucracy, it also refocused the efforts of bureaucrats. Where previously the test for employment had been political loyalty, the merit system installed the test of neutral competency. That is, the merit system stresses both political neutrality and the ability to do the job. Political neutrality is important to reduce corruption, and simultaneously stressing competency helps increase the effectiveness of the agencies.

It is interesting, however, that although much of the patronage system was eliminated by the start of the twentieth century, part of it still exists, and is important. For example, the president has the power to make many appointments within the bureaucracy, primarily among bureau leaders (and of course, the department heads, who are members of his cabinet). Thus we use a blend of merit and patronage to staff our bureaucracy. Top-level leaders are appointed by the president, and for the most part serve at his pleasure (except for those serving on independent regulatory boards and commissions). The rest of the bureaucracy is staffed through the merit system. Thus we have tried to strike a blend, recognizing that the merit system will bring more effective policy implementation, while patronage-based leaders will enhance the president's ability to manage the bureaucracy.

Why Is Public Administration 'Public'?

One final question about the structure of our administrative state is why it cannot be done by the private sector. The short answer is that for the most part, it just will not work. As Chapter 3 will show, most government services cannot be offered effectively by the private sector. Private companies exist for one purpose: to make a profit. The fundamental problem is that most goods and services provided by the government through the administrative state cannot be sold in a way to make a profit. They are **public goods**. A public good is one that is nonrival in consumption and that cannot practically be withheld from nonpayers. *Nonrival in consumption* means that your use of the good does not diminish my ability to use it. For example, national defense is a public good. You and I can be simultaneously protected by the military without diminishing each other's level of protection, and adding more people to the country would not suddenly leave one of us unprotected. Furthermore, there is no practical way to deny national defense to nonpayers. At the start of a war we cannot simply round up foreign tourists, people too young or poor to pay taxes, or even tax cheats, and shuttle them off to some desolate corner of the country in order to let the enemy attack them at will. All of this means that there is no profit to be had in trying to provide national defense through the private sector.

Even when government goods and services could be sold in the private market for profit, we sometimes feel the need for public oversight. This oversight is crucial in important activities that have broad social impact. One concern is that there is more than one way for a private business to make a profit. One way is to offer a superior product at a reasonable price. Another, easier way is to cut corners as much as possible and reduce prices in order to increase demand. This may be acceptable for many of the day-to-day products we buy, like shampoo. But for goods and services that will influence large segments of the population, it is troublesome. For example, we recently federalized airport security, which had been provided by private companies prior to September 11, 2001. This is a clear case where the private sector failed to provide adequate levels of service, and a public good (public safety) was minimized.

Privatizing other government services, such as public schools and prisons, also raises controversy because of the possibility that broader social issues might be ignored by a private company, as you'll see in Chapter 3. For example, in education we worry about equal access and feel that a degree of uniformity is desirable. In prisons, we are concerned about civil rights as well as programs that would reduce repeat offenders.

Finally, we sometimes resist privatizing government goods and services because we are interested in at least partially subsidizing them. We recognize that some services, which have benefits that go beyond the direct users of the services, could very easily be privatized. But the market price for them would increase, thus decreasing their use and eliminating those extra benefits. Bus service, public swimming pools, and public universities are three examples of using the government to partially finance the costs of desirable services.

By now it is clear that the long answer to the question of why we have public and not private administration is that there is room for limited privatization. Public goods typically cannot effectively be offered through private markets. Other goods and services are problematic because of broader social concerns. The key to the answer is that there are good reasons for having the public sector perform these tasks.

Conclusion

By now we should not be surprised about the size of the bureaucracy in the United States. Although our country was founded on the ideas of limited government, those ideas have long since been replaced by a philosophy of positive government. Recognizing that the government can be a useful tool for solving problems in society, no matter if your ideology leans left or right, we have established a large administrative state. This enables the government to do the things we ask it to do. Where did all this bureaucracy come from? The short answer to this question is easy: it comes from us. Especially over the last 100 years, we have asked the government to regulate the economy, protect the safety of consumers, secure our incomes and savings, provide education, control pollution, ameliorate racism and sexism, control people's abuse of drugs and alcohol and other sinful behaviors, build and maintain roads and infrastructure, defend the country, promote science and exploration, and on and on. In other words, we ask the government to do important things that we cannot do for ourselves, or that could not be provided by the private market.

It is true that the administrative state has grown tremendously over the last 100 years. Our demands have increased and have become more complex. Even now we are placing new demands on our government, and in the process of responding to those demands new bureaucracy is created. The Department of Homeland Security is the latest significant addition to our administrative state, one that prior to 2001 was not deemed necessary.

The bureaucracy is a hugely important part of your daily lives, and it is crucial if the government is to be able to act on our demands. The study of public administration is therefore the study of how (and how well) the government is able to solve the problems we want it to solve. It is also the study of how the government interacts with citizens and how it is able to shape the lives of those citizens. The rise of the administrative state was no accident, and it makes sense that it is important to study how it works, what powers it has, and how it might be made better.

Key Concepts

bureaucratic neutrality The principle that holds professionalism as a desirable feature of a bureaucrat. Rather than hiring bureaucrats on political grounds, we expect them to be professional, neutral experts who will make decisions based on that professionalism and expertise rather than on their political allegiances.

clientele Bureaucratic clients are those directly served by a government agency. Sometimes this is a distinct, identifiable group, such as recipients of Social Security. Other times agency clientele will be more general or broad, which usually is the case with agencies that provide widely used services or public goods.

departments Executive departments are large groupings of bureaus and offices that carry out crucial political functions and provide citizens with important services. Each of the 15 departments is led by a secretary appointed by the president, who then sits on the president's cabinet and provides policy advice.

government corporations Enterprises that are expected to be "nonpartisan," but more free to use operating procedures from the business world. Government corporations are usually expected to operate for profit.

independent regulatory boards and commissions Freestanding agencies that operate outside of executive departments. Instead, they report directly to the president or to Congress. They are typically lead by an odd-numbered group of experts who are usually thought to be more insulated from politics than the cabinet members who lead executive departments.

merit system A personnel system that uses evaluations of work to determine promotions and raises, rather than basing rewards on political grounds. A merit system in a government agency also protects workers' rights in most personnel matters (hiring, firing, evaluations, promotions, and raises).

patronage Under patronage, political loyalty is the chief criterion used to staff government agencies, as opposed to professionalism under bureaucratic neutrality. While this makes bureaucrats easier for the president to control, the quality of public administration suffers because the bureaucracy has fewer professional experts.

positive government The belief that, unlike the philosophy of limited government, there are important social and economic problems that can best be solved through government intervention. This best describes the current era of the United States, as most political discussions are centered on *what* the government should do rather than *if* it should do anything.

public goods Public goods are things that cannot be sold on the private market for a profit. These goods have no acceptable mechanism for exluding nonpayers, and there is no reduction in the goods as they are used, which make it impossible to sell them at a profit. If we are to have them at all, the government must provide them.

standard operating procedures (SOPs) Sets of rules that govern how an organization resolves recurring situations. These are developed in order to speed decision making in the organization and to provide consistent, predictable responses. Standard operating procedures ideally improve the efficiency and dependability of government agencies. ✦

Chapter 3

A Difficult Mission

Trying to Please All the People All the Time

At first glance, bureaucratic reform and oatmeal would seem to have little in common. Yet the fiber-filled breakfast grain is a good example of what critics are calling, for lack of a better description, a highly constipated bureaucracy in the state of California. Still not getting the connection? Well, consider the purchasing process of the California Department of Corrections (CDC).

CDC buys a lot of oatmeal. Well, actually it doesn't. The wardens that run its prisons buy a lot of oatmeal. How much the CDC pays for oatmeal is thus dependent upon the shopping skill of the wardens. Some pay more, some pay less. There is no centralized oatmeal-buying unit of the CDC, so the prices the agency ends up paying for oatmeal can vary, though prisoners end up eating pretty much the same thing. Wouldn't it make more sense to consolidate oatmeal purchases within the corrections system? Yes. That way the CDC could leverage its buying power into a good deal, and the taxpayers would end up paying a little less to feed felons and juvenile delinquents. This is a small example of why California Governor Arnold Schwarzenegger expressed a desire to "blow up the boxes" of the state bureaucracy. Blowing up boxes is an action hero's way of saying that a systematic reorganization of the bureaucracy could make public programs more efficient and rationally managed.[1]

Such sentiments have widespread popularity, and have made reforming bureaucracy at all levels of government a more or less permanent feature of the political landscape. The politics of such reforms are typically accompanied by tales of bureaucratic incompetence or inefficiency (like paying too much for oatmeal). In practice, though, efforts to "blow up boxes" and either rationalize the administrative side of government or contract out public services to the private sector have met with as much failure as success.

The central problem has to do with goals and objectives. The job of the CDC, for example, is not to buy cheap oatmeal. The official mission of the CDC is to "end the causes and tragic effects of crime, violence, and victimization in our communities through a collaborative effort that provides intervention to at-risk populations and quality services that from the time of arrest will assist our clients in achieving successful reintegration into society."[2] Obviously, this agency has a bit more on its plate than reasonably priced breakfast cereals. Ending "the causes and tragic effects of crime," for example, is a pretty tall order—a vast, sweeping objective. How is the CDC supposed to do this? And will cheaper oatmeal help? No one objects to getting the taxpayers a better deal on prison meals, but reforming the bureaucracy to achieve this goal is not likely to get the CDC closer to stamping out crime. Before reorganization or reform, it might be a better idea to figure out exactly what the CDC should (or should not) be doing.

A Question of Goals

If administration is the "art of getting things done," a prerequisite for effective administration is first knowing what needs to get done. For this reason, the most fundamental task of the administrative process is to identify organizational goals.[3] This core administrative task is easier for most private-sector companies than for most public-sector bureaucracies. The core purpose of business is obvious: to make money. Most businesses exist because of a desire for financial gain, and their continued survival is dependent upon consistently making a profit. There is an endless set of possibilities for making money with any given product or service, but the profit-loss statement serves as the basic administrative and managerial gyroscope. A company may have other goals: to innovate, to provide the best customer service, to provide the highest quality product, to sell at the lowest possible price, to be a fair and generous employer, to support charitable causes, to promote community service, to be a good steward of the environment. Yet all of these goals must be subordinate to making a profit, at least in the long term, for the simple reason that no other goals are possible unless the company is making money.

There is no comparable clarity about organizational objectives in the public sector. Consider: What is the purpose of a school? An army? A welfare agency? Possible answers include providing a quality education, protecting the national interest, and helping the poor. Fair enough. Yet all of these goals are vague and invite disagreement on specifics. What is a quality education? How do we know when the goal has been achieved? When test scores go up? When dropout rates go down? When students can be inculcated into a certain set of values? What actions really serve the national interest? An expensive weapons system originally designed to combat an enemy that no longer exists? What is in the best interest of the poor? Providing direct aid in the form of cash, food, and housing subsidies? Or indirect aid through job training and daycare services? There are no clear-cut answers to these questions, and without this clarity public agencies face an enormous challenge. Scan back up a few paragraphs and reread the CDC's mission statement—is its mission crystal clear? Does it clearly imply what it should (or should not) be doing? What *are* the causes of crime? If the agency's job is to eliminate these causes, how does it identify them? How does it address them? How will it know when the causes of crime are being eliminated or reduced?

Differences over what constitutes the goal of a "quality education" or "the national interest," or eliminating the "causes and tragic effects of crime," or the catchall purpose of government bureaucracy to promote "the public interest" are more than invitations to a legalistic parsing of words. These differences cut to the heart of the primary source of confusion and misunderstanding about public administration: what public bureaucracies are supposed to do and how they are supposed to do it.

The popular perception of public bureaucracy is largely negative, and there is a widespread and persistent belief that government should be run more "like a business." This assumes that a businesslike approach would result in more efficiency (cheaper oatmeal) and higher agency performance (less crime). Such popular beliefs are largely mistaken in that they tend to assume organizational objectives as a given. To assume that public agencies could be more effective and efficient if they adopted the practices of the market is to assume that the goals and motivations at the heart of market forces can be transferred to the public sector. As the CDC shows, public-sector missions are

United States Army, photo by Spc. Jeffery Sanstrum.

No one questions the need for a military, but what is the goal of an army? How do we know if a soldier is being efficient? Unlike organizations in the private sector—which primarily exist to make a profit—public agencies often have broad, hard-to-measure goals. Profits and losses tell a business how well it is achieving its primary goal. For a soldier patrolling Mosul, Iraq, success can be more difficult to measure.

more complex and harder to identify than the basic mission of a for-profit firm.

The goal of this chapter is to introduce students to the primary mission of public agencies and to make clear the enormous administrative challenge fulfilling that mission entails. Though reforming bureaucracy to make it more businesslike is a perennial issue in politics, it turns out that public and private organizations have very different purposes. The private and public sectors operate with different goals and justifications, with different expectations and environments, and the tasks and principles of one are not easily transferred to the other.

The Basic Goal of Public Agencies

The primary goal of all public bureaucracies is to implement and manage the laws passed by elected representatives.[4] This goal marks the fundamental difference in how the public and private sectors operate, because every action of a public agency must have a basis in public law. Regardless of the level of government or the particular policy area, any action undertaken by a public agency is predicated on the assumption that it has the explicit or implicit legal authority to take it. Businesses and corporations, of course, are also expected to stay within the confines of the law. But the law is not the primary source of their goals, nor their primary behavioral motivation. In the private sector, the impetus and justification for action is largely driven by the financial interests of entrepreneurs, business executives, and shareholders: in other words, profit. In the market, the law sets the boundaries for behavior rather than providing its primary motivation.[5]

Though simple in the abstract, the basic goal of public agencies turns out to be enormously complex and provides none of the gyroscopic consistency of the profit motive. Laws are the end products of a political process that typically involves a good deal of disagreement. The laws public agencies are expected to implement and abide by thus encompass an enormous variety of political preferences. This should not be surprising to anyone with a casual familiarity with the democratic process. Representative bodies rarely speak with one voice, but reflect the competing points of view across their constituencies. In brokering compromises among these competing voices, representative bodies often give public agencies multiple goals, vague goals that can be interpreted according to political or ideological perspective, or even contradictory goals.

Consider, for example, the goals the old Immigration and Naturalization Service (now a part of the Department of Homeland Security) was expected to pursue: "Keep out illegal immigrants, but let in necessary agricultural workers;" "find and expel illegal aliens, but do not break up families, impose hardships, violate civil rights, or deprive employers of low-paid workers;" "fully screen foreigners seeking to enter the country, but facilitate the entry of foreign tourists."[6] It is not hard to imagine a political constituency for any of these goals and, taken individually, all seem reasonable enough in the abstract. Overall, however, these goals doomed the old INS (and most likely the new one) to failure. The agency cannot fulfill all the tasks assigned to it for the simple reason that they are vague and contradictory. Many illegal immigrants are agricultural workers that the farming industry classifies as "necessary." Expelling illegal aliens sometimes means separating families. The process of finding illegal aliens often raises questions of civil rights. As yet there is no known method of fully screening people crossing national borders without imposing some obstacles to entry. Succeeding at one goal means failing at another. Given that the agency has limited resources, it has little choice but to prioritize some goals over others. But this invites objections and dissent from the political constituencies whose goals are allocated lower priorities. Regardless of what actions it takes, the INS will be charged with failing to adequately achieve at least some of its goals.

The INS is far from unique. Let's take a very different public agency—the Springfield-Greene County Library in Springfield, Missouri—and look at its goals. According to its mission statement, the job of the library is to "provide an environment where lifelong habits of learning, self-improvement, and self-expression are encouraged and where patrons can meet their educational, informational, and recreational needs."[7] It's hard to fault a local library for pursuing such goals. But what if, say, someone who wrote a book sympathizing with the arguments and actions of certain terrorist groups wanted their book on the Springfield library shelves and to give a public reading from their manuscript? It's a reasonably safe bet that some would see such support of self-expression in direct opposition to their educational, informational, and recreational needs. If the library allowed such a reading, would it be fulfilling its goals or abandoning them?

The point here is not to decide whether terrorist sympathizers should be given public platforms by the libraries of middle America. Rather, it is that public agencies are often at a disadvantage when it comes to figuring out what, exactly, they are supposed to do. Through law and the political process, representative bodies routinely task public agency with multiple, ill-defined, and often contradictory goals. This makes the fundamental task of administration an enormous challenge. A widget manufacturer has a clear core mission (to make a profit) and knows what needs to be done in order to achieve that goal (make widgets). The administrative challenge of a widget manufacturer is to coordinate the inputs of the organization (labor and capital) so as to maximize its outputs (widgets) in order to achieve its primary goal (profit). Because there are disagreements about the goals of public agencies, there are disagreements about the outputs it should concentrate on producing. This leaves public bureaucracies facing the administrative paradox of needing to coordinate inputs to achieve ill-defined and contested goals. Contrast the chief executive of a widget business with the superintendent of a school district or a head librarian. The business CEO may well face all manner of challenges that require considerable administrative skill and dexterity—recalcitrant unions, for example, or the headaches of implementing new manufacturing technology, or shareholders unhappy with their dividends. Yet in an overall sense, the core element of administration is unchanging for this CEO. She knows what the company needs to get done: make widgets and turn a profit. The specifics involved in the process of achieving these goals may present all manner of difficult challenges and choices, but the overall target and purpose of administration and management remains clear and stable. There is no uncontestable equivalent to widgets and profit for a library or a school, leaving the administrators running those organizations with less of a natural organizational focus. Rather than producing and selling widgets to earn a profit, libraries, schools, and most other public agencies pursue goals that are products of the political process. Such goals may be contested, subject to change, or even contradictory.

The complexities surrounding the goals of public agencies not only make it difficult to clarify the basic mission of a public agency, they also make it hard to assess their success in achieving these goals. The issue of performance in public agencies is considered in more depth in Chapter 7. For present purposes, let us consider some of the basic indexes used to assess performance and goals in the private sector: efficiency, effectiveness, and productivity. For the private sector these measures are typically used to assess how well outputs are produced. If you define profit for a widget manufacturer as the selling price of widgets minus the costs of producing the widget, then producing more widgets at lower costs (becoming more efficient) can be expected to translate into more profits. Such direct relationships between output production and goal achievement are more complex in the public sector. As a result, the yardsticks used to measure profit-related performance can give incomplete or misleading assessments of public agencies.[8]

Efficiency

Efficiency can be calculated in a number of different ways, but as a practical matter is best defined as a ratio of inputs to outputs:

$$\text{Efficiency} = \frac{I}{O}$$

So to measure the efficiency of a widget manufacturer requires computing the costs of the inputs represented by the production process (labor and capital) by the total number of widgets produced in a given period of time. The resulting number is a per-unit cost, and widget manufacturers with lower per-unit costs are said to be more efficient (and are more likely to make a profit).

In the abstract, no one opposes more efficient public agencies, bureaucracies that can do "more for less." In practical terms, however, efficiency is an extraordinarily difficult concept to transfer to the public sector because it has no equivalent to widgets. Though a number of accounting quibbles may be involved, it is comparatively easy to account for the inputs of a public bureaucracy. Just like the private sector, they can be calculated by adding up the costs of labor and capital. Outputs are a different matter. Because public agencies frequently have vague and contradictory goals, they have no obvious output measure. What is a school, or a library, or a welfare agency, or an army expected to produce?

This is a critical question, because any measurement of efficiency is dependent upon the assumption that there is a clear idea of the desired output. In the public sector, outputs are the subject of much confusion and disagreement. Consider, for example, a library. It is a relatively easy matter to calculate the labor costs for librarians, and the expenditures for book purchases and periodical subscriptions. These are obvious inputs. But what is the output of a library? There is no single, universally agreeable answer. There are a number of potential output measures: circulation, size, or quality of the collection of books; the number of and participation in library-sponsored community programs; the number of people who actually make use of library services in a given period of time. Which one of these is "best"? The question is crucial because different output measures will give very different messages about efficiency.

The problem, of course, is that people have very different ideas about what a given public agency's primary mission is, and differences about goals lead to different choices of output measure, and thus very different assessments of efficiency. Trying to measure the efficiency of public agencies has been described as like "trying to pull oneself out of quicksand without a rope. There is no firm ground."[9] The same agency can be made to look highly efficient or highly inefficient simply by choosing different outputs. Because people have different beliefs about what constitutes the most important goal of a given public agency, there are disagreements about what constitutes the "best" output measure. This means any claim of efficiency attached to that agency is a contestable political claim rather than a neutral and objective yardstick.

Effectiveness

Effectiveness can also be simply defined as a ratio, this time as an observed output over a desired output. Multiply this output ratio by

100 and the result is a statement of effectiveness expressed as a percentage:[10]

$$\text{Effectiveness} = \frac{O_{observed}}{O_{expected}} \times 100$$

An effectiveness rating of 100 percent means an organization is producing exactly the output it is expected to produce. The obvious problem with applying such concepts of effectiveness to the public sector is that it compounds the output problem encountered with measures of efficiency, this time with the output problem on both sides of the ratio rather than just one. Even assuming an agency goal and an output measure can be agreed on, the political element of this measure still remains. People who agree on the primary goals of a public agency can, and often do, disagree about what an agency can realistically do to accomplish that goal.

Imagine a school district where test scores are 80 percent of state average, and where parents, teachers, and administrators (perhaps prodded by the state legislature) agree that the primary goal for the coming academic year should be to raise test scores. Parents may expect test scores to increase to at least the state average. The teachers' union may view such an increase as unrealistic, and aim for an incremental improvement, say getting the district to 90 percent of state average.

Let's say that the state average on this test is 70 (on a 0 to 100 scale) and the school scores shift from 56 to 65 in the following academic year—in other words, school scores go from 80 percent of state average to nearly 93 percent of state average. This is how the effectiveness scores would be calculated from the parent and teachers' union perspectives:

$$\text{Effectiveness (Parental Goal)} = \frac{65}{70} \times 100 = 93$$

$$\text{Effectiveness (Teacher Goal)} = \frac{65}{63} \times 100 = 103$$

In this example, the output measure is (somewhat unrealistically) universally agreed upon, but the assessment of effectiveness is dependent upon whose desired output is used for the calculation. Did this school effectively achieve its goal? Using the parents' preferred goal for outputs (the state average) shows the answer is no—it fell short of 100 percent of its goal. Using the teachers' union preference the answer is yes—the school exceeded 100 percent of its goal. Even though everyone can agree test scores improved, the disagreement on goals lead to different conclusions about the school's performance.

To put this into concrete terms, consider New Jersey's Montgomery High School, which was judged to have unacceptable performance according to the standards set by the No Child Left Behind (NCLB) Act. By most output measures, Montgomery is a very effective school. It scores well on reading and math (in the top 3 percent of the state), has high average SAT scores, and was named by the Department of Education as a U.S. Blue Ribbon School. Why was its performance considered unacceptable by the NCLB? Well, one of the requirements of the NCLB, a bill passed by Congress to raise performance standards in schools, is a 95 percent participation rate in standardized testing (the idea being to prevent schools from padding their averages by barring marginal students from taking the test). In 2004, two of Montgomery High's 29 special-education students were absent on the day standardized tests were given. This was enough to drop Montgomery's participation rate to 93 percent. On the participation rate measure, Montgomery was not effective; the expected participation rate was 95 percent, the observed participation rate 93 percent.[11] Failing this one goal—and on arguably trivial terms—put the school in the category of unacceptable performance.

Is Montgomery High School an example of an effective or an ineffective school? Well, it depends on the goal, the yardstick used to measure that goal, and how important you think that goal is to the overall performance or mission of a school (see Sidebar 3.1).

Productivity

Productivity is a narrower form of efficiency measurement. It relates one particular type of input—labor—to outputs. The result is a measure of how efficiently labor is used to produce a given output:[12]

$$\text{Productivity} = \frac{L}{O}$$

In the manufacturing industry productivity measures often are based on relating the time it takes to produce something, so in the widget industry productivity would be assessed on the number of man hours required to produce a widget. The total number of hours librarians spend at work is relatively easy to calculate. But as outputs are again the denominator of the ratio, productivity measures face the same problems of efficiency and effectiveness measures. Time is also considered a fairly crude index of labor for certain occupations. Does time spent in the office or the classroom adequately capture the labor of a CEO or a teacher? Measuring is difficult enough in the private sector; in the public sector these difficulties increase exponentially.

Concepts such as efficiency, effectiveness, and productivity are helpful to private-sector organizations because they clearly relate to the core organizational mission and provide important information about how performance in achieving that mission can be improved. The problem for public agencies is that, unlike their private-sector

Inputs and outputs for a manufacturing company can be identified and measured with relatively high degrees of accuracy, providing good yardsticks of productivity and efficiency. Inputs and outputs in the public sector, however, are a different matter. Performance in a factory can be measured through per-unit costs; in other words, whatever is being built divided by the costs of inputs such as labor and materials. What is the output of a library?

counterparts, they cannot take goals (and therefore outputs) as a given. Whether a given agency is considered efficient or inefficient, effective or ineffective, productive or unproductive, is dependent to a large extent upon a normative or political judgement about that agency's mission priority. Legislators, interest groups, citizens, and agency employees may have very different ideas about appropriate mission priorities, and thus have very different views about agency performance.

Finding Goals

Many scholars who study public bureaucracies conclude they are highly effective organizations if they are given clear goals, appropriate resources, and the freedom to deploy their in-house expertise.[13] The keystone to this effectiveness is a clear goal, ideally one carefully crafted by a representative body. As we have already seen, more often than not this ideal is not realized. If organizational goals are difficult to define with any clarity, how do public agencies figure out what to do? Public bureaucracies devote an enormous amount of effort trying to answer this question. Scholars argue that bureaucracy compensates for a lack of clear goals in a number of ways.

Sidebar 3.1   Public Agencies and Economies of Scope

When a firm uses the same resources to produce two goods or services it experiences what economists call **economies of scope**. Producers that experience economies of scope can enjoy significant cost advantages because, in layman's terms, they get a lot more bang for the buck. Frequently, however, they also face a difficult choice: producing more of one good means producing less of the other. Because no firm can produce an infinite number of outputs from a finite amount of inputs, one output gets priority over the other.

As they are given multiple goals, and thus tasked with producing multiple outputs, public agencies frequently face economies of scope. They prioritize these outputs by making tough choices about how to allocate their available resources. Regardless of the choice made, any agency dealing with economies of scope is forced to make tradeoffs. Improving at one goal means falling short of another.

Regardless of the particular choices made, these tradeoffs leave public agencies vulnerable to criticism because they generally attract more scrutiny and comment than their successes. An agency facing economies of scope invariably is doing a good job of producing some outputs and a poor job of producing others, and the latter performance provides critics with "evidence" of the agencies failure or incompetence.

Public education provides a good example of economies of scope. Schools are tasked with a bewildering variety of goals, and are expected to produce multiple outputs in order to achieve those goals. Two of the most commonly

Figure 3.1   Per-Pupil Expenditures, 1970–71 to 1999–2000

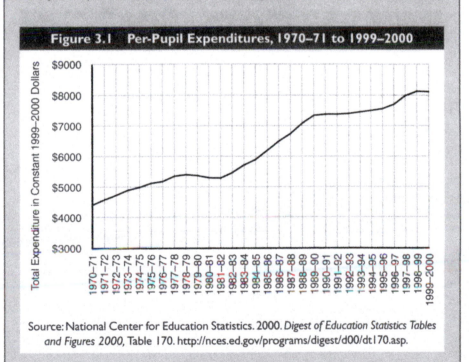

Source: National Center for Education Statistics. 2000. *Digest of Education Statistics Tables and Figures 2000,* Table 170. http://nces.ed.gov/programs/digest/d00/dt170.asp.

Sidebar 3.1 *(continued)*

used output measures in education are test scores and graduation rates. For schools, these represent competing outputs—beyond some point, increasing test scores also means increasing the dropout rate.[a] Using just one of these outputs to assess school performance provides a very incomplete picture of school performance.

Figure 3.1 shows the trend in per pupil expenditures for public schools in the United States from 1970–71 to 1999–2000 in constant (2000) dollars. This clearly shows that over three decades more resources were being invested in education. Figure 3.2 shows the average math score from the SAT during the same period. This shows a period of decline, followed by a return to historical performance levels. Using these two pieces of information, public education in the United States does not seem to be particularly efficient—it has been getting more resources, but has not increased its outputs.

Yet consider Figure 3.3. This shows the dropout rate (the percentage of 16- to 24-year-olds not enrolled in school who do not have a high-school diploma or equivalency degree) from 1970–71 to 1999–2000. The dropout rate has steadily declined, meaning graduation rates have steadily increased. Using this output measure, schools have been putting those increased resources to good use, keeping students in school longer and increasing the probabilities they will graduate. So are public schools succeeding, or are they failing?

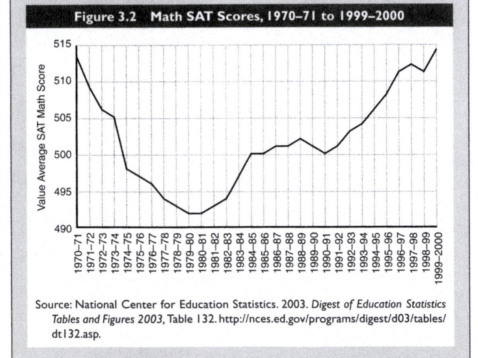

Figure 3.2   Math SAT Scores, 1970–71 to 1999–2000

Source: National Center for Education Statistics. 2003. *Digest of Education Statistics Tables and Figures 2003,* Table 132. http://nces.ed.gov/programs/digest/d03/tables/dt132.asp.

Sidebar 3.1 *(continued)*

The answer, of course, is that it depends. During the time period examined here public education has routinely been castigated for underperformance, a criticism that leans heavily on test scores for supporting evidence. Yet test scores did not decline that much (for the math SAT it was about 20 points on an 800-point test), and ended up returning pretty much to their historical benchmarks. And during this same period, dropout rates were cut by roughly a third—from more than 16 percent to around 11 percent. Public schools seem to have taken their increased resources and used them to hold the line on test scores, while increasing graduation rates.

Many argue that schools should increase test scores *and* graduation rates, but scholarly studies suggest this is not possible: "Beyond a certain point, schools may be able to increase graduation rates only by accepting lower test scores (the students retained to increase graduation rates may lower average test scores), and may be able to increase test scores only by accepting lower graduation rates (allowing those students with the lowest test scores to drop out)."[b]

Schools, like many agencies, face economies of scope. They have to make decisions among competing outputs, and increasing one means holding the line—or decreasing—other outputs.

[a]Jennie Wenger, "What Do Schools Produce? Implications of Multiple Outputs in Education," *Contemporary Economic Policy* 18 (2000): 27–36.
[b]Wenger, "What Do Schools Produce?," 28.

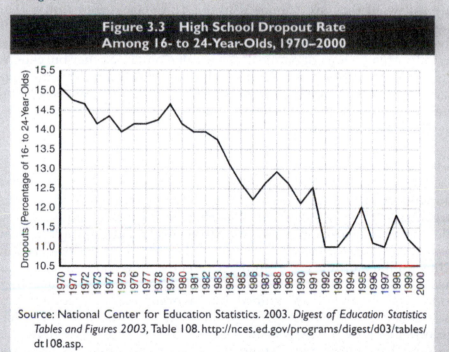

Figure 3.3   High School Dropout Rate Among 16- to 24-Year-Olds, 1970–2000

Source: National Center for Education Statistics. 2003. *Digest of Education Statistics Tables and Figures 2003*, Table 108. http://nces.ed.gov/programs/digest/d03/tables/dt108.asp.

Rules

Rulemaking is the process by which public agencies take laws or mandates from their political controllers and translate them into specific actions.[14] **Rules** are typically detailed written instructions on what public bureaucracies and public servants are supposed to do. Rules can also serve as substitutes for goals. Once they become official organizational policy, rules provide a relatively low-risk behavioral guide for bureaucrats. Most people have encountered or at least heard stories of petty bureaucrats who "go by the book," people who rigidly apply rules even when they are inappropriate to the particular situation at hand. As guides to behavior or the administrative process, rules provide a safe substitute for organizational goals when a bureaucracy or a bureaucrat has no clear organizational objective. Rather than providing a detailed set of guidelines on how a goal is to be achieved, applying the rules *becomes* the goal.

Situational Imperatives

Regardless of their detail or their direct connection to achieving an organizational goal, no set of rules can possibly cover every potential situation a teacher, a police officer, or even a student loan counselor is likely to encounter. In his classic work, *Bureaucracy*, James Q. Wilson suggests that when goals are vague, bureaucrats—especially street-level bureaucrats—use what he terms **situational imperatives** to figure out what they are supposed to do. This means that rather than working to fulfill a core goal, street-level bureaucrats simply deal with the problems they encounter on a day-to-day basis.[15] Thus, if a prison in California is short of oatmeal, the warden or some other bureaucrat deals with the problem as it crops up by buying oatmeal. This does not serve some vague, noble organizational mission such as ending "the causes and tragic effects of crime." It deals with the situation at hand—in this case, breakfast.

Culture

Every organization has a **culture**, a "persistent patterned way of thinking about the central tasks of and human relationships within an organization."[16] Culture can be thought of as the organizational equivalent of an individual's personality. Strong organizational cultures can provide a powerful sense of mission and serve as guides to behavior. Elite military units, for example, overcome long odds and sustain heavy losses in trying to accomplish their assigned tasks because their individual members are guided by an organizational culture that prizes team success, even at the cost of high individual sacrifice. While culture can provide a powerful sense of "what needs to be done," all cultures have blind spots. These are tasks or goals that are organizational responsibilities that do not fit comfortably into organizational culture. The Tennessee Valley Authority (TVA), for example, is an organization whose culture was largely formed by engineers. This created a mission focus on certain technical aspects of the organization's goals, like building dams and generating power. Other TVA goals, such as regional planning and environmental protection, were given less priority because they did not fit comfortably into the engineering-dominated culture.[17]

Self-Interest

Some scholars suggest bureaucrats take advantage of their ill-defined missions by substituting their own preferences and goals for those of the organization. The "maximizing bureaucrat" is someone who is guided by his or her own personal desire for career advancement, power, and prestige.[18] This possibility is an important issue for those concerned about the political role of bureaucracy in a democratic society. Some argue that, given unclear goals, protected by civil service regulations, and driven by career ambitions, it is only human nature for bureaucrats to pursue their self-interests by doing what they can to maximize resources by pursuing higher budgets and greater manpower, and maximizing power by "empire building" or expanding the policy jurisdictions of their agencies.

Professional or Personal Norms

Sometimes public servants are guided by their own ideology or sense of ethics, or the norms established by their profession or training.[19] Lawyers who work for a regulatory agency, for example, may be likely to pursue litigation against businesses who do not fully comply with the policies the agency enforces. Lawyers, after all, are trained to use the law. Because their training may lead them to view regulation as a burden on economic activity, economists may be less likely to pursue litigation. A personal sense of ethics may also guide behavior. Agency whistleblowers may risk ostracism from colleagues or disapproval from superiors, and perhaps even lose their jobs for reporting wrongdoing or incompetence. People can and do run these risks simply because they think it is the right thing to do.

Constituency or Public Interest

Though the law may give an agency a very vague set of objectives, the beneficiaries or targets of the programs and policies it implements may have very clear preferences about what the bureaucracy should do. Agencies that adopt the preferences of their clientele as a primary organizational mission are said to be **captured**. Captured agencies thus serve the interests of those they regulate or provide services to. Though capture is a common concern raised in writing on public bureaucracies, the evidence supporting the notion of capture is actually quite limited. Rather than being captured by a particular organization, some scholars report that bureaucracy and bureaucrats expend enormous effort trying to serve the public interest. This is done by individual bureaucrats motivated by a genuine desire to serve the public good, entire bureaucracies that respond to broad currents of public opinion, and shifts in political direction in the elected branches of government.[20] If their controlling legislation fails to provide clear goals, some bureaucracies and bureaucrats at least try to figure out what of the available options are most likely to serve the public interest.

Government Is No Way to Run a Business

Despite their crucial importance, organizational goals are rarely mentioned in popular analysis of the failures of bureaucracy. Instead, there is a popular perception that the central problem of government agencies is ineffective organization, poor management, and the general incompetence of individual bureaucrats. According to one summation of the popular image of public bureaucracies, "The lowly bureaucrat is seen as lazy or snarling, or both. The office he occupies is portrayed as plagued with incompetence or inhumanity, or both."[21]

The corollary to the popular image of government bureaucracy is the belief that private-sector organizations are better organized, better managed, and care to a greater extent about the satisfaction of their clientele. If public agencies would only adopt the methods and management practices of the private sector, they would work better, faster, and cheaper.

Though widespread, beliefs about the private sector's superiority to the public sector have, at best, mixed support from the available scholarly research. Importing the mechanisms believed to promote private-sector success (competition, a focus on consumer satisfaction, etc.) has produced a lot of claims and counterclaims, but little in the way of definitive conclusions. For example, there are numerous goods and services that are provided by both public and private sectors: education, trash hauling, and transportation are just a handful of many examples. There have been numerous studies attempting to gauge the relative effectiveness, efficiency, and productivity of public and private organizations in delivering such services. Considered as a whole, these provide no clear indication that one is better than the other.[22]

Despite the lack of clear supporting evidence, the belief that public agency performance could be significantly improved if only government would run "more like a business" is so strong that it has been termed "almost a religion."[23] A concerted effort to identify how the public sector can become more like the private sector is one of the constants of U.S. politics. During the past half-century or so, these efforts have included the following.

The Hoover Commission

Formed during the administration of President Harry Truman and headed by former President Herbert Hoover, it had the mandate of identifying how to improve efficiency and effectiveness in the executive branch.

The Grace Commission

Formed during the administration of Ronald Reagan, this organization was headed by J. Peter Grace and made up of 160 other corporate executives. Its mandate was to go over the administrative arm of government, working "like tireless bloodhounds to root out government inefficiency and waste of tax dollars."[24] The Grace Commission eventually evolved into Citizens Against Government Waste, an independent government watchdog group (check them out online: http://www.cagw.org/site/PageServer).

The National Performance Review

This was an ongoing effort to "reinvent government" during the administration of President Bill Clinton. Headed by Vice President Al Gore, it was essentially an attempt to implement the blueprint for "entrepreneurial" (more businesslike) government popularized by David Osborne and Ted Gaebler.[25]

The Bush Administration

The administration of George W. Bush had no specific blueprint to run government like a business, but he was the first MBA-holding businessman to sit in the White House, and he tapped the private sector heavily to staff his administration. Among those drafted directly from corporate boardrooms were Vice President Dick Cheney, Defense Secretary Donald Rumsfeld, Treasury Secretary Paul O'Neill, Commerce Secretary Donald Evans, Director of the Office of Management and Budget Mitch Evans, Secretary of Veterans Affairs Anthony Principi, and White House Chief of Staff Andrew Card. If the public sector could benefit from the business sector, this who's who of corporate America certainly seemed well qualified to do the job.

What all of these efforts have in common is that they did little to clarify the goals of public agencies, and little to change the fundamental operation of public-sector bureaucracies. Despite the difficulties in making government more businesslike, the continuing effort to do so is understandable. Taken as a whole, the administrative arm of government is plagued by overlap, redundancy, confused lines of authority, and poor coordination. Public bureaucracies pursue contradictory goals and are given program responsibilities that have little connection to their primary policy jurisdiction. Though all bureaucracies in a technical sense, the agencies come in bewildering varieties. As we

learned in Chapter 2, just at the federal level there are cabinet departments and agencies, independent agencies and commissions, and government corporations. Each has a variable set of organizational
characteristics and is accountable in different ways to the president
and Congress. Instead of one federal bureaucracy to regulate financial
institutions like banks and savings and loans, there are five. The Department of Housing and Urban Development not only has to report to
the president, but to 40 congressional committees that can claim jurisdiction over its program responsibilities. The Department of Agriculture does not just deal with farmers and agribusiness, it runs one of the
largest social-welfare programs in the nation—food stamps.

Consider Figure 3.4, the organizational chart of the agencies responsible for homeland security prior to the terrorist attacks of September 11, 2001. It is hard to imagine any self-respecting business
organizing itself into such a convoluted maze of overlapping jurisdiction and confused lines of communication and authority. The urge to
streamline such organizational spaghetti, to get the government to
borrow some basic organizational and management lessons from the
private sector, to "blow up boxes," is not hard to fathom.

So why do such efforts invariably fall short of their objectives? Why
is it so hard to clear up some of the "obvious" problems of government
and get it to be more businesslike? The problem is that virtually every
attempt to get the government to adopt the lessons of the private sector
is predicated on an incorrect assumption about bureaucratic goals.
Typically, reform movements assume that the prime objectives of public agencies are to effectively and efficiently achieve their assigned
tasks. In many cases, perhaps most, this assumption is wrong. As one
observer of the historical record of government reform movements put
it: "Economy and efficiency or responsiveness to customers are not the
prime objectives of public administration."[26] The primary job of public
agencies, remember, is not effectiveness or efficiency, but to implement
the law. That means serving *political* objectives, not economic ones.

As an example, consider the federal agencies that regulate the
banking industry. There at least five such agencies: Comptroller of the
Currency (COC), the Federal Deposit Insurance Corporation (FDIC),
the Office of Thrift Supervision (OTS), the National Credit Union Administration (NCUA), and the Federal Trade Commission (FTC). The
program responsibilities of these agencies crowd in upon each other,
and they have little in the way of centralized coordination because they
are housed in different areas of the executive branch and operated by
different legal and organizational arrangements. Two of the agencies
(COC and OTS) are divisions of the Treasury Department, one is an
independent government commission (FTC), one is an independent
federal agency (NCUA), and one is a government corporation (FDIC).
The result is varying organizational setups and cultures reporting to
everything from a cabinet secretary (thus, at least in theory, under the

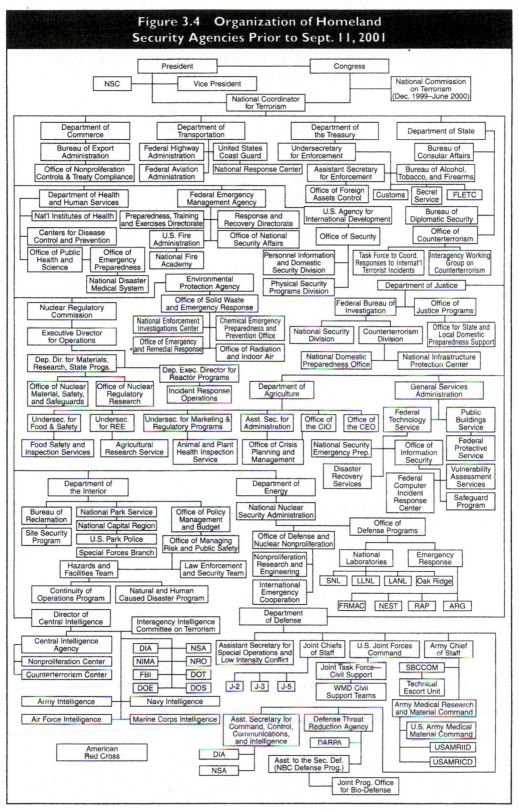

Figure 3.4 Organization of Homeland Security Agencies Prior to Sept. 11, 2001

Adapted from: Monterey Institute of International Studies. 2001. *United States Response to CBW Terrorism and Domestic Preparedness.* http://www.cns.miis.edu/research/cbw/domestic.htm# wmdchart.

more or less direct control of the president), to Congress, to an independent board with relatively little political oversight or interference (see Table 3.1).

The reason there are five federal agencies instead of one is because the banking industry does not want the regulation of financial institutions concentrated into a single agency. In other words, the banking industry has good reasons to want federal regulation to be *inefficient*. Having different agencies regulate different dimensions of the financial industry allows banks to pick regulators and regulations based on the type of activity they engage in.[27] Credit unions and traditional banks, for example, have their own regulatory agency, and an accompanying set of congressional committees interested in exercising oversight in this critical area of the economy, all of which can be targeted and lobbied. From a private-sector perspective, the organization of the financial regulatory "business" seems slightly bizarre. It is unlikely a bank would divide itself into five branches, organize each branch differently, give each branch a different director accountable to a slightly different set of feuding shareholder committees, and then limit the executive authority of the bank president to manage the overall operation. That makes no business sense because it invites inefficiency and ineffectiveness. For public administration, though, that misses the point, or to be more accurate, ignores the underlying goal. The organization of these regulatory agencies may invite inefficiency and ineffectiveness, but it also serves a set of political objectives, political objectives that have made their way into public law. It is to the latter

Table 3.1 Federal Agencies Regulating the Banking Industry		
Agency	**Type of Organization**	**Primary Function**
Comptroller of the Currency	Agency housed in the Department of the Treasury	Regulates national banks
Federal Deposit Insurance Corporation	Government corporation	Regulates state chartered banks that are not members of the Federal Reserve System
Office of Thrift Supervision	Agency housed in the Department of the Treasury	Regulates federal savings and loans and federal savings banks
National Credit Union Administration	Independent federal agency	Regulates federally chartered credit unions
Federal Trade Commission	Government commission	Regulates finance companies, mortgage companies, credit bureaus, stores, and automobile dealers

that the public agencies owe their existence and must justify their action, not efficiency and effectiveness.

In short, the goal is *not* efficiency or effectiveness. It is to mollify and abide by the conflicting political interests that make their way into law. This makes no business sense, but perfect political sense. It also means the repeated efforts to get government to run more like a business are unlikely ever to achieve their goal, because they mistakenly assume the goals of the private sector can be imposed on the public sector. Public agencies are more oriented towards equity, accountability, and the law than to efficiency or effectiveness in any particular program or policy. As one study of reform concluded: "Regardless of how many times and how loudly those who have not tried it assert to the contrary, running a government bureaucracy is not the same as running a business."[28] To assert that what works in the private sector will work equally well in the public sector turns out to be the rough equivalent of saying that a good point guard in the National Basketball Association will make an equally good defensive guard in the National Football League.

Having Business Run the Government

Though the differences between the public and private sectors can be made clear enough in the abstract—and are often frustratingly obvious in practice—there has been a steady movement toward blurring the distinction between the two. The melding and merging of the public and private sectors, however, has not been achieved by getting the government to run more like a business. Instead, business is increasingly running the government.

For several decades, governments in Western democracies have been stepping back from their role as central policy actors and have increasingly turned to the private sector to handle a number of functions traditionally the responsibility of public agencies. In the United States this is typically achieved through the process of contracting out, which simply means the government hires a private vendor to deliver a good or service rather than providing it directly. A number of states, for example, are restructuring how they administer welfare benefits. Traditionally, people visited a government agency. An emerging new model is the public-service equivalent of a corporate call center. Rather than visiting a government bureaucracy and dealing with a public employee, those seeking public assistance phone a call center run by a private corporation in much the same fashion as a computer help line. The corporation is hired by the government on a contract basis to administer welfare programs.[29]

These sorts of contracts are very lucrative for the private sector, and several vendors may get contracts to deliver the same service or administer the same program. The end result is a network of loosely coordinated private and nonprofit organizations with the direct responsibility for implementing public policy. These networks are increasingly a large part of what has traditionally been thought of as public administration. Indeed, the role of private companies in providing public services has become so large that some scholars argue the administrative state is being replaced with a "virtual" or "hollow" state.[30]

This trend has also led to what some call a **shadow bureaucracy**, a large layer of private companies whose primary business is working for the government. This shadow bureaucracy dwarfs the public bureaucracy. One study estimates that the shadow work force of the federal government, that is, the people whose jobs are dependent upon federal contracts or grants, is at least four times larger than the number of workers officially on the federal payroll.[31] Indeed, in the United States, government is more heavily dependent upon the private sector than in almost all other Western democracies. There are a number of advantages to using private companies to deliver public goods and services rather than traditional public agencies.

Flexibility

Private companies are not governed by the often restrictive personnel, operating, and accountability regulations of government agencies. This gives them flexibility and freedom of action that government agencies cannot duplicate. By using private vendors, the government can take advantage of the greater freedom of action private-sector companies enjoy.

Experience and Expertise

Using private companies means government can take advantage of organizations that are already experienced in a particular service or program area rather than building an organization or program from scratch. Through contracts, the expertise of private-sector specialists can be tapped on an as-needed basis at a fraction of the cost of hiring such experts as full-time public employees.

Reducing Costs

At least in theory, awarding contracts through a process of competitive bidding will exert downward pressure on the costs of public goods and services. Contracting also allows the public sector to leverage any natural private-sector advantages in effectiveness and efficiency to the advantage of the taxpayer.

Political

There are certain political advantages to using private companies. Lawmakers who advocate any particular policy take a political risk—the risk that the policy will fail. Failures can be politically costly. Using a network of private vendors rather than a single public agency increases the probability that any failure will be diffuse; this provides political cover. For example, if a reading program introduced into a large city school district fizzles, it is hard for those who championed this program to escape at least some political fallout. If a school district contracts with several private companies to operate individual schools and gives them a mandate to raise reading scores, blame can be deflected towards those holding the contracts.

Another key political advantage of contracting out is that it provides patronage opportunities for lawmakers. At the federal level, roughly 15 percent of government expenditures go directly to private companies through contracts, an annual payout of hundreds of billions of dollars.[32] For legislators, helping secure contracts for companies in their own districts has obvious political advantages.

Yet, while there are advantages to using the private sector to implement and operate public policy and programs, in practice there are also disadvantages.

Accountability

Compared to public bureaucracies, private companies have much fewer legal obligations to make their records, meetings, and other decision-making processes public. In theory, contracts make private vendors accountable—they are legally obligated to deliver what they promise to deliver, and by issuing a contract an agency has a powerful legal tool to ensure compliance. In practice, however, things are more complicated. Issuing a contract to a private vendor is roughly equivalent to formulating rules for a public agency; it represents an attempt to specify actions that will be taken in order to achieve a given goal or task. The involvement of a private vendor does not automatically clarify the goals of a public policy, and in some ways adds complications. For example, a private company hired to run a school with the objective of "improving the overall quality of education" does not have any clearer guidance than a traditional school district. If it is a for-profit company, however, the gyroscope of the bottom line remains. What happens when the drive for profits and a vague policy objective appear contradictory? Which goal will provide the ultimate motivation for the actions of a for-profit company? For example, replacing paraprofessionals with untrained, cheaper classroom aides might serve a company's bottom line, but its overall impact on educational quality invites dissent and debate. Such potential conflicts can lead to ever more complicated relationship arrangements as public authorities seek to write detailed "airtight" contracts. Because goals in the public sector are difficult to clarify and performance is so difficult to measure, however, contracts typically leave plenty of room for disagreement on the specifics of vendor obligations.[33]

The difficulties of insuring accountability are exacerbated by the political activities of companies that routinely do business with the government. In theory, contracting out means the private vendor is simply the agent of government policy, an organization hired to do a specific job and held accountable for delivering on its contractual promise. In practice, vendors work hard to develop strong relationships with legislators and bureaucrats, relationships that often provide them with a considerable amount of input in determining how contracts are structured. In other words, they become as much makers of policy as agents of policy. In observing contracting arrangements at the state and local level, Donald Kettl concluded that contractors often "create independent political ties with policymakers and thus outflank their administrative overseers. In such cases the contractors are less agents than partners, helping to shape the very design of the program, free of any significant oversight, and beneficiary of state and local governments' dependence on their performance."[34]

Complexity

Paradoxically, the effort to be less bureaucratic by relying on private vendors can create a byzantine network of operations and relationships that make the homeland security organization chart in Figure 3.4 look tight and neatly ordered by comparison. Governments issue tens of thousands of grants and contracts every year, covering everything from building jet fighters for the Air Force to providing janatorial services at a local school. In 2001, the federal government spent more than $200 billion on contracts with private vendors, and undertook more than 560,000 contract actions (a *contract action* is defined as awarding or modifying a contract or an actual order of goods or services).[35] This huge amount of activity involves such a broad variety of goods, services, and expenditures, raises so many issues of eligibility, fairness, security, and quality control, and attracts such a diversity of conflicting political interests, that its administrative oversight creates an enormous regulatory challenge. Federal acquisition regulations codifying the laws governing federal contracts run to more than 15,000 pages. Given the money involved, there is ample incentive to forge strong connections to those who determine the budgets, make the laws, and write the rules. The end result is a blurring of the public and private sectors, where people increasingly move from public careers to companies that do business with the government, the archetypical example being a retired military officer who goes to work for a defense contractor. The resulting shadow bureaucracy is a layer of private companies built around public agencies that issue high-dollar contracts. It is increasingly difficult to identify a clear separation between these companies and the government proper. For example, these companies are staffed to an increasing extent by those with public sector experience, people who "know the system" and have strong relationships with public agencies and public servants. Other companies are so dependent on government contracts—public money—that it is disingenuous to call them private. For example, when the storied aircraft company McDonnell-Douglas did not win approval to compete for the contract for the next Joint Strike Fighter, it went out of business and was purchased by Boeing.[36] The shadow bureaucracy is less visible, less accountable, and its place in the public or private sector more difficult to define.

Differences Between Theory and Practice

The theoretical advantages of the private sector are not always evident in practice. For example, in theory contracting out is based on competitive bidding, a process that theoretically puts downward pressure on costs. Vendors seeking to win a contract in a competitive bidding process have an incentive to keep costs low in order to avoid losing business to a competing bid. In reality, a number of forces work against competitive bidding and its associated payoffs. For example, when the Colorado legislature mandated that public bus routes in Denver had to be opened to competitive bidding from the private sector, 18 companies showed initial interest, and eight actually submitted bids. Three contracts were awarded, all to national transportation companies. The national companies submitted bids far below those submitted by local companies (they may have been below the actual costs of actually operating the bus routes), and by doing so cut local operators out of the market. Two of these companies merged, and costs soon went up. In the late 1990s, another round of bidding yielded only three bids, all of which were awarded to a single company. Over a decade of contracting out, the costs of using private vendors turned out to be not much different from using a public agency, and the downward pressure on costs had largely disappeared. The end result of the contracting-out process for public transportation in Denver seemed to be an oligopoly, one dominated by companies with pockets deep enough to lobby the state legislature hard to expanded privatization and increase the associated lucrative business opportunities.[37]

At the federal level, so many exceptions and constraints on competitive bidding have been created (often after hard lobbying by the private sector) that many contracts are negotiated rather than bid out. This process again draws the public and private sectors closer together and raises questions about how profit and the public interest can comfortably accommodate each other. Contracting out is a balancing act that involves elements of need, accountability, and political expediency. As one observer of the contracting process observed, "the primary job of the contracting officer is to balance political demands and supports with budgetary restrictions and governmental needs."[38] Employing the private sector for public services in many ways creates rather than removes the conflict and uncertainty of politics.

Questionable Efficiency Payoffs

As we have already discussed, the widespread belief that private companies are more efficient than their public counterparts rests on surprisingly little supporting evidence. Having businesses run government programs is often no more cost-effective than using public agencies, and in many cases is *less* cost-effective. Often this is simply because the profit motive creates incentives to increase rather than decrease government payouts. The classic example is a government bureaucracy overpaying for a good or service. Everyone has heard stories about the government paying five dollars for a 30-cent screw or 600 dollars for a coffee maker. Such stories are generally presented in the media as examples of the incompetence and ineffectiveness of bureaucracy. What tends to get left out of such stories is that it was private vendors who were gouging the government, and public agencies that caught and exposed the fraud.

Conclusion

The single biggest source of confusion about public administration stems from an ignorance or a misunderstanding of the goals of public agencies. The widespread belief that government operations would improve immeasurably if bureaucracy adopted more businesslike organization and management practices often overlooks the key differences between the public and private sectors. Fundamental to these differences are goals: profit versus implementation of public law. Public agencies are routinely tasked with vague, multiple, and contradictory goals. The lack of mission clarity makes it hard for public agencies to satisfy the diversity of expectations placed upon them, and creates severe difficulties in using private-sector benchmarks to assess their performance.

Despite these differences, the drive to make public agencies more businesslike is a staple of government reform movements. There is a notable lack of success in the historical track record of these efforts. From a private-sector perspective, however, the motivation to reform the public sector is understandable. The administrative arm of government is characterized by redundancy, confused lines of authority, poor coordination, spotty communication, and a bewildering variety of organizational cultures and characteristics. This produces countless examples of the prisons-could-get-cheaper-oatmeal variety, which in turn serve as constant justification to "blow up boxes" and reform bureaucracy. The problem with reform movements is that they begin with the assumption that improving efficiency, effectiveness, and productivity in public agencies is the primary goal. These goals often conflict with the political purposes of public agencies. Political goals tend to win such conflicts for the simple reason that political missions—not efficiency, effectiveness, or productivity—are the reason public bureaucracies exist, and they provide government bureaucracies with their primary motivation and justification for action.

Though attempts to make government run more like a business have met with little success, there is an increasing trend towards having businesses run the government. The private sector is increasingly involved in the formation and implementation of public policy. There are some distinct advantages to using the private sector to discharge the traditional responsibilities of public administration. There are, however, also disadvantages, especially in terms of accountability and balancing the often conflicting goals of profit and the public interest. The growth of the private sector shadow bureaucracy has not created a universal resolution to the fundamental difference between the public and private sector goals. When those goals are clear and clearly compatible, public-private sector partnerships can increase the probabilities of successful policy and programs. When goals are not clear, and certainly when they conflict, there is always the possibility that the public interest will not be served by the increasing involvement of the private sector.

Key Concepts

captured Public agencies are said to be captured when they adopt the interests and preferences of their clientele as their primary goals.

culture Organizational culture is a persistent way of thinking about organizational tasks and human relationships within the organization.

economies of scope Economies of scope exist when an organization uses the same resources to produce more than one output.

effectiveness A measure of organizational performance, typically calculated by dividing observed organizational outputs by expected outputs.

efficiency A measure of organizational performance, typically a ratio of an organization's outputs to its inputs.

productivity A measure of organizational efficiency that calculates the labor required to produce an output.

rulemaking The process by which public agencies take laws or mandates from their political controllers and translate them into specific actions.

rules Written instructions on what public bureaucracies and public servants are supposed to do.

shadow bureaucracy Private organizations whose primary business is getting contracts from public agencies. Shadow bureaucracies typically operate under much looser regulatory restraints than public agencies.

situational imperatives The characteristics of a particular situation that provide the goal or motivation to make a choice or take an action. ✦

Chapter 4

Bureaucratic Power in a Democratic State

Or, Why Government Is More Than It's Cracked Up to Be

In 2003 the Department of Education adjusted the federal needs analysis methodology, a complex formula used to calculate a family's discretionary income. The formula, not to mention the specifics of the adjustment (which dealt with how state and local taxes counted against income), sounds like red-tape minutiae best described as eye-glazing. Eye-opening is more like it. The decision—made by bureaucrats, not by elected officials—cut federal spending on higher education by hundreds of millions of dollars and shifted those costs to parents and students. Under the recalculated formula, California families earning more than $50,000 were judged to be able to spend an extra $500 on college expenses, while families in New York were judged capable of spending another $700.[1] The formula readjustment meant the Department of Education changed the financial-aid eligibility requirements for millions of college students.

If politics is the process of deciding who gets what, this is clearly a political decision. College students, after all, clearly got less financial aid. As those writing checks to cover tuition and fees can attest, that's politics writ large. What's more interesting for our purposes is the Department of Education's authority to unilaterally make such a sweeping policy decision. Where did they get that power, and how do they get to exercise it? It's not just the Department of Education, after all. Virtually all public agencies at all levels of government routinely make decisions about who gets what. Like it or not, the bureaucracy exercises political power every day.

Indeed, the bureaucracy is a focal point of government power. In order for public agencies to effectively accomplish the tasks we want done (from smooth city streets to missile defense), they rely on several different sources of political power. This political power is then used in a variety of ways, including making policy on their own (called rule-making), resolving legal disputes (called adjudication), and implementing policy. Thus, the bureaucracy can truly be called a focal point where legislative, judicial, and executive power, all of which are delegated to the bureaucracy by legislatures, are combined. It is the only institution of government that is able to combine these powers, which are otherwise separated by the Constitution across the three branches of government. These powers, and how they are used, will be the topics of this chapter.

The Traditional View of Public Administration

Even though Congress has delegated authority to make rules and regulations to the executive branch since its first sessions in the late 1700s, scholars of public administration have traditionally viewed the duties of bureaucracy as largely limited to the implementation of laws passed by legislatures. In a sense, the bureaucracy was seen as a passive institution, waiting to be directed by an elected body of government. This traditional view is the politics-administration dichotomy first mentioned in Chapter 1, the notion that politics and public administration are completely separate. The traditional view also assumes that the politics-administration dichotomy is the source of good governance and good public administration.

The source of this traditional view is typically traced to Woodrow Wilson, who was a political science professor prior to becoming the 28th president of the United States. In 1887 he wrote an influential article on public administration, where he outlined his view of the "proper" role of bureaucracy in America.[2] In the article, he clearly desires public administration to be based solely on the implementation of public law (passed by legislatures), stating that politics sets the tasks for the bureaucracy and should not be an activity that the bureaucracy engages in. The crux of his argument is that "the field of administration is a field of business. It is removed from the hurry and strife of politics."[3] If this is achieved, he implies, then the bureaucracy will function more efficiently and more ethically, in terms of serving the public good.

It is easy to see why this traditional view has remained popular (indeed, many public administration degrees are offered through the business schools in American universities). Politics is often considered to be full of corruption. People complain about the influence that lobbyists and special interest groups have, which steers public policy away from what is good for the country and toward what is good for a small number of people or corporations. Others complain about the *quid pro quo* that occurs in legislatures, where politicians "scratch each others' backs" and engage in pork-barrel spending that not only targets special interests, but also increases overall spending to unacceptable levels. Still others complain that politicians are cynical, a product of a system that does not adequately hold them accountable for promises made on the campaign trail. With all of these complaints, assuming there are grains of truth to them, who in their right mind would want to subject the bureaucracy to the same situations? This indeed was Wilson's point: public administration should be a refuge from partisanship in order to improve efficiency, speed, and quality of service. Mixing politics and administration, Wil-

Woodrow Wilson (1856–1924) was a scholar of public administration and the nation's 28th president. He advocated that politics be separate from administration, in order to achieve more efficient policy implementation.

Library of Congress, Prints and Photographs Division LC-USZ62-13028.

son argued, would only hurt governance by shifting the focus in public agencies away from finding technical and cost-effective ways of implementing policies toward advocating policy positions and supporting particular ideological or political factions. After all, there is no "Republican" or "Democratic" way of paving a street, just a way to do the job right for minimum cost. This requires the politics-administration dichotomy, where the bureaucracy passively waits for policy directives to implement, without having a political "voice" of its own.

Bureaucracy as a Political Actor

Fortunately, as we will see, for the United States, there is no politics-administration dichotomy, and there probably never was one.[4] There are several reasons for this, but the underlying reason is that legislatures themselves delegate a substantial amount of political power to the bureaucracy. There are practical reasons for doing so. In the American political system, executives, legislatures, or courts cannot govern independently. This is because the system is founded on the notion of a separation of powers, the idea being to ensure that no individual or single element of government has enough power to govern as a tyrant. Separation of powers results in a government characterized by deliberation and caution, and no small measure of inertia and inflexibility. This certainly prevents a concentration of power and shields democracy against the development of tyranny, but it's not exactly calculated to get things done. If all political decisions—all decisions on "who gets what"—were made by elected officials, the political system would be even more gridlocked and overburdened than it is. Instead, authority has been delegated to the bureaucracy in such a way so as to collapse the powers of the three separate branches into one institution. This allows some political decisions to be made quickly and efficiently, ensuring that government is capable of responding to citizen demands in a timely fashion.[5] Bureaucracy, in short, makes political decisions because legislatures want them to.

Further, the bureaucracy is a political actor because legislatures rely on it when making public policy, as you saw in Chapter 2. Legislators are generalists, almost by definition. They must know a little bit about a lot of things, in order to make them appealing to a wide range of voters, and in order to allow them to adequately serve the diverse needs in their constituency once elected. Legislators also operate under serious time constraints, particularly those who must run for office every two years. And even though their staff sizes have increased over time, learning the details of each policy issue is beyond the resources of most legislators. Consequently, they frequently do not have enough information or technical expertise to make high-quality legislation without advice from bureaucrats. This means that government agencies play an important political role in writing legislation, and are key actors even at the start of the policy process.

Besides relying upon bureaucracy for expertise, legislators may also shift political pressure away from themselves by delegating an issue to an agency, or they may delegate an issue if they are unsure about how to resolve a problem. In the second case, the agency can try different options, with the legislature holding the power to select the option it feels is best.[6] In fact, Kenneth Meier argues that a key reason for increased policymaking activity on the part of the bureaucracy is due directly to the inability or unwillingness of elected institutions in the United States to resolve political conflict.[7] Even if our democracy is not in as bad condition as Meier argues, it remains true that legislators increasingly rely on government agencies to help them make public policy.

The bureaucracy is also a political actor because of its central role as the implementer of public policy. Policy implementation, covered in more detail in Chapter 10, is important because no policy can be specific enough to cover all circumstances or future situations. Consequently, bureaucrats need to make their own decisions about how to apply the existing policy to a new situation. This means that policy implementation allows bureaucrats to use discretion. Bureaucratic discretion is essentially the ability of an agency or a single bureaucrat to determine how a law will work in certain applications. This can range from the Federal Trade Commission making a decision about what is and what is not deceptive advertising, to the police officer who has just pulled you over for speeding making a decision about whether to write you a ticket or send you on your way with a stern warning.

With important roles to play in both policy making and policy implementation, the bureaucracy is definitely an actor that is engaged in "politics of the first order"—that is, engaging in policy making and political decisions as an autonomous actor. Because the bureaucracy is a focal point of legislative, judicial, and executive authority, government agencies have the power to write policy (rulemaking authority) and resolve legal disputes (adjudication) all by themselves, in addition to influencing politics and decision making in our elected institutions.

Sources of Bureaucratic Power[8]

So where does all of this influence and power come from? Why is the bureaucracy able to take advantage of its access to elected institutions? How is it able to take advantage of the authority that is delegated by the legislature? There are two main sources of bureaucratic power: skills or "internal" sources, and political support or "external" sources.

Skills or 'Internal' Sources of Power

There are several internal sources of power, most of which rest on the skills and abilities of the bureaucrats that staff government agencies.[9] The first is **expertise.** Bureaucracies enjoy many advantages over elected institutions that serve to increase their technical information, expertise, and levels of competence. Since bureaucracies are effectively permanent, they can take advantage of the power or organization. Difficult goals can be accomplished through coordination, teamwork, and division of labor that would be otherwise impossible for individuals to do. Expertise is further enhanced in bureaucracies due to specialization. Unlike elected officials, bureaucrats have the luxury of concentrating on a single issue for long periods of time. Agencies typically have a relatively limited set of goals and policy issues on which to concentrate. As such, bureaucrats are able to develop experience and will become familiar with the details or technical aspects of a policy or problem. An additional benefit is that because most bureaucrats are careerists (in other words, they are likely to keep their jobs over the long term), concentration and consistency are enhanced.

Bureaucratic expertise is often developed to such an extent that government agencies have a virtual monopoly on information. It is difficult, for example, to imagine another policy actor with as much information on smoking than the bureaus housed within the United States Department of Health and Human Services. The Office on Smoking and Health's database houses a collection of research articles on smoking covering 35 years of publications, and nearly 2,000 items are added each year—and this is only a tiny fraction of the information it has available. This makes it unlikely that a legislator seeking advice from the Office on Smoking and Health will have a way to verify the information, which greatly enhances the influence the agency has on the policy process. These advantages in expertise and information are key reasons why elected officials, even the president, rely on the advice of bureaucrats when writing legislation or making decisions. For example, the president frequently seeks the advice of the State Department on issues related to foreign policy, consults with the Joint Chiefs of Staff on military issues, or uses recommendations from the Council of Economic Advisors when planning tax policy.

Professionalism is another internal source of power, and is related to expertise. Professionalism is acting according to a set of standards and goals for ethics, quality of service, and self-improvement that a field of work has established. Many bureaucrats employed by government agencies are highly trained professionals. Lawyers, economists, chemists, physicians, social scientists, and others bring high levels of training and technical knowledge, and act according to the expectations and obligations of their professions. Considering that, by definition, professions require a level of technical knowledge not available to those outside the profession, these bureaucrats are much more able to influence government policymaking. They simply may be the only people who understand the problem that a policy proposal is supposed to address.

Professionalism also enhances the credibility of the policy positions that bureaucrats take. If good policy advice was given by an agency in the past, then that agency will be more accepted and gain legitimacy in the future. Professionalism that leads to good performance is therefore an important source of bureaucratic power and influence. And it is undoubtedly the case that professionalism generally leads to good bureaucratic performance. For example, five scientists from the National Institutes of Health have won Nobel Prizes,[10] we rely heavily on the economists on the Federal Reserve Board to guide our economy, and although there have been setbacks, the accomplishments of the scientists at NASA over the last 40 to 50 years are astounding. We have literally sent our bureaucrats to the moon.

Discretion is another internal source of bureaucratic power. Discretion is typically defined as "the ability of an administrator to choose among alternatives—to decide how the policies of the government should be implemented in specific cases."[11] As legislators cannot pass policies that will be able to meet every situation or address every technical detail, many of these decisions about how a policy will function are left to the bureaucracy. This means that once a policy has been passed, bureaucrats still have influence over how it will be applied to society. Essentially, bureaucrats will determine how it works by making a variety of decisions about such things as enforcement levels, determining the definition of a problem, procedures for the public to follow, or even ignoring certain issues or policies.

For example, the local police department exercises its discretion for enforcing speed limits; it may set speed traps one day and choose not to the next, or it may patrol certain roads more heavily than others. Defining problems is another important way bureaucracies exercise discretion; the Consumer Product Safety Commission may choose to recall a toy because it has determined that it is a choking hazard, or the Environmental Protection Agency will define what is an "unacceptable" amount of a certain pollutant. Another key way that bureaucracies exercise discretion when implementing policy is when they set procedures for the public to follow. Professors at public universities are tasked by the state with providing higher education, and they are basically free to write their syllabi as they see fit. The National Park Service establishes rules for how the public is able to use the parks, and sets procedures for dealing with naturally caused forest fires. Another interesting element of bureaucratic discretion is that policies may not be enforced vigorously, or may simply be ignored. This is typically the result of the fact that the agency in charge does not have the ability to aggressively enforce the policy, or that the policy is self-enforcing, or both. The Internal Revenue Service rarely actually audits individual tax returns, partly because it probably lacks the capacity to "cast a wide net," and partly because citizens tend to obey the law anyway.[12] Other well-meaning laws may not be deemed important enough for enforcement, or citizen behavior may already be more or less in line with the goals of the law. Outside of large cities, jaywalking laws are routinely ignored. Many towns and cities also have laws prohibiting people from riding bicycles on sidewalks, but unless someone poses an obvious danger to pedestrians, these laws go ignored.

The political power that expertise, professionalism, and discretion bring can also be augmented by **bureaucratic cohesion** and leadership. A cohesive organization is one in which members are committed to the organization and believe in its goals. Because the policy problems that we face in the United States are complicated, solutions require dedication and hard work. A cohesive agency is much more likely to have employees who meet these requirements, and as a result will perform better. Highly cohesive agencies will give better advice to policymakers, will use discretion more creatively, and will establish more effective rules and procedures.

Similarly, well-led bureaus will be more effective in politics and policymaking. Good leadership will build cohesion and expertise, thus improving bureaucratic influence. Leadership is also important because it can build the reputation of the organization, which can serve the agency well when dealing with elected officials as well as with the public.

Political Support, or 'External' Sources of Power

The reason why leadership is so important is because the bureaucracy does not exist in a political vacuum. A bureau's actions will always influence people and groups in society. These groups and people represent the bureau's clientele: those who are directly served by the agency. For example, the clientele of the Farm Service Agency in the Department of Agriculture includes farmers (who take advantage of farm loan programs, disaster relief, and price supports), environmentalists (who are served by the agency's environmental protection and conservation programs), and businesses that deal with agriculture markets (who are served by the agency's informational programs on food warehousing, prices, and commodity markets). Of course, bureaucratic clientele can also offer political support to elected officials, and policymakers who oppose a government agency must therefore oppose the agency's clientele. Thus, the electoral concerns of policymakers effectively enhance the power of a bureaucracy, as long as the bureaucracy can cultivate a clientele that is politically meaningful. Elected officials will be less willing to oppose the bureaucracy if they think that by doing so they will lose popular support at the polls.

This means that some clientele provide more bureaucratic power than others. Some clients are actually hostile. The Environmental Protection Agency frequently faces this situation, as industries the EPA regulates bear additional costs when they must install pollution-control devices due to that regulation. Therefore, some activity on the part of government agencies will be focused on ensuring they have more clients that provide support than opposition.

The size and dispersion of an agency's clientele should also matter (although evidence is mixed). For example, the larger an agency's clientele, the less likely that elected officials will openly oppose the agency and its mission. The reason is simple political mathematics: a larger clientele equals more voters, voters who won't be happy if their favored government programs are targeted by elected officials. Indeed, elected officials are more likely to direct resources toward agencies with large clientele. The political math again makes sense: happier voters mean reelection for incumbents. Furthermore, concentration of clients in one area of the country may indicate that an agency is of only local interest. Clients who are spread across the country, on the other hand, are more likely to represent a national concern, one that will draw much more attention from policymakers.

Clientele that are committed and respected, and that possess information beyond what the agency already has, are particularly useful for

Although bureaucrats are not elected, government agencies are sensitive to the demands of their clients. Because agencies are political actors, they can take advantage of public support, and have their influence reduced when they lose it.

building bureaucratic power. A committed and respected clientele will be more energetic and successful when advocating policy in support of the agency. A clientele that can supply additional information in support of the agency to policymakers is particularly valuable.

The influence of clientele is revealed in research that demonstrates that agencies with clientele support are much more able to avoid budget cuts, and even gain increases in congressional appropriations. Clearly, bureaucratic power rests in large part in the clientele of public organizations. Of course, there is a less cynical view of bureaucratic power that comes from agency clients. Clientele make legitimate demands on government. Because policymakers wish to make good public policy to solve problems in society (otherwise why would they run for office?), they will seek to satisfy the needs of the bureaucracy's clientele.[13]

Public opinion may also be considered to be an "external" source of bureaucratic power, although it is a source that is difficult to use. Like clientele support, public opinion may actually be hostile to an agency. It is difficult, for example, to imagine an agency with greater general public hostility than the Internal Revenue Service. Also, few people actually understand the function of many or most government agencies. Without some idea of what an agency does or how it does it, general public opinion is worthless. In fact, this is perhaps the key reason why government agencies advertise and publish information.

Because public opinion is not something that agencies have much control over, it is not a consistent source of political power. For example, general public opinion in the 1960s and early 1970s provided a great deal of political power to NASA, as spaceflight began and the moon landing program was executed. Once the mission of landing a man on the moon was accomplished, however, public opinion turned elsewhere and NASA's programs were no longer national priorities. Government agencies need to take advantage of supportive public opinion when it is there, because it may vanish quickly as the attention of the nation shifts, or if the agency is involved in a disaster or scandal.

Other elites in politics can also be an external source of power for bureaucracy. Support from other elites may include individuals who can be influential due to their position, job, or expertise. Academics and professionals in the private sector have resources, information, and expertise that they can provide to agencies to help them advocate their positions. Certainly, however, elected officials are the most important elites. Individual legislators or the chief executive will frequently act as personal lobbyists on an agency's behalf. This is particularly the case if an agency's clientele is related to key portions of the elected official's constituency, or if an agency's mission is close to a particular policy goal that the individual has. Obviously, some legislators are more valuable to an agency than others. In Congress, members of substantive committees that oversee the activity of an agency will be more important, as will be members of the appropriations subcommittee for the agency. Support from substantive committees is generally easy to obtain, as they are composed of members who are interested in the mission of the agency. Support from appropriations subcommittees is more difficult to obtain, as they are charged with protecting public funds. An agency with solid internal sources of power, however, should fare better.

The importance of support from the executive branch is difficult to assess. Certainly, having an executive lobby the legislature on behalf of an agency's position is beneficial. However, much of what the president, for example, can do in terms of supporting government agencies and programs is to boost public awareness and opinion. As a result, support from executives is rarely consistent or obvious.

The Nature of Bureaucratic Power in a Democracy

With all of these sources of power, it is obvious that the bureaucracy is able to play a large role in policymaking. By using its expertise and professionalism, and by cultivating its ties with other political elites and its clientele, the bureaucracy can be considered to operate side-by-side with the legislative branch. In other words, the bureaucracy is most definitely a political actor, fully capable of influencing political decisions about government priorities, policy goals, and even the wording of legislation itself. Finally, the bureaucracy is in control over policy implementation. By exercising discretion over how policies are applied to society, the bureaucracy has political power here too.

The fact that the bureaucracy is engaged in politics of the first order raises some crucial issues for how our democracy works. The basic democratic principle is that of free and fair elections. This provides citizens with the opportunity to participate in government, and leads to a representative government that will respond to the needs and wishes of the public. To quote Lincoln's Gettysburg Address, it produces "government of the people, by the people, and for the people." Although we may grumble sometimes, we worry less about the power we vest in our elected officials, because we can replace them if needed.

This safeguard for citizens does not exist in the bureaucracy. The bureaucracy enjoys many political powers, as we have shown, and bureaucrats make decisions every day about what policy positions to support, what advice to give to lawmakers, and how laws will be implemented. These are serious decisions indeed, even more so because we do not elect our bureaucrats. Thus, bureaucrats have a lot of political power and policymaking authority, yet there is (or at least seems to be) little direct accountability to citizens. We cannot elect new people to the Department of Education if we do not like what it is doing.

This has worried the public, as well as scholars of government, for a long time. In fact, Woodrow Wilson's argument, made in 1887, about dividing politics and administration is based on this very concern. He proposed establishing control over the bureaucracy by making it a more passive institution, reacting only to the demands of elected officials. This is what is known as "overhead democracy," where voters elect candidates who support their positions (and remove from office those who no longer please the public), and those elected officials control and direct the bureaucracy. This theoretically allows for indirect bureaucratic accountability to citizens, through elected institutions. This subject will be discussed in detail in the next chapter. Suffice it to say here that while controlling the bureaucracy is an important concern, it is still the case that democratically elected officials provide bureaucrats their administrative and political power. Bureaucrats therefore are expected to operate under their authority and to be accountable to them.[14] This control provides more legitimacy to bureaucratic power in a democracy.

Over-Reliance on External Sources of Power

Another potential problem of bureaucratic political power is that government agencies may tend to rely too heavily on their external sources of power. This may lead to a situation where an agency's ties to

its clients and other political elites are so strong that the policy decisions the agency makes serve only the clientele, possibly to the detri-
ment of the rest of the public.[15] There are natural and reinforcing links
between an agency, its clientele, and key political elites, primarily
those legislators who sit on the substantive committee that oversee the
agency. A client group will obviously be interested in supporting an
agency that provides it with goods and services, just as the agency will
rely upon that clientele for political support. Members of the substantive committee in the legislature, those legislators who are interested
in the policy area of an agency, will be supportive of that agency's mission, just as the agency will rely upon those members for resources and
program assignments. And the clientele will support the substantive
committee in order to ensure favorable programs, just as the committee will rely upon the clientele for support in elections.

Thus, an agency with a politically important clientele and strong
ties to the legislature may develop a relatively closed policy network.[16]
This network will be more resilient to opposition, as all three members
have an incentive to maintain the set of relationships. It is also possible
that these networks will not act to support broad public interests but
will rather operate in order to serve the more narrow interests of the
clientele. This is because of a lack of opposition and the lack of incentive to act in ways that are not directly beneficial to one or more of the
members of the network.

These networks are called subsystems[17] or **iron triangles**. This
name aptly describes the set of relationships: there are three members
or points of the triangle (a legislative committee, an agency, and the
agency's clientele) and because the relationships are reinforcing, the
network can be long-lasting and difficult to break apart. Iron triangles
are most likely to develop when an agency provides concentrated benefits to a distinct friendly clientele, and when the costs of those benefits
are spread widely across the population. The agency also needs the
ability to exercise discretion over program implementation so it can
meet the demands of the clientele. Under these conditions, there are
greater incentives for the three members to maintain the network, and
little prospect of opposition because no other single group in society
bears a high cost.

Clearly, the implications of iron triangles are undesirable. Theodore Lowi argues that the United States has allowed these relationships to develop to such an extent that special interest groups have
"captured" government agencies and effectively determine public policymaking.[18] This leads to the unchecked growth of government
spending, particularly "pork-barrel" spending targeted at narrow interests. Lowi argues that through the over-reliance of government agencies on their external sources of power, we have policy outputs that are
less democratic and less likely to serve the broader public welfare.

Are these concerns reasonable? Probably not, at least not to the extent that Lowi argues. One mitigating circumstance should already be apparent: iron triangles are only likely to form when an agency has a distinct friendly clientele, without opposition, and when benefits to the clientele are concentrated but costs of those benefits are diffuse. These particular conditions are rarely met. At a minimum, the iron triangle only describes one type of policy network that can exist. Even when the conditions are met, it is usually not for long, and the "damage" to democratic policymaking is minimized. There are several reasons why iron triangles are rare, and more difficult to maintain than the name implies.

First, it is now easier to mobilize and organize citizens. With television, email, and the Internet, communication has been made faster, easier, and less expensive. The proliferation of computers and printing technology also makes publishing newsletters possible for even small organizations. Since it is easier to form organizations and interest groups, it is less likely that any one interest group or government agency will be without opposition.

Second, new information is provided constantly, and new definitions of policy and problems are produced as a result. The members of iron triangles cannot stop the provision of information by others, even on subjects that they normally control. If the information is important and widely available, it is possible that public opinion may change in a way that eliminates the iron triangle. This is what happened to the tobacco industry. Until the mid-1960s, the tobacco industry enjoyed a closed policy network with the Department of Agriculture and members of Congress from tobacco-growing states. However, once enough information on smoking and cancer was available, the Surgeon General issued a report on smoking in 1964. From then on, tobacco became a public health problem rather than one related simply to crop prices, and many additional groups, interested in regulating the tobacco industry, began to play a role in tobacco and smoking policy.[19]

Third, agencies have many other groups, institutions, and people they must respond to besides their clientele and members of substantive committees. Chief executives (the president, or governors at the state level) also place demands on agencies. So do courts when they rule on issues in a way that forces a change in bureaucratic behavior. Even other government agencies make it difficult to establish a closed policy network. For example, the Environmental Protection Agency, which regulates water pollution from mining, may make it difficult for the Bureau of Land Management to act in ways that will exclusively benefit mining companies.

Fourth, agency politics are not necessarily based on friendly clients, which means that not all agencies are in a position to build an iron triangle policy network. Some agencies may have client groups that compete with each other. Small farmers and large agribusiness concerns disagree over how price-support programs should be run by the Farm Service Agency. This situation is becoming more common across all agencies, as it is easier to mobilize citizens and form advocacy groups. Client groups can also be either hostile or ambivalent toward the mission of the agency. The Food and Drug Administration faces such a situation, in which regulated drug manufacturers sometimes chafe under the FDA's regulations. Car manufacturers frequently oppose the National Highway Traffic Safety Administration's positions. Other agencies may not even have an identifiable or consistent clientele. The Federal Trade Commission, charged with ensuring fair marketplace competition, serves the general public. Regulated industries or firms do not necessarily support or oppose the activities of the FTC, as they wish for a fair market and may never find themselves the target of an FTC ruling.

Fifth, discretion may not be available to the agency, even if all the other conditions for the formation of an iron triangle are met. The Social Security Administration definitely serves a specific clientele, and provides concentrated benefits to clients while spreading costs out across the country. However, the clientele has almost no ability to pressure the agency to use its discretion to increase benefits for the simple reason that it has no such discretion: benefit levels and eligibility are determined by statute. The SSA is an example of a bureaucracy that has almost no discretion over implementation. Consequently, if client groups want policy change, they lobby Congress rather than work with the SSA.[20]

Finally, client-based politics are not inherently bad, and are frequently intentional.[21] This still does not mean that agencies are completely captured by their clientele.[22] The Department of Veterans Affairs, for example, exists to serve veterans in a variety of ways, from administering the GI Bill (which provides funds for college education) to providing health care. Yet the VA does not necessarily rely on client demands to decide eligibility or benefit levels. The Federal Aviation Administration operates in the interest of airlines and civil aviation. It helps ensure safe, efficient air travel by providing crucial services such as air traffic control, and encourages the growth of civil aviation by helping develop new technology. The FAA also sets safety standards, and so can choose to respond more directly to passengers than airlines. Cases such as these reveal that there are policy issues that either require a focus on client service in order to provide services vital to the functioning of the economy and our society, or demand it out of a sense of social justice. It is important to remember that this focus need not lead to a situation where an agency is captured by a group in society.

Rulemaking and Adjudication

Agencies are certainly well-positioned to play an important political role in legislation. As you have just seen, they bring useful skills and tools to policymaking, ensuring that they are able to help guide decisions made by elected officials. Beyond this, however, the bureaucracy is also its own independent policymaking authority. This authority is used in two ways: rulemaking and adjudication.

Rulemaking

Rulemaking, as discussed in Chapter 3, is a legislative function that agencies use to make their own public policy. Rules made by government agencies carry the force of law, and are used to both implement and clarify public policy made by Congress. Rulemaking allows agencies to use their expertise, information, and discretion to codify how they will achieve the broader policy goals set forth by Congress.

Agencies follow the **Administrative Procedures Act** when making rules. This Act, passed in 1946, was intended to make decision making in government agencies more regular and predictable, as well as more open and democratic.[23] Following this Act, agencies that are interested in making a rule first develop a draft. This draft is submitted to the Office of Management and Budget for economic analysis (as well as to ensure the rule fits with the presidential administration's interests) and it may be submitted to interest groups, members of Congress, or other agencies. Once the draft is cleared, the agency then submits it as a rule proposal in the ***Federal Register*** (see Sidebar 4.1). Any party that would be affected by the rule may then provide comments to the agency, and has at least 30 days to do so. Once the comment period is over, the agency has several options: pass the final rule with no changes; pass the final rule with changes as a result of the comments; reopen the comment period; or remove the rule from consideration and either start over or abandon it altogether.[24]

The number of interested or affected parties is often quite large, and the various parties may conflict. For example, the Federal Communications Commission is under tremendous political pressure from both sides of the issue of decency on the airwaves. Parent groups and social conservatives advocate tough rules for regulating language and lewdness on television, while groups worried about censorship argue that such rules overstep the FCC's boundaries. Due to this potential for political conflict, rulemaking procedures are "designed to sort through facts from multiple sources in order to select standards that apply generally."[25] Once a rule is issued, any person or party interested or affected by the rule may petition the issuing agency for the repeal or amendment of the rule.

These rulemaking procedures are centered around democratic ideals of information, participation, and accountability. Agencies must at least provide information about the basis, purpose, and authority for a proposed rule. Other statutes may force particular agencies to provide further information about how the rule will work, its feasibility, and

---

Sidebar 4.1   A Rule Proposal From the *Federal Register*

When a government agency wishes to make a new rule, it must place a rule proposal in the *Federal Register*, in accordance with the Administrative Procedures Act. The proposal summarizes the provisions of the potential rule, provides the details of how the rule will work, identifies the authority the agency has to issue the rule, and directs anyone who is interested to provide comments. The following is a brief excerpt of a rule proposal from an agency within the Department of Housing and Urban Development. The actual proposal is eight pages long.

```
DEPARTMENT OF HOUSING AND URBAN DEVELOPMENT

24 CFR Part 598

[Docket No. FR-4853-P-01; HUD-2005-0009]
RIN 2506-AC16

Empowerment Zones: Performance Standards for Utilization of Grant Funds

AGENCY: Office of the Assistant Secretary for Community Planning and
Development, HUD.

ACTION: Proposed rule.

---------------------------------------------------------------------

SUMMARY: This rule proposes to establish certain planning and
performance standards for utilization of grant funds allocated to
Empowerment Zones, including for benefit levels and economic-development
activities. The standards are designed to ensure that the activities
undertaken by Empowerment Zones with Federal grants are consistent with
the Empowerment Zone's strategic plan.

DATES: Comment Due Date: August 8, 2005.

ADDRESSES: Interested persons are invited to submit comments regarding
this rule to the Regulations Division, Office of General Counsel, Room
10276, Department of Housing and Urban Development, 451 Seventh Street,
SW., Washington, DC 20410-0500. Interested persons may also submit
comments electronically through either:
    The Federal eRulemaking Portal at: http://www.regulations.gov
; or

    The HUD electronic Web site at: http://www.epa.gov/feddocket.
Follow the link entitled "View Open HUD Dockets."
```

Source: Office of the Federal Register, National Archives and Records Administration. 2005. *Federal Register* 70 (109):33641–33648.

---

its cost-effectiveness. The procedures, open to comments from those affected by the proposed rule, ensure public participation in bureaucratic decision making. Although there is nothing in the Administrative Procedures Act that forces agencies to heed the comments of interested parties, they run great risks by ignoring them. Agencies may have their decisions and actions on a rule reviewed if there are signifi-

**Sidebar 4.2 Rulemaking in the National Highway
Traffic Safety Administration**

Government agencies use rulemaking to regulate industry and individuals, and to clarify and aid the implementation of broader legislation. Many of these rules influence your lives in a variety of ways. Federal Aviation Administration rules prohibit you from smoking on airline flights. The Food Safety Inspection Service of the Department of Agriculture requires labels on meat and poultry products to provide you with information about nutrition and contents.

One set of agency rules has produced a product and an outcome that all of you are familiar with. The National Highway Traffic Safety Administration has a set of rules that require passive restraints. Passive restraints are devices that restrain passengers during a crash, but require no action, such as putting a seatbelt on, on the part of the passenger. These rules started in 1968, when automobile manufacturers were first required to include seatbelts in all new cars. Prior to this, seatbelts were optional equipment for consumers. During the 1970s and early 1980s, the NHTSA tried to adopt rules that would phase in passive restraints, but were put on hold due to lack of support from the Nixon, Ford, Carter, and Reagan administrations.[a] After a lawsuit against the NHTSA brought by insurance companies and consumer advocacy groups, the NHTSA passed a rule to phase in passive restraints in all newly manufactured cars by 1990.[b] These restraints started with the development of automatic shoulder belts, and a later rule phased in air bags. So the seat belts and airbags in your cars are due to the rules made by a regulatory agency.

The story of the NHTSA's rules on seatbelts and airbags is a good one to show how agencies respond to their political environment. Aside from the 1968 rule requiring seat belts, the NHTSA suffered from a lack of political support, and was not able to find backing for subsequent rules on passive restraints. However, when consumer groups and a private industry (insurance) joined to force the NHTSA to act and gave it enough political support to do so, it responded, just as elected officials respond to their constituents. The result is that it is safer for people to drive, and the required policy was made through agency rulemaking rather than legislation.

[a]Kenneth J. Meier, *Politics and the Bureaucracy: Policymaking in the Fourth Branch of Government*, 4th ed. (Harcourt Brace: Forth Worth, TX, 2000).
[b]Kenneth J. Meier, *Regulation: Politics, Bureaucracy, and Economics* (St. Martin's Press: New York, 1985).

cant public complaints. Clearly, one way to avoid those complaints is to listen and respond to interested parties during the rulemaking procedure. Finally, rulemaking procedures ensure some accountability. Because the bureaucracy must respond, at least in part, to the demands of the constitutional institutions of government (at the federal level, the presidency, the Congress, and the courts), they may review and make judgments about agency rules. Further, the democratic ideals of information and participation provide a way for citizens to hold the bureaucracy accountable. We get to see what decisions are being made, and we can take part in those decisions if we wish. This means that agencies must respond to us directly, as well as to Congress, the president, and the courts (see Sidebar 4.2).

Adjudication

Adjudication is a judicial function that agencies use to charge and try individuals or firms suspected of violating the law. Because it is a judicial function, agencies must abide by some of the requirements that exist in the courtroom. The individual or firm must be served notice, evidence must be presented, and the proceedings must be fair and impartial. The results of adjudication are not the same as the results of rulemaking. A decision reached through adjudication applies only to the case at hand. Other similar cases must be ruled on separately.

Regulated industries prefer adjudication over rulemaking, because the process is slow and it allows the industries or individuals to present a detailed case. Often, a hearing is held and some agreement is reached between the agency and the firm or individual. In particularly large cases, however, agreements may not be reached, but the process allows for resolution in a court of law.[26] Examples of adjudication abound, some of which are familiar and appear regularly in the news. For example, adjudication is used by the Consumer Product Safety Commission to recall a huge variety of products; in 2002, the CPSC recalled products ranging from bicycles, gas grills, and circular saws. Recalls of toys get the most media attention, because badly designed toys can injure or kill children. However, other product recalls can be prominent, too. The National Highway Traffic Safety Administration used adjudication to cause a highly publicized recall of certain Firestone tires in the fall of 2000.

Both rulemaking and adjudication represent the policymaking power of agencies. Thus, the bureaucracy is not only able to play a role in policymaking in elected institutions, it can also make public policy by itself (with input from interested parties, other institutions, and regulated clients, of course).

Conclusion

The influence that the bureaucracy has in politics and policymaking in the United States is enormous in scope. By relying upon internal and external sources of political power, government agencies play crucial roles in determining political agendas, making policy decisions, and influencing how policies are applied to society.

The bureaucracy plays a direct role in legislation by providing advice and technical information to lawmakers, who generally lack expertise compared to bureaucrats. By cultivating ties with clientele and key committee members in the legislature, agencies can enhance their influence on policymaking and enhance their ability to serve their clients and the general public. Government agencies can also make their own public policy, through rulemaking and adjudication, which carries the same force of law that "ordinary" legislation does.

Bureaucracy is certainly not just about implementation, separated from politics, as Wilson argued in the late 1800s. Bureaucracy is a political actor with its own political power. This helps the government function. Legislation is better because of the advice of bureaucrats. Policies are more tailored to the needs of citizens because agencies are interested in serving both the general public and specific clientele. Authority for rulemaking and adjudication is delegated to agencies so that elected officials do not have to legislate for every single contingency or special case. Positive government in the United States would not be possible today without the bureaucracy's ability to play a role in politics. This power, of course, causes us to have concerns about how to control it and make sure it is used appropriately. These issues will be discussed in the next chapter.

Key Concepts

adjudication A judicial function that government agencies use to charge and try individuals or firms suspected of violating the law. Adjudication is done on a case-by-case basis, but can still have broad implications, such as when the Food and Drug Administration recalls medication from the market due to safety concerns.

Administrative Procedures Act Passed in 1946, this act guides how government agencies make rules, adjudicate, hold public meetings, retain records, and otherwise enforce the law.

bureaucratic cohesion Commitment to an organization and belief in its goals shared by members of a public agency.

discretion A source of political power for agencies that is derived from the ability to decide how policies will be implemented. Discretion allows bureaucrats to decide how to apply the general terms of a policy to specific situations in society, and to decide what procedures will be used to accomplish the goal of the policy.

expertise A source of political power for agencies that is derived from the coordination, teamwork, and experience that arises from their being able to devote attention to a single issue for long periods of time.

Expertise gives bureaucrats an advantage in technical information that others in the policy process do not have.

external sources of power Some political power of the bureaucracy comes from sources outside government agencies. Broad public support for the mission of an agency lends it political power. On the other hand, general public opposition to the mission of an agency makes it politically weaker. Agency clientele that is committed and respected generates political support. Other elites (academics, professionals in the private sector, and elected officials such as executives and legislative committee members) can also be important sources of political power.

Federal Register The federal government's daily publication of rules, proposed rules, and notices that government agencies wish to announce. Executive orders and other presidential documents are also included.

iron triangle A name for a policy subsystem that denotes the strong bonds between a government agency, its clientele, and key members of the legislature. These bonds are durable and reinforce each other because what is good for one member is usually good for the other two.

professionalism A source of political power for agencies that is derived from acting in accordance with the standards for ethics, training, quality of service, and dedication to self-improvement established by a particular field. Professionalism gives bureaucrats legitimacy and respect, as well as special skills not available to those outside the profession. ✦

Chapter 5

Ethics and Accountability

Nebraska State Treasurer Lorelee Byrd and Army Reserve Specialist Jeremy Sivits served in very different public agencies, and had very different duties and responsibilities. What they have in common is that both were accused of taking actions in 2003 that breached the public trust. Sivits was the first soldier convicted in connection with the infamous Abu Ghraib scandal, where a number of American soldiers were found guilty of physically and psychologically abusing Iraqi prisoners of war. For his part in these actions, Sivits went to jail for a year. Byrd was accused of writing $300,000 in state checks with no intention of cashing them. Critics who called for her dismissal charged her with, in effect, hiding money to shield her agency from potential budget cuts. She ended up pleading guilty to a misdemeanor charge of official misconduct and resigned her office in early 2004.[1]

Prisoner abuse and questionable accounting practices serve, respectively, as an extreme and a mundane example of a central challenge for the administrative state: how do you ensure that public agencies and their employees act in the public's interest? The important role of public agencies in social, political, and economic life means it is essential for democratic institutions to be able to control and influence bureaucratic behavior. If public agencies and their employees can act as they please, putting their own interests above the public interest without fear of consequence, political power inevitably flows to bureaucracy. The potential for the hierarchical and authoritarian bureaucracy to act independently, to follow its own path rather than following the wishes of democratic institutions, has been a perennial concern of public administration scholars. As previous chapters point out, public bureaucracies are influential policy actors engaging in "politics of the first order." Yet while being granted broad discretionary authority to implement and enforce legislative wishes, bureaucracies are also largely insulated from the ballot box and only partially accountable to elected officials.

There are good reasons to separate bureaucracies from direct democratic processes, including minimizing the influence of special interests over public agencies and individual bureaucrats, promoting competence over popularity as the basis for public employment, and reducing the potential for corruption that comes when job security lasts only as long as the next election. Yet distancing bureaucracy from democracy exaggerates the paradox at the heart of governance: democratic states need bureaucracy to function, and to function well they need to keep bureaucracy away from democracy. This contradiction in democratic terms raises a perennial question for students of public administration: "How does one square a permanent (and, we would add, powerful) civil service—which neither the people by their vote not their representatives by their appointments can readily replace—with the principle of government 'by the people'?"[2]

The difficulty and importance of bureaucratically squaring the democratic circle is essential to understanding the role of public administration in governance. How can we ensure that bureaucracies and bureaucrats choose the public interest over self-interest? This chapter explores a range of potential answers to that question.

Ethics

The most straightforward solution to the problem posed here is to ensure that public agencies are staffed with people who can be trusted to "do the right thing." The problem, of course, is that the right thing to do in a given situation can be very much in the eye of the beholder. There is no universal definition of the public interest that provides a clear-cut course of action for all conceivable circumstances. **Ethics** is "a system or code of conduct based on universal moral duties and obligations which indicate how one should behave; it deals with the ability to distinguish good from evil, right from wrong, and propriety from impropriety."[3] Bureaucrats routinely face **ethical dilemmas**, situations where the right course of action is not clear. For example, should public agencies favor socially disadvantaged minorities in hiring decisions? On the one hand, it seems clear that public agencies should just hire the best qualified for the job and pay no attention to characteristics such as race and gender. Yet some groups undeniably have suffered discrimination, and lack of educational and job opportunities. If the government does not take positive action to address those inequities, who will? In this case, what is the right thing to do? There is no universally agreed upon answer.

Ethical dilemmas extend from the trivia of workplace decisions well into the personal life of public employees. Is it ethical for a public employee using an agency vehicle to run a personal errand on the way to or from work? Should a public employee be allowed to use the office phone to make personal calls? What if an agency employee has a gambling or drinking problem? Even if these problems are not noticeably affecting their job performance, are they reason enough to remove them from positions of public trust?[4]

The answers to a lot of these sorts of questions often boil down to "it depends." It depends on the situation, it depends on the individual, it depends on the intent behind the action, and it depends on the expectations and the rules of the agency. Since ancient times governments have struggled to provide clearer answers by establishing rules of conduct that lay down minimal expectations of behavior for public-sector employees. Such a set of rules is called a **code of ethics**—a set of guidelines that helps distinguish between "right" and "wrong" behavior.

Ethics are derived from **values**, or beliefs about what is right or wrong. There are numerous sources of values in our society, and thus a variety of different ways to go about constructing a code of ethics. Religion and political ideology, for example, are well-known and powerful sources of values. Religious beliefs often provide a set of detailed, value-based rules on how to behave (the Ten Commandments from the Old Testament of the Bible, for example). Ideology provides people with a set of consistent beliefs about the proper role of government in society, and those beliefs can be used to determine whether a particular action or decision is the right thing for a public employee to do. Many are leery, however, of using religion or ideology as the basis for a code of ethics in public administration. The obvious risk is public agencies that make decisions based on a particular set of religious or ideological beliefs. This is fine if you share those beliefs, but creates enormous concern if you do not. Sooner rather than later, the public interest will find itself at odds with any narrowly defined set of religious or ideological interests.

Other sources of values include the broad civic values shared by most Americans, such as a respect for the democratic process and tolerance of dissenting ideas, and the values embedded in professional codes of behavior. Many professions have a distinct set of values and clear ethical codes that are drawn from them. For example, doctors take a Hippocratic oath in which they promise to, above all, do no harm to their patients. Lawyers are bound to keep their private consultations with clients confidential, regardless of what the client reveals during those consultations. Ethical journalists have gone to jail rather than break that profession's core value of never revealing a confidential source. During the past 50 years or so, scholars, elected officials, and public administrators have increasingly recognized the need for a code of ethics that draws from the broad civic values of the United States that creates clear guidelines on ethical behavior for all professional public administrators. Among the oft-suggested values that should be foundational to a public administration code of ethics are truthfulness, neutrality, respect of and adherence to law, honesty, and trustworthiness.[5]

In the United States all levels of government impose some form of ethical guidelines on public servants that are based on these sorts of values. Typical local, state, and federal employees are prohibited from using their public positions for private gain, from using confidential government information, from receiving gifts offered by special interests, from representing private governments before public bodies, and from receiving fees and honoraria. In most cases these are not voluntary "honor systems," but requirements of the job backed by the force of law.[6]

A number of public administration scholars have argued that given their high levels of responsibility and their insulation from democratic processes, it is critical that public servants have more than a set of legal prohibitions to guide ethical behavior. Ideally, what is needed is some sort of consistent professional value system that distills the ethical essence of what it means to be a public administrator. For bureaucrats making decisions in difficult and uncertain environments, this value system would resolve ethical dilemmas.

One of the first scholars to advocate a systematic set of ethical standards for public administrators was Paul Appleby. Appleby sought to identify the characteristics that make up a principled administrator and distill them into a code of ethics. Appleby argued that ethical administrators are those willing to assume responsibility, take the initiative, work with people, and refuse to wield power for its own sake, and who are technically competent, able to deploy the resources of their agencies to achieve its goals, polite and courteous, and, above all, sensitive to the importance of political freedom. By the latter, Appleby meant administrators who would be responsive to the needs and wants of the public, be willing to make modifications based on those expressed preferences, and put the public interest above their own.[7]

Scholars who followed Appleby have made further contributions to our thinking on the values that should guide an ethical public administrator, and much of this work is reflected in the American Society for Public Administration's (ASPA) Code of Ethics. ASPA is the largest professional organization for public administrators, and its Code of Ethics seeks to promote the highest standards of public service. ASPA expects its members to serve the public interest, uphold the law, demonstrate personal integrity, promote ethical standards in their organizations, and to strive for professional excellence. ASPA considers ethical standards important enough to create an organizational unit solely devoted to promoting ethics in the public service. ASPA's Ethics Section publishes a research journal on ethics in public administration (*Public Integrity*), holds conferences and forums, and serves as a general clearing house for issues related to what constitutes ethical behavior in the public service (check it out online: http://www.aspaonline.org/ethics community/).

A supplement to ethical codes designed to cover the public service broadly are the other professional value systems and principles or norms of behavior that are stressed as facts of life in particular types of public organizations. A city attorney and a doctor working for the Centers for Disease Control are both expected to abide by the norms of their respective professions; client-attorney privilege and the Hippocratic oath are not put aside, or pushed to secondary importance, just because they work in the public sector. Professions that exist almost exclusively in the public sector often have high expectations of behavior. For example, firefighters and many military units have unwritten rules that "no one gets left behind," rules that are obeyed even at the risk of serious injury or even death to those who voluntarily adopt these standards as the price of belonging to the organization. The firefighters who were going up the towers of the World Trade Center as it collapsed during the terror attacks of September 11, 2001, were much more likely motivated by the values of their particular branch of the public service than by considerations such as a paycheck or the chance at promotion. Academic researchers have found that the sense of duty that often comes with public service is taken extraordinarily seriously by many who work in public agencies.[8]

A professional value system that promotes high ethical standards is appealing in the abstract, and in practice most public administrators are people of good character who are highly attuned to the public interest. Once internalized by the individual, a code of ethics or value system exerts a powerful influence on behavior. There is perhaps no stronger internal check on bureaucracy than making civil servants answer to their own consciences.

The problem with systemized value systems is that they are of limited use as guides for making specific decisions. It is all very well to stress doing the right thing and upholding the public interest, but bureaucrats are routinely faced with situations where the right thing and the public interest are not immediately clear. The utility of ethical codes is further diminished by the fact that they are often not heavily promoted or emphasized. ASPA's membership is about 10,000, meaning that most public employees are not members. Even among ASPA members, awareness of the organization's code of ethics and its contents are fairly low.[9]

A further problem is that there is not *a* code of ethics for public employment. Instead there are a wide array of ethical codes, laws, systems, and expectations placed upon public agencies. If there is a problem with ethical codes in the public service it is that too many, rather than too few, exist. Federal, state, and local governments have widely divergent sets of ethical standards and ethics enforcement mechanisms with little coordination between them. These overlap with—and sometimes even contradict—the professional value systems that go along with becoming a doctor, a lawyer, or any of the other myriad professions and occupations that set ethical expectations for their members. This lack of standardization makes it hard for a single system, such as that proposed by ASPA, to gain much traction as the ethical gyroscope for the entire public service.

Ethical codes and value systems are also limited because, no matter how detailed, they cannot cover every potential moral dilemma faced by a public servant. As the President's Commission on Federal Ethics Law Reform reported: "Laws and rules can never be fully descriptive of what an ethical person should do. They can simply establish minimal standards of conduct. Possible variations in conduct are infinite, virtually impossible to describe and proscribe by statute."[10] In other words, codes of ethics for public administrators help address the problem of getting public agencies to do the right thing. Yet they are unlikely to be a solution all by themselves.

A Question of Accountability

One of the values often embedded in values and ethical codes of public administration is **accountability**, or the belief that public agencies and their employees should be answerable for their actions. Americans have always been somewhat uneasy with the power and responsibilities given to government bureaucracies, and have expressed a strong and consistent desire for public agencies to be held strictly accountable for their actions and decisions. The idea here is that public agencies are more likely to serve the public interest if they have to answer to representatives of the public interest. While such sentiments are broadly held and easy to agree with in the abstract, translating the universal desire for strict accountability into practice turns out to be highly complex.

As mentioned above, public agencies and public servants are judged to be accountable to the extent that they are required to answer for their actions.[11] This seems reasonable enough, but our definition of accountability leaves unanswered the questions of what bureaucracies should be held accountable for, who they should be held accountable to, and by what means accountability is going to be insured.

Figuring out what bureaucracies should be held accountable for raises the problem of agency goals. In order to hold an organization accountable for something, a prerequisite is to have a clear idea of what that something is. As discussed at length in Chapter 3, this turns out to be a frustrating task because we ask public agencies to take on a variety of complex and even contradictory tasks. For example, do we hold schools and teachers accountable for test scores or graduation rates? Preparing students to become citizens or training them for useful and rewarding careers? Serving the wishes of the community or conforming to the standards of professional teacher training? Or all of these?

As we learned in Chapter 3 , simply figuring out what we want bureaucracies to do is surprisingly hard. Accordingly, holding public agencies answerable for what we want them to do is equally difficult.

Recognizing this, public administration scholars view accountability, like agency goals, as multidimensional. In other words, there are different sorts of accountability. **Bureaucratic accountability**, for example, means to hold a public agency answerable for compliance with the laws and rules that govern its operations. **Performance accountability** means to hold a public agency answerable for achieving a particular task or goal. **Market accountability** means to hold an agency answerable for the satisfaction of its clientele with its services. **Professional accountability** means to hold individual bureaucrats answerable for adhering to the norms and standards of public services and their individual professions—acting in accord with professional codes of ethics.[12] Using any one of these approaches for a particular agency has advantages and disadvantages. Because these different accountability standards are not mutually reinforcing, successfully applying them all to a single agency is virtually impossible. For example, bureaucracies that strictly adhere to the rules governing their operations can (and often do) end up with a dissatisfied clientele put off by a "by the book" approach to its particular needs. Other bureaucracies may be faced with a choice between process or outcome; that is, achieving a certain goal means bending (or breaking) some rules.

A good example of these sorts of tradeoffs comes from a study by sociologist Linda Francis of a county agency in the southeastern United States that serves as the social safety net for people who are homeless and suffer from mental health and substance-abuse problems. Case workers in this agency were consistently caught between the needs of their clients and the rules they were expected to enforce. The federal grants that helped fund these programs were designed to aid the homeless and those with substance abuse problems. But the county-level mental-health agency was set up to deal with just mental-health problems, not substance abuse or homelessness. Their rules specified that clients had to have a home address and no substance abuse problems. Given this, what would be the right thing to do when faced with a truly needy individual who is homeless and/or has a substance abuse problem? Caught between the rock of the rules governing the mental-health agency and the hard place of their clients' needs—which in many cases were immediate and truly desperate—many caseworkers took to bending the rules or breaking them outright. Because a substance abuse diagnosis could severely complicate an effort to get people the shelter and healthcare they needed, some people with substance abuse problems were simply diagnosed as suffering from depression. Why? Because people suffering from depression could get help from the county mental-health agency, while those suffering from substance abuse could not. In this case, the bureaucrats made a conscious decision to buck the rules in order to get their clients the help they needed.[13]

Given the broad range of things we want public bureaucracies to answer for and the difficult choices created by different accountability standards, some scholars have suggested that the real nature of accountability is unavoidably political. Rather than being held answerable to a clearly understood standard, "public administration accountability involves the means by which public agencies and their workers manage the diverse expectations generated within and outside the organization."[14] From this perspective, bureaucracies are accountable to the extent that they can successfully juggle the many demands placed upon them.

Regardless of the specific approach to accountability, there is little doubt that we want public agencies to serve the public interest rather than their own interests. We not only want bureaucracies to be answerable, we want them controlled by democratic institutions or processes. So, "When we speak about bureaucratic accountability, the bottom line is that we are concerned about whether or not our government agencies are under some control and oversight by us or our representative institutions. We want them to be answerable and responsive to our goals and priorities."[15]

Accountable to Whom?

Even assuming that a rough consensus exists on what a given public agency is to be held answerable for (no small assumption—see Chapter 3), a central question remains on to whom the agency should be held accountable. There are at least three possibilities.

Elected Officials

Perhaps the most common view of bureaucratic accountability holds that public agencies should be answerable to elected officials. This perspective leans heavily on the concept of **overhead democracy**.[16] Under the theory of overhead democracy, elected officials hold bureaucracies accountable and voters hold elected officials accountable.

Overhead democracy thus sets up an indirect, two-stage process for controlling public agencies. The first step requires that citizens hold public officials accountable through the mechanism of the ballot box. The second step requires that these elected officials pay close attention to bureaucracy and make sure the actions of public agencies meet with the wishes of the people.[17] In theory, this is a fairly simple system of control and accountability—if public agencies are doing things that are contrary to the public interest, public officials will act to correct the problem. If they do not, they face the possibility of being replaced by irate voters during the next election. In practice, of course, things are more complicated.

To begin with, overhead democracy assumes that elected officials have both the tools to control the bureaucracy and the political will to use them. There is little doubt that the requisite tools for bureaucratic control exist (see below), yet it is not always clear that incentive to use them exists. Most of the time public agencies do their jobs reasonably well, and elected officials have many demands on their attention. Given this, there is often little incentive for elected officials to invest much time in bureaucratic oversight, which necessarily lowers the level of accountability.

Even when the incentive to play close attention to bureaucracy does exist, it does not necessarily result in clear direction for public agencies and unquestioned control for the elected official. In a system of divided powers like the United States, bureaucracies typically have at least two elected masters—a legislature and an executive. Legislatures and executives serve different constituencies and may have very different ideas of what a public agency should or should not be doing. Even within a legislature, there may be different groups pulling a bureaucracy in different directions. The end result is a fragmented and diffuse sort of accountability that makes overhead democracy, even in the best circumstances, a complex and far from perfect undertaking.

The People

One potential solution to the difficulties inherent in making public agencies accountable to public officials is to cut out the middle man of overhead democracy and make bureaucracies directly accountable to the people. The most obvious way to do this is to establish direct democratic control over public agencies by making at least some of their leadership posts elected positions. At least in theory, this establishes a direct electoral connection between citizens and a public agency and thus gives voters the option of holding public agencies directly accountable. If an agency fails to live up to expectations or does not deliver on the promises of its leaders, the voters can install a new set of leaders.

This approach to bureaucratic control and accountability is widely employed at the state and local level, where many executive agencies are headed by elected officials. Depending on the state, these offices may include everything from attorney general to insurance commissioner, from county sheriff to local tax assessor. Nebraska State Treasurer Lorelee Byrd, who got into trouble for financial improprieties in this chapter's opening examples, was an elected official. Even if she had not resigned from office, the scandal was enough to severely limit her chances of being reelected.

The problem with making bureaucracies directly accountable to the electorate is that they tend to be less accountable to executives and legislatures. This has a number of potentially negative consequences. For one thing, it is harder to govern if key public agencies are, in effect, separate electoral fiefdoms. Strong ideological or partisan differences between key agency heads can complicate interagency cooperation and make it difficult to coordinate public policy. For another, electoral popularity is no guarantee of competence. The only qualification required to run some sheriff's departments, for example, is to get a plurality of the vote. No law enforcement credentials (or even experience) is required. And agency heads trying to be attentive to their own reelection prospects may get mixed messages from their constituents. Citizens are rarely of one mind about any given issue, and trying to respond to public opinion is a notoriously difficult task. Even when public opinion is clear, public agencies may better serve the public interest by ignoring rather than following the message it sends. Few believe that it serves the greater democratic good to have powerful bureaucracies such as law enforcement or regulatory agencies controlled by the shifting winds of public opinion, the passions of the mob, or ideological or partisan agendas.

It can be argued that the American experience shows that linking bureaucracies directly to the ballot box confuses rather than promotes accountability. Offices such as insurance commissioner or county election supervisor tend to be fairly low profile, attracting comparatively little attention and interest from voters. Dispersing responsibility through a series of elected agency heads requires citizens to be highly informed and involved in order to exercise effective control and accountability by means of the ballot box. Even then, having multiple agents to hold accountable—as opposed to a single representative and a single executive—can be a daunting and difficult task.

Clientele

One way to simplify the complexities of direct accountability to the public is to make an agency accountable to its clientele. So rather than trying to answer to the entire electorate, an agency instead focuses on trying to satisfy the demands of the subgroup of citizens with a direct interest or involvement in the agency's program responsibilities. This is a quasi-market form of accountability and control. A bureaucracy can be structured so that it is held answerable to its clientele in much the same way that a business must either satisfy its customers or run the risk of failure.

Typically this is done by giving agency "customers" a choice of service provider. School voucher programs, for example, allow parents to shop for the schools that best fit the needs and wishes of their children. In theory, schools that do a poor job will not attract students. No students, no vouchers, and no vouchers, no budget. This gives these agencies a strong incentive to respond to the demands of their primary clientele. The idea is to make public agencies answerable to the internal demands of their clientele rather than the external demands of legislatures, executives, or the public at large. Unlike broader public opinion, clientele groups are likely to send clearer and more unified messages, and have a much greater incentive than the public at large to hold bureaucracies to account for any failure to respond to these messages.

While making public agencies accountable to their clientele has some advantages, the market analogies go only so far before conflicting with the need for democratic control. Making an agency answerable to its core clientele in a very real sense sidesteps democratic accountability altogether. The preferences of a bureaucracy's clientele and the preferences of elected officials and citizens are not necessarily the same thing. A school that responds to demands for, say, racial segregation or religious indoctrination may be doing a very good job of responding to the wants of its customers, but it is hardly serving broader democratic interests. The problem with employing market-like systems of accountability and control is that they make it hard to get agencies to respond to the broader interests of the democratic process when they are in conflict with customer or clientele preference.[18]

Mechanisms of Accountability

There is a wide variety of tools that can be employed to control bureaucracies and hold them accountable for their actions. These tools can be roughly classified into external and internal checks on the bureaucracy. The main differences between these forms of control are whether the bureaucracy answers to someone inside or outside of the agency's general scope of operations.

External Checks on Bureaucracy— The Accountability Tools of Public Officials

External checks mean a bureaucracy is held accountable to someone or something outside an agency's normal scope of operations. This notion is central to concepts of bureaucratic accountability like overhead democracy. In order to work, this form of accountability requires some actor to have the tools and the power to impose effective controls on bureaucratic action from outside the agency. Generally speaking, these external actors are taken to mean public officials in the form of legislatures, executives, and the courts. Each has a different set of options for controlling bureaucracy.

Legislatures. Representative bodies such as Congress and state legislatures have five basic ways in which they can control bureaucracy.[19] First, they have the power to make law, which is the power of life and death over a public agency. Bureaucracies are brought into existence by law, and the methods and scope of their actions are dictated by law. Through their lawmaking powers, legislatures can set limits on what public agencies can and cannot do, mandate reporting and performance requirements, and determine personnel and management practices. The power to make law literally gives legislatures the power to tell public agencies what to do, how to do it, and even put public agencies out of business altogether.

Budgeting powers constitute a second important tool for control and accountability for legislatures. Typically legislatures are given the responsibility of raising the money necessary for government operations and authorizing its expenditure. In most cases legislatures have the final say in how much money a bureaucracy gets. This means that in public administration, the golden rule (he who has the gold gets to make the rules) works in favor of legislatures. Public agencies that resist legislative direction or fail to meet minimally acceptable performance and service standards risk losing some or all of their budget.

A third option for placing a powerful external check on bureaucracy is the legislative veto. Under the provisions of a legislative veto, a bureaucracy formulates a proposed plan of action and then submits this plan for legislative approval. If the legislature has objections to the proposal it can deny—or veto—the plan, and the bureaucracy is then forced to submit a revised proposal. Legislative vetoes are controversial for two reasons. First, they delegate a good deal of decision-making power to bureaucracy. The legislature's involvement in policymaking becomes a comparatively passive process of giving a thumbs up or thumbs down to plans formulated by the bureaucracy. Second, they raise the question of a violation of the separation of powers. Certainly at the federal level, it is largely the president's job to run the administrative side of government, and the legislative veto creates the possibility of Congress micromanaging the agencies the president is supposed to oversee. The legislative veto has actually been ruled unconstitutional at the federal level by the U.S. Supreme Court, though it is widely acknowledged that it is still used. A number of states formally allow legislative vetoes.[20]

The fourth option legislatures have for controlling public agencies and holding them accountable is their oversight powers. It is within the power of Congress and most state legislatures to gather information, hold hearings, and conduct investigations into the activity of the bureaucracies they create and control through law. These powers mean legislatures have the ability to check up on what bureaucracies are doing and force them to justify their actions. Oversight operations such as congressional hearings can provide a very public and high-profile forum where a public agency is required to account for its behavior.

Finally, legislatures can hold bureaucracies accountable through informal contacts between individual members and individual agencies. These informal contacts routinely occur during the process of constituency service when citizens who have encountered problems turn to their elected representatives for help and advocacy. For example, a senior citizen who has not received her social security check may contact her member of Congress. An informal phone call to the Social Security Administration from that legislator—who, remember, has input into the agency's budget and governing legislation—may bring a much speedier and satisfactory resolution to the problem than if the constituent tried to negotiate the bureaucracy on her own. At a minimum, it is likely to result in a confirmation and clarification of social security eligibility guidelines. Dedicated constituency service by legislators at any level of government can help keep public agencies accountable.

Executives. Unlike legislatures, executives cannot make law. Generally speaking, the president, governors, and local heads of government do not have the power of life and death over bureaucracy, nor can they unilaterally cut their budgets or change the laws that govern their scope and responsibilities. Nonetheless, executives typically have a number of very powerful tools available to them to help control bureaucracies and hold them accountable.

To begin with, though public executives in the United States rarely have the power to create or destroy public agencies, they typically have at least some opportunities to staff them. Staffing powers provide executives with an important tool to control bureaucracies. For example, by appointing agency heads who are advocates of his agenda, a president can exert a strong influence over the behavior of that bureaucracy. As such agency heads serve at the pleasure of the executive, and if the bureaucracy does not fulfill the president's expectations he has the option of replacing the leadership. The power to hire and fire agency leaders is an effective means of holding a bureaucracy answerable to an executive.

Most public executives in the United States—certainly the president and most governors—also have significant budgetary powers. While executives do not have the power to raise or appropriate money, in many cases they have a good deal of influence in the budget process. For example, executives often have the responsibility of preparing a budget and submitting it for approval by the legislature (this is the case at federal and state levels). The legislature will often change the proposed budget—sometimes drastically—but the power to draft the initial blueprint nonetheless gives an executive an important tool to influence bureaucracy. If nothing else, an executive who proposes significantly cutting the budget of a recalcitrant bureaucracy gets that agency's attention very quickly. Many public executives also exercise some control over spending in the sense that they can determine when (or even if) funds appropriated by the legislature are disbursed for a particular program or agency. Though weaker than the legislature in this area, the budgetary powers of most public executives are significant enough to help hold bureaucracies accountable.

Finally, and perhaps most importantly, is the fact that being head of the executive branch means being head of the majority of public bureaucracies at that particular level of government. As most public bureaucracies are executive branch agencies, the head of the executive branch is the chief bureaucrat. The president is not just commander-in-chief of the military, he holds a similar position of authority over most major federal bureaucracies. All the cabinet secretaries, for example, report directly to the president and serve at his pleasure. Governors tend to have somewhat of a less direct leadership role over some agencies—especially if their heads are independently elected—but they remain the chief executive officers of state government in a very real sense.

The formal position of authority does not automatically translate into tight control over public bureaucracies. But a chief executive with the skills and aptitude to lead government is in an unequaled position to exercise those talents and motivations to influence public bureaucracies.

The Courts. Compared to legislatures and executives, courts have a much more limited range of options for controlling public agencies and holding them accountable. To begin with, courts are passive institutions. While executives and legislatures can be proactive in overseeing bureaucracy, courts can only react to litigation. This means someone else—the government, a special interest group, or a citizen—has to take the initiative if the courts are to play a role in holding bureaucracies accountable.

Courts apply a two-pronged test to most conflicts involving bureaucracies. First, does the bureaucratic action or rule being challenged uphold legislative intent? In other words, judges ask whether the action or rule at the source of conflict is consistent with the intent of the law that authorizes it. Second, is the action or rule constitutional? Even if a bureaucracy's actions are consistent with legislative intent, this does not necessarily mean they are consistent with applicable case law and constitutional interpretation. A particular concern of courts in posing this second question is the issue of due process. Courts have repeatedly proved themselves willing to overrule bureaucracy if that agency in some fashion violates established procedures, especially if that violation involves general constitutional principles of due process.[21]

Generally speaking, public agencies are highly sensitive to court rulings. Although courts have no independent enforcement mechanisms and must rely on self-compliance, other units of government, or court-appointed agents to enforce their rulings, it is exceedingly rare for any public agency to ignore a court order. The price for ignoring the courts is a loss of democratic legitimacy in the eyes of other branches of government and perhaps in the eyes of the general public. For organizations dependent upon legislatures for funding, direction, and even their very existence, such a loss of legitimacy is potentially devastating. Court rulings have forced a wide variety of public agencies into taking actions they did not necessarily agree with. It was a Supreme Court ruling, for example, that called for the racial desegregation of public schools. This decision was widely unpopular and strongly resisted in some areas. Yet the court order was backed by the power of the federal government (up to and including the deployment of federal troops) and schools had little choice, at least over the long term, but to comply.

Should public agencies be accountable to their clientele? Some would argue yes—bureaucracy should be responsive to the demands of those it serves. But what if the clientele makes ethnically or morally questionable demands? Many whites, for example, supported racial segregation of public schools, and it took a Supreme Court decision to stop school systems from responding to that demand.

Internal Checks on Public Agencies

Internal checks are a second option for imposing controls on the bureaucracy. Internal checks are the logical opposite of external checks. Rather than having bureaucracy answer to an actor or institution outside of its normal scope of operations, the idea is to make bureaucracy answerable to someone or something within its normal scope of operations. This can be done in a number of different ways. Codes of ethics, for example, are a form of internal check on bureaucracy. They are designed to be the ultimate form of internal check on bureaucracy by making bureaucrats accountable to the values of someone they cannot escape: themselves.

Codes of ethics, however, are far from the only form of internal check on public agencies. Bureaucracy can be internally answerable to a core constituency, which can consist of a clientele group or even the public as a whole. For example, farmers are a core constituency of the United States Department of Agriculture (USDA). If the USDA takes actions detrimental to farmers, farmers will certainly know about those actions and make their concerns known. Through interest groups, elected representatives, and informal contacts, farmers as a group can exercise considerable clout in terms of making the USDA accountable for its actions.

As already discussed, the obvious mechanism to make bureaucracy directly answerable to the people is the ballot box. The advantage of this approach is that the electorate is no longer an indirect force on the bureaucracy, with its preferences filtered through legislatures and executives. By determining key leadership positions the decisions of the ballot box become a direct internal force on the bureaucracy. Yet there are good reasons above and beyond those just mentioned to insulate bureaucracy from direct exposure to elections. The start of the modern system of public administration in the United States began around the turn of the twentieth century as a reaction to the incompetence and corruption of the spoils system. The spoils system was so-called because it operated on the notion that to the winner went the government patronage spoils. Government jobs were awarded on the basis of partisan loyalty rather than competence or merit. As these positions came with no guarantees—if your political patron lost the next election you were out of a job—the whole system created incentives for powerful public servants to have their agencies work for partisan gain and to line their own pockets before the next vote put their appointments at risk.[22] The spoils system bound bureaucracy fairly tightly to the ballot box, but it politicized the bureaucracy rather than making it accountable.

The founders of the modern conception of public administration in the United States argued that merit and competence rather than partisan loyalties and political connections should be the standards for public bureaucracy. In order to achieve those standards, influential public administration scholars such as Woodrow Wilson (who went on to become the 28th president) argued that bureaucracies needed to be distanced from the ballot box. Bureaucrats should be "neutrally competent," that is, they should hold their positions on the basis of their technical skills and merits and employ those skills to competently implement and manage public policy regardless of partisan preference or who held elective office.[23] Issues of control and accountability fell to the indirect means of overhead democracy.

The external checks employed by overhead democracy, however, do little to ease concerns that a powerful fourth branch of government is being kept two steps removed from the democratic process. In response, there have been a number of suggestions for imposing internal checks on the bureaucracy.

Representative Bureaucracy. The concept of a **representative bureaucracy** is premised on the simple notion that an agency reflecting the diverse interests of the community it serves is more likely to take into account those diverse preferences when making decisions.[24] Students of representative bureaucracy accept that public agencies operate in complex environments and have little choice but to make political decisions: "The theory of representative bureaucracy begins by recognizing the realities of politics. In a complex polity such as the United States, not all aspects of policy decisions are resolved in the 'political' branches of government."[25] Bureaucrats will take into account a number of factors in making these decisions—the specifics of the situation, professional training, applicable rules and guidelines, etc. Representative bureaucracy scholars argue that because they are human, bureaucrats will also rely on their own values and interests in making these decisions. Thus one way to make sure that bureaucracies are accountable to the public interest is to make sure that public employees reflect the diverse values and interests of the society they serve.

The essence of representative bureaucracy is the idea that a bureaucracy filled with people like "us" is more likely to look after "our" interests—or at least not act against them. The first scholar to suggest that bureaucracy could serve as a representative institution in its own right was J. Donald Kingsley, who argued in his study of the British civil service that in order to carry out their responsibilities effectively public servants had to share the values of the ruling class.[26] In a democratic society these shared values have to encompass all citizens. If this is accomplished, the policymaking power of the individual bureaucrat or bureaucracy is connected to the will of the people and can stake a legitimate claim to be a representative institution in its own right.

Making a bureaucracy representative has generally been taken to mean that it is staffed by a broad cross-section of society, and considerable research has been invested into examining whether public agencies sociodemographically reflect the society they serve. Because of this, the notion of representative democracy is still somewhat controversial. One objection is that it leads to an ethical dilemma we visited earlier in this chapter: when should technical qualifications give way to characteristics such as race and gender in making hiring decisions? Despite these objections, there exists a growing body of research showing that the diversity of a bureaucracy's staff does shape its decision making. Bureaucracies with more minorities and more women, for example, have been found to be more vigorous in taking the interests of these groups into account in its decision making.[27]

A big problem for representative bureaucracy is the fact that, overall, public agencies are not particularly representative. At the turn of the twenty-first century, for example, the employees of state and local governments were about 55 percent male and 45 percent female. The population as a whole was about 49 percent male and 51 percent fe-

male. There is a considerable minority presence in public bureaucracies—nonwhites constitute more than 20 percent of all state and local
government employees—but they tend to be concentrated in the lower
ranks. Racial and ethnic minorities make up about 11 percent of the
managerial ranks in state and local government administration, but
account for 45 percent of the service and maintenance positions[28] (see
Table 5.1). In other words, the most powerful positions in the bureaucracy—those most likely to make what we consider important *political*
decisions—are disproportionately white and male. At least in the upper
ranks, public bureaucracies do not reflect the diversity of the society
they serve.

Marketplace Competition. Representative bureaucracy suggests
an internal check on public agencies can be created by equating bureaucracy with a legislature and making it representative of the society
it serves. An alternate approach is to equate bureaucracy with a business and make it responsive to its clientele. Businesses, it is argued, are
ultimately answerable to their customers. This is because in a free and
functioning market, any business that fails to satisfy customer demands puts its survival at risk. Rather than put up with shoddy service
or overpriced products, customers will "vote with their feet" and take
their business to a competitor. The mechanism of competition thus
provides a powerful incentive for businesses to pay attention to wants
and wishes of customers.

As discussed in earlier chapters, the desire to make government
more like a business is one of the perennial reform issues in American
politics. Most of these reform efforts fail because of misunderstand-
ings about the very real differences between the public and private sectors. Yet scholars have given serious thought to how to borrow some of
the lessons of the private sector and employ them in the public sector
as an effective means of accountability.

Table 5.1 Characteristics of State and Local Government Employees					
Position	**Male**	**Female**	**White**	**Black**	**Hispanic**
Managers	212,000	118,000	271,000	37,000	15,000
Professionals	649,000	790,000	1,052,000	222,000	89,000
Technicians	269,000	197,000	337,000	71,000	37,000
Protective Services	889,000	196,000	770,000	198,000	96,000
Paraprofessionals	106,000	297,000	234,000	120,000	36,000
Administrative Support	126,000	803,000	610,000	189,000	97,000
Skilled crafts	397,000	23,000	308,000	65,000	65,000
Service/Maintenance	432,000	130,000	306,000	175,000	66,000

Source: Census Bureau. 2004. *Statistical Abstract of the United States*, Table 456. http://
www.census.gov/prod/2004pubs/04statab/stlocgov.pdf.

Advocates of market-based reform of the public sector argue three things are necessary in order to make a public organization accountable to its clientele in much the same manner that a business is accountable to its customers. First, the clientele must have a choice of organizations. In other words, a public agency cannot monopolize the service it provides. If it is the sole provider of services there is no competition, and thus little incentive to pay attention to the consumers of these services. Second, these consumers must be allowed to have control of the resources sought by the competing service providers. In other words, the money follows the customer. Rather than operating under a guaranteed budget, service providers have to attract clientele or risk the real possibility of closure. Third, customers must be allowed a voice within the organization; public agencies must develop the skill of listening to their customers by copying the private sector's use of surveys, focus groups, and the like.[29]

Basing a business-based model of accountability on these principles has met with mixed success when actually applied to the public sector. For some public services it is theoretically possible to create something approaching a competitive market for public services, with multiple service agencies competing for clientele. School vouchers have already been used in this chapter as an example of an attempt to create the necessary conditions for a businesslike model of accountability. Funding goes directly to parents in the form of a voucher that they can spend at their choice of school. As schools have a bottom-line interest in attracting clientele, they have a powerful incentive to pay close attention to the opinions and interests of parents. For other public services—law enforcement, fire protection, libraries—the costs and logistics of setting up multiple service providers often do not make sense.

Even where they are theoretically possible, business-based models of accountability face a perennial problem: the inevitable conflict between money and public interest. There are powerful incentives for the agency to put its own interests and those of its clientele above the public interest. A voucher-funded school, for example, may be pressured by parents to advocate a particular religious perspective in its curriculum, or to eliminate controversial books from its library, or to exclude students with undesirable socioeconomic, religious, or class characteristics. If it faithfully follows the market model, the school listens to its customers, responds to these demands, satisfies its customers, and secures its budget. It also arguably violates the public trust and acts against broader public interests.

Structural Design. A final way in which bureaucracy can be controlled is through structural or organizational design. Perhaps the most obvious way to design a built-in accountability system is to create a bureaucracy for this specific purpose. In other words, create a bureaucracy to check up on bureaucracy.

At the federal level there are a number of agencies tasked with holding other bureaucracies accountable. The Government Accountability Office (GAO), for example, is an agency designed as the investigative arm of Congress. Its job is to evaluate federal agencies and provide reports and analysis to the legislature, all as a means of helping improve the performance of the federal government and hold it accountable for its actions. The Office of Government Ethics (OGE) is an executive branch agency created to eliminate conflicts of interest in the civil service, to design and implement uniform guidelines of ethical behavior, and to promote high ethical standards among federal government employees.

Many federal agencies also have a permanent internal watchdog—an inspector general (IG). Inspectors general are a product of the Inspector General Act of 1978, part of a wave of government reforms enacted in the wake of the Watergate scandal. An IG's job is to conduct independent audits and investigations, detect and prevent fraud waste and abuse, and keep Congress and agency leadership informed. Currently there are 57 inspectors general overseeing 59 federal agencies. Each inspector general is appointed by the president, generally on the basis of a strong reputation of personal integrity coupled with high professional qualifications in fields such as law, accounting, or public administration, and must be confirmed by the Senate.[30]

Inspectors general and agencies such as the GAO and the OGE have a mixed track record in holding bureaucracy accountable. Though the GAO has a well-deserved reputation for accuracy and objectivity, there is little doubt that some members of Congress have tried to use it for their own political purposes, requesting investigations that simply by being undertaken will help or hurt a particular agenda. The OGE is so small that few have ever heard of it, and its low profile and small size are obvious constraints on its effectiveness. Inspectors general who do their job diligently can end up being viewed as irritants by the agencies they monitor, and those who miss a problem that later blossoms into scandal can end up as scapegoats.[31] If nothing else, however, the fact that these bureaucracies and bureaucratic positions exist serve as a constant reminder to public agencies of the accountability standards they are expected to meet.

An alternate to creating bureaucracies or individual administrative positions specifically for accountability purposes is to create a system of checks and balances between public agencies. So rather than have a single agency with unquestioned authority over a particular policy or program arena, have at least two agencies that serve to check the excesses of the other. This check and balance approach to controlling bureaucracy is part of the natural order of the federal system of politics in the United States. For example, local, state, and national governments have education bureaucracies, environmental bureaucracies, law enforcement bureaucracies, and transportation bureaucracies. Because of their shared program areas these agencies often work in close cooperation, but each level of government also operates with a high degree of autonomy from the others. This constitutes an internal check on bureaucracy in the sense that public bureaucracies, after a fashion, promote accountability to each other.

It is possible to create a similar built-in structural check on bureaucracy by giving agencies at a single level of government overlapping jurisdictions, by breaking up related program responsibilities among several agencies, or by imposing multiple reporting requirements on agencies. The organization of the federal government makes little sense if the goal is to create powerful and efficient public agencies, but a good deal of sense if the goal is political control. As pointed out in Chapter 3, the fact that there are at least five federal agencies regulating the financial services industry makes it very hard to exert centralized regulatory control over banks, but it also makes it very hard for the regulators themselves to accumulate power unchallenged. In other words, it makes it easier to control the regulators.

Though there is little doubt that the decentralized nature of public administration in the United States helps check some of its potential excesses and provides incentives for public agencies to act as watchdogs on each other, it has several drawbacks. Duplication and redundancy, competition for jurisdictional authority ("turf wars"), complexity and difficulty in coordination, and a certain level of inefficiency are all part of the price of achieving this sort of internal check on the bureaucracy.

Conclusion

Because bureaucracy plays such an important role in the governance of democratic societies, it is important that bureaucracy "do the right thing" and be made accountable to democratic values and processes. Yet it is also important to establish a distance between bureaucracy and democracy to insure the bureaucracy does not devolve into an agent of partisanship, ideology, or special interests. These create two contradictory needs. First, a need to keep bureaucracy relatively independent of the political pressures that naturally arise from democratic politics, and second, a need to keep bureaucracy accountable to democratic wishes. This creates an underlying tension in public administration and a perennial question for public administration scholars: how can the authoritarian and hierarchical nature of bureaucracy be reconciled with egalitarian democratic values?

As this chapter suggests, thus far there has been no single universally agreed-upon answer to this question. There is widespread agreement that public administrators should abide by a code of ethics that reflects broadly held civic values and the high expectations of moral behavior placed on those in positions of public trust. Yet however detailed and well thought out, codes of ethics cannot cover every single situation. Even the best-intentioned bureaucrat will face ethical dilemmas for which there are no easy and universally agreeable answers. So in addition to creating systems of behavior for public administrators based on values reflecting core civic notions of how to separate "good" from "bad" behavior, the American political system also seeks accountability. Ethical or not, we want public agencies and their employees to be answerable for their actions.

Traditionally, some form of overhead democracy is employed to set up an indirect mechanism of control and accountability over bureaucracy. While other branches of government clearly have effective tools

---

Sidebar 5.1   Oliver North—Public-Service Hero or Criminal?

What would you call a bureaucrat who broke the law, lied repeatedly to Congress, helped arm a nation hostile to the United States, and then willfully tried to obstruct an investigation into his conduct?

How about hero?

Unlikely as it seems, this was at least the partial result of what is one of the most famous cases of an individual bureaucrat breaking the checks, controls, and ethical guidelines imposed on public servants. The bureaucrat in question was Marine Lt. Col. Oliver North, who was at the center of the Iran-Contra scandal that tarnished the last years of Ronald Reagan's presidency in the 1980s.

Iran-Contra was a term used to describe complicated scheme that, in essence, ran a covert and highly illegal foreign policy operation out of the White House. The two key elements of the scheme were a scheme to funnel arms to Iran in hopes of winning the release of Americans taken hostage by terrorist groups in the Middle East, and financing and supplying a revolutionary army (known as the Contras) trying to overthrow the government of Nicaragua. Both of these actions were prohibited by law, contrary to the stated policy of the United States government, and opposed by public opinion.

North was a mid-level bureaucrat working for the National Security Counsel (NSC) in the 1980s, and in the subsequent investigations emerged as a key figure in the scandal. By his own admission he ran the operation that funneled money and arms to Nicaragua, lied to Congress, accepted legally questionable gifts and gratuities, and illegally destroyed documents implicating himself and others in the wrongdoing.

Despite this, North ended up not just as a media celebrity but as a figure admired and respected by many. North *was* a genuine war hero—he was a decorated combat veteran—and the investigation into his more questionable public service at the NSC in many ways burnished rather than stained this hero status. In hearings before Congress, the telegenic Marine presented himself as a figure who went beyond the law in order to serve higher principles. He wanted

to check the bureaucracy and influence its actions, this does not automatically supply the incentive to vigilantly employ them. Recognizing the gaps that will always occur in indirect and complex accountability mechanisms like overhead democracy, numerous alternatives have been suggested and explored. These range from trying to equate bureaucracy with a representative institution to trying to equate bureaucracy with a business. All have their benefits and drawbacks, but none has thus far proved to be a universally agreeable solution to the problem of bureaucratically squaring a democratic circle.

Ultimately, then, placing public trust in public bureaucracies is always going to mean placing trust in individual bureaucrats. Given human nature, this trust is on occasion going to be betrayed, and we

---

Sidebar 5.1 *(continued)*

American hostages released, believed the Contras were engaged in a struggle comparable to America's War of Independence, and viewed the policies and laws passed by Congress on these matters as seriously misguided. Besides, North reported that he genuinely believed he was just following orders from the top—all the way from President Reagan on down.

For his part in the Iran-Contra scheme North was convicted on three counts: obstruction of Congress, illegally destroying documents, and accepting illegal gifts. All convictions were later overturned on a technicality—North had testified before Congress on a grant of immunity from prosecution, and an appeals court ruled that witnesses in North's trial were likely to have been influenced by this testimony. After Iran-Contra North campaigned for the U.S. Senate and became a media celebrity.

Even though his conviction was overturned on appeal and North ended up becoming a popular (if controversial) public figure, most public administration ethicists would have problems with his NSC service and the defense of his role in Iran-Contra. In essence the NSC usurped the power of Congress and, if Reagan's denial of all knowledge of Iran-Contra operations was wholly truthful, also usurped the power of the executive. North and/or his superiors took it upon themselves to decide the right thing to do, with the full knowledge that doing so meant contradicting the clear policy directives produced by the democratic process. They did this on the grounds of ideological disagreement with that official policy.

Scenarios can be imagined where bureaucrats will question or object to official policy on the grounds it compels them to violate moral or constitutional principles. Taking upon themselves the power to set those policies by secretly and deliberately breaking the statutory mandates of the legislature, and using ideology or "just following orders" as justification, is unlikely to hold up as a shining example of the highest standards of public service.

Source: Walsh, Lawrence E. 1994. *Iran-Contra: The Final Report.* New York: Random House.

are all familiar with stories of government employees who are lazy, incompetent, corrupt, or simply make bad decisions. Jeremy Sivits and Lorelee Byrd are far from the first public employees to take actions that brought discredit to their offices, and they will not be the last (see Sidebar 5.1). One study suggests that more than half of public employees report knowing of some ethical violation.[32] In a large-picture sense, however, it is important to note that such anecdotes and polls can paint a highly inaccurate picture of the public sector. Perhaps what is most surprising about public bureaucracies in the United States is their longstanding commitment to serving the public interest. The values of public service seem to be so deeply embedded in most public agencies that public employees somehow manage to juggle the myriad expectations placed upon them in spite of—rather than because of—the formal mechanisms of control that link them to democratic processes. Some scholars have noted that the "failures" of bureaucracy are justifiably attributed to electoral institutions who provide vague goals, inadequate resources, uneven oversight, and use the bureaucracy as an all-purpose scapegoat for whatever goes wrong. In this sort of environment, the fact that most of the time bureaucracies manage to divine something approximating the public interest and make a genuine effort to fulfill it suggests that most of the time, that trust is not misplaced or abused.

© John Nordell/The Image Works.

Principled hero or unethical crook? Oliver North has been called both. The telegenic former marine is a combat veteran whose military record reflects personal sacrifice and honorable public service. Yet North was also a central figure in the Iran-Contra scandal that tarnished the presidency of Ronald Reagan, playing a leading role in an illegal scheme to subvert laws passed by Congress.

Key Concepts

accountability The belief that public agencies and their employees should be held accountable for their actions.

bureaucratic accountability Holding a public agency accountable for complying with the laws and rules that govern its actions.

code of ethics A set of guidelines designed to help people distinguish between right and wrong behavior.

ethical dilemmas Decision situations in which the right course of action is not clear.

ethics A system of behavior based on values and moral principles designed to help people distinguish between right and wrong behavior.

market accountability Holding a public agency accountable to its clientele.

overhead democracy An indirect, two-stage method of holding public agencies accountable. The first stage requires citizens to hold elected officials accountable for the performance and actions of government. The second stage requires public officials to hold public agencies accountable for their performance and actions.

performance accountability Holding a public agency accountable for achieving a particular task or goal.

professional accountability Holding bureaucrats accountable to the norms and practices of a profession or a professional code of ethics.

representative bureaucracy A public agency whose personnel reflect the diversity of the community it serves.

values Beliefs about right and wrong. ✦

Chapter 6

Deciding and Doing

The Central Challenges of Public Administration

If administration is the art of getting things done, then at the core of the process of administration are just two basic tasks: deciding and doing. *Deciding* means choosing what course of action is best suited to achieving agency goals, completing the assigned task, or solving the problem at hand. *Doing* means translating that choice into action.

Though simple enough in the abstract, deciding and doing get more complex in practice. Consider the case of child labor laws. Most people are in favor of laws that prevent children from being exploited for cheap labor, and, at least in the abstract, would support agencies that vigorously enforce child labor laws. Tell that to Brian Glennon. In 2002, Glennon was a 12-year-old baseball umpire who planned to spend a big part of his summer calling games for the Darien (Illinois) Youth Club Baseball League. The youth club hired more than 30 umpires under the age of 14 for the princely sum of 10 bucks a game. The Illinois Department of Labor told the league it could not hire people under 14 for pay, and the league was forced to fire them all before a single pitch had been thrown. What did Glennon think of the agency that vigorously enforced child labor laws in Illinios? "It kind of stinks," he said.[1]

At first glance, this looks like just another case of an overbearing bureaucracy needlessly meddling. The Darien League had been hiring 12- and 13-year-olds to umpire its games for 40 years with no complaints. Yet the "overbearing" agency faced something of a dilemma. It received an anonymous complaint about the league. As its job is to enforce child labor laws, complaints that these laws are being broken are not lightly ignored, so it investigated the league. It found 180 violations of child labor laws and regulations—in theory, enough to justify levying $900,000 fines. A primary mission of the agency is to enforce those laws and regulations, but shutting down a summer baseball league

121

seems almost un-American. So what to do? And how to do it? The agency decided its job was to enforce the law, and insisted the league live by the child labor standards and employ no umpires under the age of 14. But it did not impose any draconian fines. The agency decided to respond to a legitimate complaint, conducted a thorough investigation, found legitimate violations, insisted they be addressed, but tried to be sensitive to the context and avoided any overly punitive actions. For its trouble, it was portrayed as a villain, and ended up the target of numerous complaints from upset parents who began lobbying state legislators to make changes in child labor laws. As said earlier, in the *abstract*, everyone is in favor of child labor laws and their vigorous enforcement. Yet what an agency decides to do in a specific case can trigger widespread disapproval.

What the agency faced was something of a no-win situation. It could ignore the complaint, or respond. It could insist the violations be addressed, or just turn a blind eye. Regardless of the option it took, someone would argue it was the wrong one. Deciding and doing in this case ranged from doing nothing to using the full weight of the law to put the league out of business. They opted for a middle course and were roundly criticized for doing so. This sort of scenario is common to public agencies. They routinely have to make decisions then translate them into action, knowing full well that whatever they do, someone will be upset. Given this, how do you best go about deciding and doing? Bureaucrats can, and often do, make decisions by relying on rules, regulations, due process, and other legal requirements that are less of a concern in the private sector.[2] As the Illinois Department of Labor found out, however, that approach is no guarantee a decision will be viewed as a good one.

What the baseball example also makes clear is that public agencies are making political decisions and taking political actions. Recall the definition of politics from an earlier chapter—the process of deciding who gets what. Recall also the notion of the politics-administration dichotomy, the idea that politics and administration should be kept separate. The Illinois Department of Labor had no choice but to make a political decision. Obviously the crux of the matter was who got what; specifically, do 30 kids get to keep their summer jobs? The agency could have ignored the complaint and the law it was supposed to enforce, and answered *yes*. It could have followed up on the complaint, done its job, and answered *no*. Yes or no, the agency made a political decision; there is no way to keep politics out of its actions. Because bureaucrats have no choice but to make political decisions, understanding public administration's broader role in social, political, and economic life requires a basic understanding of process; in other words, a basic understanding of deciding and doing.

Deciders and Doers

All organizations have a rough division of labor between "deciders" and "doers." Deciders are those in supervisory or managerial positions. Their decision-making responsibilities may include some policy setting (i.e., deciding what goals the organization will pursue) and at a minimum will include some discretionary authority over how goals or subgoals are to be accomplished. Doers are those who carry out the actual physical tasks necessary to achieve organizational objectives. While doers are at the lowest levels of the administrative hierarchy, they are "not surplus baggage . . . [and] have a critical role to play in the accomplishment of agency objectives." Without doers, deciders have no way to translate ideas into reality. A car, after all, "is built not by the engineer or the executive, but by the mechanic on the assembly line. The fire is extinguished, not by the fire chief or the captain, but by the team of firemen who play a hose on the blaze."[3] In the example above, somebody in the Illinois Department of Labor had to decide how or whether to respond to the complaint, and somebody had to conduct the actual investigation.

In bureaucracies this basic division of labor is formalized by hierarchy. Deciders are managers with direct supervisory responsibilities; in layman's terms, a boss that other people report to. The job of managers in public bureaucracies is varied and complex. They have to enforce rules, supervise personnel, and coordinate the behavior of subordinates towards organizational goals. They may have hiring and firing responsibilities, and are answerable for themselves and their particular organization or unit to their superiors in the hierarchy, agency clientele, and ultimately a legislative body, the public, and the law. This is a complicated environment for decision making: public agency managers are expected to make systematic, supportable choices that help achieve organizational goals, effectively and efficiently manage programs, serve agency clientele, uphold the law, and serve the public interest.

The public-sector employees who translate the choices of managers into action—the doers—are typically "street-level" bureaucrats, the agency employees who interact directly with citizens. The division between doer and decider in public agencies is in practice often more abstract than real. We have already talked in earlier chapters about the policymaking power of the street-level bureaucrat.[4] The greenest police rookie and the most junior teacher are, in our organizational terms, doers rather than deciders. Yet they wield the final decisions on which speeders get stopped and how quickly or attentively a curricular program is followed in the classroom. This sets up a particular challenge for public agencies. Like it or not, the leaders of public agencies have to recognize that what any agency actually does is ultimately in the hands of the doers, the street-level bureaucrats. Public-sector managers not only have to figure what to do, they have to figure out how to best get street-level bureaucrats to buy into the program.

Though the challenges are particularly difficult in the public sector, deciding and doing represent the fundamental challenge of all organizations. What differentiates public from private agencies is the broader political environment where the decisions are taken and implemented. Because it cuts to the heart of administration, scholars have devoted enormous effort to the systematic study of deciding and doing. Comprehensively covering all that has been learned requires a book (and a class) all to itself. In this chapter we are going to take a brief tour of the fundamentals of deciding and doing. Rather than offering a "how to" guide, the idea here is to convey the considerable challenge public administrators face in deciding and doing.

Decisions, Decisions

The *Public Administration Dictionary* defines **decision making** as, "A process in which events, circumstances, and information precipitate a choice designed to achieve some desired result."[5] Decision making thus involves information gathering, analysis, and prioritizing as a means to select the best course of action to solve a problem or achieve a goal. Who should we hire? What should we budget for? Where should we concentrate our effort and limited resources? These are the sorts of questions that all managers are routinely expected to answer, and those answers involve making choices. There are a number of ways to make these choices. Decisions can be made on the basis of ideological or partisan loyalty (we will cut our budget 10 percent, because that is what the Republican Party wants). Decisions can be made on the basis of pure self-interest (we will award the contract to my brother-in-law's company, so I can get a kickback). Decisions can be made on the basis of emotions (let's hire the good-looking applicant) or even divine appeals (I must pray for guidance on this one). Generally speaking, however, most public administrators are expected to approach decision making on the basis of more than ideology, self-interest, emotions, or religious motivation (see Sidebar 6.1). Most public managers are expected to make decisions that can be logically justified in the context of agency tasks and resources, the applicable law, and the public interest.

There is no single "best" way to make decisions that fit all those requirements, but decision making typically involves a process that starts with identifying objectives or problems, moves to a consideration of potential ways to solve the problem or achieve the objective, and ends when these potential alternatives are winnowed down to one. Though these steps are a fairly universal description of decision making in the public sector, in practice the decision-making process can be

Sidebar 6.1 Types of Deciders and Doers

Deciders and doers are not all alike. A number of public administration scholars argue bureaucrats can be classified into a set of categories that differentiate the behaviors and attitudes of agency employees.

Anthony Downs penned one of the best-known of these classification schemes in his 1967 classic *Inside Bureaucracy*.[a] According to Downs, bureaucrats fall into one of several personality types that help explain how and why they decide what they do.

The *conserver* is a bureaucrat who is oriented to maintaining the status quo. Conservers are less interested in building bureaucratic empires than in protecting bureaucratic turf. Accordingly, "they strongly oppose any losses in their existing power, income, and prestige," and their decision making is motivated by a desire to hold onto what they already have.[b]

Advocates, on the other hand, are not satisfied with what they have. They are motivated by a desire to expand their agencies' power and responsibilities. Accordingly, they are energetic and seek out new responsibilities and resources for their agencies.[c] *Climbers* go one better than advocates. Not only do they seek expansion of their bureaucracies' responsibilities, they want the scope and resources of public administration as a whole to increase. While advocates want a bigger slice of the existing bureaucratic pie, climbers want a bigger slice of a bigger pie.[d] The decisions of advocates and climbers, then, will be oriented toward gaining more power and resources for particular agencies and the bureaucracy in general.

What conservers, advocates, and climbers all have in common is bureaucratic self-interest—they want their agencies' programs and responsibilities expanded, or at least not cut. *Statesmen*, on the other hand, are motivated by a more general conception of the public interest rather than the activities of their particular agencies. Statesmen are who most people would like to see staffing public agencies; they are dedicated and selfless. When statesmen make decisions they do so with the goal of furthering the public good rather than increasing the power or resources of the bureaucracy.

According to Downs, however, statesmen are also unfortunately rare. The altruistic qualities that define statesmen (and -women) are uncommon characteristics. Accordingly, it is unreasonable to expect public agencies to be disproportionately staffed by statesmen. We have to assume, then, that most bureaucrats are like most everybody else. In other words, in decision making, self-interest plays a role.

[a] Anthony Downs, *Inside Bureaucracy* (Little, Brown: Boston, 1967).

[b] Ibid, 96–97.

[c] Ibid, 102.

[d] Cynthia Bowling, Chung-Lae Cho, Deil S. Wright, "Establishing a Continuum from Minimizing to Maximizing Bureaucrats: State Agency Head Preferences for Governmental Expansion—A Typology of Administrator Growth Postures 1964–98," *Public Administration Review* 64 (2004):489–499.

much less linear. There may be a good deal of back tracking, outside political pressures may limit the list of alternatives that can be practically considered, and revisions and updates can bring new information to bear on a problem or desired objective that changes the direction of decision making in mid-process.

Given that decision making is such a core element of administration it has understandably attracted an enormous amount of attention from scholars. The result is literally hundreds (probably thousands) of studies, theories, books, and monographs, all vying to explain why administrators and managers make the decisions they do, and offering advice on how these same people can improve their decision making. Much of this research revolves around a basic question: what's the best or most practical way to make systematic decisions? While there are many answers to this question and many systems of decision making, they can be broadly classified into three categories: rational-comprehensive decision making, incremental decision making, and mixed scanning.

Rational-Comprehensive

The basic objective of **rational-comprehensive decision making** is to identify the most efficient means to achieve a particular goal or solve a particular problem. This means finding the course of ac-

United States Army; photo by Spc. Bill Putnam.

As the nation's top bureaucrat, George W. Bush is known less for analyzing different points of view than for making up his mind and acting. Responding to the terror attacks of 9/11 and the threat of Iraq's weapons of mass destruction, for example, Bush put together a relatively small group whose job was less to weigh the pros and cons of a military response than to hammer out the details of prosecuting wars in Afghanistan and Iraq.

tion that maximally achieves the goal and the lowest possible cost. Rational-comprehensive decision making consists of four basic steps.

Step 1. Identify the problem or goal.

Step 2. Develop a list of all potential solutions to the problem or all potential means to achieve the desired goal.

Step 3. Systematically analyze the costs and benefits of all the options.

Step 4. Choose the option that, to the greatest extent, solves the problem or achieves the goal with the least costs.[6]

There are several distinguishing characteristics of the rational-comprehensive approach to decision making. First, there is an emphasis on the individual. Rational-comprehensive decision making is closely associated with microeconomic theory, and from there it adopts the assumption that only individuals—not groups or organizations—make decisions. Rational-comprehensive models invariably describe an individual faced with the need to make a choice, not an agency or a committee. Such decision makers are viewed as **maximizers**, people who know their goals, can rank order the preferred means to achieve those goals, and will choose the means that best achieves the goal at the lowest cost. Second, the rational-comprehensive approach emphasizes the need for complete information. In the idealized theoretical world of rational-comprehensive decision making, the individual has a clear idea of the goal to be achieved, and has all the information necessary to evaluate the costs and benefits of all possible courses of action to achieve that goal.

There are several obvious advantages to adopting the rational-comprehensive approach to decision making. Because it requires decision makers to begin with a clear idea of the objective to be achieved, it makes it more likely that public agencies will be able to fulfill the desires of policymakers. Because it requires *all* potential courses of action to be considered, it reduces the probability that the most effective or innovative option will be overlooked. Because it winnows the potential courses of action on the basis of costs and benefits, it increases efficiency.

The big drawback of rational-comprehensive theory is that it describes a world that for most decisions and for most public administrators simply does not exist. Public administrators often have only a vague notion of the objectives they are supposed to achieve, and are often forced to balance several goals at once. Consider the Illinois Department of Labor's approach to underage baseball umpires. Its goals included properly responding to a legitimate complaint, enforcing child labor laws, and being sensitive to the social and political context. In trying to steer a middle course to meet all these goals, the agency's actions arguably achieved none of them.

Public administrators also rarely have the time, resources, and excess mental capacity to bear the huge information and analytical requirements of rational-comprehensive decision making. When a department runs out of paperclips, a manager is unlikely to invest a work day or more analyzing the need for and consumption of paperclips, researching the potential alternatives to paperclips, conducting an exhaustive search of paperclip suppliers, becoming familiar with price lists, and undertaking a thorough study of the costs and benefits of buying paperclips at a local office supply store today versus buying them via an Internet wholesaler and waiting three days for them to arrive. What is much more likely in the real world is that a manager will authorize a subordinate to go buy paperclips from the same place the department always buys paperclips from. Such a decision is not rational, at least not in the strict sense of the rational-comprehensive model. The outcome of this decision may not be efficient—there may be some other paper-fastening technology that can fulfill the agency's needs more effectively and at lower cost. In fact, this "irrational" behavior has only one big advantage: it works. The department's paperclip shortage is solved in short order.

Incremental

Incremental decision making is an approach to problem solving that emphasizes using past experience and the current situation as baselines for coming up with practical solutions. More formally, **incremental decision making** is defined as "an approach to decision making in government in which executives begin with the current situation [and] consider a limited number of changes in that situation based upon a restricted range of aternatives."[7]

Incrementalism bears a superficial resemblance to rational-comprehensive decision making in that it also involves considering a range of options to solve a problem or to achieve an objective. It differs in that it places much less emphasis on gathering information and extensive cost-benefit analysis, and much more on getting something done. In contrast to the microeconomic theory and its reliance on the notion of a rational individual, incrementalism is based on the assumption that humans have a limited capacity for rational action.

This notion of limited rationality, is heavily based on the work of Herbert Simon.[8] In observing how public administrators go about their business, Simon rapidly came to the conclusion that they were not rational decision makers. They did not make decisions that fully maximized utility—i.e., they did not painstakingly search for the option that resulted in the most benefits and least costs. Utility maximization is at the heart of classic rational behavior, and from his observations Simon saw that public administrators—actually, humans generally—were not fully rational. Most humans, and certainly most administrators, have limits on their capacity for rational decision making. They frequently lack information and the time to gather it, they are guided by habit and values as much as costs and benefits, they do not always have the advantage of clear goals, and they engage in negotiation and compromise and make decisions on the basis of practical politics as much as efficiency. In other words there are limits, or bounds, to the human capacity for rational decision making.

In detailing the mismatch between theory and reality, Simon became much more interested in the real bureaucrat and the problems she faced than the abstract rational bureaucrat fashioned from microeconomic thinking. Rather than maximizers, Simon described humans as **satisficers.** He coined the term "satisficing" to describe what he actually saw administrators doing: they search the available alternatives until they come up with something that works. They do not engage in a relentless pursuit of the best

As the nation's top bureaucrat, John F. Kennedy often sought input from lots of people—even those he disagreed with. This is exemplified by the Cuban missile crisis, which brought the United States and the Soviet Union to the brink of nuclear war over the placing of Soviet missiles in Cuba. Kennedy put together a large group to analyze the situation and work through the pros and cons of different responses, a group that often disagreed. Nonetheless, from this group (called the "Ex Comm") came a solution that succeeded in removing the missiles and avoided hostilities.

option, they search until they find something that is good enough and then they stop. Unlike a maximizer, when faced with a choice a satisficer will consider a limited range of potential actions and pick the one that experience, training, values, habit, or instinct suggests is the most doable.

The incremental approach to decision making was famously formalized by Charles Lindblom.[9] Lindblom argued that what scholars observed public administrators actually doing in the realm of decision making, which by most accounts was simply getting by without any real plan, was actually systematic and very much rational in the sense of satisficing. Lindblom called incrementalism "the science of muddling through," and he argued it had identifiable characteristics and a logical process.

Step 1. Identify the problem.

Step 2. Look at how similar problems have been addressed in the past.

Step 3. Analyze a handful of solutions that seem feasible given the current context.

Step 4. Choose the solution that seems the most "doable."

Lindblom suggested this described the vast majority of decision making in public administration, and that this approach was dominant for good reason: incrementalism was much more practical than rational-comprehensive decision making. Incremental decision makers start with a known baseline, consider a limited set of changes to that baseline, dicker to a compromise on those changes with other interested parties, and the end result is a marginal shift from the original baseline. Incrementalism comfortably accommodates the political give and take that we frequently observe as public agencies go about the business of making decisions.

Incrementalism has much to recommend it as an alternative to rational-comprehensive decision making as an approach to problem solving. It places much less of an information burden on a manager, it uses what currently exists to provide structure to decision making, and the end result usually works even if it is not the best possible alternative. Our manager with the paperclip shortage of a few paragraphs ago was an incrementalist—she responded to the problem by having a subordinate order more paperclips from the same vendor the department always used. It is quite possible that paperclips could be bought cheaper from another vendor, and simply opting for what had been done in the past was not rational. But with many demands on her time, the minor irritant of running out of paperclips did not rank particularly high on her list of decision-making priorities. The department always buys paperclips from this particular vendor, this brand of paperclips does its job and places no unreasonable burdens on the budget or the staff. Problem solved.

Despite its practical appeal and its more realistic portrayal of the public administrator's world, incrementalism has disadvantages. Perhaps most importantly, compared to rational-comprehensive decision making, incrementalism is more likely to fail in the sense of not fully achieving the desired goal. Satisficing means ignoring a lot of possible options, and one of these ignored options might turn out to be the best solution to the problem at hand. This is especially the case if the best solution means making a radical break with past practices. The incremental decision maker tied to the past is unlikely to ever consider this option. Some critics have suggested that incrementalism's fatal weakness is that it relies on process rather than on analysis to achieve a goal or solve a problem. Rather than rationally assessing "what should we do to achieve this goal?" incremental decision makers let the past make that choice for them. Habit, values, and experience supply the goals and set the boundaries on how to achieve them.[10]

Budgets are the classic example of incremental decision making in action. For most public agencies, decisions on next year's budget are shaped heavily by the previous year's budget. Last year's budget is taken as a baseline, and from there a series of proposals and compromises on marginal increases or decreases is negotiated. This makes a good deal of sense. An agency head with a multimillion-dollar operation who is forced to begin the annual budget exercise with a baseline of zero—i.e., he is expected to justify every cent the agency requests regardless of the bureaucracy's previous funding level—is unlikely to do much else. The sheer amount of time and effort required to comprehensively justify every minor line item would consume an enormous amount of time and resources. The result would likely be an example of bureaucracy at its worst—lots of study, lots of reports, lots more study, and not much in the way of decisions. It is much quicker, and from a satisficing standpoint much more practical, to start with last year's budget and try to make whatever minor adjustments the current environment seems to call for.

The problem with this approach, of course, is that it may miss the broader picture. Is the agency still fulfilling its objectives? Is there a new approach to achieving those objectives that is faster and cheaper? Potentially useful answers to those questions may well get lost in the incremental approach to budget making.

Mixed Scanning

Rational-comprehensive and incremental decision making obviously have a set of complementary advantages and disadvantages. So rather than consider the choice between the two approaches as an "either-or" decision, why not try to take advantage of both? In a famous 1967 *Public Administration Review* article, Amitai Etzioni proposed doing exactly that and he called the result **mixed scanning**.[11] Mixed scanning views rational-comprehensive and incremental decision making as two ends of a continuum, and argues that public administrators should strategically decide which end of this scale to favor for a given problem.

Mixed scanning accepts the argument that humans are incapable of being fully rational—there is always going to be some piece of information that is not collected and few can divest themselves of their full measure of human foibles when making important decisions. However, it is also clear that humans can make greater or lesser efforts to be rational. Our manager with the paperclip shortage could have asked a subordinate to spend 15 minutes surfing office supply web sites and putting together a comparative cost list. A rough perusal of this list might well have resulted in a better informed decision, not to mention cheaper paperclips from a closer supplier. This does not qualify as an exhaustive, fully maximizing approach by any means. But it is a step away from satisficing and toward more classically rational behavior. What Etzioni tried to establish with mixed scanning was a systematic way to select between emphasizing the rational comprehensive or the incremental approach.

Mixed-scanning decision makers attempt to distinguish between important or "fundamental" and "nonfundamental" decisions. Rational-comprehensive decision making is employed for critical decisions, issues that cut to the core of the agency's objectives. Incremental decision making is employed for more day-to-day choices where it makes little sense to invest scarce agency resources into what amount to more mundane operational challenges. Thus, the basic approach of mixed scanning is this:

Step 1. Decide whether a decision is fundamental or nonfundamental.

Step 2. If nonfundamental, follow incremental approach. If fundamental, follow rational-comprehensive approach.

Mixed scanning thus attempts to overcome one of the key drawbacks of incrementalism. Sometimes it is better for an agency to engage in bold decisions, to make a break with the past to meet the needs and pressures of new policy challenges and a changing political environment. Incremental decision making is ill-equipped to do this. Incrementalism favors a low-key, low-risk, conservative approach that is often practical but rarely innovative.

A mixed scanner favors routinely engaging in a comprehensive review of agency purposes and operations—in other words, a periodic attempt to get a big-picture view of the organization and assess whether big-picture changes are justified. The resources and process devoted to making those big-picture decisions consciously approximate the rational-comprehensive aproach to the greatest practical extent. Once these big-picture decisions are made, the nonfundamental decisions are turned over to incremental processes.

Though mixed scanning takes the best of the rational-comprehensive and incremental approaches, it also incorporates some of their drawbacks and adds one of its own. The big question for a mixed scanner is this: what is a fundamental decision? How do you know when a decision merits the resources and effort of a rational-comprehensive approach? When is it better to be a maximizer than a satisficer? Unfortunately, there is no clear-cut rule dividing the two. At least for some issues this creates an added layer of decision making. Before doing anything else a manager has to decide whether the problem at hand is of a fundamental or nonfundamental nature. This can create some administrative wheel spinning: is it better to be a maximizer or a satisficer in making the fundamental versus nonfundamental decision? Piling decisions on decisions is a good way not to get things done. In practice, it is clear that mixed scanning does represent a roughly accurate picture of public-sector decision making. Though incrementalism explains a good deal of decision making in bureaucracy, public agen-

Table 6.1 Decision-Making Systems		
Rational Comprehensive	**Incremental**	**Mixed Scanning**
1. Identify problem or goal.	1. Identify problem or goal.	1. Identify problem or goal.
2. Develop exhaustive list of potential solutions.	2. Examine how similar problems or goals have been addressed in the past.	2. Assess whether problem or goal is "fundamental" or "nonfundamental."
3. Gather information and systematically assess the costs and benefits of all options.	3. Consider a handful of solutions that seem feasible in the current environment.	3. Adopt rational-comprehensive approach for fundamental decisions.
4. Choose option that solves problem or achieves goal with most benefits and fewest costs.	4. Adopt the course of action that seems the most "doable."	4. Adopt incremental approach for nonfundamental decisions.

cies do occasionally make radical breaks with the past.[12] Figuring out what approach is best used when, however, is still more art than science (see Table 6.1).

Putting Decisions Into Action, or Getting People to Do What You Want Them to Do

Making a decision represents only half of "the art of getting things done." Regardless of how a decision was reached, it is of little use to an administrator unless it can be translated into action. Deciding that the agency needs more paperclips does not fill the supply cabinet. Somebody has to actually contact a vendor, fill out a purchase order, and make sure the paperclips are actually delivered. Managers cannot implement most of their decisions themselves, especially when these decisions require the time, effort, and expertise of more than one person. Decision makers thus have to figure out how to get other people to take the actions necessary for implementation.

Getting people to do what you want them to do is thus the second central challenge of administration. There are a number of ways this can be attempted: persuasion, power, or appeals to self-interest or the good of the group. Because of its centrality to public administration, scholars have also invested considerable effort in trying to identify the most systematic and effective way to coordinate the behavior of humans in order to achieve a specified objective. Again, comprehensive coverage of all the findings and suggestions generated by this research would require a book—and a course—unto itself. Here, we try to highlight some of the best known solutions to the problem of getting people to do what you want them to do, along with their primary advantages and disadvantages.

Giving Orders

The most simple and direct approach to getting people to do what you want them to do is to rely on power and hierarchy. If the boss says do something, the subordinate does it because he knows his position. In bureaucratic organizations, the direct route of issuing orders has a certain appeal. One of the characteristics of bureaucratic organizations is a clear hierarchy in which everyone knows who has authority over whom. Why not rely on this clear-cut power structure? In the chain of command, superiors make decisions and subordinates do what they are told. There are advantages to this approach, especially in military and paramilitary bureaucracies such as police and fire departments. In situations where fast decision making and quick action are essential, giving orders and having them obeyed can literally mean the difference between life and death. When the captain of an engine company deploys his firefighters at a two-alarm blaze, he does not expect his subordinates to hold a caucus and take a vote on whether his instructions are reasonable.

Even in the most chain of command–conscious agencies, however, an over-reliance on hierarchy and power structures is often a bad idea. Frequently this approach is counterproductive. Bureaucratic tyrants—managers who expect their orders to be obeyed simply because they are managers—are often seen as unreasonable and are resented by their subordinates. Such situations often invite what is known as **shirking**, the process of consciously circumventing the wishes of superiors.[13] Most people at some point in their lives have been asked to do something they thought was unnecessary, silly, or frivolous, and consequently have approached the assigned task with irritation, apathy, or outright hostility. Such attitudes are obviously not conducive to getting things done, or at least getting them done well. Direct orders issued by a superior run the risk of being disobeyed.

Recognizing this, a number of scholars argue it is a fundamental mistake to rely on hierarchy as the basis for the authority to issue orders. Chester Barnard argued that in the giving of an order it is not the superior who is really important, but the subordinate. He laid down the basic framework of **acceptance theory**, which turns on its head the classic understanding of how hierarchies structure power. Acceptance theory argues that superiors derive their authority not from their place in a hierarchy—their position as "boss"—but from the willingness of subordinates to accept their orders.[14] The captain of an engine company has the power to issue orders to his firefighters with the expectation they will be obeyed not because he is a captain, but because those firefighters trust the captain's experience, skills, and judgment, and on that basis are willing to do what he says. The ultimate power here, though, lies with the subordinates. If the captain loses the confidence, respect, and trust of those firefighters, his badges of rank are reduced to mere symbols of authority. He still has his place in the hierarchy, but he is going to have a much harder time getting his subordinates to do what he wants them to do.

The notion of acceptance theory can perhaps best be summed up by an old military maxim: the first rule of command is to never give an order that a subordinate cannot obey. In a classic piece of administration scholarship, Mary Parker Follet provided a systematic explanation of the wisdom behind this aphorism. Follet argued that subordinates do not obey a superior's orders; they obey what she termed the **law of the situation**. She argued that people respond not to the dictates of a superior, but to the problem and circumstances at hand. They will obey an order if it conforms to a reasonable expectation of what the problem and circumstances demand. Thus, the job of superiors is not simply to issue orders, but to identify what the problem at hand requires and what a subordinate can be reasonably asked to do. Follet suggested subordinates will refuse to follow orders—even those that seem like reasonable requests—if they do not conform to the law of the situation.[15]

For example, if our engine company responds to an alarm and arrives to find a house wrapped in flames with people trapped inside, the captain may order firefighters to enter the house to rescue the trapped victims. Chances are, this is an order that will be obeyed even though in obeying it subordinates willingly put their lives at risk. In contrast, if at the same scene the captain orders his engine company back to the firehouse, he runs the risk of insubordination. The second order keeps his firefighters safe and out of harm's way, but it does not conform to the law of the situation. Firefighters are public servants trained to save lives and property by fighting fires, even when the risks are high. If there is a fire and people are at risk, firefighters are fully aware of the problem at hand and what constitutes a reasonable response on their part to the situation. That law of the situation compels them to fight the fire rather than to seek safety. An order to do the former rather than the latter stands a much higher probability of being obeyed, even with the risks involved, because it conforms to the law of the situation. The same basic principle, argued Follet, works in the more mundane day-to-day operations of any hierarchical organization. The job of superiors in such organizations is not to imperiously issue orders, but to find the law of the situation. It is the job of the manager to match the problem and environmental context with the behavior needed to achieve the goal. Once that match is made, orders can be given with a high expectation that they will be obeyed.

Carrots and Sticks

Rather than rely on power and authority, or search for a law of the situation that may not be immediately clear, some scholars argue a better way for managers to coordinate behavior toward a desired end is to play on human nature. All humans have "trips" or "triggers" that will cause a behavioral response. Discovering these motivations and aligning them with organizational goals provides a powerful way to channel individual desires or fears toward collective goals. In layman's terms, this can be thought of as dangling a carrot or wielding a stick. Why do people work? Well, for a wide variety of reasons. One of the most fundamental, however, is a paycheck. Stop paying wages and chances are a manager will have a hard time getting anyone to do anything. Indeed, they may not have any employees at all. In this case money is the carrot. Subordinates carry out their assigned tasks at work, even if they do not like or enjoy them, because that is what it takes to get a paycheck. If they fail to carry out these assigned tasks they face the risk of being fired. This is the stick.

The cause and effect here are intuitive—you do something I want and I will give you something you want in return. If you do what you are asked to do you are rewarded, fail to do what you are asked to do and you are punished. The study of human motivation in organizational settings, however, is considerably more refined than the notion of exchanging something of value for a desired behavior or making a credible threat about the consequences of behavior. What makes more sense for managers to get their decisions implemented—carrots, sticks, or a judicious mix of both? If it is the latter option, when is it best to employ a carrot over a stick or vice versa?

The answers to these questions have important implications for how managers approach the task of getting people to do what they want them to do. In order to get answers, public administration scholars have tried to apply the lessons of psychology to organizational settings. Broadly speaking, there are two schools of psychological thought that scholars have drawn on to establish systematic management rules of thumb.

One of these approaches is **behaviorism**, a school of psychology most famously associated with B. F. Skinner.[16] The central tenet of behaviorism is that most human behavior is a response to an environmental stimulus. If our hand touches a hot stove we snatch it away. If it gets dark we go to sleep. Building on this basic assumption, Skinner developed his ideas of conditioning. **Conditioning** is behavior learned through the process of associating an environmental stimulus with a particular behavioral response. One of the most famous examples of conditioning is Pavlov's dogs. Ivan Pavlov, a Russian psychologist, conducted an experiment where he rang a bell just before he fed dogs. The dogs came to associate the bell with food, and begin to salivate as soon as they heard its ringing. They had been conditioned to associate a stimulus (the ringing of a bell) with eating, even though that stimulus normally had nothing to do with food.

How does this help managers? As it turns out, people can also be conditioned to expect a particular result on the basis of past experience. Those who work well for management get promotions, pay raises, or some form of positive recognition. Those who do not get demotions, deductions, and negative recognition. Regardless of whether carrots or sticks are used as the basis of conditioning, however, using behaviorism to fashion a management system means making a set of basic assumptions about humans.

These assumptions were famously catalogued as the characteristics of a management system by Douglas McGregor in a book called *The Human Side of Enterprise*.[17] McGregor coined the term **Theory X** to describe a generic management approach that leans heavily on the psychology of behaviorism. Theory X assumes that subordinates are self-interested, prefer to be directed rather than being self-motivated, and prefer not working to working. Under Theory X, a manager needs to issue clear instructions and closely supervise subordinates, and motivate them to do the actual required tasks through simple and direct reward-punishment conditioning. The rewards approach (sometimes called soft Theory X) involves more pay, praise, and promises of promotion. The employee thus begins to associate successfully achieving work tasks with these positive payoffs, even if the work itself holds no intrinsic interest.

In contrast to the soft approach, hard Theory X relies more on the stick than the carrot. This has also been called the KITA (Kick in the Ass) approach to management.[18] Rather than offering benefits for good performance, hard Theory X promises punishment for poor performance. People do what you want them to do—even if they do not want to—because failure to follow instructions brings the risk of losing pay, being yelled at, getting bad evaluations, or even being fired.

Many people will recognize the Theory X approach from their own experience. Theory X offers an intuitive way to coordinate subordinates' behavior toward a desired task or goal that can be relatively easily systemized through things like merit pay or work quotas. Nonetheless, Theory X approaches, especially in their KITA variants, have significant drawbacks. They are based on a rather gloomy view of human nature (people are generally lazy, manipulative, and self-interested) and require constant vigilance on the part of the manager. Under Theory X, there is little allowance for self-motivation or innovation on the part of subordinates. As subordinates actually carry out the individual tasks that achieve agency goals, they are well-positioned to figure out how to do those tasks more effectively and efficiently. Such contributions are likely to be missed in a Theory X approach. Subordinates are conditioned not to do anything unless there is a carrot or stick, and without these as motivation the assumption is that subordinates will do nothing.

In contrast to Theory X, McGregor also systemized another management approach he called Theory Y. **Theory Y** is based on a second psychological school that emerged as a counter to behaviorism. Theory Y assumes that people are quite capable of being self-directed and self-motivated. A manager simply has to create the right conditions and work environment, and people will do a job well without the controlling micromanagement necessary in Theory X. Theory Y heralded the formalization of what came to be known as the humanistic management approach, which emphasized self-awareness, self-knowledge, and self-reliance. The basic notion underpinning Theory Y was that the most effective way to coordinate people's behavior toward a desired objective was to align individual goals with organizational goals. When this happened, individuals wanted to get the job done, no KITA or carrots required.

The basic understanding of how to align individual and organizational goals came from the work of Abraham Maslow, who formulated a comprehensive explanation of human motivation now known as **Maslow's hierarchy of needs**.[19] Maslow argued that humans are motivated by unmet needs, that these needs are ranked hierarchically, and that the lower order needs must be satisfied before the higher needs play a significant role in behavior. In Maslow's hierarchy, the most basic needs are physiological necessities: air, water, food, shelter, and sex. The next need is the psychological need for safety, the desire to establish a secure and stable living environment. At the apex of Maslow's hierarchy of needs are esteem and respect topped by self-actualization (see Figure 6.1). Maslow argued that the unmet need at the next level of hierarchy provides the primary motivation for human behavior.

To get the basic idea of Maslow's hierarchy of needs, consider how often you think about oxygen or water. Chances are, not often. This is because these basic physiological needs are freely available in the air we breathe and at the nearest faucet. Yet deprive someone of oxygen for 30 or 40 seconds, or water for two or three days, and their entire existence will be focused on fulfilling those needs. Once these basic physiological needs are met, they no longer motivate behavior—it is always the unmet needs at the next level in the hierarchy. In industrialized nations such as the United States, lower-level needs rarely motivate behavior, because they are widely met. But the higher-level needs are often unmet, and remain powerful motivators of behavior. Everyone craves respect and esteem and, ultimately, most seek self-actualization—to discover and satisfy their innermost selves.

The Theory Y manager uses this alternate conception of human nature as a basis for coordinating behavior to organization goals. From the Theory Y perspective, humans are assumed to have the capacity for self-motivation and a willingness to take on responsibility. The trick to

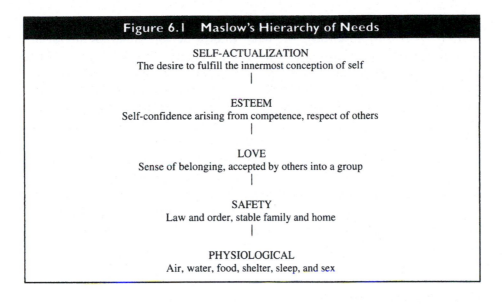

Figure 6.1   Maslow's Hierarchy of Needs

SELF-ACTUALIZATION
The desire to fulfill the innermost conception of self

|

ESTEEM
Self-confidence arising from competence, respect of others

|

LOVE
Sense of belonging, accepted by others into a group

|

SAFETY
Law and order, stable family and home

|

PHYSIOLOGICAL
Air, water, food, shelter, sleep, and sex

harnessing these capacities is to make the link between unmet needs and organizational goals. There is really no such thing as a Theory Y micromanager; the Theory Y approach involves motivating subordinates to do a job and then getting out of their way.

Your own educational experience probably provides you with examples of Theory X and Theory Y management approaches. Assume the basic goal of a college class is to get students to master course content. How can an instructor achieve this goal? A Theory X approach means assuming students are not particularly interested in mastering course content and need close supervision and a well timed mix of carrots and sticks to get them to achieve the goal. Theory X courses will have lots of quizzes and tests, with the focus on the instructor. A Theory Y approach assumes that students are quite capable of achieving mastery of course content if they are properly motivated to learn. Thus, a Theory Y instructor will attempt to convince students they have a vested individual interest in learning. A Theory Y instructor will try to gauge the interests of students and link those interests to the course. A Theory Y classroom is much more likely to be student centered. The ultimate objective of Theory Y is to create an environment where individual and organizational goals are indistinguishable. In an ideal Theory Y situation subordinates do not have to be told what to do, nor do they require external carrots and sticks for motivation. They take the actions necessary to achieve the organizational objective not because they have to, but because they want to.

Theory X and Theory Y spawned a number of management schools, which in turn were based on alternates to or extensions of the various schools of thought on the psychology of human motivation. All of these have useful applications for public administration, but as of yet there is no perfect understanding of "what makes people tick." Behaviorism turned out to be wrong in fundamental ways. People are not blank slates that can be manipulated through conditioning to be a tinker, tailor, sailor, or spy. At least some elements of human personality appear to be innate. Maslow's hierarchy of needs turned out to have so many exceptions they threatened the hierarchy's rule. People will ignore thirst and hunger to achieve esteem or self-respect; the multimillion-aire banker who discovers that digging ditches makes him happy is unlikely to follow through on the process of self-actualization by giving up the world of finance to become a day laborer. An important part of a good manager's tool box is a basic understanding of human psychology. Applying that knowledge, however, is still as much art as systematic science.

Get a System

An alternate approach to giving direct orders, or working from a particular understanding of human motivation, is to create a system that structures behavior toward organizational goals. Rules and standard operating procedures (SOPs) are good examples of such systems. Both provide clear guidelines for behavior, in effect saying "if A happens, do B."[20] Bureaucracies, with their focus on uniformity and written records, are very good at creating such systems.

Rules and SOPs have clear advantages. A good example is the preflight checklist that all good pilots follow to ensure their aircraft are safe and ready to fly. Bureaucratic organizations—the military and airline companies, for example—standardize such preflight checklists and require pilots to run through the checklist prior to taking off. The checklist becomes part of a pilot's routine, simply "what we do around here." It does not matter if an aircraft is brand new or fresh from an overhaul and certified safe by a chief mechanic and a federal safety inspector. Pilots are still expected to go through the checklist, because that is the rule. In this case the rule helps ensure the basic goal: fly from point A to point B as safely as possible. Establishing this particular SOP helps assure that a pilot methodically verifies that all major systems are operational. If something does go wrong during the flight—an engine failure, an instrument malfunction—pilots will typically follow another SOP predesigned to solve the problem and achieve the objective of arriving safely.

Managing part of a public bureaucracy is similar to flying a plane, in that SOPs can play an important role in achieving desired objectives. There have been numerous attempts to establish SOPs not just as guides for subordinate behavior, but as the fundamental guidelines or rules of management. The idea is that distilling a common set of generic management rules will enhance the effectiveness of all bureaucracies in achieving their objectives.

One of the best-known of attempts to create such a set of management rules was formulated by Frederick Winslow Taylor. Taylor is the father of **scientific management**, an early attempt to systemize the "laws" of management. There are four basic principles of scientific management.

1. Understand Fundamental Tasks. Break down the organization into its most fundamental tasks, and gain a systematic knowledge of all details of frontline work. No matter how small or trivial, the first requirement of scientific management is a complete database of even the most menial tasks in the organization. This data set is used to formulate a systematic understanding of how best to perform each individual task.

2. Get the Right People for the Job. Use the knowledge gained in step one to match the right person to the right job. Armed with knowledge of what is required to complete the task, a manager can match the physical and psychological attributes of an individual to a particular job.

3. Put Knowledge to Work. Make sure workers have the knowledge gained from step one, that is, make sure they know the most effective and efficient way to do the job.

4. Ensure Rational Division of Labor. Properly divide the work between management and labor. The task of management is to make sure workers know what has to be done and that they have the right tools for the job. Labor's task is to actually do the job.[21]

In a famous demonstration of his approach to management, Taylor did an exhaustive study of shoveling. He examined the optimum weight that a man might shovel consistently for long periods of time, designed shovels to accommodate this weight, and suggested hiring people with the right physical capabilities to handle this work load. Taylor's point was not just to do the definitive study of shoveling, but to demonstrate the importance of analyzing even the most trivial of operations. For a manager, knowing the best way to shovel, ensuring the right sort of shovel is available, and hiring the right people for the task can have a considerable payoff in productivity.

Taylor's work ushered in a broad-scale search for the "principles of management." The idea was to systematically deduce the universal laws of management, a proven set of guidelines that could be confidently followed by managers regardless of the specific goals of the organization. Famous attempts to formulate such a set of universal principles came from people like Luther Gulick and Henri Fayol, both of whom developed a set of management axioms that stressed the importance of clear objectives, logical divisions of labor, and establishing a clear chain of authority.[22]

These sorts of guidelines no doubt had some practical use for managers in the field, but as scientific principles they left a good deal to be desired. In a devastating critique, Herbert Simon pointed out that Fayol, Gulick, and others actually offered proverbs of management, not principles. For example, a basic "law" of management is to break an organization's objective into smaller goals and have people specialize in these subgoals. This idea—the efficiency of division of labor— was first formalized by Adam Smith. Simon pointed out that whatever its usefulness as a general idea, the notion of division of labor is not much use as a specific guideline. How are managers supposed to divide and specialize labor? By function? By place? By previous training? These are the important specifics managers need answered. As presented in the various principles of management formulations, the axiom of division of labor boils down to saying that "different people in the organization should specialize in doing different things." This is accurate enough as an observation. Indeed, it is a virtually inevitable byproduct of any group effort. But who should specialize in what? What counts as something worth specializing in? The axiom of "divide labor and specialize" is not much help in answering these more specific and practical questions. As a guide to help managers best specify individual missions and assign tasks, the "principle" is of little help.[23]

Whether proverbs or principles, management systems and schools continue to be formulated that are direct descendants of Taylor, Gulick, and Fayol. The "reinventing government" (REGO) and "new public management" (NPM) movements, for example, are both modern attempts to improve the efficiency of public agencies by using the principles of the market. REGO is based on 10 "principles" that Simon would no doubt call proverbs.[24] For example, one of the principles calls for public bureaucracies to be mission driven rather than rule driven. It is hard to disagree with this advice; few people would argue that bureaucracies should prioritize red tape and regulation over their primary tasks. Yet, as we have seen, the goals of public agencies are often vague. What is the mission of a police department, a library, a school? How, specifically, can a manager be assured that the decisions she makes and the actions she orders are "mission driven"? The principles have much less to offer when it comes to the day-to-day specifics of a manager's job.

Though all management principles turn into proverbs on close examination, the persistence of such systems suggests they do have some practical advantages. One review of theories of public management notes that the principles approach is "continually recycled, relabeled, and adopted by public administrators as a useful guide to action."[25] Though a long way from scientific laws, the management rules of thumb offered by the various principles approaches offer a systematic baseline for action. They usefully serve as the basis of a rough philosophy of management for many public administrators.

Conclusion

Deciding and doing are the two fundamental challenges of public administration. Like all organizations, public agencies have to decide how to achieve goals, solve problems, and complete tasks at hand. Compared to private organizations, public agencies may have a more complex and limited set of options on how to achieve their objectives. Despite the more complex political environments they operate in, public agencies are expected to make logical and systematic choices to achieve goals and solve problems and ensure these decisions are translated into action.

There are a number of systematic approaches to decision making. The rational-comprehensive approach, which emphasizes extensive information gathering and a cost-benefit analysis of all potential options, is at the heart of many decision-making systems developed or recommended for the public sector. While there is much to recommend the rational-comprehensive approach in the abstract, in practice it makes too many demands on public administrators who frequently do not have the resources (not to mention the patience or the mental capacity) to adopt it as a the primary basis for making decisions. A more realistic approach for public administrators is incrementalism. Incremental decision makers start with what is known or the status quo, consider a limited set of options to change what exists into what is desired, and opt for the course of action that seems most likely to work. Incrementalism allows for values, experience, habit, and negotiated compromise to play influential roles in decision making.

While more realistic, incrementalism is a conservative, low-risk approach to decision making. Mixed scanning tries to combine the advantages of rational-comprehensive and incrementalism. How a mixed scanner makes a decision depends on the nature of the decision—mundane, day-to-day operational decisions are handled incrementally. A more rational-comprehensive approach is adopted for making fundamental decisions, those that cut to the heart of organizational purposes.

Regardless of how a decision is made, it is an abstract intent until people take the physical actions necessary to turn it into a concrete reality. Implementing decisions means getting people to do want you want them to do. Again there are a number of options. Managers can simply issue orders and rely on power and authority to get them carried out. They can try to coordinate behavior by trying to align individual needs and goals with organizational needs and goals. They can set up a system, a list of principles or rules of thumb to guide action. There are no universal axioms of management, however, and leadership in public bureaucracies remains as much an art as it is a science.

Key Concepts

acceptance theory The idea that the authority of a superior is based on the willingness of a subordinate to accept and obey an order.

behaviorism A school of psychology based on the idea that human behavior is a response to environmental stimuli.

conditioning Behavior learned through the process of associating an environmental stimulus with a particular behavioral response.

decision making The process of information gathering, analysis, and prioritizing as a means to select the best course of action to solve a problem or achieve a goal.

incremental decision making A decision-making approach that emphasizes using past experience and the current situation as baselines for coming up with practical solutions to achieve goals or solve problems.

law of the situation The action needed to address the problem and circumstances at hand.

Maslow's hierarchy of needs The idea that humans are motivated by a hierarchically ranked set of needs. Lower-order needs must be satisfied before higher needs play a significant role in behavior.

maximizers Decision makers who know their goals, can rank order the preferred means to achieve those goals, and choose the means that best achieves the goal at the lowest cost.

mixed scanning A decision making approach that emphasizes using incremental decision making for routine decisions, and rational-comprehensive decision making for important decisions.

rational-comprehensive decision making An approach to decision making that emphasizes identifying and analyzing all possible means to achieve a given goal, and choosing the option that best achieves the goal at the lowest cost.

satisficers Decision makers whose objective is to find an option that works to achieve a goal or solve a problem. Once a practical option is found they stop searching.

scientific management A management school that seeks to distill universal laws of management by breaking tasks into their most basic components, and matching the right people and technology to these tasks.

shirking The process of consciously circumventing the wishes of superiors.

Theory X A management style that assumes subordinates are self-interested, prefer to be directed rather than being self-motivated, and prefer not working to working. Under Theory X, a supervisor gives detailed instructions, closely supervises subordinates, and motivates through reward-punishment conditioning.

Theory Y A management approach that assumes people are capable of being self-directed and self-motivated. Under Theory Y, a supervisor seeks to align individual goals with organizational ones. ✦

Chapter 7

Public-Sector Performance

Hundreds of thousands of elementary, middle-school, and high-school students are familiar with the Drug Abuse Resistance Education program, otherwise known as D.A.R.E. This program teams school districts and local police departments to teach young people to resist alcohol, tobacco, and other drugs. Pretty much everyone agrees with its goals, parents are highly supportive, and the program is widely popular. It has only one major drawback: it probably doesn't work. In fact, serious questions about the effectiveness of D.A.R.E. have been raised by a number of studies in the past decade.[1] As a result of such evaluations, D.A.R.E. has received intense political scrutiny, and as a result some schools have dropped the program.[2] This is the value of examining public-sector performance: if we place demands on government (in this case, to help kids resist drugs), and spend public money to meet those demands, it makes sense that we should make sure that we are getting what we asked for.

By now it should be clear that public organizations—the bureaucracy—in the United States do a great deal of work in the public interest. Whether you notice this work (such as watching the city snow plow move down your street) or not (if you take for granted that fresh water will come out of your tap), part of understanding public administration involves knowing when public agencies have done a good job.

Sometimes, when an agency is not doing a good job administering a program, it is obvious. A road might deteriorate quickly because it was paved improperly, or a city park may be poorly kept up. All we need to do is take a look at the roads and parks, and we can get a good sense of how those services are being delivered. Other times, it is tragic. In 1993 in Milwaukee several hundred thousand people became ill and more than one hundred people died when one of the city's water treatment plants failed to detect the presence of cryptosporidium bacteria. Unfortunately, the ineffectiveness of the city's water quality standards was all too apparent.

Usually, however, whether or not an agency is doing a good job is not readily apparent. How do we know for sure if the Department of Agriculture is successfully running its crop insurance programs? Or if the state Department of Natural Resources is making sure that people don't go fishing without a license? Or if the city's recycling program is both cost-effective and beneficial to the environment?

Even though it may be difficult to measure, it is important to know if public agencies are successful, because having this information is critical for governance and administration. Decisions about public policy need to be made with at least some information about the likelihood of a program's success. For example, if a city is considering adopting a curbside pickup recycling program, that decision is easier to make with information about the performance of other similar programs in other similar cities. Similarly, a decision about expanding, shrinking, or eliminating an existing program is better and easier to make with solid information about what the program is supposed to accomplish, its actual performance, and reasons why there might be a difference between the two. It is also important to assess the performance of agencies accurately so that we do not give them credit or blame when it is not due. For example, a decision by a town's police department to crack down on illegal alcohol consumption at college "house parties" may not actually reduce the amount of illegal alcohol consumed, but might simply move the problem to a neighboring town that does not have such an aggressive police department. One town has "solved" its problem by giving it to another town, and perhaps has unintentionally created another problem: the possibility that drunk driving instances will increase as those students drive back home because they had to travel to the party in the first place.

Making good decisions in the process of public budgeting also depends upon having good information about public-sector performance. As you will see in Chapter 8, the procedures used to make budget decisions and create public budgets themselves have changed dramatically in the last 40 years as public-sector performance measures are integrated into the process. This information goes beyond simply trying to not waste money by improving cost-effectiveness. Instead, by incorporating an analysis of agencies' performance, budget decision makers have information about the goals of government programs, what progress has been made toward those goals, and what is required to meet them. Budget decision makers can then adjust program funding levels accordingly.

Last but not least, measuring public-sector performance is important because we need to know if our government agencies have served the public interest. Part of this involves gathering information about the value of public goods and services that are provided by the bureaucracy. Programs of dubious or narrow economic or social value can be identified more readily. This not only saves public resources, but it also ensures a more fair (or at least widespread) distribution of government services. Many citizens argue that government should generally act to serve the broader population rather than concentrating benefits on a select few at the expense of the rest. When benefits are concentrated, there needs to be a good reason. For example, Social Security benefits are received primarily by the elderly, with the justification that society should ensure that people do not fall into poverty as they get older and are no longer able to work.

In addition to information about the value and beneficiaries of public programs, measuring public-sector performance also provides information about the use of agency discretion. As commonly understood, bureaucrats need some discretion in order to tailor the expectations of policymakers who established the program to the needs of the population served by that program. Properly used, discretion can be a powerful tool in improving an agency's performance. If it is improperly used, however, the agency may not meet all of its goals (it may choose to emphasize one to the exclusion of another) and may even harm the public it is supposed to serve. As an example of the former, a public-school teacher may choose to "teach to the test" in order to meet basic government-mandated benchmarks, and reduce attention to other important educational matters. As an example of the latter, police officers are sometimes criticized for the excessive use of force, harming the citizens they are supposed to protect.

The key to assessing public-sector performance, then, comes in two parts. The first is to understand the goals of the organization. As you are about to see, this is more difficult than it first seems. Government agencies rarely have a single goal. A worse problem is that it is rather common for government agencies to have goals that conflict with each other. Identifying those goals as an analyst of public-sector performance is a difficult process that frequently involves making some subjective decisions about what goal an agency "should" be working towards.

The second part to assessing public-sector performance is to understand the public's expectations of the bureaucracy. It is obvious that citizens are interested in making sure that government agencies accomplish their goals. However, the public has additional expectations regarding exactly how those goals are met. Assessing public-sector performance is therefore as much about evaluating how well agency goals are accomplished as it is about assessing whether the appropriate methods are used to reach those goals.

Organizational Goals and Evaluating Public-Sector Performance

Public organizations in the United States "lie snugly fixed between a rock and a hard place."[3] This is because we rarely assign a single goal to our government agencies. Frequently, these goals are even contradictory. When this is the case, it is almost impossible for a single agency to accomplish all of its goals. For example, our public schools are supposed to foster learning through a creative atmosphere, yet they also need to provide a secure, distraction-free environment. We expect our prison system to punish criminals and house them cheaply, and to rehabilitate prisoners, which may include offering access to educational and social programs. A more striking example is that of using the military for peacekeeping operations, such as the current deployment in Iraq. The primary goal of the military is to provide national defense. This is accomplished through the threat or use of overwhelming military power. In other words, the military accomplishes its goal by preparing to destroy potential enemies. Destruction and war, or at least their threat, are the keys to a successful military. Yet keeping the peace in certain regions of the world is also in our national security interest. As a result, we have deployed our military on peacekeeping missions, where the goals become law enforcement and maintaining friendly relations with the local population. In a peacekeeping mission, the use of force can be counterproductive. It is no wonder that many in the military are frustrated by such missions. If the organization emphasizes security and the threat of force, in line with its normal training, it becomes alienated from the local population. If the military emphasizes law enforcement goals, it runs the risk of being less able to protect its own personnel from attack, and morale may drop as a result.

Leaders in an agency with competing or contradictory goals have a difficult time fostering a sense of mission among workers. In his classic book on the bureaucracy, James Q. Wilson argues that a sense of mission is an important source of motivation for bureaucrats.[4] If an organization has a well-defined purpose, or if bureaucrats staffing the organization have a common idea of what needs to be accomplished, they are much more likely to work hard and reach the organization's goals. Competing or contradictory goals pull the organization in many directions at once. Further, sources of worker motivation are compromised by contradictory goals, and a sense of mission disappears.

Any analysis of public-sector performance therefore needs to start by examining if an organization is saddled with multiple, contradictory goals. If so, then our expectations need to reflect those goals. It is also readily apparent that one way to improve organizational performance is to remove or reduce conflict and contradiction between goals. This will help rebuild a sense of mission and increase motivation for bureaucrats.

Vague Goals and Intractable Problems

In other instances, we assign vague goals to our public organizations. This is a function of our expectations about government. The idea of "limited government" is no longer most people's fundamental view of what an appropriate government looks like. Instead, we want and use government to solve our problems. The idea of "positive government" is a more accurate way to describe our attitude about government.[5] Certainly, we differ about what government should be doing, but we all agree, basically, that it should do *something* to solve our various social, political, and economic problems.

However, we sometimes wish government to solve **intractable problems**—large, complex issues that are caused by many factors and that have many different consequences. These problems may defy definition, and therefore there may be many different ideas about the most appropriate way to deal with them. It is common for government agencies that deal with these large problems to have vague goals, such as "educating students" or "maintaining positive foreign relations" or "fighting crime." There are many ways to try to accomplish these goals, and it is possible that organizational performance may suffer as interpretations of these goals change. For example, we may tell a police department one year to focus on drunk driving and the next year to focus on drugs. Frequently redefining what an organization does frustrates its workers, forces repeated reallocation of resources, and perhaps does not allow enough time for the organization to make progress toward its current mission.

On the other hand, the need for a community to build a new bridge over a river that runs through downtown is not a vague, intractable problem. The project can be started and finished in a short amount of time, and the problem (heavy traffic on existing bridges) will be eliminated as soon as the bridge is completed. Measuring organizational performance on these sorts of issues is relatively easy. In this case, the questions to be addressed are the time and cost to complete the bridge, and the extent to which it reduces traffic congestion.

An example of an intractable problem is that of poverty. The causes and consequences of poverty are diverse. The definition of who is poor can be subjective, and one's opinion about the best way to alleviate poverty will depend on how one views the causes and consequences of poverty. Subjective definitions of a problem can create vague goals for public organizations, and may even produce contradictory suggestions about what an organization must do to remedy a problem. Often, this is as much a political opinion as anything else. For example, conservatives will choose to emphasize that poverty can be caused by an unwillingness to work hard, and thus will seek to structure welfare programs to be less generous to those who do not seek employment or who do not participate in training programs. Liberals, on the other hand, will choose to emphasize that poverty can be caused through a lack of opportunity or simple bad luck, and thus will try to structure welfare programs to reflect the fact that people may be poor through no fault of their own. These two solutions are at odds with each other, but because a definition of poverty is not easily agreed upon, welfare programs may be structured in a way that blends the two. The results are vague goals for welfare agencies, and a high probability that the results of those welfare programs will be unsatisfactory for both conservatives and liberals.

Regardless of the ideological choices that are made, poverty is not going to be "solved." So, public organizations face a stacked deck. The identification of a problem does not necessarily mean that there is a solution. Poverty, as an intractable problem, has so many causes and consequences that it is unrealistic to expect any public organization to eliminate poverty or its effects from society. This means, to appropriately evaluate public sector performance on this and other intractable issues, we need to carefully define "success" and "failure" of bureaucratic activity and government programs. Rather than defining success as the complete elimination of a problem, it should instead be thought of in terms of acceptable progress. In other words, success might be defined as being a meaningful alleviation of the problem. Public organizations can try to reduce the severity of many social problems, but rarely can they fully solve them.

Contextual Goals

Even though organizational goals may be vague or sometimes contradictory, they still serve as the source of an organization's sense of mission, and provide reasons for the existence of the organization. Those goals represent what citizens expect government to accomplish, and each public organization therefore uses its goals to define its activities. Therefore, they become the primary concern of the organization; a police department is focused first on crime prevention, and a public school is primarily concerned with education.

This does not mean, however, that government agencies do not have other goals they are expected to meet. These other goals are called **contextual goals** and are best described as expectations about how exactly government agencies are supposed to accomplish their primary goals. According to James Q. Wilson, they "define the context within which the primary goals can be sought."[6] In other words, we want our government agencies to accomplish their goals, and we want them to do so in specific ways, and accomplish other useful goals along the way.

Contextual goals can be important for the proper role of government agencies in a democracy. With democratic governance, we expect our institutions to be transparent (that is, we should be able to "see inside" to find out how government works). For public organizations, this is achieved by requiring public hearings on important issues, allowing citizens to see bureaucratic paperwork (for example, by using the Freedom of Information Act), and by requiring public notice of government activity. Democratic governance also is interested in protecting civil rights and liberties. Therefore, the actions of bureaucrats and bureaucracy are restricted by rules that ensure due process and fairness. For example, if the IRS suspects tax fraud and audits you, you are made aware of the nature of the suspicion and are given a chance to demonstrate your innocence. Rules that control government contracting are useful for protecting against unfair competition or to guard against discrimination.

Other contextual goals are important for establishing an appropriate work environment for bureaucrats. Personnel procedures that establish rules for hiring, firing, promotion, and raises are contextual goals that function to ensure that competent workers are hired and retained, and that promotion and raises are linked to job performance.

Finally, some contextual goals define what is acceptable or desirable to society. For example, sometimes it is important, politically, for a town government to contract with local businesses for services, if only to help those companies and to "keep money local." There has been a similar concern at the national level, and federal agencies are required in most cases to "buy American" when purchasing goods. Public schools have long operated on the assumption that some "social promotion" is desirable (that is, it is helpful to pass students even though they have not met academic requirements, in order to keep them with their peer or age group).

The importance of contextual goals and the number of them have increased dramatically. For example, our public schools do not simply educate students in the basics of reading, writing, and arithmetic. They provide students with access to a range of other services such as psychological diagnoses and treatment, social counseling, and public health. Further, we expect our schools to conduct their day-to-day business in particular ways. We want students to be treated fairly by teachers when grading homework, we expect personal records to remain confidential, we expect the school board to be open to the public when making important decisions about school policy, we expect the civil rights of students to be protected, and we expect the school to provide a safe environment while students are there.

All of these contextual goals are important and have value to citizens. This does not mean, however, that there is no conflict over them, or that they do not cause problems. Contextual goals, while providing some benefits, do sometimes stand in the way of an organization accomplishing its primary goal. This occurs when time, personnel, and other resources are diverted away from the main mission of the agency toward meeting contextual goals. Progress toward the primary goal can slow down or may become inefficient as an agency ensures that its procedures are in line with certain restrictions. For example, rather than following strict contracting procedures, a government agency perhaps would like to continue to use a vendor with which it has developed a working relationship.

Wilson, in his book *Bureaucracy,* argues that contextual goals can sometimes create significant management and leadership problems in public organization. This is because it is readily apparent when a contextual goal is not met, and managers worry about being held accountable (for example, when schools are not safe, or when an agency has purchased foreign rather than American goods). Managers and leaders of public organizations therefore may choose to divert more resources toward meeting contextual goals than they otherwise would like to.

Contextual goals may also be a source of serious disagreement among citizens. Some people may see little value in some contextual goals, or may even think they are completely inappropriate. Others may see value, but still feel that the primary mission of the agency is being unduly compromised. Much of the conflict over public education is related to contextual goals. Some parents feel that public schools would do a much better job, and reduce costs, if they concentrated exclusively on the basics of education. Others feel that as public institutions, schools can and should serve more diverse needs of young people, and that the value of the contextual goals outweighs any decrease in a school's ability to educate students in reading, writing, and arithmetic.

Regardless of how one feels about the particular contextual goals of an individual public organization, as evaluators of public-sector performance, we must take them into account when judging success or failure. Since contextual goals do diminish the amount of attention and resources an agency can give to its primary mission, evaluators should assess those trade-offs. The key issue becomes an evaluation of how much of an obstacle those contextual goals are. If we choose to require our public organizations to meet a variety of other goals while trying to accomplish their primary goals, then we need to adjust our expectations accordingly. Of course, we can always decide to eliminate or reduce the number of contextual goals, if we feel that the primary goal of an agency is sufficiently important (see Sidebar 7.1).

Public Expectations of Bureaucracy

Citizens are the key source of contextual goals for our public organizations. We put these goals in place for our government agencies because we have some standard expectations about how our government should function. We expect a lot from our government agencies. We want effectiveness, speed, personal service, and fairness, among other things, and all provided at low cost. Unfortunately for bureaucrats, these expectations frequently compete and as a result, as you will see, government agencies are in the words of the old truism, "damned if

Sidebar 7.1   Social Promotion in the Public Schools

One current example of a contextual goal that we give public schools is building social skills. Although the obvious primary mission of public schools is to educate and provide a certain basic set of skills, social and psychological concerns exist as well. One of these concerns is that students who are held back a grade (or more) may experience difficulties. They may struggle to fit in as their friends advance on without them, or they may suffer psychologically and become bullies, fail to improve their performance, or even drop out of school entirely. Consequently, students that may struggle in these ways are frequently promoted to the next grade, even if their school performance is inadequate. This is called *social promotion*, and it is an example of contextual goals competing with an organization's primary mission.

The practice of social promotion has obvious benefits. Students that are promoted are probably better off emotionally and socially. However, many wonder if these benefits outweigh the importance of the educational mission of schools. As a result, cities such as Chicago and New York have restricted the use of social promotion. By requiring schools to hold back low-achieving students, the hope is to produce more of a focus on providing those students with another opportunity to learn the material.

The results of restricting social promotion are unclear. Chicago even recently abandoned those restrictions after research demonstrated that holding back students did not increase test scores for young students, actually decreased scores for older ones, and increased drop-out rates. On the other hand, officials in New York City are confident their restrictions will work, because they hope to provide students that are held back with extra academic help.

they do, and damned if they don't."[7] Part of any evaluation of the performance of public organizations must assess how well all of these expectations are met. These public expectations of the bureaucracy can be divided into two categories, or standards for bureaucracy: responsiveness to the needs of the public, and competent performance.[8]

Bureaucratic Responsiveness

Bureaucratic responsiveness is a necessary and reasonable expectation because it is one way to be sure that public organizations serve the interests of citizens as well as the expectations of other government institutions in the United States. However, the diverse nature of these groups ensures that not all will be entirely satisfied with the level of responsiveness from any given agency.

Rather obviously, an agency needs to be responsive to other government institutions when making decisions. This form of responsiveness is directly due to the institutional role of the bureaucracy: it is designed

to help the other three branches of government carry out their missions. Because of this role, the bureaucracy must be responsive to the
needs of those other branches.[9] The president, as chief bureaucrat, sets
overall goals for public organizations. This is reflected primarily in the
budget process (see Chapter 8), and agencies need to try to meet those
goals. Public organizations need to also be responsive to the demands
of Congress, and they should try to follow the intent of legislation that
is passed. Sometimes this is difficult (see Chapter 3), but nevertheless,
an agency that continuously ignores the requirements of Congress is
not functioning properly in the eyes of legislators. Finally, public organizations need to be responsive to the law, and how it is interpreted.
Court decisions can either command the government to act or restrict
the government's actions, and public organizations need to adjust their
behavior accordingly to remain in compliance with the law.

Because politics and administration are blended together, public
organizations also need to be responsive to the public.[10] This form of
responsiveness includes allowing citizens access to organizational decision making, as well as a general alignment between public demands
and bureaucratic policy and decisions. In other words, we demand that
our agencies listen to our preferences (and complaints), and then make
decisions that will match those preferences (or resolve the complaints). Responding to "the public" can be difficult, however. The
general public does not speak with one voice, nor does it make its preferences clear.[11] The very fact that there are competing groups of citizens on practically every issue makes it difficult to be responsive to
"the public," particularly when it is not typically obvious which group
has the better, more practical, or more worthy preference.[12] Should the
Environmental Protection Agency respond to the demands of industry
and lower certain pollution standards, or should it respond to the demands of environmental groups that argue that the EPA takes an an-
tagonistic stance toward industry and adopt tougher sanctions? Both
options would probably be beneficial in reducing pollution, but one
way is better for industry and the other is better for environmental
groups.

Further, because political power is not evenly distributed among all
members of society, some of the public may not in fact be able to have
access to public organizations, and therefore their preferences may not
be heard, despite the fact that they may be interested in what the organization is doing. This means that an agency should also weigh the
preferences of those who are not represented. Some caution that
government agencies can in fact be *too* responsive to the needs or preferences of rather narrow groups in society. The Department of Agriculture has recently come under fire for dispersing farm subsidies in a
way that disproportionately rewards large agribusiness concerns while
small family farmers struggle with comparatively less government
help. The criticism is that the USDA is overly responsive to highly or-

ganized, wealthy agricultural businesses and less responsive to small farmers because they are less politically influential.

Flexibility is another form of responsiveness to the public. An organization is flexible when it can respond to the individual needs of clients by making exceptions to rules as well as responding to criticism (either from clients or internally, from the agency's employees) and changing rules and behavior.[13] Bureaucracy is, in the minds of many, synonymous with rigidity and is bound tightly with red tape. The stereotypical bureaucrat is unsympathetic and uncaring, one who is unwilling to bend the rules to meet the diverse, unique needs of people. There is evidence, however, that these stereotypes are inaccurate. For example, welfare caseworkers have been found to be quite flexible when meeting the various demands of clients. Generally, managers of public organizations take risks as often as managers of private firms.[14] This flexibility is also borne out of our practical everyday experience with bureaucrats. A police officer is free to make an exception if you have a good reason for exceeding the speed limit (perhaps you are rushing a friend to the emergency room), or if you are barely speeding. A public-school teacher will find ways for students who have missed class to make up work. Local sanitation departments frequently bend the rules regarding garbage pick-up, or will respond to citizen demand that services be extended. For example, city services for the removal of

Courtesy of the Agricultural Research Service; photo by Bruce Fritz.

Although the Department of Agriculture is supposed to serve the agricultural sector broadly, it has been charged with favoring the concerns of large agribusiness enterprises over those of "family farmers." Large, organized groups generally have an advantage over smaller, more loosely organized groups when dealing with government agencies.

yard waste are often expanded in the fall and spring, and sometimes performed at a reduced charge, when citizens are raking leaves and cleaning their yards after winter.

On the other hand, procedural safeguards, often derided as **red tape**, exist for a reason. This is because we want public organizations to be consistent and fair.[15] Consistent service is important because otherwise agency decisions and actions would be arbitrary. Bureaucrats should not show favoritism, nor should they treat all people equally badly. Rules and standard operating procedures—red tape—exist to ensure equal, impartial treatment. Thus there is a natural tension between the need for public organizations to be flexible and the need to treat people equally.[16] Often we do not want to be treated like everyone else. This is in fact one of the more frequent complaints about large public organizations, and specifically about large universities. Smaller universities or colleges will advertise that they do not "process" their students, and that students are not "just a number." Clearly, we like individual attention from our agencies, but we also want to be treated fairly. It is difficult for an agency to achieve both at the same time. Individual attention means making personal exceptions, which often seems unfair to those who don't receive special treatment. Fair and impartial treatment can be achieved by a rigid adherence to rules and procedures, but that ultimately disappoints those with situations that do not exactly fit those rules.

The demand that public organizations be "responsive" therefore may mean a variety of things. Responsiveness is not easily achieved, and it typically means trading one form for another. Evaluations of government agencies therefore must specify in advance what form or forms of responsiveness are important, in order to assess whether or not those agencies are performing adequately.

Bureaucratic Competence

Like responsiveness, competence may mean a variety of things. Bureaucratic competence certainly includes **effectiveness**, which is the ability of an organization to meet the policy goals that are given to it by decision makers in government. Earlier in this chapter we showed that effectiveness is often difficult to assess because public organizations have multiple goals that sometimes compete with each other. Kenneth Meier points out that it therefore is sensible to evaluate government agencies in terms of meeting policy goals, as well as in terms of developing means to achieve them.[17] In other words, agencies that learn and innovate should be considered "more competent."

Effectiveness also requires that bureaucrats know what they are doing. We should be able to depend upon them for accurate information, and we should be confident in their ability to do their jobs. Bureaucrats should also be reliable. This means their actions should not vary from case to case if those cases do not vary in nature, and suggests that bureaucrats should be predictable. If we meet the conditions set by an agency (like filling out paperwork appropriately) we should be able to know how that agency will act on our case. When we fill out a form to renew the registration for our car at the department of motor vehicles office, we expect the bureaucrat to know what to do with that form (i.e., give us the appropriate proof of registration), and we expect that, if the forms have been filled out correctly, there will be no surprises.

Competence also includes timely service.[18] "Speed" is typically not thought to be synonymous with "bureaucracy," but in fact bureaucracies enjoy significant advantages that help them provide timely service. A public organization specializes in a particular policy or program area, and therefore is not distracted by other political decisions or issues. Much of what a public organization does is also highly routine. With the experience of dealing repeatedly with the same or similar problems, a significant portion of what an agency does is not "new." For example, the registrar's office at a large public university is able to quickly process students registering for classes: specific bureaucrats are assigned to deal with registration and nothing else, and the process is highly routine, as class registration takes place several times a year. It is not surprising then that an institution serving tens of thousands of students can have them all registered in a matter of days.

In addition to speedy, effective service, we also demand that our public organizations accomplish their goals in an efficient manner. **Efficiency** and effectiveness are two different things, as it is entirely possible to be effective (that is, meet organizational goals) yet do so in a way that produces cost overruns.[19] The objective, therefore, is to meet those organizational goals at the lowest possible cost. Efficiency is an entirely reasonable demand. Rampant inefficiency is problematic because it is wasteful of tax dollars, making it likely that those tax dollars could have been more productive had they remained in the private market. Efficiency as a goal by itself, however, is frequently confounded by the other expectations we place on public organizations, or by laws that they must follow. For example, the Postal Service could be more "efficient" if it stopped delivering mail to individual houses, or to rural areas, and instead forced people to pick up their mail themselves in P.O. boxes.[20] Mail would still get to its destinations, and the Postal Service would realize tremendous reductions in its cost of operation. Few people, however, would feel this is a good idea. The operating costs of many federal agencies could probably be reduced if cheaper foreign goods could be freely purchased, or if regulatory agencies like OSHA or the EPA could ignore large complex cases and instead focus only on small, easy-to-resolve issues.

Multiple 'Layers' of Implementation

Another crucial issue to consider when evaluating public-sector performance is that policy implementation often involves many different governments and organizations. Some important organizations may not even be part of the government, such as citizen groups (like charities or activist groups), private firms, or religious institutions. When a large number of diverse organizations is responsible for policy implementation, it becomes difficult to achieve program success. Too many people and too many groups need to be in agreement about policy goals and the means to achieve those goals for there to be a high probability of successful implementation.[21] As a result, ". . . the ideal of simplicity in American administrative implementation in the United States is dead today."[22] As will be shown in Chapter 10, policy implementation typically involves complex interactions between federal, state, and local agencies, as well as interactions with nongovernmental organizations. This means policy goals are realized as the result of both operations within an organization and operations between them.

Consider the example of the policy goal of "quality elementary and high-school education." Some of the organizations involved in providing quality education in the United States are the bureaus within the Department of Education, the 50 states' education departments, the thousands of school districts in the country, and the schools in each of those districts. Add to these government organizations groups such as private education companies, parent-teacher associations, teachers' unions, and religious institutions. In order to provide quality education each of these groups needs to work together, and there needs to be some agreement on what "quality education" means and how to achieve it. Failure to reach the policy goal could be the result of a variety of problems. Perhaps some of the government organizations or nongovernmental groups involved are not functioning well. Perhaps the problem is that there is poor communication between groups, or that insufficient resources are flowing from higher levels of government to lower levels. With so many different government agencies, different levels of government, and different nongovernmental groups involved, complete success is unlikely.

These complexities also make it more difficult for those interested in evaluating the performance of government organizations. Identifying reasons for why a policy goal was not reached (or perhaps reasons for why it was reached in an inefficient fashion) becomes problematic due to the sheer number of organizations, citizen groups, and governments involved. Therefore, performance evaluations themselves can be elaborate, patterning the tangled web of interactions between layers of government and multiple organizations. There are, however, some efforts to distill some of the complexity to focus on a smaller number of key "ingredients" to evaluate public organization effectiveness.[23]

Evaluating Public-Sector Performance

By now, you may be concerned that with such a variety of goals and expectations there may not be a way to evaluate the performance of public organizations. In some senses, this is a very troubling question, as it can be fairly said that public organizations cannot hope to meet all of their policy goals and citizen demands. Therefore, public organizations are "failures" by definition. Those that meet one policy goal may do so at the expense of meeting some contextual goals. Those that are efficient and fair are perhaps inflexible. Those that are highly responsive to the needs of clients may not be responsive to the policies set forth by the legislature. Recognizing that public organizations cannot meet every citizen demand, we must instead try to focus evaluations on a more narrow range of policy goals.

Assuming we can identify a policy goal (typically the stated intent in legislation or the stated goal of the program or organization), there are several tools available for assessing public-sector performance.

Program Evaluation

Program evaluation "determines the value or effectiveness of an activity" and is used to make decisions about how that activity is done, or if it will be done at all.[24] In this sense, it is useful to bureaucrats because they can get information about the need for new programs, how their existing programs are working, and if adjustments are necessary. There are four major types of program evaluations: assessments of need, process, outcome, and efficiency.[25]

Evaluations of Need. Evaluations of need involve determining if there are needs or demands that are currently not being served. These evaluations take into account the nature and importance of those needs, as well as the variety of options available to meet them. This form of program evaluation should be done during the program planning or legislative stages so that any policy or program put into place will function well. It is also important to evaluate the legitimacy or importance of needs and demands so that irrelevant concerns do not take up public resources that could be better used elsewhere.

Evaluations of Process. After a program has started, evaluations of that program and how it functions begin. These are "process" evaluations, and involve assessing how well agency activities match the plans and goals of the program and whether the demands planned for actually still exist. In other words, these evaluations "document the extent to which implementation has taken place . . . and the degree to which the program operates as expected."[26] It is important to know how well a program is doing while it is in place so that any changes that are required can be made quickly (say, to meet a demand slightly different than anticipated, or to alter the activity of individual bureaucrats). For example, a new police program to deter drunk driving might be established involving well-advertised checkpoints on busy roads. A process evaluation of this program would involve determining how well the roadblocks fit with the mission of deterring drunk driving, if the roadblocks are still necessary, whether the roadblocks are placed appropriately to deter (and catch) drunk drivers, and if the roadblocks are used frequently enough and in proper quantities.

Evaluations of Outcome. Once a program has been in place long enough that it should have had some impact, an outcome evaluation can be done. This type of evaluation assesses whether or not the program is successfully meeting its goals, and is often done in conjunction with a process evaluation. That way, the program evaluation provides information about how the program is being implemented, and if it is successful. If it is not succeeding, the process evaluation will give hints about why.

Using the example of the drunk-driving roadblocks, if the goal is to reduce rates of drunk driving in a community, the implementation of those roadblocks should produce a drop in those rates. An outcome evaluation will provide information about drunk-driving rates after the program was put in place. If, after comparing drunk-driving rates before and after the implementation of the roadblocks, there is no drop, then the program cannot be deemed a success.

Unfortunately, this form of program evaluation is most susceptible to the problems highlighted earlier in this chapter. Vague goals, conflict over goal definitions, and even conflict over what "success" means can influence outcome evaluations. If the police roadblocks are a "failure" because they produce no decline in drunk-driving rates, they may be a "success" because they stop and arrest more drunk drivers than the police would otherwise catch. Surely, there is a benefit to the community from this, even if the same number of drunk drivers are on the roads each night. Or perhaps anti–drunk-driving advocacy groups (such as MADD) may feel that even a small drop in drunk-driving rates justifies the use of roadblocks, while others may feel that a small drop does not warrant the use of police resources. The best advice for program evaluators here is to be explicit about the goals under review, as well as what the definition of "success" is, and to be sensitive to the fact that there are competing opinions.

Another problem for outcome evaluation is that evaluators must watch for unplanned side effects.[27] Public programs rarely operate without some kind of side effect. Sometimes these are accounted for during the planning stages of a new program. Other times, however, they are unexpected, or they occur at unanticipated levels. Drunk-driving roadblocks in a college town may increase the number of house parties within walking distance of campus, and drive up the number of noise complaints from neighbors. An evaluation of using cigarette taxes to fund important government programs should expect that other smoking regulations will decrease tax collections, as people smoke less. Of course, a classic example of unintended consequences is that of Prohibition, which rather than eliminating the consumption of alcohol, created a thriving, violent black market.

Another problem for outcome evaluation is that of time. How long should a program run before results can be expected? There is no good answer to that question, and it is frequently disputed. Politicians, for example, might want to see results quickly so that they can be used in an upcoming legislative session or campaign. Citizens might expect fast results as well, because they expect public organizations to be responsive to them. The bureaucrats running the program, however, may want more time before an evaluation because they may realize that portions of the target population are not being served or that a particular program may not have immediate results. For example, an educational program for tenth graders designed to increase high-school graduation rates will not have an "outcome" for three years. Even after three years, one could argue that not enough time has passed, as the program would have graduated just one class.

Evaluations of Efficiency. Finally, program evaluation can involve assessments of efficiency. As noted earlier in this chapter, we expect our public organizations to be successful, but also to be cost-effective. Goals must be accomplished in a way that does not use too many resources. Efficiency evaluations can be as simple as comparing two programs that will meet the same goal and selecting the less expensive one. Sometimes, however, no alternative program is available. The evaluator then must assess how much it would cost to maintain current program levels, or to increase program activity, and let that information serve as a decision-making aide for legislators and bureaucratic leaders. They can take that information and decide if it is "worth it," given other demands on government, to continue the program.

A certain amount of care must be used when evaluating the efficiency of a government program. Many programs do not have efficiency as a primary goal, so it does not make sense to evaluate them according to standards that are not important. Consider again the example of the Postal Service. The delivery of mail would probably fail a rigorous efficiency evaluation, because of the high costs of providing door-to-door service six days a week. Yet in this instance we are willing to have a certain amount of inefficiency in order to have much better service. Essentially, we are not willing to let the Postal Service cut costs. Other programs are designed without much attention to efficiency at all. Programs that provide public goods (such as environmental protection) must be operated by the government *because* they are inefficient. There is no profit to be made, so private enterprise will not provide those goods.

The problems with outcome and efficiency evaluations are the result of the fact that program evaluation is inherently political.[28] All of the issues of vagueness of goals, contextual goals, and the wide variety of public expectations enter into program evaluation. Setting goals, defining success, expectations about time, and determining efficiency are often a function of political preferences. A program analyst, as a neutral observer, can usually operate at a distance from some of these problems and produce an evaluation that is rather free of overt political preferences. Therefore, analytical, rather than political, definitions can be used for evaluation. However, the interpretation or use of the evaluation by others will be conditioned by their politics. Finally, it is sometimes the case that program evaluations, while dressed up to be neutral, may actually be done in a way to support or oppose a program. Obviously, proper program evaluation is done in a neutral fashion. The fact that others may use it for political purposes is not necessarily troubling. It is simply a reflection of the fact that public administration in the United States is involved in politics of the first order.

Methods of Program Evaluation. There are several ways that programs can be evaluated. The most straightforward way to evaluate need is to survey the population.[29] Unmet citizen demands often can only be discovered if the citizens themselves are asked. For example, in 2004 the citizens of Cedar Falls, Iowa, were surveyed about city services. Nearly 20 percent of respondents were "dissatisfied" or "highly dissatisfied" with the public swimming pool.[30] The city is now renovating the pool. Another way to learn about the needs of the population is to examine social indicators, such as the unemployment rate or public health data, to identify any trends that warrant attention. Finally, focus groups and open meetings (such as city council meetings) can be valuable sources of information about community needs.[31]

Perhaps the simplest method to evaluate outcomes is to use an abbreviated **intervention analysis**. The nature of the issue at hand can be examined at one point before and at one point after the introduction of the program (the intervention). This will at least provide some basic information about whether the situation has changed, and it is a fast and relatively inexpensive method of evaluation. The danger is in whether enough information is collected about the situation before and after the introduction of the program. As a result, this method leaves us less sure that the program actually worked as expected. For example, we might observe at one point a high rate of drunk driving in a small university town. Then at one point after the introduction of more police patrols we might observe a lower rate of drunk driving. By collecting information at only two points in time, we might miss the fact that the semester ended, and the college students, who have higher rates of drunk driving, went home for the summer.

A way to guard against this is to use a time series design for the outcome evaluation. This method collects information about society at many points in time prior to and after the adoption of the program. This gives researchers a better idea of what the trend in society really was before and is after the introduction of the program. Figure 7.1 is an example of this technique, tracking cigarette sales in Michigan since 1985. Note that while the overall trend is downward, there is a substantial drop in 1995. This coincides with the fact that Michigan raised their cigarette tax from 25 cents per pack to 75 cents per pack in 1994. Thus, the graph is evidence that the large tax increase had an effect on cigarette sales in the state.

Both the abbreviated and time series intervention analyses can be considered a form of "natural" experiment, where the evaluator has no control over events.[32] A final method for outcomes analysis is a traditional experiment, where the evaluator has more control over those participating in the experiment and over when and how the intervention is introduced. Briefly, the typical experiment involves two similar groups, one of which is introduced to the intervention while the other is not. Differences between the two groups after the experiment are evidence that the program is having an effect.

Efficiency evaluations are often done using **benefit-cost analysis**.[33] This involves calculating the net benefits of each alternative program. The key question in benefit-cost analysis is if the program produces enough benefits so that the people who are paying for it could be compensated by those who benefit from it.[34] A program that does not do this is not efficient. Answering this question means that benefits and costs need to be identified and then "monetized"—that is, given a monetary value. When identifying benefits and costs, care must be taken to ensure that significant externalities are counted.[35] Increased smog in Los Angeles as a result of a new highway should be counted as a cost, while the pollution from the oil refineries needed to fuel those cars is too remote to count. Those present values are then discounted over the life of the project. This is important, because not all of the benefits and costs will occur immediately, and one dollar today will be worth less than one dollar after a number of years.

This becomes tricky when the issue is one of life or death. Frequently, our government programs are designed to save lives by preventing injury (requiring air bags in cars) and disease (requiring vaccinations). In order to evaluate the efficiency of these programs, we must place a monetary value on people's lives. We frequently hear the sentiment that "if only one life is saved, the program is worth it," but that is often inaccurate, at least according to efficiency evaluations.[36] Although distasteful, monetizing life is necessary. Other issues are also frustrating. Perhaps the most important is the fact that benefit-cost analysis does not address the issue of distributing benefits.[37] A program that transfers wealth from the poor to the rich can be more "effi-

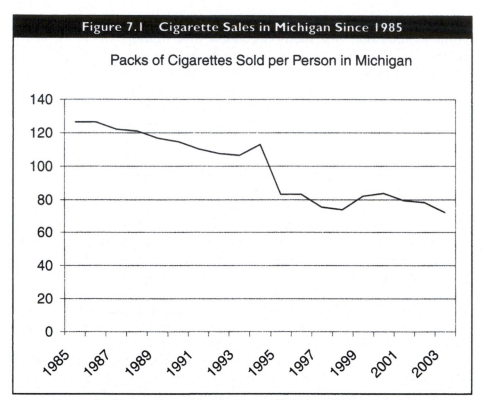

Figure 7.1   Cigarette Sales in Michigan Since 1985

Packs of Cigarettes Sold per Person in Michigan

Source: Centers for Disease Control and Prevention. 2003. *State Tobacco Activities Tracking and Evaluation (STATE) System.* http://www.cdc.gov/tobacco/statesystem.

cient" than a program that transfers wealth from the rich to the poor, as long as the first program transfers more wealth at a lower cost. This is why many government programs are not evaluated solely on grounds of efficiency.

Benchmarking

Benchmarking is a second way to evaluate public-sector performance. This involves comparing your own program with similar programs in other jurisdictions, and is particularly useful for state and local governments. A good way to assess the performance of a small town's recycling program is to compare it to the recycling program of another town of the same size. Because there are so many town, city, county, and state governments, there are many opportunities to make comparisons. A more systematic way to benchmark is to find a set of best practices that produce effective programs and compare a program to those best practices.[38] These best practices are typically the result of an assessment of all similar programs in the country, and will become the recommended policy—the benchmark that individual state or local government can use. For example, the Centers for Disease Control has a set of best practices that it suggests state governments follow in setting up tobacco-control programs.[39] Sometimes these benchmarks can be very useful in changing policy to boost program performance. In 2004, the state of Virginia increased its cigarette tax from 2.5 cents to 20 cents per pack in order to increase funding for tobacco-control programs.[40] Other times, alterations are resisted, despite obvious evidence of problems from the benchmarks. In the Spring of 2005, Iowa rejected a proposed cigarette tax increase, despite the fact that the American Lung Association's system of benchmarks gave Iowa an "F" for its efforts to control tobacco use with the cigarette tax.[41] As with program evaluation, benchmarking and how it is used are inherently political. We can choose not to change, even if we know our programs are not working as well as they could.

Organizational Report Cards

An **organizational report card** is another tool available to evaluate public-sector performance. These are defined as "a regular effort . . . to collect data on two or more organizations, transform the data into information relevant to assessing performance, and transmit the information to some audience. . . ."[42] In other words, they are evaluations of several public organizations at once, done in a way to compare how those organizations are performing, according to specific criteria that the evaluator identifies. These report cards are different from benchmarking because they are used to examine organizational performance on issues that are common to otherwise different organizations. For example, report cards can rate every state organization on how accessible information is for citizens. Thus the same report-card system can be used for the state department of transportation and the state department of education, while the two could not be compared using benchmarks because the programs that the two departments run are not similar.

Organizational report cards also differ from program evaluation in a number of important ways.[43] First, they address the organization as a whole, rather than focusing exclusively on a single program or policy. Second, they are designed explicitly for the purpose of making comparisons between organizations (just as you can use your academic report card to compare yourself, and your GPA, to other students). Third, reports are issued systematically as a matter of routine, while program evaluations are frequently done once or at irregular intervals. Organizational report cards share some of the same problems of program evaluation, however. The definition of the criteria that will be used in the reports can be highly contentious, and often reflect the political expectations of those using the report cards.

Assuming that organizational report cards are done in a neutral manner, they may be used to measure progress toward agency goals, the impact of new methods or procedures (such as the use of Internet technology to serve clients), or efficiency and cost-effectiveness. Used as such, the report cards can identify organizations that are performing well (as well as those that are not), and because of the comparisons that are made, identify reasons why. It is entirely likely that an organization that is performing differently (either better or worse than the others) will differ in how it performs its tasks. For example, report cards on public schools can help us understand why two schools receiving the same funding per pupil perform differently; perhaps one school is better at applying its resources.

This type of information is valuable to both policymakers and leaders in public organizations. Organizational report cards can be used by legislators and chief executives as accountability tools. As you have already seen, elected officials try to hold the bureaucracy accountable for its actions, and try to direct the bureaucracy's efforts to implement the policies they pass. One of the problems that frustrates political oversight of the bureaucracy is that legislators often do not have enough information about the activities of public organizations. Organizational report cards provide at least some of this information. Thus, a report at regular intervals comparing bureaucratic efforts is useful in oversight efforts, and can serve as the basis for future policy and budget decisions. For example, a report card showing that an agency is not applying its resources efficiently may lose some of them in the next budget or have its programs reorganized. This is what happened to the Commerce Department, when the president used the department's poor scores to justify consolidating the Community Development Block Grant program and the Economic Development Assistance programs. Rigorous accountability standards are also now set for the new program[44] (see Table 7.2).

Information provided by organizational report cards is also valuable to leaders in public organizations. Although the audience for these reports is external to the organization (i.e., elected officials or the public), the information is often helpful to leaders who seek to improve the performance of their organizations.[45] At a minimum, by holding public organizations more accountable to elected officials and the public, report cards offer incentives for leaders to behave in ways that enhance their organizations' reputations. For public organizations, this means trying to stay "in line" with the expectations and demands of legislators, the chief executive, and clients. Besides simply trying to enhance an organization's reputation, organizational report cards truly provide value if they produce real reforms. Report cards can be used by organizational leaders to assess and change procedures and activities.[46] If, for example, a report card indicates that an organization lags behind others in terms of offering online service for clients, this can be im-

Sidebar 7.2 Federal Government Organizational Report Cards

To evaluate the management of federal agencies, the Office of Management and Budget (OMB) uses a scorecard that rates each cabinet department and selected independent agencies in terms of meeting the President's Management Agenda. According to that agenda, President Bush's ". . . vision for government reform is guided by three principles. Government should be: [c]itizen-centered, not bureaucracy-centered; [r]esults-oriented; [m]arket-based, actively promoting rather than stifling innovation through competition."[a] These report cards show two pieces of information: how the organizations are currently performing, and if progress is being made toward goals. The information is then reported in a chart, which allows comparisons to be made among organizations.

In the chart, white indicates success, grey signifies mixed results, and black is an unsatisfactory or failing grade (green, yellow, and red in the original).

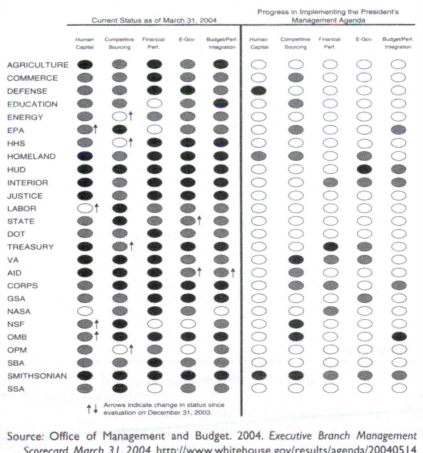

Executive Branch Management Scorecard

Source: Office of Management and Budget. 2004. *Executive Branch Management Scorecard, March 31, 2004.* http://www.whitehouse.gov/results/agenda/20040514 scorecard.pdf.

Sidebar 7.2 *(continued)*

Human Capital scores reflect how well the organizations have planned for human resource challenges. This includes managing human resources (hiring, firing, promoting, evaluating) so that the workforce is more able to meet the organization's goals. Competitive Sourcing scores are assessments of how well organizations utilize the private market for services. A hallmark of President Bush's administration has been a focus on privatization. His management agenda argues that significant cost savings can be realized by using the private sector for more tasks, such as data collection or payroll services. Financial Performance scores reflect attempts to reduce fraud, erroneous payments, and wasteful spending, as well as to hold organizations accountable for their spending. E-Government scores are assessments of how accessible organizations are to citizens via the Internet, and if they are using technology to find new solutions to problems (rather than simply automating existing procedures). Finally, Budget and Performance Integration scores reflect whether organizational budgets are linked to performance. This means defining goals more concretely and it rewards programs that are run efficiently.

You can see the Commerce Department's failing grade for financial performance and a yellow rating for budget and performance integration. This is the result of having too many programs that were thought to be inefficient and operating without a sufficient system to produce accurate and timely financial reports linking spending to program outcomes. As a result, some of the department's grants face consolidation and new performance criteria.

[a]Office of Management and Budget, "President's Management Agenda," http://www. whitehouse.gov/omb/budget/fy2002/mgmt.pdf.

---

proved. Of course, as we show in Chapter 6, leaders of organizations who want to introduce changes are hampered in many ways. This does not mean that we should not expect improvement, but organizational report cards should not be viewed as silver bullets that will suddenly provide large improvements in public administration.

Conclusion

Evaluating public-sector performance is an important endeavor, but one that is frustrated by complexity and controversy. Program evaluations and organizational report cards can provide useful information about how government agencies are performing to policymakers, the public, and the organizations themselves. This sort of analysis is crucial if we are to hold our public organizations accountable for their actions, and expect their performance to improve. Good evaluations will be useful to elected officials when making policy and budget decisions. They will be useful to organizational leaders looking for ways to improve the functioning of their agencies. And they will be useful to citizens who desire better service from the agencies they deal with.

Producing good evaluations, however, is difficult. We expect so many different things from our government agencies that it is unlikely that all of those expectations can be met. Nor is it usually the case that our policies and programs fall under the jurisdiction of a single agency, or even a single level of government. Any evaluator of the No Child Left Behind Act will be frustrated by its myriad goals and the fact that, although it is a federal policy, most of it is implemented by state and local governments. Finally, evaluating public-sector performance can be a politically charged activity. Since public organizations are political actors, it is not surprising that people will fight over what they should do, how they should do it, and how they should be evaluated. Obviously, the most valuable evaluations are those that are done by perfectly neutral observers, but sometimes this is simply not possible. Once again, the fact that public administration is inherently political is an important consideration.

Key Concepts

benchmarking A method of program evaluation that makes comparisons between similar programs in similar circumstances.

benefit-cost analysis An evaluation of efficiency that assigns monetary value to all benefits and costs of the program.

bureaucratic responsiveness The idea that government agencies should be accountable to other government institutions, as well as to the public.

contextual goals Goals that shape how an agency will accomplish its primary mission.

effectiveness The ability of an organization to meet its policy goals.

efficiency Meeting the primary organizational goal at the lowest possible cost.

flexibility A form of responsiveness that emphasizes the ideal of meeting the individual needs to citizens.

intervention analysis An experimental design to measure the impact of a program by gathering information prior to and after the introduction of the program.

intractable problems Complex, difficult-to-define problems with many causes that defy any single policy solution.

organizational report card A method of evaluating organization-wide performance, often on managerial issues. Useful for comparing the performance of several organizations.

program evaluation Analysis to determine the value or effectiveness of a government program. The four types are evaluations of need, process, outcome, and efficiency.

red tape A pejorative term used to describe what are perceived as unnecessary or inefficient rules and procedures. ✦

Chapter 8

Public Budgeting

Government budgets are often thought to be too complex for the ordinary person to understand. Many think it isn't even worth studying, because the government's budget just doesn't seem to influence their daily lives very much anyway. So what if the federal government buys new tanks for the Army, or if the state government hires another welfare caseworker, or if the local government opens a new public golf course? Most people aren't in the Army, nor do most people need welfare services. And most people don't golf. So, many people think it's not worth the effort to try to understand public budgeting.

Tell that to Jenny Rokes, the student representative to the Iowa Board of Regents, which oversees the three public universities in that state. Five years ago, the state paid for 63 percent of a student's education. Now, it is down to 49 percent and dropping. While some budget reductions were absorbed by the universities by holding down expenses on salaries and maintenance, much of the budget cuts translated into tuition increases, which hit students where it hurts the worst: their checkbooks. Jenny feels that most students have swallowed the bitter pill that their tuition will go up yet again. "I feel it. They feel it. For most of them it seems pretty hopeless," she said. "The consensus is we don't have a choice. The universities have to function and without [another tuition increase], they won't."[1] The result of the new state budget is at least another 4 percent tuition increase, on top of the 71 percent increase already experienced since 2001.

In many ways, public budgeting focuses on the politics of public administration. Public budgets literally decide "who gets what." Scan back to the first paragraph. Somewhere, somebody decided that the Army needed more tanks, that more welfare caseworkers were needed, and that another golf course was desirable. The Army, people on welfare, and golfers "got something" from the budget. The decisions to give to those groups probably meant that there was less to give to other groups, maybe even a group that you're in, like Jenny's group. That's the essence of public budgeting. If that's the case, then the process of public budgeting can be defined as making decisions about the allocation of public resources in order to carry out government decisions. This definition highlights the role of the bureaucracy in public budgeting. As one of the bureaucracy's key functions is to implement government decisions, budgeting is obviously an integral part of that job. An agency's budget determines, to a great extent, what that agency will do during the year. Money can be allocated for specific programs and policies, and as a result the bureaucracy will be more likely to follow legislative, executive, and judicial demands and decisions. More generally, government agencies use their budgeted resources to make rules, adjudicate on important issues, and make decisions about how to enforce policy based on their budgets.

But we also know that the bureaucracy is not merely a passive institution, waiting to carry out the decisions of other branches of government. As you will see, the bureaucracy is also an important participant in developing the budget. The same advantages and sources of power that make government agencies so influential in policymaking give them influence in the budget process. Although public university tuition may be increasing again in Iowa, the increase is smaller due to the concerted efforts of the university presidents to strike a funding agreement with the state legislature. Effectively, bureaucratic leaders were able to influence (although not totally control) what the state will spend on higher education for the next year.

Public budgeting not only influences what agencies will do during the year, it also influences how well they will do it, or what levels of service they can provide. In most respects, the adage that "you get what you pay for" holds true in public budgeting. Sometimes there are good reasons for reducing an agency's budget, such as an economic crisis, but that reduction should also come with a realization that the service the agency provides will probably be diminished. For example, when one quarter of Oregon's public schools had to shorten their 2002–2003 school year after state funding ran out, it reduced the quality of the education that students received, and it left teachers without paychecks. After several years trying to absorb budget cuts, Jenny Rokes is finding that Iowa's public universities are still raising tuition in order to meet the eduational needs of their students, despite cutbacks in many areas. While running a cost-effective government is a reasonable goal, it is still true that without adequate resources, it is unlikely that government agencies will be able to do their jobs well. Severe or repeated budget cuts may even damage the bureaucracy's long-term effectiveness and actually decrease efficiency rather than promote it.[2]

Of course, determining the definition of "adequate resources" is one of the reasons why public budgeting is so difficult, and why it brings political conflict to the forefront. Much of this chapter will be devoted to an examination of the process of public budgeting in order to understand that political conflict and the effect it has on public administration.

The Nature of Public Revenue and Spending

Before we start discussing how we make our budgets, we should examine where government money comes from and where it goes. That will help you understand why conflict exists, why sometimes it's hard to satisfy eveyone, and why the budget of your local, state, and federal governments influences public administration and your daily lives.

The Federal Level

Most federal **revenue** comes from personal income tax and payroll taxes. You're familiar with the income tax. Payroll taxes are just as important, but receive less media attention because you don't have to file a tax return every year to pay them. They're deducted out of each paycheck, and fund programs like Social Security, Medicare, and unemployment insurance. For **fiscal year** 2004, the federal government collected $1.88 trillion, and just $338 billion of that (about 18 percent) was from sources other than personal income tax and payroll taxes (see Figure 8.1).

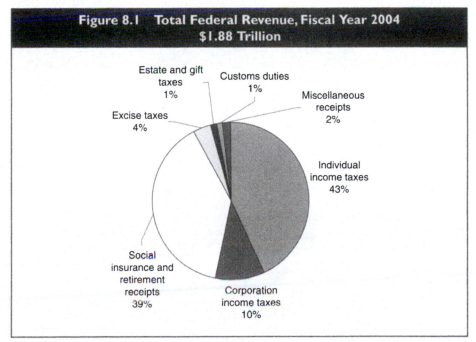

Figure 8.1 Total Federal Revenue, Fiscal Year 2004 $1.88 Trillion

Estate and gift taxes 1%

Customs duties 1%

Miscellaneous receipts 2%

Excise taxes 4%

Individual income taxes 43%

Social insurance and retirement receipts 39%

Corporation income taxes 10%

Source: *Analytical Perspectives, Budget of the United States Government, Fiscal Year 2006.* Washington, DC: Government Printing Office.

The largest single program that the federal government spends money on is Social Security (see Figure 8.2). Nearly a quarter of all federal spending goes to this one program. That's why the payroll tax is so important for federal revenue. Other **entitlement programs**, such as Medicare, Medicaid, and welfare programs, make up another 30 percent of spending. This means that about half of all federal spending goes to programs that require automatic spending if individuals meet eligibility criteria. Spending on interest on the national debt and other mandatory obligations means that we are able to make budget choices on only a little more than a third of federal spending. That is **discretionary spending**: during the budget process, Congress chooses how that money will be spent. That's still a lot of money ($893 billion in fiscal year 2004), but the fact that almost two-thirds of our budget is made up of **mandatory spending** means we have less ability during the budget process to determine where our money will go. For example, the only way to change spending on entitlement programs is to change the criteria to make fewer people eligible (such as raising the retirement age for Social Security benefits), something that is hard to do. Changing policy to cut spending on programs that put cash into the pockets of millions of people is not something that Congress does lightly, as is evidenced by its reluctance to go along with President Bush's Social Security reform in 2005.

The fact that the discretionary portion of the federal budget is shrinking makes it harder to balance the budget, harder to satisfy pub-

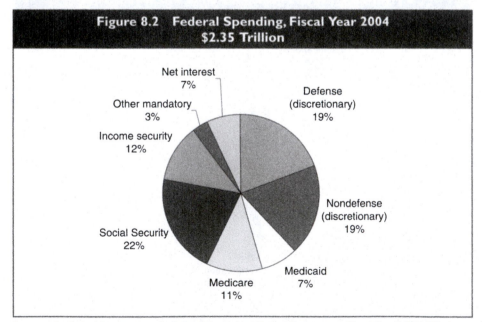

Figure 8.2 Federal Spending, Fiscal Year 2004
$2.35 Trillion

Net interest 7%

Defense (discretionary) 19%

Other mandatory 3%

Income security 12%

Nondefense (discretionary) 19%

Social Security 22%

Medicaid 7%

Medicare 11%

Source: *Analytical Perspectives, Budget of the United States Government, Fiscal Year 2006.* Washington, DC: Government Printing Office.

lic demands for new or expanded programs, and harder to control overall spending. Borrowing money in order to satisfy all the demands for spending is something that the federal government frequently does, but this only makes things worse in the future. Borrowing adds to the national debt. As interest payments on that debt increase, they take up a larger share of our total expenses, and there is less discretionary money to pay for other things. As you can see, all of this makes the political battles more intense, even as the "slice of the budgetary pie" is shrinking.

The State Level

Although there is great variation among the states, on average about half of state government tax revenue comes from sales and excise taxes, while another third of tax revenue comes from personal income taxes. State governments also rely heavily upon nontax sources of revenue (see Figure 8.3). Some of this is in the form of grants to the states from the federal government. This is an important problem for state governments, because it means that federal budget cuts will almost certainly reduce the amount of money that state governments receive. Because about one-third of total state revenue comes from the federal government, significant decreases in aid are difficult for state governments to make up elsewhere.

Two types of nontax revenue that are becoming more important are user fees and user charges. **User fees** are paid by citizens in order to engage in some activity that is otherwise prohibited—a driver's license fee, for example, or payments for hunting and fishing licenses. You can not drive, hunt, or fish without these licenses and paying the state allows you to do so while at the same time providing the state with revenue. **User charges** are paid by citizens to have access to some government service. Public university tuition, bus fare, and water charges are examples. Many of these are voluntary payments, and the amount you pay is linked to the amount of service you receive. If you spend an extra year at school, or ride the bus more, or take longer showers, you end up paying more of these charges.

State spending is typically centered on a set of core services that the state provides.[3] These services are generally: education (both elementary and higher education); Medicaid and welfare programs; social services such as public hospitals and health programs, transportation, and state prisons; and things like property-tax credits[4] (see Figure 8.4).

These are important and popular services, which means that state budget makers are faced with tough choices when revenues fall short of demands for expenditures. None of these spending areas can be eliminated. Even reducing spending in these areas is hard to do. Cutting spending for higher education may free up money to replace dilapitated and dangerous bridges, but it also means that students like

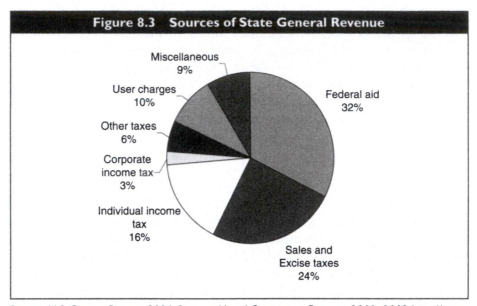

Figure 8.3 Sources of State General Revenue

Miscellaneous 9%
User charges 10%
Other taxes 6%
Corporate income tax 3%
Individual income tax 16%
Federal aid 32%
Sales and Excise taxes 24%

Source: U.S. Census Bureau. 2004. *State and Local Government Finances 2002–2003*. http://www.census.gov/govs/estimate/03gp00us.html.

Jenny Rokes are left paying more out their own pockets for tuition. Repeated cuts may mean that the state is unable to provide effective service or meet the policy goals of these areas: the bridges remain dangerous, fewer students can attend college, prisons become overcrowded (which is illegal), or elderly citizens face mounting property-tax bills, which may force them from their homes. Finally, producing an acceptable state budget is pretty tricky. By being so dependent on the federal government, and by concentrating so much spending on necessary or popular areas, it is difficult to meet expectations for increased spending or to deal with an economic downturn that decreases state revenue.

The Local Level

As at the state level, there is great variation among local governments in terms of revenues and spending. This is because there are so many local governments in the United States, and because there are so many types. County, city, and township governments, along with special districts (like school districts) are all local governments. On average, however, by far the most important source of local government revenue is the state government (see Figure 8.5). About a third of total local revenue in the United States comes from state governments. Of revenue collected by the local governments themselves, the most important source is the property tax. For example, about half of all locally collected tax revenue for cities comes from the property tax. For gov-

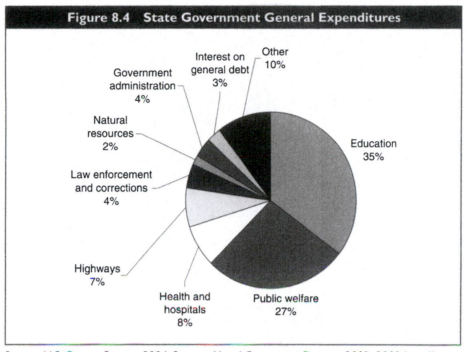

Figure 8.4   State Government General Expenditures

Other 10%

Interest on general debt 3%

Government administration 4%

Natural resources 2%

Law enforcement and corrections 4%

Highways 7%

Health and hospitals 8%

Public welfare 27%

Education 35%

Source: U.S. Census Bureau. 2004. *State and Local Government Finances 2002–2003.* http://www.census.gov/govs/estimate/03gp00us.html.

ernments like school districts, it is nearer to 100 percent. Twenty-six percent of all local revenue (that is, all sources of revenue for all local governments) comes from the property tax. Local governments also collect revenue through user charges, which are beginning to rival property taxes in overall importance. Local user charges and fees are familiar things like greens fees for public golf courses, bus fare, and garbage collection charges. Other sources of local revenue, like sales taxes and income taxes, are small in comparison to property taxes and user charges.

Because local governments are so dependent upon state aid and the property tax, budgeting is difficult. Shortfalls are difficult to make up because there are a limited number of options to increase revenue. Most local governments are not allowed to collect income taxes, and there are often limits to how much property taxes can increase. Cities and counties frequently turn to sales taxes, but even these represent just about a quarter of tax revenues for those governments. This puts a tremendous amount of pressure on local budget makers, particularly because the services that local governments provide are so important to our daily lives.

Local government spending, like state spending, is concentrated on a variety of important services. Most local spending goes to what are called **essential services**, things like police and fire protection, public

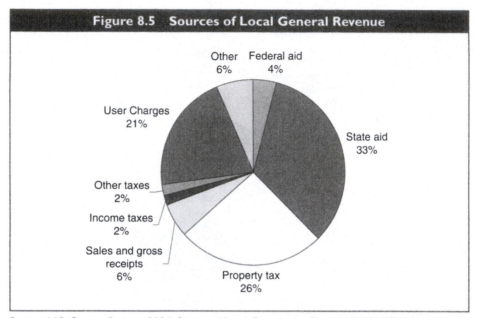

Figure 8.5 Sources of Local General Revenue

Source: U.S. Census Bureau. 2004. *State and Local Government Finances 2002–2003.* http://www. census.gov/govs/estimate/03sp00us.html.

education, public health and welfare, transportation, and sewer and water services (see Figure 8.6). Without these, it is unlikely that the community would be a particularly desirable place to live, and probably would be downright dangerous. Other spending, on nonessential services, goes to things like parks, libraries, arts, and entertainment. Although a community can function without them, these services are usually very popular. This means that when faced with having to reduce spending, local budget makers must choose to either reduce services that are critical to the community or end up looking mean-spirited by cutting youth sports programs or forcing libraries to operate on reduced hours.

What Do Public Budgets Do?

It should be clear by now that budgeting at all levels of government influences our daily lives. It also should be clear that budgeting, even for small local governments, can be complex and difficult. Public budgeting is complex because we want the process of creating the budget, as well as the budget itself, to do a variety of things. Our expectations of public budgeting are varied and diverse, and not always in agreement. This means it is unlikely that everyone will be satisfied with the results, and possibly that *nobody* will be completely satisfied.

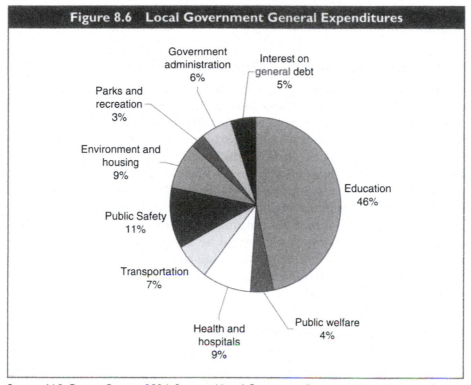

Figure 8.6   Local Government General Expenditures

Government administration 6%

Interest on general debt 5%

Parks and recreation 3%

Environment and housing 9%

Education 46%

Public Safety 11%

Transportation 7%

Health and hospitals 9%

Public welfare 4%

Source: U.S. Census Bureau. 2004. *State and Local Government Finances 2002–2003.* http://www. census.gov/govs/estimate/03sp00us.html.

Public Budgets Allocate Resources[5]

Public budgets determine how much money will be spent, as well as where and how it will be spent. This means that the process of public budgeting is when lawmakers decide "who gets what, when, and how,"[6] which is a classic definition of politics and political power. Because there is a finite amount of money, the public budget goes a long way to decide who wins and who loses. Public resources, while not infinite, are certainly plentiful. Total federal expenditures in 2001 were over $1.86 trillion dollars, or 18.4 percent of the gross domestic product (GDP is essentially the size of the national economy).[7] This is an unfathomable amount of money. If you could have just 1 percent of it, you would still have over $18.6 billion dollars, which is *51 times* the size of the largest lottery jackpot ever won in the United States. Yet we still fight over "slices of the budget pie" and have trouble balancing government budgets. This is because individual citizens are largely responsible for paying for public services. If people do not feel they are getting an adequate amount of goods and services for the taxes they pay, they will either fight for a larger share of the budget or fight to have their tax payments reduced. Because public budgets allocate resources, the size of the budget is only one component: how it is spent relative to how much people pay in taxes is another important component.

Public Budgets Set Policy Goals and Focus Policymaking[8]

Because how public money is spent is just as important as how much is spent, public budgets define the goals and priorities of the government (and indirectly, society). Doing this is difficult because collectively we usually want more government service than we are individually willing to pay for through our taxes. The classic problem faced by legislators is that we demand the goods and services of positive government, but do not want to pay for them. Because there is no free lunch (or government program), policymakers have to decide what goods and services should be emphasized. This also means that they have to decide what programs should be deemphasized or even eliminated in order to fully fund the ones that deserve more support. In effect, policymakers set relative values on all of the different services provided by government.[9]

Public Budgets Ensure Accountability

As public documents stating policy goals and priorities, and as statements of how government agencies will use money, public budgets ensure accountability to elected officials and to the public. Public budgets are commitments, and elected officials, citizen groups, and individuals can compare the budget that was passed with the budget that was implemented to see if the government did what it intended to do.[10] Accountability thus includes the proper, effective, and efficient use of public money. The proper use of public money refers to how, by law, money is supposed to be spent. Public budgeting places restrictions on what money can be spent on what agency or program, and agencies must not exceed authorized levels of spending. Public money should also be spent in ways that most help agencies be effective in providing public services. Policymakers expect to see program goals reached, and the public demands effective government service in exchange for tax payments. Programs that do not meet goals and agencies that are perceived as functioning poorly are frequent targets of criticism during the budget process. Of course, meeting program goals and providing effective service is only part of the equation. Those goals and that service must be provided in an efficient fashion. In other words, accountability includes making sure that government agencies spent public money in a cost-effective manner. We want to get the "most bang for our buck."

The accountability provided by public budgeting is important because of the political power government agencies have. They must be responsive to our elected institutions as well as the public, and the budget is a good way to ensure this, as the budget size of any agency or program is not set in stone and can be reduced if necessary. In fact, all governments in the United States now use some form of report cards for agencies (external evaluations of agency performance). It is easy to see the link between public budgeting and these assessments. Not surprisingly, the more that is spent on a particular program or policy area, the more interested policymakers will be in using these report cards.[11]

Political Priorities in Public Budgeting

The stakes are high in public budgeting, for two reasons. First, as we have seen, a public budget is a statement of goals and priorities. Those who win the battles in the budget process have their goals and priorities emphasized. Those who lose the battles have to wait until the next budget cycle to try again. Second, once the goals and priorities have been set, the amount of money spent can be both politically and economically important. Public money can help an elected official bring government services to constituents. That money can also have positive economic effects, boosting investment levels and job growth. Since the stakes are so high, public budgeting becomes a source of conflict in government.

Conflict as a Result of Different Preferences

Agreement on any large issue, but especially government budgeting, is difficult because there are so many competing preferences. Agreement is even harder to reach when more people participate in the decision. This is precisely the case with public budgeting. Competing preferences are the result of a variety of factors. First, they can be caused by the fact that people's principles differ. Public budgeting involves trying to resolve conflict over different ways of viewing what is just and right in life.[12] For example, some people may argue that it is morally wrong to fund defense programs. Others may argue that it is morally wrong for the government to fund sex-education programs. Second, competing preferences can be the result of ideological differences. Liberals and conservatives have very different views of the proper role of government, and these differences are heightened in the budget process. Government budgets are statements of what the government will do, and at what price it will do it.[13] Conservatives are more likely to reduce the price of government activity (through lower taxes), and in some cases will also try to reduce the role of government as well. Liberals have a more expansive view of what government should do, and are generally more willing to tax to pay for that role.

Conflict as a Result of Constituency Service

Elected officials use public budgets to provide government goods and services to their constituencies. Conflict arises because benefits that are targeted to a particular constituency are not enjoyed by others. Each member of Congress, for example, tries to secure a "slice of the pie" for his or her constituency, but will label every other member's attempt as **pork-barrel spending**. Constituency service will frequently cut across ideological preferences. A member of the legislature may support programs that he or she would otherwise oppose for ideological reasons, if they benefit constituents.[14] For example, advocates of reduced government spending will still support new weapons programs that would be developed in their constituencies. Similarly, those ideologically opposed to military spending will still support new defense contracts if they benefit their constituents. Since sharing the same ideology does not necessarily create agreement, this adds complexity to the budget process and makes it more difficult to find consensus.

Conflict as a Result of Institutional Positions and Roles

Public budgeting is not the same thing to all people. Much of how different people and institutions view public budgeting is a result of the role they play in the budget process. Most individual citizens probably have a rather superficial view of government budgeting, where a balanced budget becomes the overriding concern,[15] without understanding what budgets do or how the process works. Although this view may be simplistic, it is not without merit: we want the government to be in control, and a balanced budget is a good indicator of that.

Government agencies see budgeting as the way to secure resources in order to function. Without effective participation in the budget process, agencies starve and services are less effective. Government agencies may also compete with each other if funds are scarce. Public interest groups see government agencies as either allies or obstacles in the process as they try to get their favorite programs funded (or their despised programs cut).

Budgeting committees in legislatures derive their power and influence from the budget process, and try to protect that power, just as chief executives do. Institutions have their own preferences, and members identify with their institution and defend its preferences. Thus, it is common to have disagreements between the legislative and executive branches.

Balancing the Budget

Having a **balanced budget** is a perennial goal of the federal budget process. It is also very difficult to achieve. There are a variety of reasons for why a balanced budget is a goal at all. As you have seen, one reason is that ordinary citizens project their own personal situations onto the government. The sentiment is usually that "if I have to balance my family's budget, then the government should balance its budget"—

despite the fact that our own individual budgets typically do *not* balance, and we rely heavily on borrowed money for things such as college, cars, and houses. Even if this is an unsophisticated assessment of the need to balance the government's budget, it is still important because public opinion is ignored only at the peril of elected officials.

More importantly for our concerns here, the popular sentiment that a balanced budget is a worthy goal is correct for a variety of administrative reasons. An unbalanced budget seems to be inefficient, full of pork spending on programs of dubious national concern. Further, repeated **deficits** can create economic problems, such as inflation and difficulties in securing additional financing in the future. Adding to the **federal debt** also means that **debt service payments** will increase, which leaves us with an even smaller portion of our budget available for discretionary spending. The size of the debt is already staggering: $7.8 trillion. As we add to it, it means that in future taxes will have to be higher or spending will have to be cut. After all, somebody has to pay for our borrowing. That raises the last concern about excessive borrowing: it is unfair to future generations because they will have to pay for the goods and services we are enjoying now on credit.

Despite these good reasons to balance the budget, it is still difficult. For many legislators, the desire to serve constituents places real pressure on them to fund projects that will benefit them. As we already noted, this even causes legislators who are otherwise opposed to certain government programs to spend money anyway. Deficit spending is also a way for legislators to avoid making tough political decisions on taxing and spending. Raising taxes to pay for programs is just as hard as cutting program funds to meet tax revenue. Having low taxes and higher spending makes eveyone happy, at least in the short term. Borrowing money is also useful on occasion for dealing with emergencies and truly unexpected needs. Recessions are an example of when the United States borrows heavily. Recessions are particularly difficult to deal with, as revenue declines (fewer people have good jobs, or jobs at all) while demands for services increase (more unemployment insurance payments, for example). Often we justify borrowing money in these circumstances because we say we can spend our way out of them. George W. Bush justified his tax cuts in his first administration on the grounds that people needed money in their pockets for us to break out of the economic slump of 2001–2002.

Another problem we face when trying to balance the budget is that most of our expenditures are mandatory.[16] Some, such as debt service, are unavoidable. Others, such as spending on Social Security, Medicare, and welfare programs are linked to the number of people who are eligibile. The only way to make sure that spending on such programs is reduced is to change the eligibility criteria so that fewer people collect benefits. This is much harder to do, because it must take place in the normal policy process and cannot be buried in the budget process. This means that proposed changes will receive much more media attention. Further, many of these programs are aimed at senior citizens, one of the most politically influential groups in the United States.

Balancing the budget is so difficult that Congress has even passed laws to force itself to be more fiscally responsible.[17] One, the Gramm-Rudman-Hollings Act, was passed in 1985 and was supposed to force Congress to balance the budget in five years. It was designed to set deficit reduction targets for each year. If the proposed budget did not meet the target, it triggered across-the-board spending reductions (which are very destructive, and which every legislator strives to avoid). Unfortunately, there were so many loopholes to exploit that no serious attempt was ever made to apply the spirit of the law, even if the letter of the law was followed.

A more successful policy was passed in 1990: the **Budget Enforcement Act**. This set discretionary spending caps, and adopted a **Pay-as-You-Go (PAYGO)** system. This meant that to stay within the caps, any increase in discretionary spending had to be immediately offset with a spending reduction elsewere, or a tax increase. Likewise, any reductions in revenue also had to be immediately offset by spending reductions. PAYGO forced decision makers to directly link tax policy with government spending, by ensuring that any tax cuts would have to be met with equivalent spending cuts. The BEA was used throughout the 1990s and into the first few years of the twenty-first century. However, In 2000, 2001, and 2002 the spending caps were raised, and have now expired. PAYGO has also functionally expired (not technically, but there are no enforcement requirements).[18] It is not surprising that moving away from the regulations of the BEA, coupled with a sluggish economy, have led to the reappearance of budget deficits (see Figure 8.7).

The Federal Budget Process

There are five major steps in the federal budget process. First, each government agency prepares a budget request. Second, using the agency requests, the president's budget is prepared by the OMB, with guidance from the president and his staff. Third, the president's budget proposal is delivered to Congress. Fourth, Congress analyzes and acts on the president's budget, and enacts legislation that appropriates money. Fifth, the budget is executed (money is spent on government activity). Each step in the process has its own set of procedures, most of which are technical. Rather than going into detail for each step, a more general overview is provided here.

Agency Budget Requests

Each year in July, the OMB asks all government agencies to prepare and submit their budget proposals by September. These proposals are

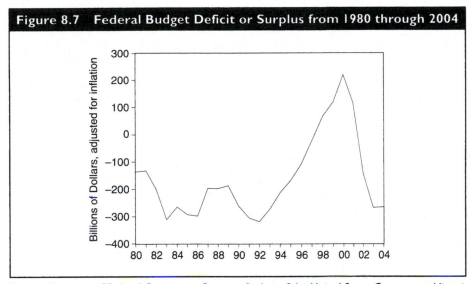

Figure 8.7   Federal Budget Deficit or Surplus from 1980 through 2004

Source: *Overview of Federal Government Finances, Budget of the United States Government, Historical Tables.* Washington, DC: Government Printing Office. The data for 2003 and 2004 are estimates.

known as budget requests. An agency's budget request is the dollar amount required for its activities in the next fiscal year. Consequently, these budget requests are based on a set of assumptions about what it will cost in the future to provide government goods and services. These assumptions are related to material and labor costs for producing those goods and services, as well as expectations about how many people will use them. For example, the cost of operating health care through the Veteran's Health Administration will fluctuate based on the costs of medicine and health care technology, the costs of paying doctors, nurses, and staff, and the number of patients the VHA will serve in the next fiscal year. The requests are also structured to respond to instructions from the OMB. These instructions are based on the president's expectations, economic assumptions, and policy priorities. For example, if the president wishes to reduce spending on a program, the OMB will instruct the agency that implements that program to reduce that component of its budget request. Alternatively, programs that have presidential support will allow agencies that oversee them to increase the size of their budget request.

The President's Budget

In the federal budget process, the president "gets the ball rolling" (see Sidebar 8.1). He uses this position in the process to prepare his own budget proposal, which is a statement of his preferences for policy, taxing, and spending. The development of the president's budget is the result of the Budget and Accounting Act of 1921. This Act did two

Sidebar 8.1	The Timeline of the Budget Process

Deadline	Action
1st Monday in February	President's budget submission
February 15	CBO Budget and Economic Outlook report
6 weeks after the President's budget	Committees submit views and estimates to the Budget Committees
April 1	Senate Budget Committee reports budget resolution
April 15	Congress completes budget resolution
May 15	Appropriations bills may be considered in the House, even in the absence of a budget resolution
June 10	House Appropriations Committee reports last appropiations bill
June 30	House passes all annual appropriations bills and completes reconciliation bill
July 15	President submits mid-session review
August 15	CBO sequester update report
August 20	OMB sequester update report
October 1	Fiscal year begins
10 days after end of session	CBO issues revised projections
15 days after end of session	OMB issues revised projections
15 days after end of session	GAO compliance report

Source: House Budget Committee's Budget Timeline. 2004. http://www.budget.house. gov/budgcalendar.pdf.

important things that are still prominent features of the budget process today. First, it requires that government agencies prepare and submit budget requests directly to the president, as you have seen. The president then can place those requests in his budget proposal, or change them to fit his policy priorities. Before the 1921 Act, agencies submitted their requests to congressional committees, which meant that the president had been largely cut out of the budget process. Second, the Act created the Bureau of the Budget (now titled the Office of Management and Budget, or OMB) to serve the president by providing economic advice, analysis, and help with creating the budget. The president's budget and the OMB have now become crucial components of the federal budget process.

Once all of the budget requests have been collected, the OMB analyzes them. The OMB has two main objectives at this stage. One is to trim the amount of spending requested by the agencies. As part of this, the OMB will frequently challenge the assumptions about costs and clientele demands made by the agencies. In many cases, the agencies will have to provide additional information to the OMB to back up their assumptions and requests. The other objective is more political, and focuses on making sure the president's policy preferences are reinforced. The OMB, on the advice of the president's advisors (and perhaps the president himself), prepares the president's budget in accordance with his policy goals and spending priorities. Thus, the president's budget is part of the process that tries to build in efficient government spending, but it also allows the president a way to build his political preferences into the budget.

Presenting the President's Budget to Congress

Although the president dominates the first two steps of the budget process, his influence does not necessarily extend to Congress. The presentation of the president's budget is interesting because it signals to Congress and the general public what the president wants. However, his budget is simply an advisory proposal, and the importance of the president's budget depends on the amount of influence he has on Congress. Congress, as a result, may do one of three things with the president's budget. First, Congress may enact it "as is," or with only minor changes. This never happens, as it would require an unlikely amount of agreement between the White House and Congress, and it would require an unlikely amount of agreement among members of Congress themselves. Second, Congress may choose to use the president's budget as a starting point for analysis and decision making. This is probably most common, but it does not necessarily indicate that the president's preferences will all be preserved. Finally, Congress may simply disregard the president's budget. President's budgets have indeed been "dead on arrival" on numerous occasions in the recent past. President Clinton's was in 1995, as were several of President Reagan's.

Congressional Decision Making

The budget process in Congress is quite complex, but it can be broken down into three sets of actors: the Budget Committees in the House and Senate, the Appropriations Committees, and other substantive committees (see Figure 8.8).

Once the president submits his budget to Congress, the Congressional Budget Office provides an analysis of the assumptions and projections made in the president's budget. The substantive committees in Congress then draw up their "views and estimates" concerning revenue and spending for the upcoming fiscal year. These proposals, along with the CBO analyses, are transmitted to the Budget Committees in each house. The Senate Budget Committee reports a **budget resolution** by April 1, which sets a maximum for the total budget authority that can be passed. The House and Senate Budget Committees then complete the resolution by April 15. The spending limits set by the budget resolution are **crosswalked** back to the substantive committees. Any adjustments by the committees are made in the form of reconciliations in the budget resolution. A reconciliation is simply an adjustment to the committee's initial view and estimate that was sent to the Budget Committee.

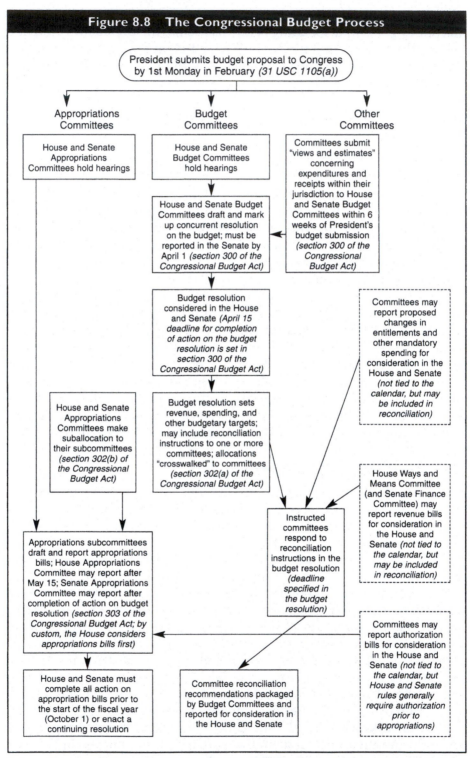

Figure 8.8   The Congressional Budget Process

President submits budget proposal to Congress by 1st Monday in February *(31 USC 1105(a))*

Appropriations Committees

House and Senate Appropriations Committees hold hearings

House and Senate Appropriations Committees make suballocation to their subcommittees *(section 302(b) of the Congressional Budget Act)*

Appropriations subcommittees draft and report appropriations bills; House Appropriations Committee may report after May 15; Senate Appropriations Committee may report after completion of action on budget resolution *(section 303 of the Congressional Budget Act; by custom, the House considers appropriations bills first)*

House and Senate must complete all action on appropriation bills prior to the start of the fiscal year (October 1) or enact a continuing resolution

Budget Committees

House and Senate Budget Committees hold hearings

House and Senate Budget Committees draft and mark up concurrent resolution on the budget; must be reported in the Senate by April 1 *(section 300 of the Congressional Budget Act)*

Budget resolution considered in the House and Senate *(April 15 deadline for completion of action on the budget resolution is set in section 300 of the Congressional Budget Act)*

Budget resolution sets revenue, spending, and other budgetary targets; may include reconciliation instructions to one or more committees; allocations "crosswalked" to committees *(section 302(a) of the Congressional Budget Act)*

Instructed committees respond to reconciliation instructions in the budget resolution *(deadline specified in the budget resolution)*

Committee reconciliation recommendations packaged by Budget Committees and reported for consideration in the House and Senate

Other Committees

Committees submit "views and estimates" concerning expenditures and receipts within their jurisdiction to House and Senate Budget Committees within 6 weeks of President's budget submission *(section 300 of the Congressional Budget Act)*

Committees may report proposed changes in entitlements and other mandatory spending for consideration in the House and Senate *(not tied to the calendar, but may be included in reconciliation)*

House Ways and Means Committee (and Senate Finance Committee) may report revenue bills for consideration in the House and Senate *(not tied to the calendar, but may be included in reconciliation)*

Committees may report authorization bills for consideration in the House and Senate *(not tied to the calendar, but House and Senate rules generally require authorization prior to appropriations)*

Source: Congressional Research Service Report RS20095. 2004. *The Congressional Budget Process: A Brief Overview.* http://www.house.gov/htbin/crsprodget?/rs/RS20095.

Meanwhile, the House and Senate Appropriations Committees are holding hearings. The appropriations subcommittees draft and report appropriations bills. There are 10 appropriations subcommittees in the House, reorganized from 13 for fiscal year 2006. The full House Appropriations Committee also produces one appropriations bill, for a total of 11. The Senate now has 12 appropriations subcommittees, each reporting one bill. Although the jurisdictions of the Senate's committees are similar to those of the House, the fact that the two chambers differ is the source of some confusion. These subcommittees cover a variety of policy issues and portions of government (see Table 8.1). The House has until June 30 to pass all of its appropriations bills, as well as to complete the reconciliation bill. During this time, substantive committees may also report new authorization bills to be considered in the House and Senate. This is not technically part of the budget calendar, but both the House and Senate typically require authorization before appropriations. The Senate may complete its appropriations activity after the reconciliation bill is finalized, but both the House and Senate must finish before the start of the fiscal year on October 1. Otherwise, they must enact a continuing resolution to fund government functions.

Authority and Authorization. It is crucial to understand the difference between these two terms. **Authorization** is substantive legislation; it commands the government to do something. Authorization creates government programs and agencies. Authorization also lets programs and agencies continue to exist, assuming they adhere to the rules by which they were established and there is support for what they do. Obviously, government programs and agencies need money to work. Authorization bills do not include this money; they simply allow such programs and agencies to exist. **Budget authority** is required to actually provide funding. This authority is provided in five ways.

Appropriations authority covers all discretionary spending. It sets the limit on outlays for programs and agencies for the upcoming fiscal year. Essentially this authority tells each agency how much cash can be spent.

Borrowing authority allows agencies to take on debt. Borrowing authority sometimes is included in appropriations acts, but it can also be permitted through other legislation. Agencies can be permitted to borrow from the Treasury, the Federal Financing Bank, or the public. The appropriations act or legislation that grants borrowing authority limits the amount that can be borrowed.

Contract authority allows agencies to enter into agreements for work or services before appropriations are actually made. Appropriations are made once the work is done or services are provided by the contractor. This is how the military buys weapons. The Air Force may use this type of authority to contract an aircraft company to provide new fighter jets. Because it will take several years for those jets to be built and delivered, the Air Force uses contract authority to start the

Table 8.1   House Authorization Committees and Appropriations Subcommittees

House Authorization Committees

- Agriculture
- Armed Services
- Education and the Workforce
- Energy and Commerce
- Financial Services
- Government Reform
- Homeland Security
- House Administration
- International Relations
- Judiciary
- Resources
- Science
- Small Business
- Transportation and Infrastructure
- Veterans' Affairs
- Ways and Means

House Appropriations Subcommittees

- Subcommittee on Agriculture, Rural Development, Food and Drug Administration, and Related Agencies
- Subcommittee on Science, State, Justice, and Commerce
- Subcommittee on Defense
- Subcommittee on Energy and Water Development
- Subcommittee on Foreign Operations, Export Financing, and Related Programs
- Subcommittee on Homeland Security
- Subcommittee on Interior and Environment
- Subcommittee on Labor, Health and Human Services, and Education
- Subcommittee on Military Quality of Life and Veterans Affairs
- Subcommittee on Transportation, Treasury, and Housing

Source: U.S. House of Representatives. 2005. http://www.house.gov.

program, then secures appropriations to pay the aircraft company at a later date.

Entitlement authority is granted through legislative actions that do not take place in the appropriations process. This authority allows agencies to spend money when no authority has been given in advance. This is important for programs that provide payments based on eligibility criteria. This means that spending is automatic, as long as people meet those criteria. Examples of this are Social Security and Medicare, which need to provide payments without having to wait for Congress to act.

Loan guarantee authority allows for the government to pay some or all of the interest and principal to a lender if the borrower defaults. This means the authority might not be used; money is spent only if bor-

An F-22 is built for the U.S. Air Force. When government agencies purchase items or services that will not be delivered right away, contract authority is used. This allows agencies to enter into contracts with private businesses to start the programs. When the items or services are delivered, appropriations are passed to pay for them.

rowers default. Student loans for college education are backed with loan guarantee authority, which is why lenders can offer them in large amounts and at relatively low interest rates.

Types of authority besides appropriations are often called "back-door authority." This is because no money is spent right away, it involves spending money not yet appropriated, and it is often granted outside the normal appropriations process. Many people are skeptical about this type of authority because it can be easy to hide government spending, or force government spending at later dates (for example, when contracts must be paid, or payments must be made on borrowed money). Of course, there are many good reasons for using these types of authority. Defense contracting and student loans have already been given as appropriate uses of contract and loan guarantee authority. Borrowing authority is also sensible for expensive projects that will last a long time. Highways and other infrastructure components are best financed through borrowing, as they will provide public service for many decades. This ensures that people in the future who use those services also help pay for them.[19]

Budget Execution

Because there are five different types of authority, some of which may not be used right away, actual outlays of a government agency for a fiscal year will not equal its authority for that year. Figure 8.9 shows the relationship between budget authority and **outlays** for the fiscal year. Most of the outlays will be based on authority from the current year, but a significant portion of outlays is from unspent authority enacted in previous years.

Budget execution is basically done by government agencies carrying out their duties. Services are delivered by using their budget authority, and money is spent. The budget document is also important in the execution stage, because it allows for monitoring and control of spending. Agencies walk a fine line when spending money. Under the Anti-Deficiency Act of 1906, their expenditures must not exceed the level they have been appropriated, under threat of criminal prosecution. However, *not* spending all of their appropriated money is often taken by Congress as a sign of deficiency as well. While it might be the result of efficient work, it also might be that the agency did not do as much as it should have, or it might indicate that its appropriations were unnecessarily high. In any case, it almost always results in more scrutiny, both from the OBM and Congress in the next budget cycle.

Agencies do have some control over how money is spent, even in light of appropriations bills that specify funding for each program. This flexibility is required, because the budget process is so long. Agency requests for spending are made at least a year in advance of the actual execution of the budget. Circumstances obviously will change, and there are times when money is tied to one program, but the agency

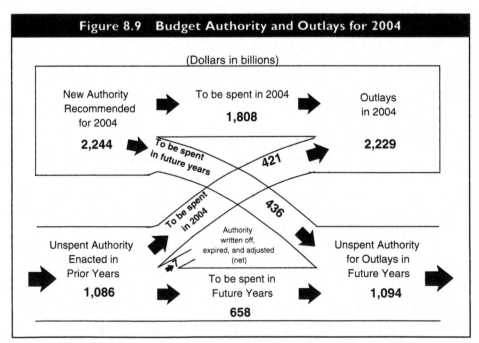

Figure 8.9 Budget Authority and Outlays for 2004

(Dollars in billions)

New Authority Recommended for 2004
2,244

To be spent in 2004
1,808

To be spent in future years

Outlays in 2004
2,229

421

436

To be spent in 2004

Authority written off, expired, and adjusted (net)

Unspent Authority Enacted in Prior Years
1,086

To be spent in Future Years
658

Unspent Authority for Outlays in Future Years
1,094

Source: Budget of the United States Government, Fiscal Year 2004, *Analytical Perspectives.* Washington, DC: Government Printing Office.

feels it could be better spent elsewhere. There are two tools agencies use to ensure a measure of flexibility over their expenditures. First, transfers can be used to move money from one purpose to another, as long as Congress has allowed for it in advance. If Congress has done so, the agency may transfer money by itself as it sees fit. Second, agencies can reprogram money. This is done in consultation with committees in Congress, in order to secure congressional approval.

Audit and Evaluation. Audits and evaluations are crucial elements of the execution of the budget. At the federal level, the Government Accountability Office (GAO) conducts audits and evaluations of government agencies. This information is provided to verify to Congress that agencies are following the rules of their appropriations. This ensures that agencies remain accountable to Congress. The GAO's audits also provide information to citizens, so that we can be aware of how the government is spending public money.

There are two types of audits: financial and performance. Financial audits determine if agencies have spent their money in accordance with the law. They also determine if agencies have retained the proper financial records to document their spending and financial situations. Financial audits by the GAO can also uncover theft from government agencies, although there are usually internal audits done by the agencies themselves to guard against this.

Performance audits seek to evaluate agencies on two issues: program success and efficiency. Program audits provide information about how well an agency's programs are performing, relative to the agency's stated goals. These audits also look for reasons why a program may not be as successful as hoped, in order to try to offer advice to the agency. Efficiency audits examine if a program is run in the most cost-effective manner possible. If inefficiency is found, the audit tries to uncover the reasons. Efficiency audits are complementary to performance audits, because a program may reach its goals, but still be run inefficiently. On the other hand, inefficient use of resources may be a reason for why a program is not reaching its goals. Once audits are finished, the budget process is ended for that fiscal year.

Budgeting in State and Local Governments

Although each state and local government has its own budget process, some broad trends and similarities can be identified. Most states have an overarching process that is very similar to the federal budgeting process, even though there can be important differences across the 50 states. For example, 21 states budget biennially—that is, every two years—and two states (Missouri and Kansas) have a portion of their budget done annually with another portion done biennially.[20] Local budgeting is significantly more varied, and often is also much less formal. Although firm generalizations are difficult to make, this section will introduce the common features of both budgeting processes, as well as the common problems that both levels of government face when making budgets.

State Budgeting

Most state budget processes are very similar to the federal process, and follow the same cycle, starting with the submission of agency requests, then moving to the development of the executive budget, legislative deliberation, and budget execution. Despite this resemblance to the federal process, some general themes of state budgeting have been identified.[21] These general features are common to most states, and they also set the politics of state budgeting apart from federal budgeting.

State Budgets as Public Policy. One key feature is that state budgets are useful to make significant changes in public policy. This is because, unlike the federal budget, state budgets are more flexible due to the fact that larger portions of them are made up of discretionary spending.[22] Although there are always state debts to pay (see capital budgeting below), having more discretionary spending means greater ability to start new programs or change existing ones. State budgets are also useful as policy vehicles because state legislators often have authority to place substantive policy language in the budget.[23] Thus, at the same time, state budgets appropriate money and instruct state agencies how to run their programs (that is, spend the money). The federal budget process does not allow this.

Gubernatorial Power. Another common feature of state budgeting is the power of the governor. Typically, governors are more influential in their states' budget processes than the president is in the national process, for several reasons. First, the governor enjoys a very prominent position, compared to state legislators. The attention that the office gets allows the governor to have tremendous influence over the policy direction of the state. In fact, most of the state's policy and budget priorities are initiated by the governor's office.[24] Additionally, governors enjoy a wide range of formal budgeting powers that give them influence in the process. For example, governors in most states can set funding targets for agencies when they are making their requests, reorganize departments without legislative approval, spend unexpected federal funds without legislative approval, and reduce the budget without legislative approval.[25] Another important tool that most governors enjoy is the **line-item veto**. This allows the governor to strike out specific policy language or individual spending lines out of the state budget, while approving the rest of the budget. Only six governors do not have this power (in Indiana, Nevada, New Hampshire, North Carolina, Rhode Island, and Vermont). Although the line-item veto was originally intended as a way to slice waste out of the state budget, it is more frequently used by governors to eliminate spending that they oppose for political reasons.[26] Regardless of how it is used, all of this authority makes governors powerful independent budget decision makers.

   Competitive Environment. Each state budgets with an eye toward its competition—other states, particularly neighboring states. Since state budgets are so useful as policy vehicles, this allows state legislatures and governors to advocate for spending that will hopefully make their state more attractive to businesses and residents. Consequently, the budget is used to find ways to promote economic development, tourism, and programs that improve the quality of life in the state, such as education or state parks. Using the budget in this manner is increasingly important in states that are experiencing long-term economic difficulties (such as Michigan or Pennsylvania, as they transition from heavy industry), or that are losing population (such as Iowa). Economic difficulties and population loss are trends that need to be reversed if those states are to continue to enjoy the level of government services they currently have.

   Fiscal Responsibility. Unlike the federal government, which has practically unlimited ability to borrow money, most state governments are restricted from passing budgets that are not balanced. Only Indiana and Vermont have no such requirements. The other 48 states have some constitutional or statutory provisions that force them to have balanced **operating budgets**.[27] These budgets cover the day-to-day workings of the state, and include things like salaries for state employees, equipment and building maintenance, utility bills, payments (such as welfare benefits), and supplies. Furthermore, most states have a statutory or consitutional limit on how fast state expenditures and taxation can grow. For example, in Montana, New Jersey, Oregon, South Carolina, Tennessee, and Texas, state appropriations cannot grow faster than

www.governor.state.mn.us.

Tim Pawlenty (1960–), the governor of Minnesota, battled with Democratic leaders in the state legislature over health and welfare spending during the budget process for the 2005–2006 fiscal year. The disagreements lasted so long that the state government partially shut down when there was no budget at the start of the fiscal year on July 1, 2005.

the growth of personal income in the state. In Missouri, state revenue is limited to 5.64 percent of the previous year's personal income in the state.[28] These requirements to balance the budget and that limit growth in expenditures and revenue force state budget makers to make some tough decisions about how much—and where—to spend money, as well as how much taxation the population will tolerate in order to pay for state programs. Typically, these restrictions mean that there is never enough money to meet all of the demands on the state, and many state agencies will not get all the money they requested. In practical terms it means more groups—like college students in Iowa—will be disappointed.

Capital Budgets. You might be wondering, if states must pass a balanced budget, how do they pay for big, expensive projects? To be able to fund large long-term items, like buildings, bridges, or things like flood control projects, state governments use **capital budgets**. So each state actually has two budgets: one to fund day-to-day operations, and another to fund large projects, usually geared toward improving infrastructure. Unlike operating budgets, capital budgets do not need to be balanced—in fact, that is the point. They allow the state to borrow money by issuing bonds to finance those expensive projects. If done correctly, the financing continues for the life of the project. That is, if a bridge is expected to last 25 years, the term of the loan will be for 25 years, and the state will make 25 annual payments which will then erase the debt. This allows states to pay for projects that would be impossible if their full costs had to be built into the operating budget. Stretching payments over the life of a project is also more fair, because if people today pay the full costs of a bridge that will last 25 years, people in the future will be using that bridge without paying for any of it. Care must be used, however, when planning capital projects, because new buildings and expanded infrastructure increase annual operating budget expenses (such as for maintenance and utilities). Increased capital expenditures also means increased debt service payments that have to come out of the operating budget.

Local Budgeting

It is very difficult to identify a single local budget process, simply because there are so many local governments with such a wide variety of forms and functions. In other words, it is hard to compare budgeting in New York City with that of Mille Lacs County, Minnesota. The former has a population of about 8 million people and has an annual budget of more than $43 billion, both of which are larger than many states. The latter has a population of 23,000 people, is mostly rural, and has an annual budget of less than $20 million. Nevertheless, some key features of local budgeting can be identified.

Lack of Flexibility. Local governments, as creatures created by the states, must abide by the same budgeting restrictions that require balanced operating budgets. This, along with the heavy dependence of local governments on state aid (see Figure 8.5) means that local governments are almost always in danger of a fiscal crisis. This situation is made worse by the fact that local governments usually have little flexibilty in reducing spending. Most local expenditures are for essential services, which are difficult to cut. Additionally, on average at least three-fourths of municipal and county budgets are tied up in salary (which is typical for governments that are oriented toward service delivery), leaving little room for large spending cuts without eliminating employees.[29] Finally, local governments are usually restricted in their ability to tax their citizens. For example, only five states (Alabama, California, Missouri, New York, and Ohio) allow local governments to have both a sales and an income tax. As a result, they engage in **revenue budgeting**, which strongly links revenue projections to spending and builds in a surplus in case of emergency.[30]

This lack of flexibility spurs local governments to find other ways to increase revenue and cut spending. Economic development receives a lot of attention in local budgeting decisions, as a growing economy leads to more residents and increased property values; in other words, property-tax revenue is increased. Local governments therefore use their budgets to offer incentives for business development, such as subsidized loans, property-tax exemptions, and access to cheap or free land.[31] In order to cut spending, privatization is an increasingly important feature of budget decision making in local governments. As you saw in Chapter 3, however, this is usually not the silver bullet solution that it is made out to be. By itself it will not solve the fiscal problems of a local government. However, there are often opportunities to contract out for some services, such as garbage disposal and janitorial services.[32]

Regional Competition. Local governments often exist in competition with each other. Because people move, it is possible that some will move to a certain area that offers them the mix of taxes and services that they prefer,[33] called "voting with your feet." Consider a city ringed with suburbs. If you work in the city, you have a variety of choices of where to live. You can live in the city itself, or choose among the many suburbs. Perhaps you are willing to drive the extra distance and live outside of the suburbs in the country. The services available (good schools, for example), and the taxes to pay for them, might be part of the reason why one place is more attractive than another. Although not everyone votes with their feet,[34] it is clear that local budget makers take this potential for competition seriously by trying to hold taxes down and offering competitive incentives for economic development. It is also important to sustain high quality essential services to keep the quality of life high so that residents do not move away and new residents will be attracted. These pressures from competition only add to the problems from having less flexibility in budget decision making.

Local Budget Processes.[35] Local government budgeting is too varied to go into in much detail here. Indeed, courses just on public budgeting often don't even have time and space to cover many specifics. Examining just municipal and county budgets, however, three themes emerge. First, the executive usually dominates the process in more populous municipalities and counties. Mayors and city managers of larger towns and cities usually set budget guidelines for city agencies and draw up the budget for approval by the city council. It is rare for a city council to offer proposals of its own that are large departures from the executive's proposal. County executives of populous counties have similar influence. Both types of executive also enjoy professional advice from a budget staff. Executives of less populous counties, on the other hand, are less influential in the budget process than city council or county board. In these counties (typically with less than 25,000 people), the county board draws up the proposal and acts to approve it.

Finally, most municipal and county budgets are incremental in nature. This is because so much of municipal and county spending is for salaries, and because of the reasons why there is less flexibility in local budgeting discussed above. Large shifts in spending are not possible, and significant new sources of revenue are often not available.

Analysis in Public Budgeting

As you can see, public budgeting at any level of government is very complex. Many different institutions and actors are involved, and the entire process is highly political. Despite the complexity and the politics, there have been many efforts to better manage the process, in order to create efficiency and better government. This can be seen as far back as 1921, with the Budget and Accounting Act, which dramatically altered the budget process by establishing what is now the Office of Management and Budget in order to try to introduce analysis into decisions made about government spending. More recently, several theories of public budgeting have been developed and tried, to varying degrees of success, to introduce analysis into public budgeting in order to replace the traditional **line-item budget**, which frequently is nothing more than a "shopping list" of things the government would like to buy.

Most of these new theories have been introduced in reaction to how decisions are thought to be made in the budget process. The federal budget is complex, and it requires the coordination of hundreds of people. The information needed to make decisions is overwhelming, and it often comes in the form of educated guesses rather than hard facts, particularly when trying to predict future spending and revenue needs. Time is short for such a huge project. And all the while, members of Congress, bureaucrats, agency clientele, lobbyists, interest groups, and concerned citizens are all trying to avoid losing their slice of the budget pie.

Shortcuts in Public Budgeting

Due to all of these problems, many have argued that budget makers use a variety of decision-making shortcuts in order to speed up the process and to make decisions without as much information. One of these shortcuts is "satisficing," which was discussed in Chapter 6.[36] A decision maker first establishes a set of "givens" about goals and how to reach them. Any alternative that is not consistent with the givens is automatically disregarded. The first option that comes along that meets the givens is selected. Others have developed this idea further. Based on the problems of insufficient time and information, as well as the political problem of coordinating so many people with different goals, some argue that the previous budget itself is the key "given." It serves as the starting point for all decisions about the new budget. Rather than making decisions by comprehensively analyzing every piece of information and considering every possible alternative, decision makers instead just make small adjustments to the existing budget.[37] This is **incrementalism**; minor adjustments are made to previous decisions. This is a more flexible way to make decisions, and it also avoids some of the more serious ideological and value-driven conflict that would erupt if the process started from scratch each year. It also allows the variety of actors (budget committees, agencies, the president and the OMB, interest groups, etc.) to more easily focus on the changes made by others.[38] This simplifies the task of coordinating people and actors with different goals.

Introducing Analysis

Incrementalism does not seem very analytical. Indeed, it functions as a way to reduce the amount of analysis that is needed to make budget decisions. As a way to counter this, there have been several attempts to change the budget process in order to force decision makers to adopt an analytical perspective.

Performance Budgeting. **Performance budgeting** was intended to link spending on specific activities with the goals of the agency by abandoning the traditional line-item budget format (which provides information only about where money is spent, rather than what is accomplished with the money). An agency's performance budget has several components.[39] First, it includes a plan of action for the year that specifies its activities and programs, the reasons for them, and how those activities will be done. Second, costs and resources are linked and an assessment is made about what can be accomplished with the given resources. Third, the plan is carried out. In this step, the first two components allow for an analysis of the effectiveness of the programs, because there is a definite plan and an evaluation of resources. Although performance budgeting is used widely, it is not strictly followed for several reasons. First, the complexity and size of the federal and state budgets make it very difficult to create plans of action and relate costs with resources. Second, even within agencies, many diverse programs and activities defy attempts to clearly state activities and plans to carry them out. Finally, the control that a line-item budget provides is missing, making it more difficult for the legislature to hold agencies accountable for spending.

Program Budgeting. Due to these problems, **program budgeting** grew out of performance budgeting in the 1960s. It became so popular that in 1965, President Lyndon Johnson made it a requirement for most federal agencies. The key difference between the two is that program budgeting, or planning-programming budgeting (PPB), is that PPB was designed to examine the purpose of government programs, rather than just the activities of government. Performance budgeting, for example, would focus on highway patrols. PPB would instead focus on reducing fatalities on the highways by a set percentage, with increased highway patrols as simply one tool (activity) to produce fewer fatalities from car accidents. Program budgeting also is explicitly done from a cost-effectiveness point of view. There are many ways for the government to provide a single benefit or service. PPB incorporated cost-benefit analysis to examine the different options available in order to provide those benefits and services at the lowest cost.

One other distinguishing feature of PPB was that it could span agency boundaries and analyze long-term components of government programs. Traditional budgets are designed specifically for each agency and mostly provide short-term analysis of costs and benefits. PPB, on the other hand, focused on the purpose (or final result) of programs. Because several agencies may have something to do with any given purpose, and because these programs are ongoing, PPB tried to shift the focus away from annual agency-based budgets. Returning to the goal of reducing highway fatalities by a set percentage, we see that the state highway patrol would contribute to this. However, so would the state transportation department (for road maintenance and snow or ice removal), various research agencies (that do testing on roadbeds), the state department of natural resources (to prevent animal-related accidents), and state data centers (that track road usage, accidents, and fatalities). Decision makers using PPB were supposed to focus on the contributions of each of these agencies over the long term in order to select the most cost-effective mix that will reach their goal.

PPB lasted only a few years. By 1971 it had been abandoned, no longer required by federal agencies. There are many reasons for why it was so short-lived. First, the goals of many government programs are too vague to be defined in a manner required by PPB. "Promoting free trade" or "securing world peace" are examples that defy the procedures in PPB. Second, cost-benefit analysis is notoriously difficult. It requires the assignment of dollar values to all costs and benefits. What is the dollar value of the benefit from a public swimming pool? An after-school program for teenagers? A federally protected forest? Third, budgeting decisions had to cut across government agencies and programs. This served to increase the difficulties in reaching agreements on goals, because budgets were still drawn up for each agency and program.[40] These failures drove further reform at the federal level, which led to **zero-base budgeting** (ZBB).

Zero-Base Budgeting. ZBB was intended to be a clean break away from satisficing and incrementalism. The concept is to force agencies to justify their programs each year. This allows decision makers to review program effectiveness and alternatives in a comprehensive fashion. In its pure form ZBB offers the threat of no funding if justification cannot be found. Hence the name ZBB: each agency starts from zero, and funding is added as appropriate justification is made.

ZBB has three basic elements: identification of decision units, formation of decision packets, and ranking.[41] Decision units are the lowest-level units in organizations and programs for which budgets are created. Each unit has a manager who is responsible for that unit's budget justifications. Each year, the decision units are reviewed, starting with asking what would happen to the organization if the unit were not funded, or if it were partly funded (at, say 25 percent, 50 percent, or 75 percent). Further, a "survival level" of funding is also identified, below which the decision unit might as well be eliminated. These questions explore how the operation of the decision unit will be affected, and whether there is room to cut funding while maintaining effectiveness. Each unit's evaluation and answers to these questions is a decision packet. These packets are collected and ranked by the top managers in the organization. Ranking of each decision packet is decided on the basis of importance of the decision unit's activities. However, the ranking also includes choices on different levels of funding for each unit.

Problems with ZBB made it short-lived at the federal level. It began under President Carter and died with the end of his administration in 1980. One key problem with ZBB was its cumbersome, complex process. Identifying decision units and creating decision packets proved to be difficult and time consuming. It requires clearly defined operations and goals for decision units. As with PBB, however, this is hard to do, as goals and programs span decision units. As applied, decision units were identified in such a way as to keep them within agencies rather than attaching them to government programs. Finally, despite the name, ZBB did not involve resetting budgets to zero, but was a more limited tool that searched for areas where budget cuts could be made without seriously disrupting public services.

Although ZBB died at the federal level, it is still used in modified form by some state and local governments. In Iowa, for example, agency requests for the next fiscal year start at 75 percent of the previous year's budget, which becomes the base for that agency. Then, the agency develops a set of decision packets that restore the budget to the previous year's level. If the agency is requesting additional funding, decision packets can be developed for new initiatives.[42] This modification still allows the state to take advantage of the analytical features of ZBB without forcing every agency to actually start from scratch each year.

Budgeting for Results, or New Performance Budgeting. The Government Performance and Results Act of 1993 (GPRA) is the most recent effort to link agency performance to budget decision making. The GPRA instructs agencies to establish long-term (five-year) strategic plans, which include performance goals and measurable achievement benchmarks. Annual performance plans are also created that link programs with budget requests. As part of these plans, any overlap between programs and agencies is explicitly included in the strategic plans, the performance plans, and budget requests. This is a major improvement over past performance budget attempts, where there was little attempt to actually draw connections across programs and agencies.

President George W. Bush has made adjustments to the GPRA, on his assessment that the act was not functioning as intended. Starting with the 2004 budget, the OMB added a new method to assess the performance of federal agencies. The **Program Assessment Rating Tool (PART)** strongly links program performance in a number of areas with budget decisions by holding agencies increasingly accountable for the successfulness of their specific programs. The PART assesses the purpose, management, and results of federal programs, and produces an overall rating. Even though it modifies the GPRA, the PART is explicitly a "budgeting for results" tool, as it retains most of the key elements of new performance budgeting. Sidebar 8.2 shows some of the specific questions the PART asks of agency managers. The PART allows the OMB to gauge overall performance of agencies or departments, as well as gauge more specific programs and activities of those agencies and departments. This helps the OMB prepare the president's budget by demonstrating where resources might be targeted or subtracted, based on how well the various agencies are performing.

Conclusion

The continued search for analysis in the budget process is an indication of how important the budget is for policymaking and policy im-

Sidebar 8.2 The Program Assessment Rating Tool (PART)

How the PART Works

The PART evaluation proceeds through four critical areas of assessment—purpose and design, strategic planning, management, and results and accountability.

The first set of questions gauges whether the programs' design and purpose are clear and defensible. The second section involves strategic planning, and weighs whether the agency sets valid annual and long-term goals for programs. The third section rates agency management of programs, including financial oversight and program improvement efforts. The fourth set of questions focuses on results that programs can report with accuracy and consistency.

The answers to questions in each of the four sections result in a numeric score for each section from 0 to 100 (100 being the best). These scores are then combined to achieve an overall qualitative rating that ranges from Effective, to Moderately Effective, to Adequate, to Ineffective. Programs that do not have acceptable performance measures or have not yet collected performance data generally receive a rating of Results Not Demonstrated.

While single, weighted scores can be calculated, the value of reporting, say, an overall 4 out of 100 can be misleading. Reporting a single numerical rating could suggest false precision, or draw attention away from the very areas most in need of improvement. In fact, the PART is best seen as a complement to traditional management techniques, and can be used to stimulate a constructive dialogue between program managers, budget analysts, and policy officials. The PART serves its purpose if it produces an honest starting point for spending decisions that take results seriously.

The four sections of the PART are:

1. Program Purpose and Design — to assess whether the program's purpose and design are clear and sound

2. Strategic Planning — to assess whether the program has valid long-term and annual measures and targets

3. Program Management — to rate program's management, including financial oversight and program improvement efforts

4. Program Results/ Accountability — to rate program performance on measures and targets reviewed in the strategic planning section and through other evaluations

Across these four sections, the PART asks approximately 30 questions that responsible federal managers should be able to answer. Examples include:

- Is the program designed to have a significant impact in addressing the intended interest, problem, or need?

- Are federal managers and program partners (grantees, sub-grantees, contractors, etc.) held accountable for cost, schedule, and performance results?

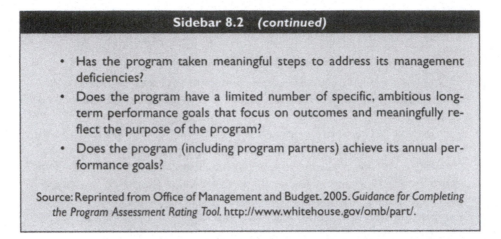

Sidebar 8.2 *(continued)*

- Has the program taken meaningful steps to address its management deficiencies?
- Does the program have a limited number of specific, ambitious long-term performance goals that focus on outcomes and meaningfully reflect the purpose of the program?
- Does the program (including program partners) achieve its annual performance goals?

Source: Reprinted from Office of Management and Budget. 2005. *Guidance for Completing the Program Assessment Rating Tool.* http://www.whitehouse.gov/omb/part/.

plementation. It is not an exaggeration to state that public budgeting is the key to governance in the United States. Poor decisions in budgeting will almost necessarily lead to less effective government.

One actor in the process, the bureaucracy, is involved from start to finish. Although it is a key actor, it is not necessarily the most influential. In fact, one key goal of the budget is to hold government agencies accountable for their programs and the money they spend on them. Improving this accountability has been the chief goal of all of the attempts to introduce analysis into the budget process.

The bureaucracy is not powerless in the process, however, despite these drives to better examine their activities. An agency that has many internal sources of power, a strong clientele, and other external sources of power can be very influential. Neither the president nor members of Congress will be willing to seriously reduce the resources of an agency that is politically powerful. Since budgets reveal policy preferences, agencies that enjoy popular and political support will reap benefits in the budget process. NASA in the 1960s and the defense department in the 1980s are good examples of portions of the bureaucracy whose budgets increased due to political support.

Public budgets are also plans of action. They lay out what the government intends to do, how much it will pay for those activities, and how (by taxing or borrowing) it will pay for those activities. By allocating social resources, public budgets determine the role of the federal government in the economy and society.

If we "get what we pay for," then public administration turns on public budgeting. The search for a way to define "adequate resources" for government agencies has followed a long road. Many reforms to the process have been attempted, and the current administration's score cards and PART will not be the last. This is because, as this chapter has shown, the process of budgeting itself is as important as, and shapes, the final budget document.

Key Concepts

authorization An act of Congress that establishes or continues a federal program or agency, and sets forth the guidelines to which it must adhere.

balanced budget A balanced budget occurs when total receipts equal total outlays for a fiscal year.

budget authority The authority provided by law to incur financial obligations that will result in outlays. This authority comes in several forms: appropriations, borrowing authority, contract authority, entitlement authority, and loan guarantee authority.

Budget Enforcement Act (BEA) A law designed to limit discretionary spending while ensuring that new entitlement programs or tax cuts do not increase deficits. It set annual limits on total discretionary spending and created Pay-as-You-Go (PAYGO) rules for changes in entitlements and taxes.

budget resolution The annual framework that Congress uses to set targets for total spending, total revenues, and the deficit, as well as allocations, within the spending target, for discretionary and mandatory spending. A budget resolution does not become law and is not binding on the executive branch.

capital budget Used by state and local governments to finance expensive long-term projects.

crosswalk A procedure that applies budget resolution spending limits to individual congressional committees.

debt service payments The amount paid annually in interest and principal on outstanding government debt.

deficit The amount by which outlays exceed revenue in a fiscal year.

discretionary spending At the federal level, what the president and Congress decide to spend through the 13 annual appropriations bills.

entitlement programs Programs in which the federal government is legally obligated to make payments or provide aid to any person who meets the legal criteria for eligibility. Examples include Social Security, Medicare, Medicaid, and Food Stamps.

essential services Local government services for the basic functions of the community.

federal debt Money owed by the federal government, divided into two types: debt held by the public, which is the cumulative amount of money the federal government has borrowed from the public and not repaid; and debt held by government accounts, which is the debt the Treasury owes to other accounts within the federal government. Most of it results from surpluses of Social Security and other trust funds, which are required by law to be invested in federal securities.

fiscal year The government's accounting period. The federal government's begins on October 1 and ends on September 30.

incrementalism A decision-making shortcut in budgeting that uses previous spending as the starting point, from which small adjustments are made for the next fiscal year.

line-item budget A budget that simply lists spending items for an agency, without examining what that agency accomplishes with that spending.

line-item veto A type of veto that allows the executive to remove specific items, while still passing the remainder of the budget.

mandatory spending Spending that is authorized by permanent law rather than annual appropriations.

operating budget Used by state and local governments to budget for day-to-day operations.

outlays The amount of money the government actually spends in a given fiscal year.

Pay-as-You-Go (PAYGO) Refers to requirements that new mandatory spending proposals or tax reductions must be offset by cuts in other mandatory spending or by tax increases, to ensure that the deficit does not rise or the surplus does not fall. These requirements are no longer enforced.

performance budgeting A type of budgeting that allocates budgetary and human capital resources by comparing historical and expected future performance levels with the full cost of producing desired program outcomes.

pork-barrel spending Public spending targeted at specific jurisdictions, used for constituency service.

Program Assessment Rating Tool (PART) Designed to help the federal government meet the expectations of the Government Performance and Results Act. Scores that agencies receive help link program performance with budget decisions, and agencies are held increasingly accountable for the successfulness of their specific programs.

program budgeting A budgeting technique that examines the purpose of government programs, rather than just their activities, including programs' cost-effectiveness.

revenue Money collected by the government as taxes, fees, charges, and other government activities such as transfers and grants.

revenue budgeting A type of budgeting that ensures spending falls substantially below revenue projections, which builds a surplus into the budget.

user charges Prices paid by citizens in exhange for some government good or service.

user fees Prices paid by citizens to engage in activity that is otherwise prohibited.

zero-base budgeting (ZBB) A budgeting technique that in its pure form sets agency budgets back to zero, forcing a thorough review of all spending each fiscal year. ✦

Chapter 9

Managing People

As an assistant city manager in Des Moines, Iowa, Michael Armstrong earns $125,000 a year. Sound like a lot? Consider that there are not many people with Armstrong's technical expertise; it's a relatively small group of people that have the knowledge and experience to successfully coordinate and supervise multipartner projects in a large urban area. Phoenix, Arizona, and Prince William County, Virginia, know this all too well. In 2004 they were offering tens of thousands more to lure people like Armstrong to work for them. There is a steady demand for talented public executives, competition for them can be fierce, and like any labor market, competition drives up salaries. Consider just a few examples: the Miami-Dade County School Superintendent earns an estimated half-million dollars a year, the chief information officer for the city of Philadelphia earns close to $200,000, and the fire chief of Little Rock, Arkansas, earns more than $100,000.[1]

These people are a small elite of public administrators; most public employees do not make six-figure salaries, regardless of their qualifications and experience. Virtually all public-school teachers, for example, have bachelor's degrees and many have graduate degrees. This highly educated labor force earns an average salary of around $45,000.[2] Nonetheless, the competition for top public executives highlights a general challenge for public-sector organizations: people. The public sector produces services rather than goods, which is labor intensive. To do their jobs bureaucracies need large numbers of competent and qualified people with an enormous variety of skills and talents.

Filling that need is a considerable challenge. First, the right people must be found. Then they need to be persuaded to take a job in the public sector. Once employed, they often have to be trained. If they develop into good workers, public bureaucracies have to figure out a way to retain them, a difficult prospect when private-sector companies can offer more prestige and higher paychecks. If they turn out to be incompetent, they have to be dismissed. This creates problems of its own. No one wants public agencies to keep employees who are unwilling or incapable of doing their jobs well. Yet public agencies, especially regulatory agencies, are often subject to a lot of external political pressures. Few want public employees dismissed simply because doing their jobs displeases politically connected businesses or individuals. This creates the need for a difficult balancing act: public managers need enough flexibility to dismiss or reassign sub-par employees, yet it makes sense to offer public employees a strong measure of job protection to ensure they are not unduly influenced by political considerations.

Meeting all these challenges is the job of personnel or human-resource systems. In this chapter we are going to explore the human side of civil service, the process by which people are recruited into public employment, compensated, evaluated, and promoted. Because public programs depend to a large extent on the quality of the people working in the public sector, these issues are directly related to policy effectiveness and success. Get, train, and keep the right people, and a public agency is highly likely to be successful. Get the wrong people, or get the right people and treat them badly, and a public agency is likely to fare considerably worse.

Public Versus Private Personnel Systems

Every organization needs a way to handle and process people. If the organization's goal is to produce goods and services, people with the right qualifications or attributes to produce those goods and services have to be located, hired, and compensated. After recruiting, selecting, and paying employees, an organization has a vested interest in evaluating their job performance as the basis for promotion and wage increases—or as the basis for firing an employee and finding someone who can do the job better. In other words, virtually every public- and private-sector organization has the need for a personnel system—a well-thought out means of managing people.

Managing people is one of the most challenging tasks facing any large organization, and also one of the most critical for organizational success. At the heart of any personnel system is recruitment, selection, compensation, training, and evaluation. Each of these has an enormous impact on the ability of an organization to achieve its desired objectives. Regardless of whether it is in the public or private sector, any organization that cannot find and promote competent, qualified people will struggle.[3]

Yet while the public and private sectors share the same need for effective personnel systems, they typically have very different approaches to handling human beings. Though private-sector personnel systems can be highly complex in specifics, the underlying goal is fairly straightforward: hire the people who will best help the organization make money. Managers are given broad flexibility to hire and fire people to serve that goal.

In contrast, jobs in the public sector serve several purposes. They are, of course, used to produce public goods and services. Yet the goal of producing public goods and services is to serve the public interest, not to make a profit. As discussed elsewhere in this book, the objectives involved in "serving the public interest" are wide ranging. It should be of little surprise, then, to discover that jobs in the public sector are used for more than producing goods and services. They are also used to repay political favors or reward partisan loyalty (the process known as patronage), to provide aid and benefits to favored groups (e.g., veterans are frequently favored in public agency hiring), and for a broad variety of policy purposes (e.g., putting people on the payroll as a means of stimulating the economy).[4]

In addition to having more than one reason for hiring employees, public agencies typically have more than one boss. Federal agencies, for example, are technically all subordinate to the president. Yet they also must serve the expressed wishes of Congress. To top it all off, those who lead the executive branch are much more likely to be amateurs with relatively little executive experience compared to the private sector. Many agency heads and executive branch employees serve at the pleasure of the president, governor, or mayor. They are, in effect, patronage jobs where political loyalty is more highly prized than qualifications or technical competence. Certainly no public-sector executive experience is required to be president, governor, or mayor, just a campaign that attracts more votes than the opponents'. Indeed, the public sector is probably the only place where people can apply for a job as the chief executive officer of a multibillion-dollar operation and present their complete lack of experience as a qualification *for* the job. Private-sector executives who run their companies well are prized and are often paid handsomely as an inducement to stay; the average CEO of a major corporation earned almost $10 million in 2004.[5] Presidents, governors, and mayors are paid considerably less, and term limits often force them out even if most people agree they are doing a good job and want them to stay.

Legal Framework

While there are clearly important differences in underlying goals, hiring, firing, qualifications, and compensation, probably the most important difference between public- and private-sector personnel systems is the legal framework under which they operate. Public employees, for example, generally have more due-process rights—most civil service systems require an agency to show "just cause" for firing an employee, and employees have a right to appeal such decisions and their justification. Public employees are granted these due-process rights mainly in an attempt to keep bureaucracy as politically neutral as pos-sible—as we will discuss more in depth below, most public personnel systems are based on the idea that people should be hired and fired on the basis of qualifications and merit, not on the whims of politics.

The net effect of such due-process rights gives public employees a higher level of job security compared to the private sector. Public em-ployees, however, may face restrictions on their personal behavior as a condition of their employment. This is best exemplified by the **Hatch Act**, which was passed in 1939 and regulates the relationship between federal employees and partisan politics. Among other things, the Hatch Act prohibits federal employees from running for office in parti-san elections and wearing partisan political buttons while at work. Employees in some agencies have even tighter restrictions on any form of partisan political activity. Employees of Federal Bureau of Investiga-tion and all members of the Senior Executive Service are prohibited from holding office in political clubs or parties, distributing campaign material in partisan elections, making campaign speeches, or publicly endorsing candidates running under a partisan label.[6]

Public employees may also face restrictions on the sort of labor ac-tions they can take. Many public employees, for example, have a very limited legal right to strike. The reasoning for denying or restricting such rights for public workers is simple: society suffers enormously if key agencies such as law enforcement are shut down. For example, in 1981, despite a law that prohibited strikes by government unions, the Professional Air Traffic Controllers Organization (PATCO) called a strike and nearly 12,000 air traffic controllers walked off the job. The union argued that growth in air travel had increased demands on their members, putting them under enormous stress. They wanted better working conditions, higher salaries, and a reduced work week. While recognizing that some of their grievances were legitimate, the Reagan administration viewed the potential to shut down the nation's air trans-portation system as the bigger issue. Reagan declared PATCO's action illegal and a threat to national safety and ordered the strikers back to work. When they refused, Reagan fired 11,359 controllers and did so with wide public support.[7]

What all this adds up to is that personnel systems differ signifi-cantly in the public and private sectors. Because the public sector has different goals, different reasons for hiring people, more complex lines of authority, and must work within a different legal framework, it needs a different way of managing people.

Public Personnel Systems

Like all management subfields, there are numerous approaches, systems, and fads associated with handling people. Basically, however, there are only two fundamental personnel systems in the public sector: systems based on political appointment or election and systems based on merit. There is a mix and match of both of these systems at all levels of government. The United States probably leans more heavily on the political appointment/election system more than any other industrialized democracy, even though most public employees fall under the umbrella of a merit system.

Administration by Aristocracy

Historically, personnel systems have gone through three distinct stages in the United States; two fall directly under the heading of political appointment and/or election, and the third represents the rise of the merit approach. The first was what might be called **administration by the aristocracy**. In the first few decades of the United States government, executives selected and appointed lesser officers from what amounted to a pool of the country's aristocratic elite. George Washington, for example, stressed "fitness of character" in making appointments. Essentially what this meant is that Washington picked people he thought could be trusted to serve with integrity and trust. Washington's immediate successors followed his example, which practically translated into the bulk of those holding significant government positions coming from a small wealthy and educated elite.[8] The key to getting a good government job was a long-standing relationship with those holding high office. An obvious means of having such a relationship was to be kin, so this approach to managing people also meant a high degree of nepotism in government.

Administration by aristocracy obviously had its drawbacks. For one thing it almost certainly meant that a lot of talented people were never even considered for public office because they were not "members of the club," that is, they were neither by family nor social background connected to the governing elite. For another, competence was a secondary consideration. Just because someone is known and trusted by those holding high elective office does not mean he or she is a qualified and competent administrator.

Patronage and the Spoils System

Administration by aristocracy lasted for a relatively short time, giving way to a more extreme form of political appointment and election known as the **spoils system**. The start of the spoils system is usually marked with the election of Andrew Jackson in 1828. The spoils system rested on the notion of patronage (discussed in Chapter 2), the idea that government jobs should be controlled by those who held elective office and awarded on the basis of political loyalty. Jackson's notion of what qualified someone for a government job was considerably broader than Washington's notion of "fitness of character." According to Jackson, "The duties of all public servants are, or at least admit of being made, so plain and simple that men of intelligence may readily qualify themselves for their performance."[9] In other words, education and social position were no longer considered prerequisites of a government job. Government jobs became tokens of partisan loyalty, with electoral winners rewarding their supporters and getting rid of those who had been foolish enough to back the losing slate.

The Jackson presidency heralded the dawn of a great democratization of public office. In the first 50 years of the nineteenth century, the number of eligible voters increased by something like 600 percent as the **franchise**, or right to vote, was expanded from property-owning white males to the (still mostly white and male) masses.[10] One of the byproducts of this massive expansion of the electorate was that the small intellectual elite that had run the government since the country's founding lost its exclusive grip on power. Given limited forms of mass communication and relatively rudimentary transportation systems, electioneering in the newly expanded electorate was a highly labor-intensive process. In order to win election, a candidate needed a high degree of organization and discipline, which in practical terms meant that political parties became critical to electoral success. The party footsoldiers who performed these services often expected something in return: a job.

The Jacksonian revolution not only instituted the spoils system, it also resulted in many administrative offices being put directly to the ballot box. Throughout the nineteenth century a wide variety of executive positions at the state and local levels became elected rather than appointed offices. Everyone from state attorneys general to county sheriffs had to run for of-

Library of Congress, Prints and Photographs Division, LC-USZ62-117137.

William Marcy "Boss" Tweed provides a cautionary tale about the drawbacks of a spoils and patronage system. His New York political machine controlled a web of government contracts and jobs that were doled out to those who served the machine's political interests, regardless of their qualifications or competence.

fice, and each position and each election created more opportunities and expectations of patronage.

The spoils systems has its advantages. Most important are the flexibility it offers managers in the upper reaches of government and its ability to make the public bureaucracy more responsive to elected leaders. If government employees serve at the pleasure of their elected masters, they either carry out the wishes of those chosen to represent the people, or risk being summarily dismissed. The spoils system, however, clearly has disadvantages. It promotes high rates of turnover as electoral winners clear house and install their own partisan loyalists. It puts partisan loyalty above competence as the basis for public-sector employment. It reduces efficiency (from a political standpoint, two jobs were better than one, even if only one was needed). It is often very time consuming—after winning office an executive office holder was faced with the daunting prospect of appointing hundreds or even thousands to government jobs, leaving less time for policy considerations. Finally, a spoils system also increases corruption—as jobs are only secure until the next election there is the constant temptation to use public office for personal gain while the opportunity is available.

Historically, the spoils systems created a good deal of irritation for electoral winners, who were often inundated with pleas for government jobs as soon as the ballots were counted. Abraham Lincoln became so frustrated with these requests that when he suffered an attack of smallpox, he told an aide that all job seekers should be allowed a personal audience with the president. His reasoning was that with an infectious disease he could finally give everyone something.[11]

In many cases, however, patronage was viewed not as an unpleasant necessity, but as fundamental to the operation of the political system. The best-known examples of the spoils system are the big city political "machines" that flourished in the nineteenth century, many of them surviving well into the twentieth. These machines were headed by a party committee or a "boss," who controlled access to the key electoral offices of a particular municipal or state government, and by controlling the electoral posts they also controlled who got government jobs and contracts. Under the party bosses of a machine were a subset of ward or precinct leaders whose job it was to make sure voters in their district supported machine candidates. Supporters of the machine who got jobs or contracts were expected to kick in a set percentage of their salary or government award to the machine. This was all hugely lucrative, and concentrated an enormous amount of wealth and power into relatively few people's hands. Machines operated on a well-regulated continual cycle (hence the term machine)—votes in one end, power and patronage out the other.[12] They operated so well and for so long for the simple reason that they could effectively trade government jobs and contracts for votes. Unsurprisingly, many machines were rife with corruption. Because the machine ultimately decided whether they had jobs, elected and appointed public officials had a strong incentive to serve the interests of the machine rather than those of the public.

Merit Systems

In the latter half of the nineteenth century there were increasing pressures to reform or replace patronage as the basis of the public-sector personnel system. The first success reformers scored was an 1853 amendment to an appropriations bill requiring competency exams for clerical positions in the federal government. But the law was often circumvented or ignored—the spoils system was too entrenched and provided lucrative benefits to too many people for fundamental reform to occur without some pressing and dramatic reason.

That reason came in 1881, when President James A. Garfield was assassinated by Charles Guiteau, a disgruntled and unsuccessful seeker of a patronage appointment (see Sidebar 9.1). The national shock and alarm created by the gunning down of a president galvanized Congress into pursuing serious reform, and in 1883 they passed "A Bill to Regulate and Improve the Civil Service of the United States," better known as the **Pendleton Act** (named for Senator George A. Pendleton). The Pendleton Act heralded the beginning of the **merit system**.

The main features of the merit system established by the Pendleton Act were these:

1. Competitive examination requirements for federal jobs.

2. Security from political dismissals—people could not be fired simply because they belonged to the "wrong" party or supported the "wrong" candidate.

3. Protection from being coerced into political activities— workers were no longer expected or required to contribute a portion of their salary to a political party or candidate.[13]

The basic principles of the merit system have since been expanded to include equal pay for equal work; recruitment, hiring, and promotion without regard to race, creed, national origin, religion, marital status, age, or handicap; and protection against reprisal for lawful disclosure of lawbreaking, mismanagement, abuse of authority, or practices that endanger public health (so-called "whistle blower" laws).

Most states and many localities followed the federal government and adopted merit-based civil service systems of their own. Today the vast majority of states and most large municipalities have personnel systems characterized by the basic merit principles first laid down in the Pendleton Act.[14] Merit systems gradually replaced spoils systems because they offered a reasonable cure to the worst of patronage excesses. Under merit systems, the basis for hiring, evaluation, promo-

The assassination of President James Garfield by Charles Guiteau, who was enraged at being denied a patronage job, galvanized the Congress into reforming the rules and expectations of federal employment. Thus began the modern Civil Service, with its core expectation that government workers would be hired and promoted on the basis of qualifications and competence rather than on the basis of a favor from a powerful political patron.

tion, and dismissal is some reasonably objective determination of merit. This stands in stark contrast to the spoils system, where partisan loyalty played a determinative role in all of these considerations. As a result, merit systems tend to be less susceptible to corruption and political abuse than spoils systems. They also tend to have less turnover, and as competence and qualification are (at least in theory) paramount, merit systems promote a more effective bureaucracy.

While offering some clear advantages over the spoils system, the merit approach to managing people is not without its drawbacks. For example, merit systems provide less flexibility for managers in public agencies. Because of civil service protections against unfair dismissal, it can be harder to get rid of employees who are not performing well. As managers must go through a lengthy and sometimes tedious screening procedure to fill open positions, public agencies are often at a recruiting disadvantage compared to private companies. Merit systems can become very rule-bound and bureaucratically cumbersome, making it more difficult for managers to handle personnel issues efficiently. As we shall see, in contrast to the nineteenth and twentieth centuries, the key personnel system reforms of the twenty-first century are shaping up to be movements away from rather than toward merit systems.

Sidebar 9.1 The Unintentional Reformer

When President James Garfield moved into the White House in 1880 he found hundreds of office-seekers waiting for him, people circling for patronage jobs "like vultures for a wounded bison." Like his predecessors before him, Garfield quickly learned that one of the drawbacks of winning the presidency was dealing with the hundreds of party hangers-on who wanted their partisan loyalty rewarded with cushy federal jobs.

The spoils system approach to filling the ranks of the federal service produced more than an irritant for presidents who had to deal with the deluge of job seekers. Federal agencies were plagued by high turnover, incompetence, and outright corruption. New technologies meant new skills were required, even for fairly mundane jobs. The introduction of the typewriter, for example, meant literacy and decent handwriting were not enough for a humble clerk's position. The spoils system, however, paid little attention to the practical skills a job required—it was all about who you knew and what you did for them.

Though many agreed that the federal civil service was in dire need of change, no one had the combination of political will and political power to force through meaningful reform. That is, until Charles J. Guiteau. Guiteau was an unlikely candidate to precipitate the most significant shakeup of the civil service in the nation's history. He was, by all accounts, a failure at most things in life. He was an unsuccessful attorney, newspaper publisher, and evangelist. He almost certainly was insane.

His erratic interests settled on politics in 1880, and after a brief flirtation with the Stalwart wing of the Republican Party (who wanted Ulysses S. Grant to serve a third term as president), he decided to support Garfield. This support mainly took the form of making speeches in the New York streets to whoever would listen.

After Garfield was elected, Guiteau relocated to Washington, D.C., and sought a patronage appointment, sending numerous letters to Secretary of State James G. Blaine requesting a consular appointment. Blaine ignored these entreaties. Enraged, on July 2, 1881 Guiteau went to the Baltimore and Potomac Railroad Station, where Garfield was about to leave for a vacation in Baltimore. He shot Garfield twice, once in the arm and once in the back. Garfield died two months later.

The killing of a president by a disgruntled job seeker provided the critical momentum for reform of the civil service. In 1883 the Pendleton Act was passed, establishing merit principles as the personnel management foundation of the federal government. Guiteau, the psychologically unbalanced seeker of a patronage job, thus bequeathed the country a most ironic legacy. Though he hoped to take advantage of the spoils system, his actions provided the reason to end it.

Sources: Georgetown University Libraries. *Charles Guiteau Collection: Collection Description.* http://www.library.georgetown.edu/dept/speccoll/cl133.htm.

U.S. Department of State, Bureau of International Information Programs. "Backgrounder on the Pendleton Act." http://usinfo.state.gov/usa/infousa/facts/democrac/28.htm.

Merit and Politics

Though the vast majority of public employees at all levels of government are now covered by a civil service system based on merit principles, merit never fully replaced the political approach and its variants, such as the spoils system. Most elected executives, whether the president, a governor, or a mayor, still fill a wide range of offices with appointments. Generally, such appointments are thought to be a reasonable prerogative of office because they help the chief executive exert authority over the bureaucratic agencies he or she technically leads. As such appointees typically serve at the pleasure of the executive—in other words, they have no civil service protections and can be fired more or less at will—they also help make bureaucracy responsive to elected officials. Agency heads who "go native," who become advocates for their agencies rather than agents of the executive's policy agenda, risk losing their jobs.

In addition to appointments, the United States more than any other industrialized democracy relies on elections to fill bureaucratic positions. This is less the case at the federal level, where virtually all major agency heads are appointed by the president and confirmed by the U.S. Senate. At the state and local level, however, there are a broad variety of bureaucratic offices that are elected, everything from state attorney generals to county sheriffs. For many of these, the only real requirement to hold office is a successful political campaign. So though most public employees are governed by a merit-based personnel system, this is far from universal. The political approach to personnel management is also entrenched in the public bureaucracy at all levels of government.

Recruiting, Selecting, and Hiring

The first and most basic challenge of any personnel system is finding and hiring people. In the political approach to managing people, recruiting and selecting is fairly straightforward. If a position is elected, for example, job candidates are usually self-nominated (they run for office) and selected by the ballot. The job is a little tougher for executives making appointments because of the need to balance political concerns (reward for partisan loyalty or recognition of a particular constituency) with the desire to get competent administrators who can lead a particular agency or bureaucratic unit in the direction desired. At least under the political approach there is a clear notion of who is *not* wanted—those who supported the other side in the last election.

Recruiting under merit-based personnel systems is harder both because of efficiency concerns and because the objectivity at the heart of the merit approach has to compete with broader goals placed upon the public sector. The efficiency concerns spring from competing goals in recruitment: the desire to get the best people, and the desire to keep recruiting costs down.[15] For some public bureaucracies (the military, for example), expensive recruiting campaigns are all but unavoidable. In order to get enough qualified people, the military uses highly professional ad campaigns and runs dedicated recruiting offices all over the country. For most bureaucracies the costs of such an approach are prohibitive.

The objectivity at the heart of the merit system means the primary recruiting goal is finding people that are qualified for the job on the basis of their skills, knowledge, experience, and qualifications. Yet public-sector agencies are also charged with recruiting a diverse set of job applicants, required to favor some groups over others (veterans, for example), and bound by a fairly stringent set of laws regulating dis-

U.S. State Department.

Colin Powell is a good example of someone who succeeded in the bureaucracy on the basis of competence and merit. A career army officer, Powell was an excellent junior combat commander (serving two tours in Vietnam), and was promoted to increasingly important leadership posts. He eventually rose to be the Commander of the Joint Chiefs of Staff, and after leaving the army was selected by President George W. Bush to serve as Secretary of State.

crimination in hiring. All these factors are hard to balance, and make it virtually impossible to make recruiting, selecting, and hiring in the public sector 100 percent neutral and objective.

Recruiting Approaches

Generally speaking, public agencies invest considerable effort in reaching out to people and trying to inform them of job opportunities. This effort is not particularly coordinated, however, and takes many forms. Perhaps the simplest, most direct, and most common recruiting tool is the public announcement. Public announcements are simply brief descriptions of employment opportunities (usually including position qualifications and salary range) that are posted in some public forum. This can be as simple as pinning a notice to a bulletin board, though it typically also includes ads in newspapers or periodicals and online announcements. Many public agencies make use of their own websites to get the word out about job opportunities. There are also a number of websites devoted to being more centralized portals to government employment. The United States Office of Personnel Management, for example, runs a site called USAJOBS (http://www.usajobs.opm.gov/) that offers a fairly easy way to search thousands of job opportunities in the federal government. A related website (http://www.studentjobs.gov/) is aimed specifically at people in high school or college, and lets users build a personal job-search profile to match their interests and qualifications for job openings in the federal government. Govtjobs.com (http://www.govtjobs.com/) performs a similar service to USAJOBS for city, county, and state governments. This site charges governments a small fee to post public-sector job announcements in its data base, which can be searched for free.

Public agencies do not rely solely on public announcements. Other common recruiting techniques are job fairs. Such events are not uncommon on college campuses and offer public agencies an obvious way to connect with a highly educated labor pool. Dropping down from college to high school, public agencies also commonly send brochures to high-school counselors, essentially using counselors to make the potential labor pool aware of the careers and job opportunities in the public sector. Some public agencies also make use of in-person recruiters who meet face to face with citizens to persuade them to take public-sector jobs (e.g., permanent, staffed recruiting stations run by the military). Government agencies also recruit through contacts with professional organizations and ads in related publications.

One of the more effective ways to recruit college students is through internships. All levels of government offer a wide range of internship opportunities that allow students to work for a public agency for a limited period, usually a summer or a semester. Internships may be paid positions, and in some cases they may also count for college credit. They can offer valuable work experience and provide a relatively low-risk way for individuals to "test drive" a public-sector career. Internships are not all go-fer positions. Some internship programs offer entree to reasonably well-paid positions of considerable responsibility. Perhaps the best known of these is the Presidential Management Fellows (PMF) Program. PMF is a highly competitive program for graduate students that aims to recruit highly educated white-collar workers into management positions within federal agencies (see Sidebar 9.2). It has been highly successful; since its inception in the late 1970s, more than 6,000 PMF interns have been hired by cabinet departments and more than 50 federal agencies.[16]

Regardless of the particular method, recruiting poses a number of challenges for the public sector. Most important is the fact that government competes directly with the private sector for the same labor pool.

Government has a number of advantages in this competition. For example, public-sector employment generally offers more job security than the private sector. Yet government also has a number of disadvantages. Generally speaking, the pay for public-sector jobs is less than comparable private-sector jobs. Public agencies also have to fight the image of bureaucracy in recruiting. Government workers are often stereotyped as engaged in trivial tasks and pointless paper shuffling.[17] This is hardly an image that helps attract qualified and motivated peo-

---

Sidebar 9.2 The Presidential Management Fellows Program

Running the nation's public programs and policies creates a constant demand for talented people with a highly diverse set of skills and qualifications. Where does the government find them? And once it finds them, how does it persuade these people—who may have more lucrative opportunities in the private sector—to choose a career in the federal civil service?

The Presidential Management Fellows (PMF) Program is one of the federal government's responses to such questions. PMF is one of the most successful recruitment programs of the past quarter century—since its inception in 1977, more than 6,000 PMF interns have gone on to permanent jobs in more than 50 federal agencies and departments. The idea behind the PMF is to find talented people from a variety of social, academic and cultural backgrounds, and groom them for upper-management responsibilities in the federal government.

PMF pursues this goal by offering two-year postgraduate internships to those completing master's or Ph.D. degrees from accredited universities. The internships have a strong focus on career development, and typically include management and field rotations in a number of agency operations, plus seminars, briefings, conferences, and a strong dose of on-the-job training. During the first year, interns are appointed to a GS-9 level (i.e., a minimum starting salary of approximately $35,500). After successfully completing the first year, they are eligible for promotion to GS-11 with a salary range of approximately $50,000 to $65,000. After successfully completing the second year, PMF fellows are eligible for a promotion to GS-12—with a salary of up to $75,000—and a full-time position in the civil service. In short, the PMF is a good way to get a fast start to a career in the upper-management levels of the public service.

Many federal agencies participate in the PMF program, and they have a good deal of leeway in who they pick from the available pool of PMF fellows. Getting one of these slots is highly competitive. Individuals must be nominated by their schools (who are typically limited to two nominations per year), submit a package of application materials, and go through a screening process that includes an in-person interview with interested agencies. The competition to secure one of the limited nominations can be fierce, something that works to the recruiting advantage of the federal government.

More information on the PMF program, including eligibility and application rules, can be found online at http://www.pmf.opm.gov/.

ple to pursue a career in the public sector. The government tends to face its toughest recruiting challenge in attracting high-end administrative talent, as well as professional and technical personnel whose skills are in high demand in the public sector. The lure of higher paychecks and the comparatively higher levels of prestige and glamor associated with the private sector often outweigh the higher levels of job security and professional anonymity that tend to accompany a white-collar career in the public sector.

Public-sector recruiting is sometimes criticized for being too insular. Virtually all public agencies have internal publications or newsletters that advertise job openings, and public employees can informally know about upcoming openings long before they are publicly posted. This can be seen as giving those inside the agency a built-in advantage that violates the spirit, if not the letter, of the merit system. This problem is particularly acute for mid-career openings where "hooks"—friends higher up the chain of command—can provide inside information not just about an opening, but about what characteristics are being particularly sought for the position.

Selection and Hiring

Generally speaking, merit-based personnel systems select and hire on the basis of a competitive examination of the education, experience, professional qualifications, and background of job applicants. Usually job applicants are required to fill out a standardized form that requests this information, and these and any accompanying materials are screened either by a formal or informal search committee, a human-resources department, or an individual manager who makes the hiring decision (see Figure 9.1). It is common for job applicants to be ranked using a standardized scoring system, with points awarded for qualifications and experience relevant to the position that needs to be filled.

Certain positions may also require applicants to take a **civil service exam**, a written test designed to gauge job-related skills and aptitude. Federal government positions that may require a civil service exam include everything from park rangers to building managers, and states and localities may also impose exam requirements for a wide range of occupations. Competitive exams have long been considered a key element of public-sector hiring because they are seen as a way to objectively determine merit. No one, for example, wants to hire a secretary who cannot read or write English, the primary language of government, and a written test is one way to judge an individual's vocabulary and grammar skills. Standardized exams, however, have become a controversial way to select who is given priority in government hiring. A number of studies suggest that standardized tests are relatively poor predictors of job skills or performance, and may be racially or culturally biased.[18] If this is the case, written exams lose their justification in

Figure 9.1   Optional Application for Federal Employment

Form Approved
OMB No. 3206-0219

OPTIONAL APPLICATION FOR FEDERAL EMPLOYMENT - OF 612

You may apply for most jobs with a resume, this form, or other written format. If your resume or application does not provide all the information requested on this form and in the job vacancy announcement, you may lose consideration for a job.

1 Job title in announcement	2 Grade(s) applying for	3 Announcement number

4 Last name	First and middle names	5 Social Security Number

6 Mailing address	7 Phone numbers (include area code)
	Daytime ( )
City State ZIP Code	Evening ( )

WORK EXPERIENCE
8 Describe your paid and nonpaid work experience related to the job for which you are applying. Do **not** attach job descriptions.

1) Job title (if Federal, include series and grade)

From (MM/YY)	To (MM/YY)	Salary $	per	Hours per week

Employer's name and address	Supervisor's name and phone number
	( )

Describe your duties and accomplishments

2) Job title (if Federal, include series and grade)

From (MM/YY)	To (MM/YY)	Salary $	per	Hours per week

Employer's name and address	Supervisor's name and phone number
	( )

Describe your duties and accomplishments

GENERAL INFORMATION

Optional Form 612 (September 1994) (EG)
U.S. Office of Personnel Management

You may apply for most Federal jobs with a resume, the attached *Optional Application for Federal Employment* or other written format. If your resume or application does not provide all the information requested on this form and in the job vacancy announcement, you may lose consideration for a job. Type or print clearly in dark ink. Help speed the selection process by keeping your application brief and sending only the requested information. If essential to attach additional pages, include your name and Social Security Number on each page

■ For information on Federal employment, including job lists, alternative formats for persons with disabilities, and veterans' preference, call the U.S. Office of Personnel Management at **912-757-3000, TDD 912-744-2299,** by computer modem **912-757-3100,** or via the Internet at **http://www.usajobs.opm.gov.**
■ If you served on active duty in the United States Military and were separated under honorable conditions, you may be eligible for veterans' preference. To receive preference if your service began after October 15, 1976, you must have a Campaign Badge, Expeditionary Medal, or a service-connected disability. Veterans' preference is not a factor for Senior Executive Service jobs or when competition is limited to status candidates (current or former career or career-conditional Federal employees)
   Most Federal jobs require United States citizenship and also that males over age 18 born after December 31, 1959, have registered with the Selective Service System or have an exemption.
■ The law prohibits public officials from appointing, promoting, or recommending their relatives.
   Federal annuitants (military and civilian) may have their salaries or annuities reduced. All employees must pay any valid delinquent debts or the agency may garnish their salary.
■ Send your application to the office announcing the vacancy. If you have questions, contact that office.

■

THE FEDERAL GOVERNMENT IS AN EQUAL OPPORTUNITY EMPLOYER

Designed using Adobe Acrobat. USOPM. April 1998

Figure 9.1 (continued)

PRIVACY ACT AND PUBLIC BURDEN STATEMENTS

■ The Office of Personnel Management and other Federal agencies rate applicants for Federal jobs under the authority of sections 1104, 1302, 3301, 3304, 3320, 3361, 3393, and 3394 of title 5 of the United States Code. We need the information requested in this form and in the associated vacancy announcements to evaluate your qualifications. Other laws require us to ask about citizenship, military service, etc.

■ We request your Social Security Number (SSN) under the authority of Executive Order 9397 in order to keep your records straight; other people may have the same name. As allowed by law or Presidential directive, we use your SSN to seek information about you from employers, schools, banks, and others who know you. Your SSN may also be used in studies and computer matching with other Government files, for example, files on unpaid student loans.

■ If you do not give us your SSN or any other information requested, we cannot process your application, which is the first step in getting a job. Also, incomplete addresses and ZIP Codes will slow processing.

■ We may give information from your records to: training facilities, organizations deciding claims for retirement, insurance, unemployment or health benefits; officials in litigation or administrative proceedings where the Government is a party; law enforcement agencies concerning violations of law or regulation; Federal agencies for statistical reports and studies; officials of labor organizations recognized by law in connection with representing employees; Federal agencies or other sources requesting information for Federal agencies in connection with hiring or retaining, security clearances, security or suitability investigations, classifying jobs, contracting, or issuing licenses, grants, or other benefits; public and private organizations including news media that grant or publicize employee recognition

and awards; and the Merit Systems Protection Board, the Office of Special Counsel, the Equal Employment Opportunity Commission, the Federal Labor Relations Authority, the National Archives, the Federal Acquisition Institute, and congressional offices in connection with their official functions.

■ We may also give information from your records to: prospective nonfederal employers concerning tenure of employment, civil service status, length of service, and date and nature of action for separation as shown on personnel action forms of specifically identified individuals; requesting organizations or individuals concerning the home address and other relevant information on those who might have contracted an illness or been exposed to a health hazard; authorized Federal and nonfederal agencies for use in computer matching; spouses or dependent children asking whether the employee has changed from self-and-family to self-only health benefits enrollment; individuals working on a contract, service, grant, cooperative agreement or job for the Federal Government; non-agency members of an agency's performance or other panel; and agency-appointed representatives of employees concerning information issued to the employee about fitness-for-duty or agency-filed disability retirement procedures.

■ We estimate the public reporting burden for this collection will vary from 20 to 240 minutes with an average of 40 minutes per response, including time for reviewing instructions, searching existing data sources, gathering data, and completing and reviewing the information. You may send comments regarding the burden estimate or any other aspect of the collection of information, including suggestions for reducing this burden, to U.S. Office of Personnel Management, Reports and Forms Management Officer, Washington, DC 20415-0001.

■ Send your application to the agency announcing the vacancy.

9 May we contact your current supervisor?

YES [ ]   NO [ ]▶ If we need to contact your current supervisor before making an offer, we will contact you first.

EDUCATION

10 Mark highest level completed.   Some HS [ ]   HS/GED [ ]   Associate [ ]   Bachelor [ ]   Master [ ]   Doctoral [ ]

11 Last high school (HS) or GED school. Give the school's name, city, State, ZIP Code (if known), and year diploma or GED received.

12 Colleges and universities attended. Do **not** attach a copy of your transcript unless requested.

Name		Total Credits Earned		Major(s)	Degree - Year
City	State ZIP Code	Semester	Quarter		(if any) Received
1)					
2)					
3)					

OTHER QUALIFICATIONS

13 **Job-related** training courses (give title and year). **Job-related** skills (other languages, computer software/hardware, tools, machinery, typing speed, etc. **Job-related** certificates and licenses (current only). **Job-related** honors, awards, and special accomplishments (publications, memberships in professional/honor societies, leadership activities, public speaking, and performance awards.) Give dates, but do not send documents unless requested.

GENERAL

14 Are you a U.S. citizen?   YES [ ]   NO [ ]▶ Give the country of your citizenship. _____

15 Do you claim veterans' preference? NO [ ]   YES [ ]▶ Mark your claim of 5 or 10 points below
   5 points [ ]▶ Attach your DD 214 or other proof.   **10 points** [ ]▶Attach an *Application for 10-Point Veterans' Preference* (SF 15) and proof required

16 Were you ever a Federal civilian employee?

		Series	Grade	From (MM/YY)	To (MM/YY)

NO [ ]   YES [ ]▶ For highest civilian grade give

17 Are you eligible for reinstatement based on career or career-conditional Federal status?

NO [ ]   YES [ ]▶ If requested, attach SF 50 proof

APPLICANT CERTIFICATION

18 I certify that, to the best of my knowledge and belief, all of the information on and attached to this application is true, correct, complete and made in good faith. I understand that false or fraudulent information on or attached to this application may be grounds for not hiring me or for firing me after I begin work, and may be punishable by fine or imprisonment. I understand that any information I give may be investigated.

SIGNATURE   DATE SIGNED

merit systems because they institutionalize rather than minimize favoritism. In response to such concerns, the federal government has moved away from making written exams a mandatory part of the selection process and others, to varying degrees, have followed suit. No mandatory written test is necessary in more than 80 percent of federal jobs.[19]

Whether or not a written test is part of the application, the initial screening process is usually aimed at narrowing the list of qualified candidates rather than actually making a hire. What typically comes out of the initial screening process is a list of those eligible and qualified for the position, and from this a subset of candidates is picked for job interviews. Most public agencies follow the "rule of three," meaning that at least three people are interviewed from the list of eligible candidates. However, this is often more a rough guideline than a hard and fast rule. If only two people apply for the job, for example, it makes it hard to interview three.

Interviews are perhaps the most subjective part of the selection process in merit-based personnel systems. Here things like personal appearance and "chemistry" between potential employee and supervisor become important. These are not necessarily good indicators of job performance. Accordingly, when people are hired at public agencies they typically must serve a **probationary period**. This is essentially a full-blown tryout, when a supervisor can observe and evaluate someone in the position that needs to be filled. Though working and receiving a paycheck, public employees serving through probationary periods are not fully covered by civil service protections. If their performance is for some reason deemed unsatisfactory, or even if they are deemed to be just not "fitting in," they can be fired. Probationary periods may also involve a training requirement. For example, someone hired to do bookkeeping may be required to successfully complete a workshop or course on the accounting software used by the agency. Failure to satisfactorily complete this training may be considered evidence of unsatisfactory performance.

While public employees can often be fired without cause during a set probationary period, once past this they often have a higher degree of job security than their private-sector counterparts. A cornerstone of the merit system is the notion that government employees are hired or fired on the basis of their abilities, knowledge, skills, and performance, not on the basis of their partisan loyalties or the political agendas of their superiors. Accordingly, public agencies with merit-based personnel systems are generally required to demonstrate a clear reason for firing an individual (documented poor performance, budget constraints, etc.) and employees are granted a measure of due process—a means to appeal their dismissal and make the case for their retention. This helps prevent public employees becoming the agents of partisanship, though it also makes public personnel systems much less flexible than in the private sector, where employees can be fired (and hired) with little more justification than the preferences of the boss.

Special Considerations in Hiring and Selection

Though merit systems promote the notion of recruiting, hiring, retaining, and promoting employees on the basis of performance, skills and abilities, they are not fully objective. **Equal opportunity laws** prevent public agencies from discriminating in their hiring practices on the basis of race, gender, religion, age, disability, or national origin. These laws trace their roots to the 1960s (particularly the Civil Rights Act of 1964) and have been subsequently expanded by laws such as the 1972 Equal Opportunity Act and the Americans with Disabilities Act. For public-sector recruiting and hiring, the combined force of these equal opportunity laws boils down to this: if you are qualified and capable, you are entitled to an even playing field when you compete for a government job.

Yet there are exceptions to equal opportunity. In some cases, favoritism for some groups is not only tolerated, but written into laws and personnel policies. Veterans, for example, are given preference for a wide variety of federal, and many state and local, jobs. This preference is often put into practice by giving veterans a certain set of points on a scoring scale used to rank job applicants (the actual number of points depends on the scale and the nature of military service). Military dependents, the spouses and children of those serving on active duty, are also given preference for some civil service vacancies. Public agencies may also give preference to former employees who lost their jobs for nonperformance reasons (budget cuts, for example) who are seeking another position.

Favoritism for veterans and those who lose their agency positions through no fault of their own are relatively noncontroversial forms of hiring bias. Most citizens accept that those who have put themselves at risk through military service—especially those who have been disabled as a result—are owed a little extra consideration. More controversial is **affirmative action**, hiring preferences given to disadvantaged groups such as women and ethnic minorities. There are a number of arguments in favor of affirmative action, including redressing historical patterns of discrimination and increasing opportunities for groups who do not have the same social, economic, and educational opportunities as more advantaged populations. A demographically balanced public sector is also considered a worthy goal because in democratic societies public agencies are held to be more effective if they reflect the diversity of the communities they serve.[20]

Affirmative action traces its roots back to the same laws that cover equal opportunity policies. The term itself comes from Executive Order 11246, signed by President Lyndon Johnson in 1965, which required federal contractors to "take affirmative action to ensure that applicants are employed, and that employees are treated during employment, without regard to their race, creed, color, or national origin." This language strongly implies that affirmative action is to be proactive, an approach that separates affirmative action from equal opportunity policies. The basic difference between the two is that equal opportunity policies are passive—they govern what personnel systems *cannot* do. Affirmative action policies are active—they govern what personnel systems are required or strongly encouraged to do.

Supporters of affirmative action argue it is necessary because the passive approach to eliminating discrimination in hiring does not fully extend opportunities to historically disadvantaged groups. Critics of affirmative action see these policies as discriminatory and undermining the core principles of the merit system. As one public personnel management text puts it, ". . . some qualified white males respond angrily or allege reverse discrimination when they discover that a job for which they applied was awarded to a female or a Native American because the agency allocated 'affirmative action points' to applicant rankings."[21] Affirmative action may also promote the stigma of tokenism, even for employees who are hired and promoted purely on the basis of merit.

Opponents have made considerable headway in rolling back affirmative-action policies during the past decade or so. One of their most notable successes was the passage of Proposition 209, which banned the use of affirmative action in California state government. Affirmative action, however, is a long way from being eliminated, and continues to be seen by many as critically important to government agencies serving a multiracial society. Most large public institutions—including universities and virtually all federal agencies—continue to include some form of affirmative action in their recruiting and hiring policies.

Compensation, Evaluation, and Promotion

The public sector faces a difficult balancing act in setting salaries for its employees. On the one hand, salaries and other forms of compensation have to be high enough to attract good people. On the other hand, they have to be low enough for the taxpayer to afford. It is often the case that public employees believe they get too little compensation for what they do, and taxpayers believe they get too much.

Position Classification and Pay Plans

Salaries in the public sector are usually based on pay plans that are integrated with a position classification scheme. **Position classification** is simply the process of grouping similar sorts of jobs into a particular class or grade. Jobs are usually classified on the basis of position requirements or expectations such as skills, qualifications, supervisory responsibility, scope and effect of job, work environment, and physical demands.[22] Position classification allows public agencies to generate a detailed description of the duties, responsibilities, and requirements of a job. This serves two purposes. First, it allows public agencies to make recruiting more systematic by allowing them to match people with different qualifications and backgrounds to particular jobs. Second, by linking position classification to pay grades, it allows public agencies to fairly compensate their employees. Jobs that have similar requirements are assigned to the same pay grades to ensure that equal work receives equal pay and that employees receive a salary commensurate with their position. Thus the underlying justification for classification plans is to match the duties and responsibilities of a job with an appropriate salary.

A good example of a pay plan based on position classification and pay grades is the federal government's General Schedule (GS) system. This pay plan consists of 15 pay grades, and in each pay grade there are 10 "steps" (see Table 9.1). Moving up a pay grade increases pay, as does moving up a step within a pay grade. The difference between pay grades and pay steps is essentially the difference between merit and seniority. Generally speaking, advancing a grade level means a job promotion, taking on an increased set of responsibilities and duties. Moving up a step is based on seniority—how long an employee has been in the pay grade. Steps reward experience rather than additional expectations or new job responsibilities. For example, employees who pass their probationary period typically move up a step in their pay grade.

The GS schedule is fairly representative of salary systems throughout the public sector, and demonstrates both the advantages and disadvantages of the general approach. The clear advantage of position classification and linked pay schedules is their ability to systematically achieve several important personnel goals: fair pay, equal pay for equal work, and clear guidelines and expectations about who should get paid what. Perhaps the biggest disadvantage is a high degree of complexity and inflexibility. Position classifications can multiply and create headaches for personnel managers who may have to deal with literally hundreds of job classifications and figure out where they belong on the pay scale. For example, the federal government has 22 occupational groups covering 441 white-collar jobs that are linked to the GS.[23] Some of these jobs may reach a "dead end" once they hit step 10 of the GS grade allocated to that particular job. Personnel managers, not to mention employees themselves, get frustrated with pay schedules that lock them into compensation tracks that may not reflect their true worth to the agency. In order to advance their careers and get paid more, individuals may have to get another job classification. All of this, as you

Table 9.1 Salary Table 2005-GS

Incorporating the 2.50% General Schedule Increase

Effective January 2005

Annual Rates by Grade and Step

Grade	Step 1	Step 2	Step 3	Step 4	Step 5	Step 6	Step 7	Step 8	Step 9	Step 10	Within-Grade Amounts
GS-1	$16,016	$16,550	$17,083	$17,613	$18,146	$18,459	$18,984	$19,515	$19,537	$20,036	Varies
GS-2	18,007	18,435	19,031	19,537	19,755	20,336	20,917	21,498	22,079	22,660	Varies
GS-3	19,647	20,302	20,957	21,612	22,267	22,922	23,577	24,232	24,887	25,542	655
GS-4	22,056	22,791	23,526	24,261	24,996	25,731	26,466	27,201	27,936	28,671	735
GS-5	24,677	25,500	26,323	27,146	27,969	28,792	29,615	30,438	31,261	32,084	823
GS-6	27,507	28,424	29,341	30,258	31,175	32,092	33,009	33,926	34,843	35,760	917
GS-7	30,567	31,586	32,605	33,624	34,643	35,662	36,681	37,700	38,719	39,738	1,019
GS-8	33,852	34,980	36,108	37,236	38,364	39,492	40,620	41,748	42,876	44,004	1,128
GS-9	37,390	38,636	39,882	41,128	42,374	43,620	44,866	46,112	47,358	48,604	1,246
GS-10	41,175	42,548	43,921	45,294	46,667	48,040	49,413	50,786	52,159	53,532	1,373
GS-11	45,239	46,747	48,255	49,763	51,271	52,779	54,287	55,795	57,303	58,811	1,508
GS-12	54,221	56,028	57,835	59,642	61,449	63,256	65,063	66,870	68,677	70,484	1,807
GS-13	64,478	66,627	68,776	70,925	73,074	75,223	77,372	79,521	81,670	83,819	2,149
GS-14	76,193	78,733	81,273	83,813	86,353	88,893	91,433	93,973	96,513	99,053	2,540
GS-15	89,625	92,613	95,601	98,589	101,577	104,565	107,553	110,541	113,529	116,517	2,988

Source: Office of Personnel Management. 2005. *Salary Table 2005-GS*. http://www.opm.gov/oca/05tables/html/gs.asp.

might imagine, involves a degree of inefficient and mostly unproductive paper shuffling.

The inflexibility of pay schedules can create other problems. If two people working for the federal government hold the same job and have the same duties and responsibilities, are they really equally paid if one works in New York City and the other in Lincoln, Nebraska? The civil servant working in Lincoln is likely to get a lot more for her paycheck because of the cost of living differential. Is this really fair? Recognizing the drawbacks of rigid pay scales, the federal government has instituted salary adjustments based on geography. This more flexible arrangement may result in a fairer pay system, but it adds yet another layer of complexity to the salary system.

Though public-sector salary schemes must constantly seek to balance the tradeoffs between being too generous and too miserly, between fairness and flexibility and complexity, paychecks are not the only form of compensation received by public employees. Though pay tends to be lower than in the private sector, many public-sector jobs come with attractive **benefit packages** that include health care, pension plans, generous vacation allotments, a greater measure of job security, and various training opportunities. These benefits serve the same basic purpose as a paycheck: to attract qualified people to public-sector jobs. Benefits are an increasingly important component of compensation in the public sector, and can account for up to 40 percent of the total value of a compensation package.[24]

Pay increases in the public sector are usually based on seniority or merit. **Seniority** simply means time in service. Wage increases are often based on seniority. **Merit pay** rewards performance rather than time on the job. Both approaches have advantages and disadvantages. The advantage of seniority is that it is objective, promotes equity, and requires little in the way of evaluation. Salary increases simply come at specific time points. The big disadvantage of seniority is that basing pay on how long an employee holds a job tends to focus comparatively less attention to how well he or she does that job. Merit pay bases salary increases on job performance rather than job experience, and by doing so reverses the advantages and disadvantages of the seniority system. The big advantage to merit pay is the incentive it creates to do a job well. Its key disadvantages are the potentially subjective nature of how performance is determined and the salary inequities it can create among people with the same job responsibilities and duties. This last issue is a particular concern in the public sector where the money available for pay increases may be relatively small.

As an example, consider an academic department in a public university that uses a merit system to determine annual salary increases. This department is given a pool of money every year that reflects the overall pay increase approved by the university's governing body. So, if the combined salaries of all the faculty in this department total

$500,000, a pay increase of 3 percent means the department has $15,000 to distribute in pay increases. If the department uses a merit-pay system, the portion of the $15,000 received by each faculty member will be determined by a performance evaluation. Typically this means an annual evaluation of each faculty member that takes into consideration things such as teaching evaluations, scholarly publications, and university service. A scoring system is attached to this evaluation to allow faculty to be ranked on the basis of performance, and this score is used to determine what percentage of the merit-pay pool is assigned to each faculty member.

The problem here is that those in the bottom half of the performance evaluation may end up with a very small salary increase, or even no increase at all. Accounting for inflation, this means some will actually get *less* money. This can create resentment, especially if performance scores fall into a relatively narrow range. In effect, it means those who are doing a pretty good job can get punished rather than rewarded. This can skew job incentives. For example, faculty members may be tempted to inflate grades in an attempt to increase student teaching evaluations. They may also simply give up on trying to be better teachers or scholars—why bother to be a good professor if you are in a good department where even average performance requires a lot of effort for little to no reward?

These sorts of problems often lead to using a mix of seniority and merit to determine pay increases. For example, our hypothetical university department may split its salary pool, using half to give everyone a 1.5 percent salary increase and distributing the other half on the basis of a performance evaluation. The big drawback to this approach is that merit increases—even for those with top performance scores—can end up being quite small. Such modest rewards may not provide the incentive to higher job performance that merit-pay systems promise.

Performance Evaluations

Performance evaluations are not exclusive to merit-pay systems; virtually all public employees undergo periodic job reviews. These evaluations serve several purposes beyond deciding pay increases. A performance evaluation is often used at the end of a probationary period to assess whether an employee should be retained. Evaluations are also used to determine who deserves promotion or extra job responsibilities. They are used to determine which employees should be laid off either because of poor job performance, agency downsizing, or budget reductions. Similarly, they are used to document and justify disciplinary actions. Finally, performance evaluations are used as a way to help employees do their jobs better. A regular assessment of the strengths and weaknesses of each employee allows managers and their subordinates to identify ways to improve their job performance.[25]

There are numerous evaluation approaches and methods, but all are based on a common assumption—that the evaluator understands the job of the evaluated. A manager not only needs an understanding of a subordinate's duties and responsibilities, but a clear idea of the challenges of a particular work environment. At the heart of most evaluations is an assessment of job performance performed by a supervisor. If that supervisor does not have a thorough "eye-level" understanding of what the subordinate's job requires and entails, he or she has no real basis to make informed judgments about performance.

Regardless of the particular approach, most job evaluations explore at least one of three employee characteristics:

1. Individual traits (e.g., work ethic, initiative).

2. Behavior (e.g., putting in overtime without being asked).

3. Results.

As an assessment of the worth or performance of an employee, each of these characteristics has pros and cons. Basing an evaluation on traits assumes there is a connection between these and results, an assumption that is not always correct. Someone who has an excellent work ethic, for example, may have no aptitude for their assigned tasks and have difficulty completing them. Using behavior as the basis of an evaluation uses a similar set of assumptions between what is observed and results. For example, someone who always shows up for work on time and is willing to work extra hours without being paid is assumed to be a valuable employee and an asset to the organization. Yet the most punctual and dedicated employees do not necessarily complete their assigned tasks satisfactorily.

Though using results as the basis to judge job performance is perhaps the most intuitive and obvious approach to evaluating job performance, in the public sector it can also be the most difficult. For one thing, the services produced by many public employees can be maddeningly difficult to measure, making it hard to assess results. What are the results of, say, a librarian's job? For another, most public employees contribute collectively rather than individually to agency goals. Assuming those agency goals can be defined and measured (as seen in Chapter 5, no easy task), how do you assess one individual's contribution to achieving those goals?

Regardless of what particular mix of traits, behavior, and results are emphasized in a job evaluation, they are typically graded using a **rating scale**. Rating scales have anywhere from three to seven levels running from unsatisfactory to exceptional performance. Raters use these scales to record a judgment about performance in a particular area, for example, to indicate whether an employee's punctuality, reliability, and communication skills (among others) are judged by the evaluator to be exceptional, good, average, below average, or unsatisfactory.

There are a number of well-known problems to virtually all methods of job evaluation. Most prominent among these is **rater bias**, the tendency of those doing the evaluation to make subjective or uninformed judgments. In worst-case scenarios, raters may use evaluations to discriminate on the basis of gender, race, or religion, or to punish and reward based on personal likes or dislikes. Rater bias does not have to take the form of explicit discrimination, as it can even be done unconsciously. The central problem here is that humans have a difficult time being totally objective in their evaluations of each other. We all tend to form perceptions of other people, and those perceptions—no matter how strongly we believe them—are not necessarily accurate.

Rater bias takes a number of forms besides outright discrimination. **Central tendency bias** is the process of assigning average ratings to everyone regardless of the actual variation in job performance. For supervisors who are uninformed, rushed, or know little about the subordinates they are evaluating, an average rating can be "safe," even if it is inaccurate. **Halo bias** occurs when a rater is overly influenced by a positive past event rather than evaluating the record relevant to the rating period. A good example of this is a professor who has a student who performs exceptionally well in a class and receives an A-plus. This performance may influence the student's grades if he takes a second and third class from the same professor. In these later courses, the professor may see an A student even if he is doing B-level work.[26] The opposite of halo bias is **horns bias**, which occurs when a rater is overly influenced by a negative past event, and igores subsequent performance, which may have improved dramatically. A final form of bias is what might be termed **Lake Wobegon bias**, after the fictional Minnesota town where all the children are above average. Lake Wobegon bias occurs when evaluators rate everyone highly, and often becomes institutionalized. In some studies, as few as three in 1,000 public agency employees are given unsatisfactory ratings.[27] In schools and universities, grade inflation is the result of Lake Wobegon bias. This suggests that the agencies studied are either extraordinarily competent or lucky in their recruiting and hiring, or that raters are devaluing the evaluation process by giving everyone good grades.

Promotion

Opportunities for promotion can be very limited in the public sector. The basic problem with promotions is that, especially in the higher executive ranks of the civil service, there is little room at the top. If you have a particular job speciality within an agency—attorney, economist, engineer—and your immediate supervisor is competent and relatively young, advancing to a higher position within your job field may require a long wait. The opportunity to move up may not come at all.

Laurence Peter and Raymond Hill provide a famous (and funny) explanation for why many bureaucrats have problems getting promoted: the Peter Principle. The **Peter Principle** states that people in hierarchical organizations rise to the level of their incompetence. At the heart of the Peter Principle is the assumption that if people start off at the bottom of the hierarchy and work hard, get good evaluations, and are good at their jobs, they will be rewarded with promotions. As they move up the hierarchy taking on new responsibilities and duties, more and more demands are made on their skills and talents. At some point, most ambitious bureaucrats end up getting promoted to positions that demand more than their skills and talents can deliver. In short, they get promoted to a job they are not competent to handle, and because they are incompetent, they get stuck and aren't offered further promotions. Tongues firmly in cheek, Peter and Hill argue this also explains why virtually all bureaucracies are ineffective—they are all run by people who are incompetent.[28]

For many talented and ambitious public-sector employees, however, scarce promotion opportunities are no laughing matter. In order to secure promotion opportunities, employees may have to shift job classifications, move between departments within an agency, or jump to another agency altogether. Public-school vice principals, for example, often move to other schools in order to secure jobs as principals. If they want to move up to a superintendent's position they may have to focus their ambitions in other districts. At the federal level career "plateaus" or "ceilings" have long been recognized as a problem for those who have their sights set on moving up the hierarchical ladder. At some point in their careers many federal, state, and local government workers reach a point where the opportunities for promotion, in effect, dry up.[29]

Promotion bottlenecks are exacerbated by other issues public agencies face in filling the ranks of upper management. Diversity concerns and the affirmative-action policies adopted to address them, for example, often play a significant role in promotion decisions. As already discussed, there are good reasons for public agencies to have these concerns and policies, but they can end up promoting not just people but resentment. The real problem with promotions in the public sector, however, is not discrimination. It is simply the fact that there are more qualified and talented people than there are well-paid and professionally rewarding jobs in the upper ranks of agency hierarchies.

The challenges of performance evaluation and promotion in the public sector are almost certainly a main reason why many public-personnel systems are heavily centered on seniority rather than merit. Despite its drawbacks, time in service is easy to objectively measure, and thus easy to reward in terms of pay and promotion.

Unions and the Return of the Spoils System: Personnel Reform

Personnel systems are one of the most common targets of public-sector reform. There are two main reasons why personnel systems attract such attention. First, because most public agencies produce services rather than goods, they tend to be labor intensive. This means much of the investment made in the public sector is an investment in people, and where tax money goes so does a lot of political attention. Second, many continue to see flaws in the merit system variants that are at the heart of the civil service in the United States. Though the merit system has produced a professionalized civil service staffed by qualified and competent people who are, at least for the most part, paid and treated fairly, it can also be seen as rule-bound and inflexible.

A good example of how these two factors can combine, spill into the political arena, and rebound as a wave of new reforms is the history of labor unions in the public sector. Organized labor is a comparatively new phenomenon for the public sector, union activity being primarily restricted to the private sector until the 1960s. President John F. Kennedy changed this by issuing an executive order allowing federal employees to join unions and federal agencies to recognize these unions as the collective bargaining agents for their members. This kicked off a wave of public-sector union activity at all levels of government, and today a public-sector worker is about three times more likely to belong to a union that her private-sector counterpart.[30]

Labor unions have made significant contributions to the lot of public workers. Historically, public workers suffered low pay and had to put up with favoritism even in supposedly merit-based systems, all while performing some of the toughest and most thankless jobs in society. Unions gave public employees a means to address these issues. For example, by giving an organized voice to public employees they attracted the attention of those seeking office—unions raise money, mobilize voters, and even run independent campaigns. All these things tend to translate into political clout. That clout is exercised every time a union collectively bargains for pay increases, job security, or changes in work conditions on behalf of its members.

Yet unions are often seen as an example of the problem with public-personnel systems. Unions that negotiate for pay raises are, in effect, making a claim on the public treasury—the taxpayer's pocket—without ever having to face a ballot box. Unions tend to push for seniority as the basis for promotion, pay increases, and deciding who is fired in tight budgetary times. Unions vigorously seek to protect job tenure and often are effective advocates for those threatened with dismissal. The net result, critics argue, makes it hard for executives to manage their own agencies, and creates a civil service that is simultaneously too involved in and too insulated from politics. Too involved because unions can exercise such electoral and lobbying clout, and too insulated because they have helped grow a protective thicket of rules and regulations that shields their members from justified dismissal or supervisory direction.

What reformers typically want are personnel systems that will give public executives more freedom to hire, fire, and move people from one position to another than existing civil service and position classification allow. In short, they want public-sector personnel systems to be more like private-sector personnel systems. This is exactly what President George Bush wanted in 2002 when he sought broad powers to employ, dismiss, and reassign the more than 170,000 workers in 22 agencies that constituted the newly formed Department of Homeland Security. This kicked off a divisive battle between the Bush administration, which claimed the powers were needed to better protect national interests, and organized labor unions, which saw the move as a thinly disguised attempt at union busting. Eventually, the labor unions and Homeland Security executives collaborated on a personnel policy, though the Bush administration did get the upper hand in the sense that the department legally got the right to write its own personnel rules with minimal input from unions.[31]

What unions and defenders of the merit system fear is that the "freedom" sought by elected executives and the agency heads they appoint will, in effect, reinstitute a spoils system. Rather than an efficient corporate personnel model, personnel systems will revert to championing partisan loyalty and political clout over competence and workers' rights. There is some evidence to support these fears. On May 14, 2001, Governor Jeb Bush (the president's brother) signed into law a radical reform of Florida's civil service called "Service First." Service First eliminates civil service job protections and makes Florida one of just a handful of states that have chosen to eliminate the merit system.

Service First did away with the merit system by doing three things: it eliminated seniority; it reclassified a large number of state employees into a serve at will category, allowing their superiors to hire or fire them at will; and it promised to give public managers the power to determine the salaries and benefits of subordinates through a massive reorganization of job titles, classifications, and their connection to a pay system. Backers of Service First see it as overdue reform of an inflexible system choking on red tape, and the harbinger of a leaner and more nimble approach to personnel management that gives managers the leeway to hire the best people, quickly shift them to the jobs best suited for their talents, and rid public agencies of dead wood and incompetents. The idea is a more rational and business-like personnel approach that is oriented towards results and performance rather than rules and regulations.

Critics of Service First see it as the second coming of a spoils system. Certainly, one of the more interesting aspects of Service First is its exemptions. Several large groups of public employees, ranging from police officers to dieticians, are not covered by the new personnel rules. What these groups have in common are unions that supported Bush's reelection campaign. To critics this looks more like machine politics than smart business practice. Even setting aside the controversy over why some seem to be getting a better deal than others, Service First is seen as having a chilling effect on how public employees do their job. If you serve at the bosses pleasure, the argument goes, it is much harder to do something that will incur a superior's displeasure, even if that something is doing your job. For example, employees of regulatory agencies may be reluctant to take on politically well-connected businesses that are bending or breaking the rules. To do so may mean risking their jobs.[32]

Similar controversies have arisen in Georgia, which in 1996 passed the Merit System Reform Act. Under this law, newly hired employees serve "at will," and the responsibility for recruitment and position classification was decentralized to individual agencies. Backers of the reform see it as making it easier to hire and fire people, aggressively pursue diversity in the civil service ranks, and generally make the personnel system more rational and business like. Its detractors see it as promoting a conservative "managerialist" ideology that tramples workers rights, makes agencies more top down and authoritarian, and produces no appreciable gains in efficiency or performance.[33]

Florida and Georgia are exceptions in terms of how far they have shifted away from the merit systems that have dominated public-sector personnel management for the better part of a century. There is little doubt, however, that at the beginning of the twenty-first century there is a fairly strong movement towards reforming public personnel systems that stress eliminating job protections and giving agency managers the power to determine position classifications, duties and responsibilities, and a freer rein to hire, fire, and reassign personnel. Especially at the state level, there has been a noticeable shift away from centralized personnel systems. The reform movement, however, is being effectively slowed (if not completely halted) in states with strong public-sector labor unions.[34] Public-sector personnel systems are probably going to become more businesslike or more political—the terminology tends to depend on perspective—in the foreseeable future. But a wholesale abandonment of the merit system as the guiding principle of public-sector personnel management is unlikely.

Conclusion

Public programs are mostly service-oriented and create a large demand for qualified employees. As the success of public programs is dependent to a large extent on the people who work in the public sector, attracting competent workers and determining fair job responsibilities, working conditions, compensation, evaluation, and promotion opportunities emerge as some of the core functions of public administration.

There are a number of ways to accomplish these goals. Historically, governments in the United States have relied on a small pool of elites to fill the ranks of the civil service, and have also employed a spoils system where public employees serve at the pleasure of those who are victorious at the ballot box. Both of these approaches have considerable drawbacks. Relying on elites means ignoring a large pool of otherwise qualified workers. The spoils system promotes turnover, puts partisan loyalty above job competence, and invites corruption. Accordingly, the personnel systems of the modern federal, state, and local civil service are for the most part based on merit principles. This means hiring, evaluation, and promotion are based on a reasonably objective assessment of qualifications, skills, experience, and performance.

The development of merit systems, however, has created its own set of problems: inflexibility, complexity, and, with the rise of organized labor in the public sector, a set of powerful political actors who enjoy an unusual measure of insulation from the ballot box. These problems have created a virtually constant cycle of reform proposals, some of which call for all but eliminating the merit system. In a handful of places (such as Georgia and Florida) the merit system has largely been abandoned, and the pros and cons of such moves are fiercely debated. Though there clearly seems to be a trend towards simplifying personnel systems and making them more rational and "businesslike," it seems unlikely that merit-system principles will be broadly abandoned at any time in the foreseeable future. Merit systems undoubtedly have their problems, and all could use improvement, but of the available options they continue to offer the best set of compromises to meet the difficult challenges of managing people in the public sector.

Key Concepts

administration by the aristocracy The process of staffing bureaucracies with political elites.

affirmative action Policies that give hiring preferences to disadvantaged groups such as women and ethnic minorities.

benefit packages Nonsalary job compensation that can include health care, pension schemes, vacation allotments, and promises of job security.

central tendency bias The process of assigning average job evaluation ratings to everyone regardless of the actual variation in job performance.

civil service exam A written test designed to gauge job-related skills and aptitude for employment at a public agency.

equal opportunity laws Laws that prohibit public agencies from discriminating in their hiring practices on the basis of race, gender, religion, age, disability, or national origin.

franchise The right to vote.

halo bias Bias that occurs when a rater is overly influenced by a past positive event rather than evaluating the record relevant to the rating period.

Hatch Act A federal law passed in 1939 that regulates the partisan political activity of government employees.

horns bias Bias that occurs when a rater is overly influenced by a past negative event rather than evaluating the record relevant to the rating period.

Lake Wobegon bias The process of rating most people "above average."

merit pay Salary increases or bonuses based on job performance.

merit system A personnel system that uses evaluations of work to determine promotions and raises, rather than basing rewards on political grounds. A merit system in a government agency will also usually protect workers' rights in most personnel matters (hiring, firing, evaluations, promotions, and raises).

Pendleton Act An 1883 law that established a merit system for the federal government.

Peter Principle States that people in hierarchical organizations are promoted to their level of incompetence.

position classification The process of grouping similar sorts of jobs into a particular class or grade.

probationary period A fixed term when new employees do not receive full civil service job protections.

rater bias The tendency of those doing a job evaluation to make subjective or uninformed judgments.

rating scale An evaluation tool used to record a supervisor's assessment of an employee's performance in a particular area. For example, a supervisor may rate an employee's punctuality, reliability, and communication skills on a scale of good, average, below average, or unsatisfactory.

seniority Time in service. Pay raises in the public sector are often based on seniority.

spoils system An approach to staffing bureaucracies that allows electoral winners to hire and fire government employees as they see fit. A spoils system means government employees get and retain jobs on the basis of partisan loyalty. ✦

Chapter 10

Implementation

There is a quip in most northern states that there are really just two seasons: winter and road construction. This statement is often made as a complaint, and it's actually more directed at the traffic jams resulting from road construction rather than at having to endure months of freezing temperatures. In fact, the Minnesota Department of Transportation states bluntly that it "makes a lot of highway improvements during Minnesota's short summer season" and that drivers in the state should plan ahead to avoid hassles.[1] Chances are no matter where you live you have been delayed or detoured as a result of road construction. However, it's unlikely that you thought about it in terms of public administration, even though that's exactly what it is: implementing a decision to construct or maintain roads.

In fact, policy implementation is so common that we usually don't even stop to think about it—not even when we are literally stopped in our cars waiting to snake our way through a construction zone on the highway. Remember back to Chapter 1, when the typical citizen woke up to a bacon-and-egg breakfast, made a phone call, and listened to the radio during the drive to work. The safe food, the price of the phone call, the smooth roads, the safe car, and the radio station are all monitored by various government agencies. This means there are bureaucrats who are in charge of ensuring the delivery of these services— implementing the decisions to provide them—even if nobody sees those bureaucrats in action.

Even when we do see bureaucrats in action, we often fail to realize that they are implementing public policy. The police officer walking the beat is implementing public safety and criminal codes of your town. Soldiers on peacekeeping missions are carrying out our country's foreign policies. The person processing the renewal of your driver's license is implementing a part of your state's transportation policy.

In this sense, policy implementation is the key to public administration. Traditionally, the bureaucracy has been assumed to exist first and foremost to carry out the policy decisions made in other institutions of government. As you saw in Chapter 2, we need the administrative state in order for our government to function. Legislatures, executives, and courts rely on the bureaucracy for help in carrying out their constitutional duties. After all, decisions made by courts or legislatures are meaningless if they are not fulfilled, enforced, or carried out. Legislatures and courts do not have the capacity (or the constitutional authority) to carry out their decisions themselves. This means that we cannot govern ourselves without some other set of organizations to perform these tasks. The bureaucracy fulfills this need. Of course, as we have shown, the bureaucracy also makes its own policy decisions. These are also implemented by government agencies. This is why public organizations are said to contain all elements of the policy process under one roof, from agenda setting, to policy formation, to policy implementation.

The fact that policy implementation is the central mission of the bureaucracy should not lull you into thinking that bureaucrats always carry out policy exactly as desired by the legislature or court, without any controversy. That common misperception harkens back to Woodrow Wilson's desire that the bureaucracy should be a neutral policy implementer, simply carrying out the wishes of the legislature.[2] In this hierarchical view, policy implementation becomes automatic and simple; the bureaucracy simply does what it is told, and the "real" decisions are made elsewhere.

In fact, it is likely that a given policy will *not* be implemented by the bureaucracy exactly as desired by those who wrote and passed it. This chapter shows why that is the case; suffice it to say here that there are three basic reasons. One is that agencies act to improve policy by applying their expertise to change the policy so that it will work better.[3] Another reason is a set of unavoidable problems, such as legislation that is overly ambitious or that comes with insufficient resources to carry it out. And occasionally there are deliberate acts by groups in society (and even, although comparatively rarely, by the bureaucracy itself) that undermine the policy.

Policy implementation is an important job, and it makes up much of what bureaucrats do on a daily basis. So what is it? **Policy implementation** can be defined as the actions taken by public organizations to ensure that policy decisions are put into effect. It is the art of turning words into action—that is, turning policy decisions on paper into actual goods and services for citizens.

Of course, as this chapter will show, this is a rather simple definition, and so far some rather simple examples have been given. The "actions taken by public organizations" can include making arrangements with private or nonprofit organizations to carry out policy decisions. For example, the Defense Department does not build its own weapons, but implements procurement policies by contracting with private manufacturers. Sometimes, many different organizations and levels of government are involved. Carrying out the No Child Left Behind Act involves the Department of Education, state education departments, local school districts, and each school. Finally, policy implementation is complex because bureaucrats are not neutrally carrying out legislative intent, even if they are technically subordinate to the legislature.[4] Policy decisions made by other institutions are not always clear, sensible, or realistic. Consequently, implementation sometimes diverges from the stated intent of the law. Government agencies also make their policy, often to aid them in carrying out other legislation. Therefore, studying policy implementation is much more than just examining the letter of the law.

Because public bureaucracies are not simply "neutral implementers" of public policy, we should not expect policy implementation to happen automatically. In fact, we should not be surprised to find out that effective policy implementation is often difficult to achieve. Because the stylized vision of implementation offered by Woodrow Wilson does not exist, understanding the implementation process is also difficult. The remainder of this chapter will help clear away some of this confusion about how policies are put into practice. The first part discusses the requirements of effective policy implementation and the second offers reasons why policies are often not implemented successfully or as legislators expect them to be.

Requirements of Effective Policy Implementation

There is often a gap between the expectations of a new policy and what the policy actually achieves upon implementation. Sometimes this is due to unrealistic goals or from expecting too much from new legislation. For example, this performance gap may be due to trying to address problems that are intractable (that is, large and complex). Poverty, crime, and drug use cannot be swept away with a single policy. Large, complex problems require large, complex solutions. These solutions are often difficult to create and use. Other times, the effects of a new policy may not be noticed immediately, even though the general public and elected officials often expect instant results. Public organizations should not necessarily be blamed for "failing" in either of these instances. Instead, it is perhaps more accurate to say that we think government agencies are failing, even though it is our lack of understanding of policy implementation that creates this perception.

What we *should* expect is that public organizations implement policies as best they can. This itself can be difficult because effective policy implementation requires that a set of conditions be met. If these requirements are not met, then the policy may not be as successful as hoped, or it might be a complete failure. Sometimes, failure to meet

them actually makes the situation worse. There are four basic requirements: having a valid causal theory, selecting an appropriate course
of action, securing adequate resources, and effectively coordinating
personnel.

Valid Causal Theory

The first requirement for effective policy implementation is to base
public policy on sound theoretical reasoning. Public policy must have
". . . a **causal theory** of the manner in which its objectives are to be at-
tained."[5] If X causes Y, and we want to implement a new policy that
will produce Y, then that policy should be based on ways to create X. To
be successful, a new policy must be based on the causes of the problem, activity, or situation that is to be addressed (see Sidebar 10.1).

Thankfully, things in society and politics happen for a reason. Once
we determine the reason (the cause) for a problem, activity, or situation, then our policies should be tailored to address that reason. For example, a factory owner does not pollute a nearby river because he
thinks pollution is a good thing. Rather, the factory pollutes as a byproduct of production, and dumping waste in the river is a cheap way
to dispose of it. The underlying causal mechanism here is the straightforward economics of the profit motive: the factory owner is looking
for the way to operate at the lowest possible cost. A policy that seeks to
reduce pollution, therefore, might logically be based on that economic
theory and increase the cost of polluting the river (through a pollution
tax) to make polluting the river more expensive than seeking a new
production method that reduces the amount of pollution.

Economic Causal Theories. Much of government policy operates
on **economic theories**, because they are relatively simple and easy to
understand. Fines, imprisonment, and other sanctions can be used to
eliminate or reduce an activity that is determined to be bad. On the
other hand, transfers of cash through grants and subsidies can be used
to reward an activity that is determined to be good. Fines and imprisonment for breaking the law (whether it is speeding, stealing, or worse)
all exist to increase the cost of that illegal activity, hopefully then making it too expensive to be worth it. Is it worth a $75 speeding ticket to
get to your destination a few minutes earlier? Why steal a $500 televi-
sion if the penalties are far greater? Grants and subsidies work in the
opposite direction: they provide rewards for doing certain things.
Farmers are paid not to produce certain crops that are already in abun-
dance. Local governments get money to create public health programs
or build libraries. You may have received government-backed student
loans, which operate as an incentive to go to college. All causal theories
based on economics are relatively straightforward: people are less
likely to do things that may cost them money, time, or their freedom,
and they are more likely to do things that produce rewards. Of course,

the costs or benefits must be large enough to matter. A $3 ticket won't deter speeders, and a $50 grant to a community for a multimillion-dollar library won't be very helpful. Those problems are relatively easy to sort out, and economic theory thus forms the basis for many public policies.

Information. Another popular causal theory for public policy is based on **information and decision making**. Here, the premise is that people often lack enough information to make sound decisions. We frequently are faced with having to make decisions without as much information as we would like: what professors to take next semester, what jobs are available with a certain degree, how the candidate for office *really* stands on the issues. This can mean that we will make poor choices, or perhaps no choice at all. This is because often, what we don't know *can* hurt us. Those negative consequences can be avoided if people have information about risks. This is why your lawnmower is plastered with labels warning you to make sure the engine is off before putting your hand underneath it to clear a clump of grass: sometimes people just need one last reminder. This is also why there is nutrition

---

Sidebar 10.1 Causal Theory of Cigarette Taxation

Economic theory of price and demand states that as the price of something increases, consumption decreases. This makes sense: people will be unwilling or unable to spend additional money to continue to buy the product. This is the underlying theory of how cigarette taxes are supposed to deter people from smoking. By forcing a price increase by raising the tax rate, the government hopes to dissuade people from purchasing as many cigarettes as they otherwise would.

You might have already come to the conclusion that it is not that simple. You are right: it is not. When the fact that most smokers are addicted to nicotine is considered, tax increases may not create much of an immediate drop in cigarette smoking. So, we have to expect two things: a smaller decrease in smoking (some smokers will not reduce the amount they smoke), and that the decrease will not be instant (because addicts may need time to adjust their behavior).

But it is even more complicated than that. As additional policies to deter smoking, such as smoking bans or public health information, are added, more and more smokers will quit or reduce the amount they smoke; other would-be smokers will be dissuaded from smoking at all. Over time, this leaves a smaller group of smokers who are likely to be the most addicted, those who are unlikely to reduce the amount they smoke unless prices skyrocket. This means that eventually, price increases will have to become much larger in order to continue having the same effect.

Thus, even for policies based on relatively simple economics, identifying the proper causal theory can be more complex than initially thought.

information from the USDA on the side of food packages, why cigarette packages have warning labels, and why the music you buy sometimes has parental advisory stickers. We try to warn people that certain foods are better or worse for you, that smoking leads to a variety of health problems, and that listening to rock music will warp your mind.

The likelihood of successful implementation often turns on whether people pay attention to it. There are several requirements for information policy to work: a clear and consistent message, "catchy" delivery, and credible information. A message that is difficult to understand, or one that seems to equivocate, is less likely to be heeded. Clarity of message is more difficult to achieve than it would initially seem. Sometimes the information to be provided is fairly complicated, which makes it difficult to condense into a brief, clear message. For example, the USDA has revised its "food pyramid" because people did not understand it, and so simply ignored it. However, the new pyramid is at least as confusing, so it is unlikely that the nutrition information it contains will help people make decisions about what to eat. Inconsistent messages are also problematic, which was an issue with the first warning labels on cigarette packs. The wording stated that smoking "may"

Cigarette warning labels were conceived in the mid-1960s as a way to provide smokers with information about the health risks of smoking. Although now well-known, the link between lung cancer and smoking was only recently established when the labels were originally adopted. Ideally, information helps people better appreciate the risks associated with their behavior.

be hazardous, which left smokers wondering if the government really knew what it was talking about.

Efforts to make messages more eye-catching, surprising, or shocking can improve the effectiveness of information policy. Warnings about the potential for injury are usually bright red. Slogans and mascots can be useful to make information more memorable (remember, only *you* can prevent forest fires). Sometimes, information needs to be shocking or disturbing in order to work. Most smokers ignored the original mild warnings on their cigarette packs, so the wording was changed to make them more stern.[6]

Credibility is also required. Antidrug policies based on scare tactics are problematic because kids see through the exaggerations and do not believe the information presented to them.[7] Additionally, many "information" policies actually contain no information at all. This occurs when policy relies too heavily on sloganeering without also providing any substantive information. Messages that are memorable but useless hardly accomplish anything (such as the well-intentioned but hollow "Just Say No to Drugs" campaign). Sometimes information even backfires. Parental advisory stickers on music fail because the music is actually sought out; if someone thinks your mom won't like it, it must be good.

Complex Causal Theories. Often, however, causal theories are not obvious. In fact, there may even be competing theories for why a condition exists. The theories for improving the performance of public schools are hotly contested, and are usually driven by ideology as much as by actual evidence.[8] Some argue that public-school systems suffer because there is no competition to force schools to improve, which is a market-based theory. Others argue that funding is inadequate, which is the theory that "you get what you pay for." Still others argue that declining parental involvement means that families have no stake in the system, which is based on political theories. All of these are plausible by themselves, but it is likely that school performance is a function of all of them combined. Crafting a policy that blends the three has proven to be exceedingly difficult.

Similarly, the causes of poverty are also debated. While both liberals and conservatives want to reduce poverty and its effects on society, the programs each side supports are very much a function of the causal theories they agree with. Liberals argue that people often live in poverty through no fault of their own. Perhaps they have not had the same opportunities as others, or maybe they lost their jobs because the companies they worked for went out of business. Therefore, more liberal welfare policies are more generous. Conservatives, on the other hand, emphasize that poverty can often be avoided through hard work or by improving job skills. Therefore, more conservative welfare policies link benefits to job-hunting and may require recipients to attend job-training sessions. In fact, both sides are partly right. This means that no matter what form welfare policies take, there will never be complete success.

Crime is another problem that involves multiple causal theories. Although many of our criminal justice policies are based on economic theory, not all crime or criminals will be deterred through fines and imprisonment. Crimes that are the result of intense poverty, of political disenchantment or disenfranchisement, or of social problems such as drug and alcohol abuse are unlikely to be deterred by sanctions based on economics. If someone has nothing to lose, then paying some penalty is irrelevant. Or, perhaps an addiction has made it impossible to make calculations of cost and benefit. These situations require other policy solutions.

These examples show that ensuring that a new policy is on solid theoretical footing is not always easy. Situations that can be based on economic theory and information are probably the easiest to deal with. However, many of our most pressing policy issues today are more complex. Terrorism, crime, poverty, and education can hardly be addressed through simple policies that create short-term economic gains or losses for those involved.

Appropriate Course of Action

In order to achieve the intent of a policy, the **appropriate course of action** must be determined. There are many ways that policies can be implemented, as well as a variety of political contexts that can potentially exist. Policy can be implemented by public or private organizations (or a combination of both), public opinion can be hostile or receptive, and policies can be assigned to hostile or sympathetic agencies. Finally, how an agency handles implementation is often a function of its rules and procedures. Frequently, these issues regarding selecting an appropriate course of action are addressed while the policy is still being drafted. Some of these decisions, however, are also made by the government agency in charge of the policy once it is passed.

One key decision to be made is whether or not implementation should be done by public or private organizations (through grants and contracts). Privatization of government service is very much an implementation issue. A town may have a publicly stated goal of weekly trash collection, but the actual collection (that is, the implementation of the policy decision) may be handled by a private sanitation company. Frequently, these decisions are based on cost; it might be cheaper for the town to contract with the private company than to hire public sanitation workers and to operate a fleet of garbage trucks. Perhaps charitable organizations already exist to meet certain needs of poor people in the community, and government subsidies can be used to more cost-effectively provide continued access to those services. Sometimes, however, there may be motives besides cost-effectiveness. President Bush's **faith-based initiatives** for providing some social services through religious organizations are at least partly designed to expose people to those organizations' moral values, which would be prohibited if the services were implemented by government organizations.

Private organizations and individuals may also be relied upon for implementation through government grants. For example, the National Science Foundation, charged with promoting the quality and amount of scientific research done in the United States, does not have a staff of its own researchers. Rather, one of its primary activities is to award grants to fund research efforts of individuals, typically those at universities.

If a policy is assigned to a public, rather than private, organization for implementation, it is important to assign it to a sympathetic agency if we are to expect success. This recognizes that policy implementation is inherently political, and is not necessarily a neutral process as expected by Woodrow Wilson. In fact, the foes of the policy will try to recover political ground in the implementation process by attempting to have the policy assigned to an agency that is not sympathetic to the goals of the policy.[9] For example, both the Environmental Protection Agency (EPA) and the Department of Energy (DOE) have programs to reduce air pollution. Presumably, the EPA would be more sympathetic to the goals of such legislation than the DOE, which is charged primarily with protecting and developing energy resources.

Of course, determining an appropriate course of action for implementation also involves public opinion and client support. Client support (that is, support from the target or beneficiaries of the policy) is crucial. When this support exists, these groups can help the agency implement its policies by providing feedback about implementation efforts, and information about the nature of the issue being addressed.[10] For example, Mothers Against Drunk Driving (MADD) is a client organization of drunk-driving laws. This group helps the police implement these laws by providing information to the public about the dangers of drunk driving and by helping identify ways to reduce the ill effects of alcohol consumption. More broadly, general public support will lead to successful policy implementation because people will be more likely to react (in the expected way) to the policy. A controversial policy may create groups in society that try to undermine its effects, have it overturned in court, or have it nullified by further legislation. For example, several states have tried to undermine the federal government's position on marijuana by passing laws that explicitly allow marijuana possession and consumption for medicinal purposes. Although federal law technically trumps state law in this case, the Department of Justice's Drug Enforcement Administration has tacitly allowed this exception, and probably will continue to do so, despite a 2005 Supreme

Court ruling reaffirming the ability of the federal government to prohibit the use of medicinal marijuana.

Finally, an agency tasked with implementing a policy must decide what sorts of activities will be required. This frequently involves agency rule making, in order for the organization to have a set of procedures to follow, to set standards for the target of the policy, and to establish consequences for failing to obey the law. For example, the Occupational Safety and Health Administration (OSHA) must decide what actions are necessary to ensure that factories comply with a new regulation and pass rules to ensure the new regulation is put into effect. Perhaps site visits are needed; perhaps a simple booklet of information will do. Note that this implies that there are two basic methods for implementation: noncoercive and coercive forms of action.[11]

Noncoercive Action. **Noncoercive methods** do not impose penalties or costs from the government for those who do not comply with the policy (that is, those who do not obey the law). Information or education provided by the government is an example of noncoercive implementation. Smokers can ignore the health warnings on their cigarette packs and the government does not punish them for it. The government also frequently tries to establish voluntary agreements. These are useful because they may create a more cooperative atmosphere, producing the policy goals with less conflict. However, these arrangements are sometimes criticized because they may fall far short of what could be accomplished through coercive measures. For example, when many smoking regulations in the United Kingdom were voluntary arrangements with the tobacco industry, the government there was criticized for not sending a stronger message.

Loans, subsidies, and benefits are also noncoercive methods of implementing policy.[12] Farmers receive crop subsidies as part of programs designed to protect the agricultural industry and economy. Retired people receive Social Security payments. College students receive subsidized or insured loans as part of an effort to increase access to college education. Businesses are frequently aided by local governments that provide development incentives or tax relief. Much of noncoercive policy implementation is thus simply transferring cash or in-kind benefits to individuals or groups.

Finally, noncoercive methods may involve doing nothing at all. Many policies basically implement themselves, as a mere statement of the law is enough to get people to obey it.[13] After all, people pay their taxes, on time and accurately, even though the IRS rarely performs audits. Smoke-free indoor air laws also operate without active enforcement. Smokers obey them, even if there are no "smoking police" (or even aggressive nonsmokers) ready to pounce if they light up a cigarette.[14] Policymakers and bureaucrats can take advantage of people's sense of duty to follow the law (in the case of taxes) or of people's desire to not be social outcasts (in the case of indoor smoking). As long as they know what the rules are, people generally behave well and follow them. These examples of **voluntary compliance** suggest that policymakers and bureaucrats should seriously consider whether any positive action beyond informing the public of the law is required at all to achieve a desired goal.

Coercive Action. **Coercive methods** of implementation, on the other hand, are designed to punish those who do not follow the law. Monetary penalties are frequently used as a coercive form of implementation. The Occupational Safety and Health Administration fines businesses for unsafe work environments. Police officers write tickets that force speeders to pay fines. Other forms of coercive implementation include product recalls, seizure of property, revocation of licenses (say, for a restaurant to sell alcohol), or initiating the criminal justice process to impose penalties such as fines and prison sentences. Coercive measures are often politically difficult to use, except for relatively small fines and certain criminal laws such as those for violent crime.[15] Generally, we try to avoid the image of the "heavy hand of government" and impose punishments as a last resort. By relying on noncoercive, cooperative, and voluntary methods we can also reduce some costs of policy implementation. We do not, for example, need to audit every tax return to the IRS because the vast majority of people accurately report their income even without Big Brother watching over them.

Photo by Mark Ide.

Speed limits are typically implemented by coercive measures. The fine for speeding is designed to punish the driver for breaking law, as well as to act as a deterrent from speeding in the future.

To summarize, choosing the appropriate course of action for implementation is not simple. It involves figuring out if the private sector or nonprofit organizations are able to help. If a policy is to work, it must be assigned to an agency that is sympathetic toward its stated goals. Public support also aids in selecting the appropriate course of action: agencies need information about how their efforts are received in order to make adjustments. Finally, coercive or noncoercive measures must be chosen, depending on the behavior of the target population.[16] For example, if we do not think that noncoercive measures will be strong enough to change people's behavior, then coercive action should be considered. Sometimes this is done while the legislature is passing policy (for example, the size of a tax increase on cigarettes will be specified in the policy). Other times, individual agencies are free to choose the measures to be used. Public-school discipline policies are a good example: a principal may first try to work out some voluntary agreement, and use sanctions such as detention or expulsion as a last resort.

Securing Adequate Resources

The next requirement for successful policy implementation is to secure enough resources for the agency to properly administer the policy. This is obviously important; a policy to reclaim land from strip mining is useless if there is no money to actually go about doing it. Recent and proposed shifts of money away from certain NASA programs are degrading the agency's ability to continue promising research in several areas.[17]

As you saw in Chapter 8, public budgeting is a highly political process. In order for an agency to get adequate funding, several situations must be met. First, there obviously needs to be political support in the legislature and from the executive. Second, there must be support from the clientele of the agency (and hopefully broad public support as well). This support will help the agency make its case in the legislature. Finally, the overall budget situation needs to be favorable for money to be spent. If the economy is bad or if there are problems with unbalanced budgets, it will be more difficult to provide adequate funding. For example, this has been a problem at state universities over the last several years. States have a policy goal of providing subsidized university education, but the recent economic downturn put extreme pressure on most state budgets. Consequently, funding to public universities was cut dramatically, forcing spending reductions and tuition increases. From the standpoint of university administrators and students paying increased tuition, "adequate funding" was not secured.

Effective Coordination of Personnel

The final requirement for successful policy implementation is the effective coordination of agency personnel. The agencies and individual bureaucrats involved in implementing the policy must all be working toward a common goal. The professionalism of career bureaucrats can be used effectively to enhance coordination. As long as the policy to be implemented is consistent with professional obligations and goals, it will be comparatively easy to make sure individual bureaucrats implement the policy correctly. Essentially, bureaucrats view such policies as legitimate and essential to their jobs of working toward the overall goals of the agency. This means, of course, that coordination of personnel is easier when the policy has been assigned to a sympathetic agency.

Furthermore, coordination implies that multiple agencies should be working in ways that complement each other, rather than competing with each other or duplicating services. In other words, multiple agencies implementing the same or similar policies must communicate and cooperate. One of the key reasons for creating the Department of Homeland Security (DHS) in the wake of the September 11, 2001, terrorist attacks was to increase the coordination of intelligence and other security agencies. By housing previously diverse organizations (such as the Border Patrol, Customs, the Coast Guard, and the Secret Service) under one common leader, it is hoped that increased cooperation, communication, and coordination will result. Further, the DHS is supposed to coordinate intelligence gathered from a variety of agencies such as the CIA, the FBI, and the Defense Intelligence Agency.

Coordination is particularly important when multiple levels of government are used to implement policies.[18] Because this is so common, such coordination is key to successful implementation. In this case, coordination is gained by establishing a strong hierarchy, or chain of command, for the implementing agencies. For national policy, state and local agencies should not have the ability to block or change implementation procedures. This is obviously a two-edged sword. With a strong hierarchy, the national government gets what it wants, but at the expense of not allowing state and local governments to tailor policy to their needs. The No Child Left Behind Act has been criticized on these grounds. By establishing a rigid hierarchy for implementation, few exceptions are made for judging the progress of individual schools, despite the fact that state governments and local school districts may have valid objections to how student testing is done or scored.

The Reality of Policy Implementation

By now you may be wondering how, with all of the requirements, agencies manage to implement policies at all. You are right to wonder. The reality of policy implementation is that it almost never goes as planned or hoped. The four requirements of effective policy implementation are, quite frankly, very difficult to achieve (see Sidebar 10.2).

Sidebar 10.2 An Assessment of the Implementation of Prohibition

On January 17, 1920, the United States ratified an amendment to the Constitution that prohibited the mass production and sale of alcohol. The Volstead Act, written to put the amendment into practice, assigned enforcement (implementation) to the Treasury Department. We all know that Prohibition was a dismal failure. By examining it using the requirements of effective policy implementation, we can see why.

First, Prohibition was based on a questionable causal theory: that it was immoral to drink alcohol. The expectation was that banning it would be seen as a valid social cause and people would follow the law. This was not the case. Most people did not see alcohol as immoral, and banning it was widely opposed (or, at least its continued consumption was widely supported!). This situation soon gave rise to widespread smuggling, moonshining, and illicit drinking in speakeasies.

Second, an inappropriate course of action was selected for the implementation of Prohibition. The Treasury Department was a poor choice to implement the law. It simply was not interested in enforcing Prohibition, revealed by the fact that in its annual reports, Prohibition activities received only 5 to 10 pages out of more than 800.[a]

Third, inadequate resources were devoted to enforcing prohibition. The budget was small, and the number of agents was pathetically low (starting out at only 1,500) given that the entire country and thousands of miles of border had to be policed.[b] Low salaries for agents also meant corruption, as bootleggers would pay officials to look the other way.

Finally, there was inadequate coordination between the Treasury Department and state law enforcement agencies. State governments were simply not willing to pay for increased efforts. Cooperation further disintegrated when local and state governments complained about federal agents using excessive force.

Considering that Prohibition failed to meet any of the four requirements for effective policy implementation, it is not surprising that it was a disaster. In December of 1933, the 21st Amendment was ratified, formally repealing Prohibition.

[a]Kenneth J. Meier, *The Politics of Sin* (M.E. Sharpe: Armonk, NY, 1994).
[b]Ibid., 142.

This means that there is often a gap between the goal of the policy and what the policy actually accomplishes. Understanding the problems encountered in policy implementation can go a long way in explaining why this gap occurs. It also can serve as a way to help improve how our policies are written, as well as how they are implemented. If a key function of public administration is to find ways to improve government performance, then identifying problems in policy implementation is a crucial component of that function. There are five general problems that can be encountered: problems with the identified target population, problems of interpreting legislative intent, lack of political support, organizational problems, and problems of timing.

Target Population

Defining the **target population**—the individuals, firms, or groups that will be directly influenced by the policy—is an important element of effective policy implementation. A policy that identifies a relatively small, distinct set of people as the target stands a greater chance of successful implementation.[19] For example, child vaccination requirements work because children in a community are identifiable and the problem is easily isolated by requiring vaccinations in order to attend school.

Frequently, however, the problem that needs to be solved is widespread, and the target population is large and diverse. This means that any legislation that is passed will have to be fairly broad and without many specifics. It is up to the agencies implementing these policies to determine, often on a case-by-case basis, the best course of action. For example, the various prohibitions on workplace discrimination that we have are not as successful as we would like. The target population—firms and managers—is so large and varied that legislation cannot be written to account for every different circumstance.

The target population may also be viewed positively or negatively. Target populations can be divided into four categories: advantaged, contenders, dependents, and deviants.[20] Policies aimed at a particular target population will have unique implications for implementation, because policies will be designed differently for each group.[21]

Legislating in favor of advantaged groups serves elected officials, but makes policy implementation difficult. Elected officials benefit from providing goods and services to powerful, highly regarded groups (wealthy elites or large corporations) even if the public interest is not broadly served. Bureaucrats then must struggle to salvage as much from the policy as they can in order to serve their public-interest goals.

Policies aimed at contenders (middle-class individuals or small businesses) often address extreme cases, which are made examples. Gun-control policies that ban automatic weapons and other firearms are an example. The result is narrow legislation to treat the worst, but not the most common, case. Extremely tough penalties for businesses that violate pollution regulations are another example. These penalties are so tough that they cannot be used for fear of bankrupting industry.

Policies targeted at dependents are usually welfare policies and other entitlements. With these policies, the strict implementation goal is to ensure that eligible people receive benefits while those who are not eligible do not. However, caseworkers often find ways to provide benefits to those who are needy but who fall outside the legislated eligibility criteria.

Finally, policies aimed at deviants are usually criminal justice policies, and are clear and specific in their punishments. Yet removing flexibility in sentencing simply moves that flexibility elsewhere, often to police forces and prosecutors, who then operate with an eye toward minimizing prison overcrowding and reducing the burden on the court system.

All of these examples show that the target population of a public policy greatly influences how that policy will be implemented by government agencies. Target populations that are distinct and relatively small lend themselves to successful implementation. However, each type of target population is linked to a specific set of implementation problems that must be overcome.

Problems of Legislative Intent

Unfortunately for those interested in effective policy implementation, legislators often legislate without much information or thought about causal theories.[22] Policymakers of course have the best intentions in mind, but sometimes problems are so large, complex, or controversial that really understanding the causal mechanisms is difficult. We continue to legislate on these intractable problems, such as education, poverty, and crime, mainly because they are so important. However, because the causes of those problems are not fully understood, any legislation has to be broad in scope, perhaps incorporating several causal theories at once, if it is going to address the entire issue. If an issue does not have a single specific cause, then it is more difficult to have specific legislation that will actually work. This means that it is often difficult for an agency to act according to **legislative intent**: what the lawmakers meant when they passed the policy. It may even be difficult for the agency to figure out what the legislative intent is.

Education policy suffers from these problems. We have broad, complex policies that cover everything from increasing competition between schools, to student testing, to improving teacher professionalism. This breadth makes it difficult for school districts to focus adequately on any single one. Federal policy, instituted with the No Child Left Behind Act, tries to increase the performance of schools by doing all three, but focuses mostly on student testing. Of course, testing policy does not address the variety of other issues that face public schools. Consequently, teachers might decide that in the absence of other solutions, the best course of action is to teach to the test. This undermines the true intent of the policy, and while it might improve test scores, it does so at the expense of a more diverse, creative education for students.

Another problem is that political competition over how policy is- sues are defined creates an environment where linking policy to clear causal theory is difficult. Both sides of a policy debate tend to oversim- plify the causes of a problem to fit their party's platform and their ideo- logical view. Due to this competition, as well as the fact that the causes are imperfectly understood, we have policies that typically are only partially successful because they are simplistic attempts to solve large problems. Our antipoverty policies suffer from this problem. Conser- vatives argue that a generous approach, favored by liberals, creates sit- uations where there is an incentive to stay on welfare. Liberals argue that a more punitive approach stressing efforts to leave welfare, fa- vored by conservatives, creates situations where poor people are worse off than before. Both sides tend to oversimplify the problem of poverty and offer simplistic solutions. Our policies then tend to emphasize one side's argument, even though it is too narrow. The result is that the pov- erty rate in the United States has been virtually unchanged for more than 30 years, hovering between about 12 and 15 percent of the popu- lation since 1970.[23]

Partisan competition and an increasing attention toward election campaigns also frequently causes vague legislation. The shift toward constant campaigning for office perhaps impedes the ability of legisla- tors to deliberate and produce clear policy based on sound causal the- ory.[24] Frequently, what is produced instead is legislation with vague goals and unclear directions for the administering agency. This type of policy is often required in order to achieve some compromise to pass legislation.[25] It is far easier for legislators to agree on abstract ideas than on specific duties that an agency will carry out, if only because if things go wrong, it is easier to blame the agency. In essence, it may be that elected officials pass the buck to the bureaucracy to avoid having to make controversial decisions.[26]

While this is useful for elected officials seeking reelection, it makes it difficult for the agency in charge of implementing the policy to do a good job. Instead of being told in certain terms what to do, the agency must make its own interpretations about what the policy intends. This in turn leads to frustration on the part of legislators. To them, bureau- crats become "shirkers" who try to avoid doing what they are told. In truth, those bureaucrats may honestly believe they *are* doing what they have been told to do. However, if it is difficult for an agency to deter- mine the precise goals of a policy, it is unlikely that implementation will proceed as the proponents of the policy expected. Affirmative- action programs are a good example of this problem. In the abstract, they are uncontroversial—no legislators are in favor of discrimination. However, as the programs have been implemented over the last 40 or so years, government agencies have been repeatedly criticized for ev- erything ranging from inadequate enforcement to discriminating against whites. Lacking clear direction from policymakers (who probably did not have a single goal as a group anyway), it was unlikely that the implementation of affirmative-action policies would be popular.

This inability to produce policy with clear goals may be symptomatic of a larger trend. As standards for government action become more abstract (such as taking on goals of equality, fairness, and "the public interest"), legislation becomes necessarily more vague.[27] For example, the Equal Employment Opportunity Commission (EEOC) was established by the Civil Rights Act of 1964. Among other things, it is charged with carrying out "educational" and "promotional" activities. Just what these are is not specified in the policy. Another common example is the unclear mission now frequently given to law enforcement agencies. The legislated mission of a local police department in Iowa is to enforce the law in a "fair and impartial" manner.[28] Definitions of "fair" and "impartial" are not offered, and probably vary from officer to officer.

Finally, legislators may send mixed messages to government agencies, even when individual policies are straightforward on their own. This occurs if new legislation competes with existing policy. Examples of this abound. Most states have official state lotteries charged with generating revenue for the state, but that revenue also helps fund gambling treatment programs. Antismoking policies such as banning smoking in public places compete with cigarette tax policies designed to increase government revenue. Do we want people gambling or not? Do we want to rely on smokers for additional tax revenue, or do we want them to quit? Contradictions or mixed messages can only serve to hinder the successful implementation of public policy.

Lack of Political Support

The second problem frequently encountered during policy implementation is a lack of continued political support after a program has started. Political battles do not end with the passage of a policy. Instead, opponents of the legislation seek to undermine it during the budget process or may try to have it assigned to a hostile agency for implementation.[29] An opponent of a new policy to regulate pollution from fossil fuels will probably want it to be assigned to the Department of the Energy's Office of Environment, Safety, and Health rather than the Environmental Protection Agency—the Department of Energy is more likely to be friendly to the concerns of business than the EPA. One extreme example is that of President Reagan's attempt in his first term in office to change the organizational culture at the EPA in order to make it more hostile to environmental protection policies. He appointed Anne Gorsuch, a lawyer who had represented clients hostile to the EPA, to administer the agency. Other top EPA positions went to a lobbyist for the paper industry and a top attorney for Exxon. Clearly, the leadership was unsympathetic to the agency's mission, and was able to reduce the size of the staff. As the leadership shrank the staff of the EPA, the agency became less able to properly implement its policies.

Opposition to a policy in the budget process is a significant obstacle to successful implementation. As noted above, if adequate resources are not secured, then a policy or program is meaningless. When the IRS came under attack from Congress in the mid-1990s for excessively harsh auditing practices, the agency's budget was slashed, impeding its ability to enforce the tax code. Budget reductions to block implementation are relatively common, and are a popular way to effectively "kill" a program without necessarily legislating it away. Many Defense Department programs are attacked this way. For example, as George H.W. Bush's Secretary of Defense, Dick Cheney tried more than once to cut funding for the V-22 Osprey tilt-rotor aircraft the Marines were building. Secretary of Defense Donald Rumsfeld had the Army's latest self-propelled artillery program terminated in 2002 after recommending the money be spent elsewhere.

Lack of popular support can also make implementation difficult, even if there is adequate funding. Opponents of a policy try to build a case against it, attempting to persuade the media and elected officials.[30] Sometimes, this popular dissatisfaction works and elected officials react, as indicated by the successful congressional sanctions of the IRS in the 1990s. Other times, opponents will file negative feedback

U.S. Air Force.

Public budgets are often used to attack or defend government programs. Plagued with technical problems and budget over-runs, the V-22 Osprey had its funding cut in 1992 by then-Secretary of Defense Dick Cheney, only to be revived under President Clinton and continued under President George W. Bush.

as part of the formal rulemaking process. Small farmers frequently criticize the USDA this way on the issue of farm subsidies, arguing that the Department favors large agribusiness concerns and diverts most subsidy money toward those companies (which probably do not need it). Opponents may even try to have a policy overturned in the courts, or otherwise try to distract the efforts of the agency in charge of the policy.

Organizational Problems

Although the effective coordination of personnel is important for successful policy implementation, it is difficult to achieve. There are several types of organizational problems: coordination and communication difficulties, inadequate administrative authority, problems of identifying an appropriate course of action, and an overreliance on standard operating procedures.

Coordination and Communication. One important reason for the difficulty is our federal system of government. With multiple levels of government frequently involved in implementation (which means multiple agencies), coordination is hard to achieve. Although the formation of the Department of Homeland Security has helped to coordinate and organize federal implementation of national security policy, the department must also establish relationships with each state, as many of the duties of assessing vulnerabilities of power plants, infrastructure, and transportation networks have fallen on state agencies. In turn, each state government must develop relationships with local governments to ensure that disaster-preparedness programs are carried out, and that local emergency response agencies (police, fire, and ambulance services) are trained in everything from bomb disposal to chemical decontamination. Communication between levels of government and between different agencies can be slow and imprecise. This makes sense, because as information needs to be passed to more people and offices, it is less likely to be transmitted quickly and accurately. The result is a confusing network of governments and public organizations, and it is unlikely that any one person knows exactly what is going on in each jurisdiction. Furthermore, each time another level of government or another agency is involved, the likelihood of successful implementation is reduced. In other words, each time a new set of decisions has to be made, another agreement must be reached before implementation can proceed.[31] Of course, this opens the door for changes, more vague policy statements, and new opposition.

Inadequate Administrative Authority. Formal agency powers, such as rulemaking and adjudication, are important tools for policymaking and implementation, as you saw in Chapter 4. It is possible, however, that government agencies may not have the necessary power to implement a policy successfully. In some cases, this lack of power is a function of elected officials trying to control the bureaucracy. For example, in 1999 Florida passed a set of amendments to the state's Administrative Procedures Act to restrict rulemaking to issues specifically included in the enabling legislation of an agency. Previously, Florida's agencies could pass rules to implement the enabling legislation more broadly.[32] At the federal level, in 2004 Congress blocked the Federal Communications Commission from implementing its rule allowing a single company to own TV stations reaching 45 percent of the national audience. The Congress passed budget appropriations for fiscal year 2004 prohibiting the FCC from granting licenses to companies owning TV stations reaching greater than 35 percent of the national audience. These examples again raise the paradox of public administration: striking a balance between having an effective bureaucracy and democratic controls over it.

In other cases, adequate authority may not have been granted to the agency in the first place. The Equal Employment Opportunity Commission, which began operations in 1965, was initially unable to implement workplace discrimination laws effectively because it could not initiate lawsuits against suspected offenders. In fact, because almost all it could do was document employment discrimination, most civil rights groups called the commission a "toothless tiger."[33] The EEOC finally got the authority to sue in 1972, seven years after it began operations.

Determining a Course of Action. Another organizational issue is that, ideally, decisions about determining an appropriate course of action are easy to make. That is, if an agency operates as a single actor with no disunity in decision making, and there is no distinction between the goals of agency leaders and those of lower-level bureaucrats, then deciding a course of action is simple.[34]

This ideal situation, unfortunately, rarely occurs. Instead, government agencies, as we point out in Chapter 6, are groups of individuals with goals and attitudes that sometimes diverge. Some organizations have competing professional cultures. The Federal Trade Commission, for example, is staffed by both lawyers and economists who are supposed to protect consumers from unfair trade practices. Lawyers, who professionally stress winning in the courtroom as an indicator of success, may choose to go after relatively small cases that will be easy to win. Economists, who professionally stress securing the most benefits possible, may forgo small cases because they will not provide much economic gain to the consumer, and choose to go after complicated cases.[35] One might even argue that competing professional cultures exist in public universities. State-subsidized universities are supposed to provide greater access to college education (a teaching mission), as well as provide services to the broader public (research and outreach or extension missions). Many professors, professionally trained to do research, see this as their primary mission. Others, on the other hand, may be drawn toward the teaching mission. It is thus difficult to find a faculty body at a public university that is truly united in a vision of what its primary duties should be. Both groups, however, firmly believe that they are properly implementing the policy goals of the state.

There is also a frequent disconnect in expectations between agency leaders and lower-level workers. Getting workers to do what managers want them to do was the subject of Chapter 6, but it is important here as well. "Street-level" bureaucrats (the cop walking the beat, the public-school teacher in the classroom, the welfare caseworker)[36] frequently have different opinions on what needs be done than organizational leaders. Sometimes, this is due to situations that these bureaucrats find themselves in (for example, a teacher may deviate from a lesson plan in order to regain control of a unruly class, or the primary goal of a cop on the beat becomes diffusing violent situations rather than strictly upholding the law).[37] Other times, implementing policy according to the demands of agency leaders seems unreasonable or is impossible. Despite demands to crack down on speeding, not all speeders are caught, and even those who are do not always get a ticket, for a variety of reasons. Local welfare caseworkers may seek ways to provide special treatment if a family is in dire need, despite cautions by agency leaders who worry about staying within the letter of the law in order to avoid punishment from the state or federal government.

Some even argue that street-level bureaucrats implement policy differently from what agency leaders expect because they have been captured by the interests of the clients they serve.[38] The argument is that due to routine and repeated contact with clients, bureaucrats begin to sympathize with them, and take on their attitudes and opinions. The Food and Drug Administration in the 1950s and 1960s was criticized as being too close to the drug industry, and the Department of Agriculture is currently criticized as being too close to large agribusiness companies. Although these critiques will never disappear, it is unlikely that any gap between what agency leaders want and what street-level bureaucrats do is largely due to being captured. Indeed, you saw in Chapter 4 that as it becomes easier to be politically active, coupled with increased bureaucratic professionalism, it is unlikely for such cozy relationships to survive long.[39]

Over-Reliance on Standard Operating Procedures. Over-reliance on standard operating procedures also contributes to the difficulties of effective policy implementation. Standard operating procedures (SOPs) are used by organizations to improve efficiency. After establishing a process or response to deal with a particular situation, the next time that situation occurs the organization will not have to treat it as new. This helps serve clients quickly and cost-effectively. However, SOPs can also hinder successful policy implementation, particularly if a deviation from the SOP is required. Organizations often have trouble "breaking away" from their SOPs, choosing to define genuinely new problems in such a way as to fit them into existing procedures. In short, although they can aid organizational efficiency, SOPs frequently act as impediments to implementing new policies appropriately, and turn into red tape.[40] Perhaps the most popular example is that of the Navy during the Cuban Missile Crisis. President Kennedy ordered a naval blockade of Cuba, but wanted it set closer to the island (and thus further from the approaching Soviet ships) in order to give the Soviet government more time to reconsider its actions. Navy standard operating procedure, however, was to establish the blockade at a distance further from the island than Kennedy ordered, and it initially set its blockade according to its SOP. Eventually, the Navy had to be explicitly ordered to set their blockade according to the president's wishes.[41] Kennedy's placement of the blockade allowed the Soviets the extra time to change their minds before the two navies came into contact.

The key effective implementation, then, is for agencies to recognize when it is appropriate to break from standard procedures. This can be difficult, as SOPs are widely used as a replacement for much of the decision making in large organizations, as you saw in Chapter 6. The other issue is that SOPs are designed to serve an agency's goals, not necessarily the goals of elected officials. The Navy assuredly had valid tactical and strategic reasons for its SOP on naval blockades. Kennedy's goal for the blockade, however, was different from the purpose of the Navy's SOP. So, it is possible that agencies might not even pause to consider a new course of action, or if they do, they may consider their own goals first rather than the policy goals of elected officials.

Bad Timing

Finally, effective implementation is difficult because the government's timing is frequently off.[42] Sometimes, the government is simply too late. This is often a function of the slowness of the policy process, or it is the result of an inability—perhaps unwillingness—to identify and tackle potential problems that have yet to materialize. This means that legislation is not usually developed in time to head off a problem. Perhaps the timing of the problem overtook the rather slow policymaking procedures of our government. Perhaps we would rather deal with fixing existing problems than pay now for programs to prevent problems that may or may not occur in the future. Our inability to permanently solve the financing problems of Social Security and Medicare seem to indicate this problem. Or perhaps government agencies are simply not equipped to act independently in order to adapt to potential situations. So instead, many of our policies are bandages placed on existing problems rather than actions to prevent them from developing in the first place. An all-too-frequent example is that flood control programs are not passed until after a town is swept away by a river, and in the meantime we rely on disaster relief programs run by the Federal Emergency Management Agency.

The vagueness of legislative intent, coupled with political opposition, organizational problems, and problems of timing, all contribute to imperfect policy implementation. Policies are typically not poorly implemented as a result of lack of effort from government agencies. Given the complexity of policy implementation and the number of potential difficulties that can be encountered, it should not be surprising at all to find out that policy goals are rarely perfectly met.

Conclusion

It was once written that regarding policy implementation, most people "cannot appreciate how difficult it is to make the ordinary happen."[43] Most people do not even stop to think about policy implementation. They simply do not consider it to be worth their time, or they are completely unaware that it is a stage in the policy process and a crucial component of public administration. If people do think about it, they usually assume it to be automatic, and that the real difficulties lie in the legislative process. The legislature passes its policy; it has a goal and tells what is expected of the agency that will put it into practice. What could be simpler than that? As a result of these misconceptions, people are frustrated when the expected results of a policy do not materialize.

Considering the difficulties of policy implementation, we should instead judge many policies to be "successful" even if their goals have not been fully met. Understanding the implementation process provides perspective on why government agencies do the things they do, and why policies turn out how they do. It is basically impossible to understand how government functions without understanding policy implementation.

This also implies that by carefully studying the implementation process we can find ways to improve government performance. An important part of public administration is normative: we want to find out how government *should* operate and figure out how to achieve that. By studying policy implementation, we can assess why policies sometimes fail. We can compare the actual situation with the four ideal requirements for successful implementation and hopefully, using our knowledge of the problems that can potentially occur, identify why there are discrepancies. Too often, legislators and ordinary citizens assume that if a policy fails it is because the agency in charge of implementation avoided the job, or because the bureaucrats were inept. This is certainly possible, but it is more likely that one of the other problems, from the long list of things that can go wrong, is to blame.

Key Concepts

appropriate course of action The means by which a policy will be implemented.

causal theory An understanding of the relationship between a public policy and the goal it is to achieve.

coercive methods Implementation that relies on punishments to those who do not follow the law.

economic theories Popular causal theories that expect individuals or groups to behave in ways to avoid punishments and to seek rewards.

faith-based initiatives A course of action that utilizes religious organizations for policy implementation, usually to expose people to moral teachings and religious values.

information and decision-making theory A causal theory that expects individuals or groups to make better decisions if they have more information about the outcome of their choices.

legislative intent The goal of the policy, and the means to the goal, that are desired by the policymakers who pass a law.

noncoercive methods Implementation that relies on things such as information, benefits, or loans. It may also involve no government action at all.

policy implementation The actions taken by public organizations to ensure that policy decisions are put into effect.

target population The set of individuals or groups at which a policy is directed.

voluntary compliance A situation in which individuals or groups respond to a policy even without government action. ✦

Chapter 11

The Future of
Public Administration

The first decades of the twenty-first century will be a time of challenge and change for public administration. New technologies, increasing diversity, and evolving expectations about what government is and what it should do are going to reshape the politics, process, organization, and study of public administration.

In this final chapter we examine the trends and issues that we believe are most likely to shape public administration in the twenty-first century. Though peering into the future is by definition a speculative exercise, there is little risk in predicting that public administration will face reform and change. The real trick is not in saying things will change, but in figuring out what will change, and how, and why. Answering those questions represents one of the most fundamental challenges facing public administration. The answers will not only shape how public programs and services are delivered, but in no small part determine the number and nature of those programs and services.

These changes are almost certainly going to reshape the marriage between bureaucracy and democracy that has been at the heart of this book. The marriage is not going to end, though predictions of a painless, no-fault divorce will undoubtedly continue to be made. It is a pretty sure bet that public agencies are going to be pressured to change how they manage public programs and services, and some of this will undoubtedly mean shifting away from traditional notions of bureaucracy. Yet there is nothing on the horizon that promises to address all of bureaucracy's drawbacks without giving up some of its advantages. There will be no irrevocable parting of the ways between democracy and bureaucracy for the simple reason that bureaucracy continues to do more things better for democracy than any other available alternative. The paradox that began this book will remain, but it will be modified and altered in significant ways.

The ATM Bureaucracy

Perhaps the most obvious force for change that has crashed into public administration during the past few decades is the rise of new information technology. That technology is continuing to develop and evolve at an astonishingly rapid rate. Public agencies not only have to adapt to advances in hardware and software, but to changing expectations from the users of the new technology. For example, the current generation of college students grew up with the Internet and the World Wide Web and expect information about public services to be available at the click of a mouse. Increasingly, they take for granted that public transactions can (and should) be done online at their convenience. A significant portion of those who read this textbook certainly went online to find information about colleges and universities before choosing which school to attend. Many may have actually applied electronically. Few will think it unusual to register for courses online. Meeting those sort of online service expectations requires an enormous investment of money, time, manpower, and knowledge by public agencies. The result of those investments is expanding and changing the traditional notion of bureaucracy.

For many citizens a public agency is increasingly a page or a link on the web, a virtual organization that is open 24/7 and seamlessly connected with a wide range of related services and programs. Contrast this with the traditional notion of bureaucracy—a hierarchical organization located in bricks-and-mortar physical space that is not easily (at least for the citizen) connected to other agencies. The difference in access and perception is forcing public agencies to rethink what they are, what they do, and how they do it. The result has been termed the **ATM Bureaucracy**, or **e-government**. Both descriptions "refer to the delivery of information and services online via the Internet or other digital means."[1] The federal government, all 50 states, and the vast majority of local governments now have at least some e-government operations. In Ventura, California, you can apply for city building permits online; in New York state you can download the form to get a mortgage banker's license; and anyone with an Internet connection can send tax returns to the IRS electronically.

There are some obvious advantages in a public agency shifting from a traditional bureaucratic model to the e-government model. Paramount is convenience. Citizens can carry out any number of interactions with government any time they want to while in the comforts of their own homes—no more hunting for the right office and waiting in line. Many government agencies also make their websites available in Spanish as well as English, making it easier for nonnative speakers to get the information they need. For example, in Texas every state government website has an "en español" button.[2] Virtually every government of any size now has an online presence, making everything from bus schedules to job notices available without waiting in lines and with no need to travel further than the nearest computer.

Many people believe e-government represents not just a new way to communicate with citizens, but a new way of delivering programs and services that is beginning to replace the traditional bureaucracy. Centralization, standardization, hierarchy, and clearly defined jurisdictions are all characteristics of traditional bureaucracy. In contrast, e-government emphasizes customer service and the creation of linked networks. So rather than going to one bureaucracy to get a building permit and a completely separate bureaucracy to get a dog license, e-government integrates these services with hyperlinks on a single city government web page. The end result for citizens are "one stop" service centers in cyberspace rather than different bureaucracies (and very likely different buildings) in the bricks-and-mortar world. E-government also makes it easier for citizens to communicate with public officials—most government web sites post email contact information, and some solicit citizen input on various projects or problems via the Web.

Because of all this, information technology is reshaping the traditional bureaucracy in significant ways. For one thing, information technology is now automatically an agency priority, regardless of what programs or services the agency runs. For another, having their agencies linked to others in cyberspace may force bureaucrats to think about ways to integrate their programs and services with those other agencies. Agencies also may get much higher levels of citizen input once they go online; it is far easier to fire off an email than to wait in line or play telephone tag with a bureaucracy.

Scholars tracking how public agencies are adapting to information technology recognize that the transition from a traditional to an ATM bureaucracy does not happen in one sudden, dramatic shift. Instead, there is a clearly identifiable progression in the development of e-government:

1. The "billboard stage," which basically means a web page that provides one-way communication—it contains information about programs or services but no opportunity to interact with government.

2. The two-way stage, which provides a means for citizens to actually communicate with government (e.g., via email).

3. The portal stage, where transactions such as paying taxes or applying for permits can be done online.

4. The interactive democracy stage, where the Internet provides a means of public outreach for the government, and a means of participation for the public. The ultimate in interactive democracy are features such as online voting and in-

teractive discussion boards that allow a frank exchange between citizens and public officials.[3]

Most public agencies at all levels of government are at stages one or two of e-government, though it is almost a sure bet that in the not-too-distant future virtually all public agencies will face increasing pressure to move into stage three, or even stage four. Moving beyond two-way communication, however, presents some significant challenges. First, there is the need for high-level technical skills—skills that constantly have to be updated as the technology (hardware and software) improves. If financial transactions (such as paying for a permit or license) are going to be done online, there is the need for a secure server and some means of electronic payment (such as an electronic bank transfer, credit card transfer, or some online version of "cash," like a PayPal account). Doing this requires electronically integrating with another set of institutions, something that can easily create additional technical and administrative work for the bureaucracy. Second, there is the cost. Hiring or contracting high-level technical skills and buying servers and software that have to be periodically upgraded does not come cheap.

Given the significant investments required, it is ironic that many see e-government as a way to make public agencies leaner and more cost-effective. The basic thinking here is that if everything is done online, fewer bureaucrats are needed. If paying fees is more convenient online, it probably means government can become a more efficient revenue collector, right? Actually, this is not clear at all. E-government may require fewer of some types of employees (people at counters to hand out and receive forms), but it certainly requires more of others (software and hardware experts), and the latter often earn more than the former. And while computers may make it easier to contact a public official, there still have to be officials there to contact, officials who may be overwhelmed by the inquiries they get from their agencies' clientele.

College instructors may be a good example of the pros and cons of how information technology has increased the workload of public employees by fostering more two-way communication between agencies and clientele. The authors of this book get roughly 20 to 30 emails a day from students (many more as finals approach). Email is convenient for students; they can ask a question outside of class without having to worry about office hours or trekking over to a building on the other side of campus. Email has pushed the classroom into cyberspace, in effect making "mini-tutorials" available with the presence of a computer and a modem. Yet even if reading and responding to each email only takes a couple of minutes, that is roughly an hour a day just answering emails. That adds up to 80 hours per 16-week semester, which means that each semester we spend the equivalent of two 40-hour work weeks doing nothing but answering student emails. The convenience here is undeniable—and we like hearing from our students—but information technology does not necessarily translate into less work. In fact, quite the opposite.

The bottom line is that the revolution in new technology is putting a new set of pressures and expectations on public agencies and public officials. E-government means expensive new investments, the mastering or hiring of new skills and knowledge, and increased work loads for public employees. E-government is a long way from maturing, and for at least the next decade those involved in public administration are likely to be learning as much from their mistakes as their successes.

The Great Governance Debate

A second major force for change in public administration is changing attitudes towards government. The discussion of new information technology provides one example of how changing expectations can have important implications for what public agencies do and how they do it. However, it is much more than technology that is changing attitudes about government.

This shift in attitudes is a product of what might be termed **the great governance debate**. Roughly since the mid-1970s, most Western nations have undertaken a serious reexamination of two questions of fundamental importance to public administration: What is government? What should it be expected to do? The answers to these questions are far from settled, but for the traditional public bureaucracy the implications of the debate are already far reaching.

To understand those implications it helps to have a little historical context. The origins of the great governance debate date to the 1970s and 1980s. During that era a series of events combined to create a broad-ranging debate about the role of bureaucracy and government in virtually all industrialized democracies. The first of these was an increasing concern with the size and responsibilities of the public sector, which had increased enormously in the decades following World War II. As the size of government and its responsibilities grew, so did the size and scope of public agencies. Conservatives, especially, began to question the increasingly powerful role of bureaucracy in almost every facet of economic and social activity, arguing that government had taken on too much responsibility and should be pared back.

This conservative critique of government coincided with a fiscal crisis that gripped many nations, including the United States. Supporting the public sector and all its programs and services is enormously expensive, and long periods of recession and rising government deficits meant the desire for public services crashed headlong into the increasing reluctance to pay for them. By the 1980s the federal government was having problems funding these programs; in essence, it had maxed out its credit cards. To make matters worse, a grass-roots tax revolt swept the nation, as citizens used ballot initiatives to cap or roll back tax rates. Governments at all levels were stuck trying to deliver programs and services that many wanted, but few were willing to pay for.

Economic stagnation, deficits, and increasing concerns about the power and role of the bureaucracy led many to begin questioning both the methods and purposes of government. Conservative electoral victories (notably the election of Ronald Reagan as president in 1980) put the two fundamental questions squarely into the mainstream political arena. What should (or should not) government do? How should (or should not) government do it? In the United States the general response to these questions was that government should do less, and rely more on the private sector to deliver public programs and services and less on traditional bureaucracies. This is a response that by the early twenty-first century was less ideological and much more mainstream—there is broad agreement that the methods and means government uses to manage public programs and services needs to change.

What has emerged from the great governance debate are a set of widely held beliefs about how public administration should change:

1. Public agencies should "do more with less," becoming more productive in the sense of providing public services with fewer resources.

2. The private sector should become more heavily involved in delivering public services.

3. Public agencies should become more "customer" focused, oriented more toward their clientele.

4. Public agencies should become less hierarchical, pushing decision making down as close as possible to the people who will be affected by those decisions.

5. Those responsible for public programs should be held to high levels of accountability.[4]

This set of beliefs forms a common philosophical foundation for many recent public administration reform movements (remember reinventing government from Chapter 3?). In this book we have tried to promote what we believe is a healthy skepticism towards management reform fads that promise to make government "more like a business." Their historical track record gives little reason to vest much confidence in such promises. Yet while individual reform movements come and go leaving behind (at best) mixed results, the underlying change in attitudes is permanent.

Yet while shifting attitudes create expectations that public administration should change, they provide little in the way of specific guidelines of what those changes should be and how they should be carried out. Think about the five characteristics listed above—taken together they all sound pretty reasonable, right? Yet they do not really coalesce into a clear picture of how the public sector should reorganize itself or change the way it does business. For one thing, pursuing one of these characteristics may mean abandoning another. Contracting out public programs and services to the private sector may enable government to do "more with less." Yet contracting typically means losing a measure of accountability. Rather than a public bureaucracy delivering a public program, there is a web or network of private organizations, all operating independently. It is virtually impossible to monitor a diffuse network of private-sector companies in the same way as a single public bureaucracy. Similarly, street-level bureaucrats and key agency heads are now private-sector managers. They assume the policymaking powers of their public-sector counterparts.

The ultimate result of contracting out public programs and services to the private sector is what we referred to in earlier chapters as the hollow or **virtual state**. This describes a government that still funds many programs and services, but does not deliver them. Theoretically (though not always in practice) these services can be delivered more efficiently through the private sector. The tradeoff is that the government gives up a measure of control, accountability, and policymaking power. One of the key risks is that the profit motive will become the major factor in decision making and, as we have already seen, the profit motive sometimes conflicts with the public interest. This obviously is not a situation conducive to improving accountability.

Thus the current result of the great governance debate is a state of uncertainty for public administration. The traditional notion of a public agency is a bureaucratic organization with a centralized set of responsibilities and boundaries. That notion is clearly under pressure from the change in attitudes about government. Less clear is how the traditional bureaucracy should change (see Sidebar 11.1). Should it become a "hollow" organization, contracting for services rather than delivering them directly? Should the merit system be modified or entirely abandoned so as to allow public-sector managers the flexibility to be more responsive to their clientele? If so, how can we retain high levels of accountability or prevent the problems of the spoils system (corruption, incompetence, and, especially, partisan bias) from reappearing? These are some of the big questions public administration is facing in the twenty-first century and, thus far, there are no universally agreed-upon answers.

Political and Policy Change: The Rise of the Disarticulated State

Problems such as maintaining clean air and water, regulating traffic flow, and dealing with sales tax bases migrating from main street to

Sidebar 11.1 Faith-Based Initiatives: Substituting Church for Bureaucracy

If you want to get rid of traditional public bureaucracies, what should replace them? How about a church? That is the basic idea behind President George W. Bush's faith-based initiative program, one of the more controversial attempts to reform how and who delivers and manages public programs and services.

Federal, state, and local governments have long used nonprofits to address problems ranging from homelessness, to drug addiction, to early childhood education. Generally, the government recognizes a need or problem and responds by providing financial, facility, or material support to a charitable organization already addressing the issue. There are a number of good reasons for working indirectly through nonprofits rather than directly tackling the problem with a public agency. Nonprofits often have experience and expertise that existing public agencies do not, and as nongovernmental agencies they have more flexibility to respond to changing needs. There is also the question of cost—providing a grant to a nonprofit can provide a lot more "bang for the buck" than setting up an independent public agency or program.

One set of nonprofits with considerable experience and expertise in addressing community-based social issues are faith-based organizations such as churches, synagogues, and mosques and their various community outreach operations. Traditionally, however, the public sector has been leery of providing resources to religiously affiliated institutions. There are constitutional, political, and practical reasons underlying this reluctance.

Many acknowledge the important work of religiously affiliated organizations in addressing public problems, but remain uncomfortable with mixing government and religion. On one side are religious leaders concerned about the strings that come attached to federal grants, and on the other are those who argue that large transfers of federal money to religiously affiliated groups violate the separation of church and state. The politics of funneling public money through religious organizations are potentially explosive. For example, some faith-based institutions discriminate (in action, if not explicitly in word) in their hiring practices. For government to underwrite with public money an organization that only hires people of a certain religious faith invites controversy (and maybe lawsuits) that will consume resources that could be put to better use elsewhere.

Adding to the controversy is the fact that Congress did not approve the faith-based initiative program. It was implemented by executive order, i.e., by direct action of the president without approval of the legislature. Whether faith-based organizations can take some of the bureaucracy out of public programs remains to be seen. They certainly won't remove the politics.

Sources: Mary Leonard, "Bush Presses Funding for Faith Groups," *Boston Globe*, November 30, 2003.

Dana Milbank, "Bush Legislative Approach Failed in Faith Bill Battle; White House Is Faulted for not Building a Consensus in Congress," *Washington Post*, April 23, 2003.

the strip mall to the Internet, are all interjurisdictional issues. In other words, they are hard to confine to the geographical boundaries of a single government. Addressing these problems comprehensively and effectively requires high levels of cooperation between localities, states, and even nations.

This need is forcing public agencies to become less provincial and more oriented towards creating networks and cooperative arrangements with their counterparts in other jurisdictions. The net result is what has been called the **disarticulated state**, a term that describes the decreasing importance of geographical borders to political jurisdictions. For example, consider the typical city or suburb. In most major urban areas the issues that affect one community affect all. The mayors might still be elected within city limits, but economic and social activity for most cities of any size is now multijurisdictional.[5] People often live in one community, work in another, and shop in yet another.

It is hard to serve such a highly mobile society by relying on public agencies that remain confined to small local jurisdictions that respond to the wishes of a single government. As the mayor of a city cannot dictate the policies of an adjoining suburb, public agencies often cooperate informally and formally with their counterparts across jurisdictions. Following society's lead, bureaucracy has, in its own fashion, become mobile. Some urban areas resemble mini-United Nations in the sense that addressing problems effectively requires cooperation among governments. At the forefront of this diplomacy are the bridges built between similar public agencies in different jurisdictions. These allow the necessary traffic in information and cooperation to occur.

It is not just the boundaries of municipalities or states that are becoming less meaningful. Increasingly, public administration has to think globally. In one sense this makes public administration no different from the private sector. Businesses have been grappling with the problem of how to act in a multinational marketplace for some time. For public administration, the experience is comparatively new. Yet semipublic institutions that are rooted in multinational agreements are becoming more and more important. The North American Free Trade Agreement (NAFTA), the World Trade Organization (WTO), and the General Agreement on Tariffs and Trade (GATT) have implications for a broad range of American public agencies. Everything from the Border Patrol, to the Coast Guard, to individual state revenue departments are affected by such agreements. As this sort of globalization occurs, public agencies are for the most part thinking about how their traditionally bureaucratic organizations can operate in a global context. At some point it is likely that they will have to think about whether those traditionally bureaucratic organizations are the best choices for such an environment. A new model—perhaps a full-blown, stage four

ATM bureaucracy—might be a better choice. This may make it easier for public agencies to deal with each other across national borders.

The exact nature of these changes remains to be seen. The pressure to make change coming from the changing nature of the problems and issues public agencies are being asked to face, however, is probably only going to increase.

Homeland Security

The war on terror that began with the terrorist attacks on September 11, 2001, precipitated one of the most significant and far-reaching organizational public-sector shake-ups of the past half-century. A key element of this shake-up was the recognized need for public agencies to integrate their operations across jurisdictions. This is because in the federal political system of the United States, much of the first-response capability to any disaster or emergency is concentrated in state and local governments. Prior to September 11, there was little preparation or capability to mount a centralized and coordinated nationwide response to a terror threat. The nation's preparations for war were largely predicated on the military engaging the armed forces of another nation-state.

Terrorist organizations, however, are not nation-states, and they are unlikely to engage the armed forces in any conventional sense. Homeland security depends less on the military and more on civilian law enforcement and emergency-response agencies. Consider that the response to the attacks on the World Trade Center did not initially involve the armed forces (except as victims—the Pentagon was attacked on the same day). It was local police and firefighters—in other words, municipal and county public agencies—who were the first responders.

There is much to praise about these local public agencies—certainly the professionalism and heroism they displayed in the wake of the initial attacks. From an organizational standpoint, however, there is a potentially large weakness in the security and emergency first-response capabilities of these agencies. Because they are agencies in separate jurisdictions, created and run by different governments, their ability to work together, or even communicate with each other, varies enormously. This means creating a centralized and coordinated homeland security policy, a challenge that is mind-boggling in its complexity. Any comprehensive homeland security program poses four key challenges to public administration.

Coordination

Bringing together the various levels of government and effectively coordinating their resources and capabilities is an enormous administrative challenge. These challenges range from giving law enforcement agencies in adjoining jurisdictions the ability to effectively communicate with each other (e.g., the same sorts of radios operating on common frequencies), to sorting out jurisdictional issues. For example, who has jurisdiction if the mode of a terror attack is anthrax sent through the mail? Is it the Post Office? The FBI? The police department in the jurisdiction where the mail was opened? The Federal Emergency Management Agency (FEMA)? If an infectious agent is unleashed, should a health rather than a law enforcement agency—the Centers for Disease Control, for example—be in charge of the initial response? Most likely all of these agencies, and perhaps more, will be involved in the response and investigation of such an attack. But who should be in charge?

This is not a question with an obvious or easy answer. Effectively matching the capabilities of each agency to the tasks at hand requires someone with the authority to make decisions. In other words, the key ingredients needed to effectively coordinate a response to terrorist attacks are things like hierarchy, authority, centralization, and division of labor. These are virtually a verbatim description of the characteristics of bureaucracy—the same characteristics of government that the great governance debate has more or less resolved to dilute to the greatest extent possible.

Department of Defense.

Organization

If homeland security means getting public agencies to effectively work together across jurisdictions and different levels of government, then obviously local, state, and federal governments need to seriously rethink how some of their agencies are organized.

The best-known example of such a reorganization effort undertaken in response to the war on ter-

The future almost certainly will see more interagency cooperation, and more cooperation between public agencies and nongovernmental organizations such as the Red Cross. Here members of the Alabama National Guard and the Red Cross work together to deal with the aftermath of Hurricane Katrina.

ror is the creation of the Department of Homeland Security (DHS). This new cabinet-level department in the national government was created directly in response to the attacks of September 11, with the express purpose of protecting the United States from any future attacks. DHS represents the most significant reorganizational effort of the executive branch in more than a half-century.

The DHS is made up of about 170,000 federal employees from 22 different agencies. The agencies shifted under the DHS umbrella include the Coast Guard, the Secret Service, the Immigration and Naturalization Service, and Customs. The department's goal is to centralize, coordinate, and improve the government's intelligence and response capabilities. This sounds simple enough, but merging 22 different agencies, who in many cases are not used to working with each other, is a challenging administrative task. These issues are not simply administrative, but political.

This is amply demonstrated by the struggle to create the DHS. Originally, the idea was pushed by Democrats, especially those serving on the U.S. Senate's Governmental Affairs Committee. President Bush was initially critical of the idea, arguing against creating a new bureaucracy. The idea gained bipartisan support, however, and Bush threw the weight of the White House behind its creation. In doing so, however, he added a twist: he wanted to remove the civil service and union protections of a significant portion of DHS employees, as well as put an end to their collective bargaining rights. The administration argued that this was necessary to give the secretary of the DHS the personnel flexibility necessary to fight the war on terror. Democrats cried foul, arguing it was a transparent attempt at union busting, and represented an end to the merit system that would end up politicizing (think spoils system) a department with broad-ranging law enforcement, intelligence, and security responsibilities. Bush was adamant, however, and threatened to veto any legislation that did not satisfactorily address these labor issues.

Congress—under pressure from a public demanding government do something about terror—passed a law creating the DHS that included most of the provisions Bush wanted. The end result was a new agency with unrivaled power to organize itself without congressional oversight. The new agency is much more oriented toward the president and appointed executives than to Congress. Since its approval there has been further political skirmishing. Democrats accuse the Bush administration of underfunding key responsibilities and DHS programs such as providing training grants to police officers and firefighters.[6]

Even setting aside the political battles over the agency, fully organizing the DHS and integrating the agencies under its umbrella is a multiyear task. Among the biggest challenges is integrating the computer and email systems of the various department agencies. Without such integration it is difficult to share information, not just internally but with the state and local governments who provide much of the nation's first-response capability. Sorting out these challenges requires significant investments of money, time, and expertise. On top of the information technology problems are personnel issues. Agencies with long histories, unique organizational cultures, and their own traditions and ways of doing things have to change in order to work together. This is hard enough, but on top of that, many employees have been stripped of the labor protections expected and enjoyed by most other federal employees. The potential for resentment and alienation is significant, and from a personnel standpoint it will take talented and committed leadership to make everything work.[7]

What DHS demonstrates is that while it is easy to say that the government should better organize itself to prevent further terrorist attacks, the administrative challenge in practice is enormous. Integrating communication technologies and computer systems, merging personnel systems (or creating new ones), changing hierarchies, and pushing tighter working relationships between agencies are not things that will be accomplished overnight. They take time, money, and commitment, and like all reorganizations of the public bureaucracy, they will be unavoidably tangled up in politics. If nothing else, the creation of the DHS shows that partisan interests will never be far away.

Funding

There is considerable debate about who should bear the financial responsibility for homeland security. Local governments often see the federal government quick to take charge of homeland security, and slow to cover the costs. The financial burden to state and local governments for the increased focus on homeland security is considerable. What we are talking about are extra personnel, equipment, and training, as well as new infrastructure investments, all high-dollar items. In the two years following 9/11, for example, the city of Seattle spent about $6 million extra on training, improving coordination, and overtime pay for first responders. Baltimore, Maryland, spent roughly $11 million to upgrade security, and is expecting to pay an extra $10 million a year. Sometimes local governments simply do not have the money to adequately fund security programs. In Iowa, for example, healthcare workers received about 1,000 units of smallpox vaccine, but did not have the money to cover the costs of learning how to properly and effectively administer the vaccines.[8]

Nationwide, new homeland security costs in the form of increased training, more personnel, new equipment, new programs, and new responsibilities run into billions. These costs coincide with burgeoning federal deficits and tight fiscal times for state and local governments. The federal government's approach has largely been to offer block grants to cover the costs of equipment and training. These block grants

284 ◆ *Chapter 11*

fall considerably short of the actual totals being spent by state and local governments, who often resent the federal government's trying to assume a position of command without fully sharing fiscal responsibility. Terror alerts issued by the federal government mean more police officers on patrol and heightened awareness at fire stations, but the federal government has shown little sustained interest in helping to pay for the extra manpower the terror alerts demand. Balitmore Mayor Martin O'Mally voiced the concerns of many local officials when he said, "Our nation cannot fund America's homeland security on the backs of local property taxes and fire hall bingo proceeds."[9]

Legalities

Changes in the law following 9/11—both in terms of passing new laws and interpreting existing laws—raise new questions about the power and authority of public agencies. These legal questions are particularly important in the area of civil rights. Following the September 11 attacks the federal government passed laws giving certain law enforcement agencies sweeping search-and-seizure powers and stripping civil rights away from individuals charged with—or even simply suspected of—engaging in terrorist-related activities. To some extent this reaction is understandable—it simply reflects the feelings of Americans at the time that the safety of the many trumps the civil rights of a few. From a public-administration standpoint, however, the implications of new laws providing unelected bureaucrats sweeping new powers is considerable.

An obvious concern raised about these new powers is the loss of civil liberties, and in the first few years following September 11, a number of groups argued that federal law enforcement agencies had been given too much power, and that individual rights needed to be reaffirmed and reestablished, either through new legislation or court challenges to laws such as the Patriot Act. A not-so-obvious concern is the dilemma the conflicting expectations put on public officials. Being the enforcement arm of the homeland security effort involves a delicate balancing act. No one wants to repeat the mistakes of 9/11 and let terrorists slip through the regulatory net, but no one wants to punish the innocent. The problem for everyone, from police officers, to airport screeners, to immigration officials, to customs agents is that in the field the difference between the good guys and the bad guys is not always apparent. Should they be aggressive, figuring it is better to err on the side of being overly suspicious rather than run the risks of missing a terrorist? Or should they be more deferential to the rights and liberties of the individual, figuring the overwhelming majority of people are law abiding and should not have the shadow of suspicion cast upon them because of, say, their ethnicity, national origin, religion, or even their skin color and looks?

The easy answer, of course, is that public officials should do both—aggressively enforce the rules and go after terrorists while respecting the rights and dignity of individuals. In practice, that balancing act is hard to achieve, and many agencies involved in the homeland security effort are still learning how to identify wrongdoers who do not want to be found without violating the rights and liberty of law-abiding people.

Personnel

One of the practical challenges facing public administration is the continuing need to attract highly qualified people into public-sector careers. A hard reality facing government in the twenty-first century is that the vast majority of Americans prefer to work for the private sector. Asked whether they would prefer working for a private firm or a government agency, roughly two-thirds of poll respondents favor the private-sector job. Less than a quarter express a preference for the public sector.[10]

Perhaps even more disconcerting is that those who do express an interest in public-sector jobs are less educated and have fewer skills than those interested in private-sector jobs. College graduates, for example, overwhelmingly express a preference for private-sector careers, even though as a group they are more likely to find work in the public sector than those with less education. Moreover, the number of people who express interest in public-sector careers is declining rapidly. During the 1990s, the number of people expressing preference for a public-sector job dropped by a third. This problem is especially acute among younger Americans, who as a group are less likely to want or to have a government job.[11]

The bottom line here is that public agencies are facing a huge problem in attracting the best and the brightest. How should they respond to this problem? There are some fairly straightforward potential responses. For example, public agencies could make finding and applying for a job easier, perhaps by moving all job listings and application forms online. They could do more recruiting. Readers of this textbook, for example, make an obvious and desirable recruiting pool for public agencies. As authors, we are willing to wager that only a small percentage of you have ever been contacted about potential public-sector job opportunities, though no doubt some of you have sought the information out yourselves. With notable exceptions (e.g., the armed forces), the public sector does a poor job of reaching out to young and talented people to convince them of the benefits of a career in public service.

Marketing and making jobs easier to find and apply for, however, are unlikely to be enough. Governments need to approach the problem from the job seeker's rather than the agency's perspective. What sort of jobs are likely to be attractive to people with the skills, education, and characteristics that public agencies prize? Would they involve merit-based pay or build compensation around seniority? Would they be 9-to-5, punch-a-clock jobs, or be more flexible and embrace trends such as work sharing and telecommuting? Would they even require formal employment? Might it be better to rely more heavily on independent contractors who see public agencies as clients rather than employers? We leave the reader to ponder the best answers; the point we are trying to make here is that given the evolution of the labor market, the government has little choice but to seriously pose the questions.

The Study of Public Administration

It is appropriate to close this look at the challenges and changes of public administration in the twenty-first century by looking at the ongoing evolution of how our subject is studied. For much of the twentieth century the study of public administration was viewed through the lens of the politics-administration dichotomy. Those who studied public administration focused on the technical elements of public administration such as management and organization. Politics was kept at arms length.

This is no longer the case. Those who study public administration now largely acknowledge that Dwight Waldo, one of the preeminent public administration scholars of the past century, was right: the study of bureaucracy and its administration of public programs and policies *is* the study of politics.[12] Rather than focusing on the purely technical aspects of administration, a large portion of modern public administration scholarship is squarely centered on political questions. At the heart of much of the

Library of Congress.

Getting the "best and the brightest" into public service is a perennial challenge for government that shows no sign of diminishing. A classic example is the military; the modern all-volunteer force has struggled to recruit highly qualified candidates to its ranks while fighting an increasingly unpopular war. Pay differences, flexibility, and the career mobility of the private sector often put public agencies at a recruiting disadvantage.

professional study of the bureaucracy today are questions of political control, or how to ensure that bureaucracy remains a servant of democracy. Rather than the politics-administration dichotomy, current public administration scholarship is heavily influenced by principal agent theory. **Principal agent theory** seeks to explain how one actor (the principal) can get another actor (the agent) to act in the principal's best interests, even though the principal cannot fully control or monitor the agent's actions and effort. The principals for public administration scholars are democratically elected office holders, and the agent is the bureaucracy.

Yet while the bureaucracy's role in a democracy has become a central issue for the study of public administration, it is far from the only issue. Many public administration scholars are less focused on the grand theoretical questions of bureaucracy's role in a democratic society and much more focused on the applied and practical issues of how to make public programs and policies more effective, more efficient, and more accountable. In some ways, those who study public administration have perpetuated the politics-administration dichotomy, with some focusing on the applied issues of administration such as management and performance evaluation while others focus on broader theoretical questions and their implications. The latter include issues such as the inherent tension between democracy and bureaucracy, the difficulty in making bureaucracy a representative form of government, and the task of making bureaucracy the servant of democracy rather than serving its own interests. The end result is that public administration has become something of a schizophrenic academic discipline, with widely divergent opinions on what public administration is and what are the primary issues it must face.[13]

These differences leave the field of public administration, at least as an academic discipline, facing big challenges for the twenty-first century. Some scholars see public administration as a discipline in trouble, without unifying theories or issues, and in danger of being broken up and dissolving into related disciplines such as business administration, political science, and academics. Others see a healthy pluralism rather than a dangerous fragmentation, a field that is "engaged in a healthy introspection, not tied to any paradigmatic dogma, constantly experimenting with fresh approaches, and beginning to formulate original ways of thinking about its arena of study."[14] We tend to side with the latter perspective, but also recognize that there are no guarantees. In the twenty-first century public administration will either find its feet as an independent field of study, be broken up and taken on as appendages in other fields, or stagger along as something in between. The jury is very much out on which of these three directions will actually materialize.

Despite such uncertainty, we can confidently say that whatever its ultimate academic fate, public administration as we've described it in

288 ◆ *Chapter 11*

this book will continue to be an important arena of study, and that politics will remain at its heart.

Conclusion

What we have covered in this chapter represents just a portion of the issues and challenges public administration must face in the near future. They should suffice, however, to convey the main point: at the beginning of the twenty-first century, public administration is facing pressure to change from many quarters. Some of these pressures are extensions of issues bureaucracy has been dealing with for a long time (e.g., to be more businesslike and less bureaucratic), and others come from new technologies and unforeseen events (e.g., the rise of the World Wide Web, the terrorist attacks of September 11, 2001).

Responding to this disparate set of challenges is doubly difficult. The demands being made on public administration require new skills and technologies, new ways of thinking about public programs and services, and more organizational experimentation. These demands are asking public agencies to do contradictory things. Consider the rise of the ATM bureaucracy and the shift in attitudes arising from the great governance debate. These demand public agencies become less bureaucratic; in essence, they are telling the public sector to swap centralization for networks, hierarchy for accessibility, rules and red tape for customer service. The changing nature of the policy problems public agencies deal with, and the lessening importance of defined political jurisdictions, push public administration down the same path.

Yet consider the pressures being created by the demand for homeland security: greater centralization, clearer lines of authority and responsibility, more power for public agencies to set and enforce rules. All of this sounds a lot like a call for good old-fashioned bureaucracy. What should be recognized as riding on the tails of the calls for both less and more bureaucracy is politics. A new agency is used as an opportunity to alter merit-system rules. There are demands for less regulation until some scandal or failure arises, then there will be calls for more. And so it goes. Regardless of its twenty-first century characteristics, the changes add up to something familiar for public administration. It is what we began this textbook with: a paradox. Democracy is still trying to find a way to get along without bureaucracy, and in some ways it is actually making headway. Yet it is far from being able to manage without bureaucracy, and in some ways is looking for more, rather than less. This highlights that studying public administration unavoidably means studying politics, and politics is what professional students of public administration are increasingly putting at the heart of their studies.

So, whatever changes come its way in the coming century—and undoubtedly there will be many—it is a sure bet that public administration will remain the all-important connection between democracy and bureaucracy. It will remain the process, the organization, and, above all, the politics that make that paradox work.

Key Concepts

ATM bureaucracy The delivery of public programs and services electronically, typically via the Internet.

disarticulated state A term that describes the decreasing importance of geographical borders to political jurisdictions. In the disarticulated state, problems ranging from traffic congestion to water conservation management are addressed by cooperation and coordination among public agencies in different political jurisdictions.

e-government Another term for ATM bureaucracy.

the great governance debate A wide-ranging reexamination of what government is and what it is expected to do. This debate has been a central concern to public administration scholars since the 1970s.

principal agent theory Principal agent theory seeks to explain how one actor (the principal) can get another actor (the agent) to act in the principal's best interests, even though the principal cannot fully control or monitor the agent's actions and effort.

virtual state A government that funds public programs and services, but does not provide them directly. Instead, it contracts out delivery of programs and services to private vendors. Also called a hollow state. ✦

Notes

Chapter 1

1. Kevin Fullerton, "Who You Gonna Call?," *The Austin Chronicle*, February 23, 2001, http://www.austinchronicle.com/issues/dispatch/2001-02-23/pols_feature3.html.
2. Find out more about the agency online: http://www.orca.state.tx.us/.
3. Quoted in Allison Cook, "ORCA—Not a Killer, but a Whale of a Texas Agency," *State Legislatures* July/August (2004):46.
4. William Richardson, *Democracy, Bureaucracy, and Character* (University Press of Kansas: Lawrence, 1997), 5.
5. Kenneth J. Meier, *Politics and the Bureaucracy: Policymaking in the Fourth Branch of Government* (Brooks/Cole: Pacific Grove, CA, 1993), 2.
6. Census Bureau, *The Statistical Abstract of the United States* (2004), Table 454, http://www.census.gov/prod/2004pubs/04statab/stlocgov.pdf.
7. Dan Rutz, "Milwaukee Learned Its Water Lesson, but Many Other Cities Haven't," *CNN.com*, September 2, 1996, http://www.cnn.com/HEALTH/9609/02/nfm/water.quality/.
8. National Center for Education Statistics, *Digest of Education Statistics* (Department of Education: Washington, DC, 2001).
9. F. King Alexander, "Private Institutions and Public Dollars: An Analysis of the Effects of Federal Direct Student Aid on Public and Private Institutions of Higher Education," *Journal of Education Finance* 23 (1998): 390–416.
10. Ibid.
11. Herbert Simon, *Administrative Behavior*, 4th ed. (The Free Press: New York, 1997), 1.
12. Census Bureau, *The Statistical Abstract of the United States*, Table 417.
13. Charles Goodsell, *The Case for Bureaucracy* (Chatham House Press: Chatham, NJ, 1994), 8.
14. Max Weber, *From Max Weber: Essays in Sociology*, eds. H.H. Gerth and C. Wright Mills (Oxford University Press: New York, 1946).
15. Meier, *Politics and the Bureaucracy*.
16. Harold D. Lasswell, *Politics: Who Gets What, When and How?* (McGraw-Hill: New York, 1936); David Easton, *A Systems Analysis of Political Life* (Wiley: New York, 1965).

17. Dwight Waldo, *The Administrative State* (The Ronald Press Company: New York, 1948).
18. Michael Lipsky, *Street-Level Bureaucracy* (Russell Sage Foundation: New York, 1980).
19. Cornelius Kerwin, *Rulemaking: How Government Agencies Write Law and Make Policy,* 2nd ed. (CQ Press: Washington, DC, 1999).
20. John Gaus, "Trends in the Theory of Public Administration," *Public Administration Review* 3 (1950):161–168.
21. Ronald Moe and Robert Gilmour, "Rediscovering the Principles of Public Administration: The Neglected Foundation of Public Law," *Public Administration Review* 55 (1995):135–146.
22. Richard Box, Gary Marshall, B.J. Reed, and Christine Reed, "New Public Management and Substantive Democracy," *Public Administration Review* 61 (2001):608–619.

Chapter 2

1. Charles Goodsell, *The Case for Bureaucracy,* 4th ed. (CQ Press: Washington, DC, 2004).
2. Kenneth J. Meier, *Politics and the Bureaucracy: Policymaking in the Fourth Branch of Government,* 4th ed. (Harcourt Brace: Fort Worth, TX, 2000).
3. A good discussion of the structure of the bureaucracy is found in Meier, *Politics and the Bureaucracy,* 15–25.
4. Max Neiman, *Defending Government: Why Big Government Works* (Prentice Hall: Upper Saddle River, NJ, 2000).
5. Marc Allen Eisner, *Regulatory Politics in Transition,* 2nd ed. (Johns Hopkins University Press: Baltimore, 2000).
6. Meier, *Politics and the Bureaucracy.*
7. Brian J. Cook, *Bureaucracy and Self-Governance* (Johns Hopkins University Press: Baltimore, 1996).
8. Ibid.
9. Hal Rainy, *Understanding and Managing Public Organizations* (Jossey-Bass: San Francisco, 1997).
10. Francis Rourke, *Bureaucracy, Politics, and Public Policy,* 3rd ed. (Little, Brown: Boston, 1984).
11. Theodore Lowi, *The End of Liberalism,* 2nd ed. (W.W. Norton: New York, 1979).
12. Paul Quirk, "Food and Drug Administration," in *The Politics of Regulation,* ed. James Q. Wilson (Basic Books: New York, 1980).
13. William Berry, "An Alternative to the Capture Theory of Regulation," *American Journal of Political Science* 28 (1984):524–58.
14. John Kingdon, *Agendas, Alternatives, and Public Policies,* 2nd ed. (Longman: New York, 2003).
15. Brian J. Cook, *Bureaucracy and Self-Government* (Johns Hopkins University Press: Baltimore, 1996).
16. Lawrence Gostin, *Public Health Law: Power, Duty, Restraint* (University of California Press: Berkeley, CA, 2000).
17. Paul Sabatier, "An Advocacy Coalition Framework of Policy Change and the Role of Policy-Oriented Learning Therein," *Policy Sciences* 6 (1988):301–42; Kenneth Meier and Lael Keiser, "Public Administration

as a Science of the Artificial: A Methodology for Prescription," *Public Administration Review* 56 (1996):459–66.

18. Ronald Sylvia and C. Kenneth Meyer, *Public Personnel Administration*, 2nd ed. (Harcourt: Orlando, FL, 2002).

19. N. Joseph Cayer, *Public Personnel Administration*, 4th ed. (Wadsworth: Belmont, CA, 2004).

20. Richard Jensen, *Winning of the Midwest* (University of Chicago Press: Chicago, 1971).

Chapter 3

1. Alan Greenblatt, "A Rage to Reorganize," *Governing* 18 (March 2005): 30–35.

2. California Department of Corrections, *Department of Corrects' Vision, Mission, Values and Goals* (2005), http://www.corr.ca.gov/CDC/mission.asp.

3. Herbert Simon, *Administrative Behavior*, 4th ed. (The Free Press: New York, 1997), 1.

4. Ronald C. Moe and Robert S. Gilmour, "Rediscovering Principles of Public Administration: The Neglected Foundation of Public Law," *Public Administration Review* 55 (1995):135–146.

5. Ibid.

6. James Q. Wilson, *Bureaucracy: What Government Agencies Do and Why They Do It* (Basic Books: New York, 1989), 158.

7. Springfield-Greene County Library (2004), http://thelibrary.springfield.missouri.org/about/mission.cfm.

8. George W. Downs and Patrick D. Larkey, *The Search for Government Efficiency* (Temple University Press: Philadelphia, PA, 1986), 6–11.

9. Deborah Stone, *Policy Paradox: The Art of Political Decision Making* (W.W. Norton: New York, 1997), 64.

10. Downs and Larkey, *The Search for Government Efficiency*, 6–11.

11. Alan Greenblatt, "The Left Behind Syndrome," *Governing* 17 (September 2004):38–43.

12. Downs and Larkey, *The Search for Government Efficiency*, 6–11.

13. Kenneth J. Meier, "Bureaucracy and Democracy: The Case for More Bureaucracy and Less Democracy," *Public Administration Review* 57 (1997):193–199.

14. Cornelius Kerwin, *Rulemaking* (CQ Press: Washington, DC, 1999).

15. Wilson, *Bureaucracy*, 37.

16. Ibid., 91.

17. Ibid., 103.

18. William Niskanen, *Bureaucracy and Economics* (Edward Elgar Publishing: Brookfield, VT, 1994).

19. Wilson, *Bureaucracy*, 70.

20. Meier, "Bureaucracy and Democracy."

21. Charles T. Goodsell, *The Case for Bureaucracy* (Chatham House Publishers: Chatham, NJ, 1994), 8.

22. Elliott D. Sclar, *You Don't Always Get What You Pay For* (Cornell University Press: Ithaca, NY, 2000).

23. Harold Seidman, *Politics, Position, and Power: The Dynamics of Federal Organization* (Oxford University Press: New York, 1998), 3.

24. Citizens Against Government Waste, http://www.cagw.org/site/Page Server?pagename=FAQ.

25. David Osborne and Ted Gaebler, *Reinventing Government: How the Entrepreneurial Spirit Is Transforming the Public Sector* (Plume: New York, 1993).

26. Seidman, *Politics, Position, and Power*, 12.

27. Ibid., 14.

28. Downs and Larkey, *The Search for Government Efficiency*, 3.

29. Jonathan Walters, "Going Outside," *Governing* May (2004):23–29.

30. B. Guy Peters and John Pierre, "Governance Without Government? Rethinking Public Administration," *Journal of Public Administration Research and Theory* 8 (1998):223–254.

31. Paul Light, *The True Size of Government* (Brookings: Washington, DC, 1999), 38.

32. Donald Kettl, *Sharing Power* (Brookings: Washington, DC, 1993).

33. Sclar, *You Don't Always Get.*

34. Kettl, *Sharing Power.*

35. Federal Procurement Data Center, http://www.fpdc.gov/.

36. Public Broadcasting Service, "Battle of the X-Planes," *NOVA* (originally aired February 4, 2003).

37. Sclar, *You Don't Always Get*, 84–88.

38. Phillip J. Cooper, "Government Contracts in Public Administration: The Role and Environment of the Contracting Officers." *Public Administration Review* 40 (1980):462.

Chapter 4

1. Greg Winter, "Change in Aid Formula Shifts More Costs to Students," *New York Times* (June 13, 2003).

2. Woodrow Wilson, "The Study of Administration," *Political Science Quarterly* 2 (1887):197–222.

3. Ibid.

4. Paul Appleby, *Policy and Administration* (University of Alabama Press: Tuscaloosa, 1949).

5. David Rosenbloom, "Public Administrative Theory and the Separation of Powers," *Public Administration Review* (1983).

6. Kenneth J. Meier, *Politics and the Bureaucracy*, 4th ed. (Harcourt Brace: Fort Worth, TX, 2000).

7. Kenneth J. Meier, "Bureaucracy and Democracy: The Case for More Bureaucracy and Less Democracy," *Public Administration Review* 57(3) (May/June 1997):193–199.

8. This section draws from the works of Francis Rourke and Kenneth J. Meier; Francis Rourke, *Bureaucracy, Politics, and Public Policy*, 3rd ed. (Little, Brown: Boston, 1984); Meier, *Politics and the Bureaucracy.*

9. Jeanne Nienaber Clarke and Daniel C. McCool, *Staking out the Terrain: Power and Performance Among Natural Resource Agencies*, 2nd ed. (SUNY Press: Albany, 1996), 7.

10. You can read about their exploits at the National Institutes of Health's website: http://www.nih.gov/about/almanac/nobel/#scientists.

11. Rourke, *Bureaucracy, Politics, and Public Policy*, 36.

12. John Scholz and Neil Pinney, "Duty, Fear, and Tax Compliance: The Heuristic Basis of Citizen Behavior," *American Journal of Political Science* 39 (1995):490–512.

13. For a succinct summary of the role and importance of clientele as a source of bureaucratic power see Clarke and McCool, 7.

14. Beryl Radin, *The Accountable Juggler: The Art of Leadership in a Federal Agency* (CQ Press: Washington, DC, 2002); William Gormley and Steven Balla, *Bureaucracy and Democracy: Accountability and Performance* (CQ Press: Washington, DC, 2004).

15. Rourke, *Bureaucracy, Politics, and Public Policy*, 58.

16. Emmette Redford, *Democracy in the Administrative State* (Oxford University Press: New York, 1969), Ch. 4

17. J. Leiper Freeman, *The Political Process*, 2nd ed. (Random House: New York, 1965).

18. Theodore Lowi, *The End of Liberalism: The Second Republic of the United States*, 2nd ed. (W.W. Norton: New York, 1979).

19. A. Lee Fritschler and James M. Hoefler, *Smoking and Politics: Policy Making and the Federal Bureaucracy*, 5th ed. (Prentice Hall: Upper Saddle River, NJ, 1996).

20. James Q. Wilson, *Bureaucracies: What Government Agencies Do and Why They Do It* (Basic Books: New York, 1989).

21. Ibid.

22. Meier, *Politics and the Bureaucracy*.

23. Corneilus Kerwin, *Rulemaking: How Government Agencies Write Law and Make Policy* (CQ Press: Washington, DC, 1994).

24. Kerwin offers a highly detailed outline of the process on pages 76–77.

25. Ibid., 51.

26. Meier, *Politics and the Bureaucracy*.

Chapter 5

1. *CNN.com*, "Voided Check Scandal Is Rare for Nebraska Politics," December 17, 2003, http://www.cnn.com/2003/US/Central/12/17/nebraska.scandal.ap/; Jackie Spinner, "Soldier Gets 1 Year in Abuse of Iraqis," *Washington Post* May 19, 2004, http://www.washingtonpost.com/wp-dyn/articles/A38672-2004May19.html.

2. Frederick Mosher, *Democracy and the Public Service* (Oxford University Press: New York, 1982), 7.

3. M. Josephson, *Power, Politics, and Ethics: Ethical Obligations and Opportunities of Government Service* (Government Ethics Center: Marina del Rey, CA, 1989), 2.

4. See John A. Rohr, *Ethics for Bureaucrats* (Marcel Dekker: New York, 1978).

5. P.G. Brown, "Ethics and Public Policy: A Preliminary Agenda," *Policy Studies Journal* 7 (1978):132–137; T.L. Cooper, *An Ethic of Citizenship for Public Administration* (Prentice Hall: Englewood Cliffs, NJ, 1991).

6. Carol W. Lewis, "Ethics Codes and Ethics Agencies: Current Practices and Emerging Trends," in *Ethics and Public Administration*, ed. H. George Frederickson (M.E. Sharpe: Armonk, NY, 1993).

7. Paul Appleby, *Morality and Administration in Democratic Government* (Louisiana State University Press: Baton Rouge, 1952).

8. James L. Perry, "Antecedent of Public Service Motivation," *Journal of Public Administration Research and Theory* 7 (1997):181–197.

9. Kenneth J. Meier, *Politics and the Bureaucracy: Policymaking in the Fourth Branch of Government* (Brooks/Cole: Pacific Grove, CA, 1993), 194.

10. The President's Commission on Federal Ethics Law Reform, *To Serve With Honor* (U.S. Government Printing Office: Washington, DC, 1989).

11. Barbara Romzek and Melvin Dubnick, "Accountability in the Public Sector: Lessons From the Challenger Tragedy," *Public Administration Review* 47 (1987):228.

12. Gregg Garn, "Moving from Bureaucratic to Market Accountability: The Problem of Imperfect Information," *Educational Administration Quarterly* 37(40) (2001):571–599.

13. Linda Francis, "Conflicting Bureaucracies, Conflicted Work: Dilemmas in Case Management for Homeless People with Mental Illness," *Journal of Sociology and Social Welfare* 27 (2000):97–112.

14. Romzek and Dubnick, "Accountability in the Public Sector," 279.

15. R. Kearney and C. Sinha, "Professionalism and Bureaucratic Responsiveness: Conflict or Compatibility," *Public Administration Review* 48 (1988):281.

16. Grace Hall Saltzstein, "Conceptualizing Bureaucratic Responsiveness," *Administration & Society* 17(3) (1985):289.

17. Meier, *Politics and the Bureaucracy,* 144.

18. Richard Box, Gary Marshall, B.J. Reed, and Christine Reed, "New Public Management and Substantive Democracy," *Public Administration Review* 61 (2001):608–619.

19. V.O. Key. "Legislative Control," in *Elements of Public Administration,* ed. Fritz Morstein Marx (Prentice-Hall: Englewood Cliffs, NJ, 1959), 312–346.

20. Meier, *Politics and the Bureaucracy,* 154.

21. Ibid., 163.

22. Dwight Waldo, "Development of Theory of Democratic Administration," *American Political Science Review* 46 (1948):81–103.

23. Woodrow Wilson, "The Study of Administration," *Political Science Quarterly* 2 (1887):197–222.

24. Sally Selden, *The Promise of Representative Bureaucracy* (M.E. Sharpe: Armonk, NY, 1997).

25. Kenneth J. Meier, "Representative Bureaucracy: An Empirical Analysis," *American Political Science Review* 69 (1975):527.

26. J. Donald Kingsley, *Representative Bureaucracy* (Antioch Press: Yellow Springs, OH, 1944).

27. Selden, *The Promise of Representative Bureaucracy.*

28. Percentages calculated from: Census Bureau, *Statistical Abstract of the United States* (2004), Table 456, http://www.census.gov/prod/2004pubs/04statab/stlocgov.pdf.

29. David Osborne and Peter Plastrik, *Banishing Bureaucracy* (Plume: New York, 1997), 184–185.

30. Federal Inspectors General, *An Introduction to the Inspectors General Community,* http://www.ignet.gov/igs/igbrochure.pdf.

31. Paul C. Light, "Federal Ethics Controls: The Role of Inspectors General," in *Ethics and Public Administration,* ed. H. George Frederickson (M.E. Sharpe: Armonk, NY, 1993).

32. Robert W. Smith, "Corporate Ethics Officers and Government Ethics Administrators: Comparing Apples With Oranges, or a Lesson to be Learned?" *Administration & Society* 34 (2003):632–652.

Chapter 6

1. Ted Gregory, "Labor Agency Plays Hardball With 12-, 13-Year-Old Umps," *Child Labor News* (Illinois Parks and Recreation Association, 2002), http://www.il-ipra.org/resources/ChildLaborNews.cfm.
2. Ronald Moe and Robert Gilmour, "Rediscovering the Principles of Public Administration: The Neglected Foundation of Public Law," *Public Administration Review* 55 (1995):135–146.
3. Herbert Simon, *Administrative Behavior* (The Free Press: New York, 1997), 2.
4. Michael Lipsky, *Street-Level Bureaucracy* (Russell Sage Foundation: New York, 1980).
5. Ralph C. Chandler and Jack C. Plano, *The Public Administration Dictionary* (ABC-Clio: Santa Barbara, CA, 1988), 127.
6. Ibid., 127–131.
7. William Fox and Ivan Meyer, *Public Administration Dictionary* (Juta & Co.: Cape Town, South Africa, 1995).
8. Simon, *Administrative Behavior.*
9. Charles Lindblom, "The Science of Muddling Through," *Public Administration Review* 19 (1959):79–88.
10. Sharon Smith and Ronald J. Stupak, "Public Sector Downsizing Decision-Making in the 1990s: Moving Beyond the Mixed Scanning Model," *Public Administration Quarterly* 17 (1994):359–379.
11. Amitai Etzioni, "Mixed Scanning: A 'Third' Approach to Decision Making," *Public Administration Review* 27 (1967):395–392.
12. Frank R. Baumgartner and Bryan D. Jones, *Agendas and Instability in American Politics* (University of Chicago Press: Chicago, 1993).
13. John Brehm and Scott Gates, *Working, Shirking, and Sabotage* (University of Michigan Press: Ann Arbor, 1997).
14. Chester I. Barnard, *The Functions of the Executive* (Harvard University Press: Cambridge, MA, 1938).
15. Mary Parker Follett, "The Giving of Orders," in *Scientific Foundations of Business Administration,* ed. H.C. Metcalf (Williams and Wilkins Company: Baltimore, MD, 1926).
16. B.F. Skinner, *Science and Human Behavior* (Macmillan: New York, 1953).
17. Douglas Murray McGregor, *The Human Side of Enterprise* (McGraw-Hill: New York, 1957).
18. Frederick Herzberg, "One More Time: How Do You Motivate Employees?," *Harvard Business Review* 46 (1968):1.
19. Abraham Maslow, "A Theory of Human Motivation," *Psychological Review* 50 (1943):370–396.
20. Graham Allison and Morton Halperin, "Bureaucratic Politics: A Paradigm and Some Policy Implications," *World Politics* Spring (1972):40–79.
21. Frederick Winslow Taylor, *The Principles of Scientific Management* (Harper and Row: New York, 1911).

22. Luther Gulick, *Papers on the Science of Administration* (Institute of Public Administration: New York, 1937); Henri Fayol, *General and Industrial Management* (Pitman Printing: London, 1949).
23. Simon, *Administrative Behavior.*
24. David Osborne and Ted Gaebler, *Reinventing Government* (Addison-Wesley: Reading, PA, 1992).
25. H. George Frederickson and Kevin B. Smith, *The Public Administration Theory Primer* (Westview Press: Boulder, CO, 2003), 238.

Chapter 7

1. Government Accountability Office, *Youth Illicit Drug Use Prevention* (2003), http://www.gao.gov/new.items/d03172r.pdf#search='D.A.R.E. %20program%20evaluation'. The report shows that many program evaluations have not revealed any lasting influence in terms of reducing drug use as a result of participating in the program.
2. "Minneapolis Discontinues Schools' D.A.R.E. Effort," *Alcohol and Drug Abuse Weekly* 11 (1999):8.
3. Charles Goodsell, *The Case for Bureaucracy* (CQ Press: Washington, DC, 2004).
4. James Q. Wilson, *Bureaucracy: What Government Agencies Do and Why They Do It* (Basic Books: New York, 1989).
5. Kenneth J. Meier, *Politics and the Bureaucracy,* 4th ed. (Harcourt: Orlando, FL, 2000).
6. Wilson, *Bureaucracy,* 129.
7. Goodsell, *The Case for Bureaucracy.*
8. Meier, *Politics and the Bureaucracy.*
9. William Gormley and Steven Balla, *Bureaucracy and Democracy: Accountability and Performance* (CQ Press: Washington, DC, 2004), especially Chapter 4.
10. Beryl Radin, *The Accountable Juggler: The Art of Leadership in a Federal Agency* (CQ Press: Washington, DC, 2002).
11. John Kingdon, *Agendas, Alternatives, and Public Policies,* 2nd ed. (Longman: New York, 2003).
12. Paul Sabatier and Hand Jenkins-Smith, *Policy Change and Learning: An Advocacy Coalition Approach* (Westview: Boulder, CO, 1993), 213.
13. Meier, *Politics and the Bureaucracy.*
14. Charles Goodsell, "Looking Once Again at Human Service Bureaucracy," *Journal of Politics* 43 (1981):763–778; Barry Bozeman and Gordon Kingsley, "Risk Culture in Public and Private Organizations," *Public Administration Review* 58 (1998):109–118.
15. Herbert Kaufman, *Red Tape: Its Origins, Uses, and Abuses* (The Brookings Institution: Washington, DC, 1977).
16. Goodsell, *The Case for Bureaucracy.*
17. Meier, *Politics and the Bureaucracy,* 114.
18. Ibid., 115.
19. Gormley and Balla, *Bureaucracy and Democracy.*
20. Meier, *Politics and the Bureaucracy,* 6.
21. Jeffrey Pressman and Aaron Wildavsky, *Implementation* (University of California Press: Berkeley, 1973).
22. Goodsell, *The Case for Bureaucracy,* 66.

23. Chilik Yu, Laurence O'Toole Jr., James Cooley, Gail Cowie, Susan Crow, and Stephanie Herbert, "Policy Instruments for Reducing Toxic Releases: The Effectiveness of State Information and Enforcement Actions," *Evaluation Review* 22 (1998):571–589.

24. Susan Paddock, "Evaluation" in *Introduction to Public Administration: A Book of Readings*, eds. J. Steven Ott and E.W. Russell (Addison Wesley Longman: New York, 2001).

25. Emil Posavac and Raymond G. Carey, *Program Evaluation: Methods and Case Studies*, 6th ed. (Prentice Hall: Upper Saddle River, NJ, 2003).

26. Ibid., 7.

27. Ibid., 6.

28. Dennis Palumbo, *The Politics of Program Evaluation* (Sage: Newbury Park, CA, 1987).

29. Posavac and Carey, *Program Evaluation.*

30. Gene Lutz, Michael Philipp, Ki-Hyung Park, and Natalie Jensen. *City of Cedar Falls 2004 Citizen Survey* (University of Northern Iowa: Center for Social and Behavioral Research, 2004).

31. Posavac and Carey, *Program Evaluation.*

32. Kenneth Bickers and John Williams, *Public Policy Analysis* (Houghton Mifflin: Boston, 2001).

33. David Weimer and Aidan Vining, *Policy Analysis: Concepts and Practice*, 4th ed. (Prentice Hall: Upper Saddle River, NJ, 2004).

34. Ibid., 378.

35. B. Guy Peters, *American Public Policy: Promise and Performance*, 6th ed. (CQ Press: Washington, DC, 2004).

36. Ibid., 428.

37. Ibid., 435.

38. Grover Starling, *Managing the Public Sector*, 6th ed. (Harcourt: Orlando, FL, 2002).

39. Centers for Disease Control and Prevention, *Best Practices for Comprehensive Tobacco Control Programs* (Centers for Disease Control and Prevention: Atlanta, 1999).

40. Centers for Disease Control and Prevention, *Sustaining State Funding for Tobacco Control: Snapshot From Virginia* (Centers for Disease Control and Prevention: Atlanta, 2005).

41. American Lung Association, http://lungaction.org/reports/tobacco-control04.html.

42. William Gormley and David Weimer, *Organizational Report Cards* (Harvard University Press: Cambridge, MA, 1999), 3.

43. Ibid., 3–5.

44. Office of Management and Budget, *Analytical Perspectives for the Fiscal Year 2006 Budget of the United States* (Office of Management and Budget: Washington, DC, 2005).

45. Ibid., 123.

46. Ibid., 135.

Chapter 8

1. Emily Christensen, "Gartner Holding Hope Tuition Increase Won't Be Necessary," *Waterloo-Cedar Falls Courier*, June 15, 2005, A1.

2. Irene Rubin, *Balancing the Federal Budget: Trimming the Herd or Eating the Seed Corn?* (Chatham House/Seven Bridges Press: New York, 2003).

3. James Gosling, *Budgetary Politics in American Governments*, 3rd ed. (Routledge: New York, 2002).

4. Ibid.; also see Ronald Fisher, *State and Local Public Finance* (Irwin: Chicago, 1996).

5. Gosling, *Budgetary Politics in American Governments*.

6. Harold Lasswell, *Politics: Who Gets What, When, How?* (World Publishing: New York, 1958).

7. U.S. Census Bureau, *2002 Statistical Abstract of the United States* (Government Printing Office: Washington DC, 2002).

8. David Nice, *Public Budgeting* (Wadsworth: Belmont, CA, 2002); see also Gosling, *Budgetary Politics in American Governments*.

9. Gosling, *Budgetary Politics in American Governments*.

10. Ibid., 11.

11. William T. Gormley Jr. and David L. Weimer, *Organizational Report Cards* (Harvard University Press: Cambridge, 1999).

12. Aaron Wildavsky and Naomi Caiden, *The New Politics of the Budgetary Process*, 5th ed. (Pearson Longman: New York, 2004).

13. Gosling, *Budgetary Politics in American Governments*.

14. Ibid., 8.

15. Wildavsky and Caiden, *The New Politics of the Budgetary Process*.

16. Rubin, *Balancing the Federal Budget*.

17. Irene Rubin, *The Politics of Public Budgeting* (Chatham House: Chatham, NJ, 1997).

18. Ibid., 213.

19. John Mikesell, *Fiscal Administration*, 6th ed. (Wadsworth: Belmont, CA, 2003).

20. Government Accountability Office, *Biennial Budgeting: Three States' Experiences* (Government Printing Office: Washington, DC, 2000).

21. Gosling, *Budgetary Politics in American Governments*.

22. Don Cozzetto, Mary Grisez Kweit, and Robert Kweit, *Public Budgeting: Politics, Institutions, Processes* (Longman: White Plains, NY, 1995).

23. Gosling, *Budgetary Politics in American Governments*.

24. Ibid.

25. Greg Von Behren and Paul Korfonta, *Budget Processes in the States* (National Association of State Budget Officers: Washington DC, 2002).

26. Glen Abney and Thomas Lauth, "The Line-Item Veto in the States," *Public Administration Review* 45 (1985):373.

27. National Association of State Budget Officers, *Budget Processes in the States*.

28. Ibid.

29. Gosling, *Budgetary Politics in American Governments*.

30. Ibid.

31. Ibid.

32. E.S. Savas, *Privatization: The Key to Better Government* (Chatham House: Chatham, NJ, 1987).

33. Charles Tiebout, "A Pure Theory of Local Expenditures," *Journal of Political Economy* 64 (1956):422.

34. See criticism in Ronald Fisher, *State and Local Public Finance* (Irwin: Chicago, 1996).

35. This section draws upon Gosling, *Budgetary Politics in American Governments*, 187–189.

36. Herbert Simon, *Administrative Behavior* (Macmillan: New York, 1958).

37. Charles Lindblom, "Decision Making in Taxation and Expenditures," in *National Bureau of Economic Research Public Finances: Needs, Sources, and Utilization* (Princeton University Press: Princeton, NJ, 1961).

38. Wildavsky and Caiden, *The New Politics of the Budgetary Process*.

39. Catheryn Seckler-Hudson, "Performance Budgeting in Government," *Advanced Management* 18 (1953):5–9, 30–32 (reprinted in *Government Budgeting*, 3rd ed., ed Albert C. Hyde [Wadsworth: Belmont, CA, 2002]).

40. Allen Schick, "A Death in the Bureaucracy: The Demise of Federal PPB," *Public Administration Review* 33 (1973):146–156.

41. Graeme Taylor, "Introduction to Zero-Base Budgeting," *The Bureaucrat* 6 (1977):33–35 (reprinted in *Government Budgeting*, 3rd ed., ed Albert C. Hyde [Wadsworth: Belmont, CA, 2002]).

42. Iowa Department of Management, *Budget Process Overview* (2005), http://www.dom.state.ia.us/state/budget_proposals/files/general/process_overview.html.

Chapter 9

1. Jonathan Walters, "Worth the Money?," *Governing* July (2004):34–37.

2. CNN, "Teachers Paid an Average Salary of $46,752, Survey Finds" (June 24, 2005), http://www.cnn.com/2005/EDUCATION/06/24/teacher.salaries.ap/.

3. Don A. Cozzetto, Theodore B. Pedeliski, and Terence J. Tipple, *Public Personnel Administration: Confronting the Challenges of Change* (Prentice Hall: Upper Saddle River, NJ, 1996), 3–4.

4. Robert D. Lee Jr., *Public Personnel Systems* (Aspen Publishers: Gaithersburg, MD, 1993), 3–4.

5. AFL-CIO, "Executive Paywatch," 2004, http://www.aflcio.org/corporateamerica/paywatch/.

6. U.S. Office of Special Counsel, "Hatch Act for Federal Employees" (2004), http://www.osc.gov/hatchact.htm.

7. CNN, "The Air Traffic Controllers Strike" (2005), http://www.cnn.com/SPECIAL/2001/reagan.years/whitehouse/airtraffic.html.

8. S.H. Aronson, *Status and Kinship in the Higher Civil Service* (Harvard University Press: Cambridge, MA, 1964).

9. Paul Van Riper, *History of the United States Civil Service* (Harper & Row: New York, 1958), 36.

10. U.S. Census Bureau, *Historical Statistics of the United States: Colonial Times to 1970* (U.S. Census Bureau: Washington, DC, 1975), Tables 13, 1072, and 1074.

11. D.R. Harvey, *The Civil Service Commission* (Praeger: New York, 1970), 6.

12. Alfred Steinberg, *The Bosses* (MacMillan: New York, 1972).

13. Lee, *Public Personnel Systems*, 20.

14. Keon S. Chi, "State Civil Service Systems," in *Handbook of Human Resource Management in Government*, ed. Stephen E. Condrey (Jossey-Bass Publishers: San Francisco, 1998).
15. Lee, *Public Personnel Systems*, 109–110.
16. Office of Personnel Management, "Presidential Management Fellows Program," http://www.pmf.opm.gov/.
17. Charles Goodsell, *The Case for Bureaucracy: A Public Administration Polemic* (Chatham House: Chatham, NJ, 1994).
18. Christopher Jencks, "Racial Bias in Testing," in *The Black-White Test Score Gap*, eds. Christopher Jencks and Meridith Phillips (The Brookings Institution: Washington, DC, 1998).
19. Dennis V. Damp, *The Book of U.S. Government Jobs*, 7th ed. (Brookhaven Press: Moon Township, PA, 2000), 87.
20. Sally Selden, *The Promise of Representative Bureaucracy: Diversity and Responsiveness in a Government Agency* (M.E. Sharpe: Armonk, NY, 1997).
21. Cozzetto, Pedeliski, and Tipple, *Public Personnel Administration*.
22. Lee, *Public Personnel Systems*, 52–53.
23. Damp, *The Book of U.S. Government Jobs*, 225.
24. Dennis M. Daley, "An Overview of Benefits for the Public Sector," *Review of Public Personnel Administration* 18 (1998):5–22.
25. Lee, *Public Personnel Systems*, 147–148.
26. Cozzetto, Pedeliski, and Tipple, *Public Personnel Administration*.
27. Lee, *Public Personnel Systems*, 152.
28. Laurence Peter and Raymond Hill, *The Peter Principle: Why Things Always Go Wrong* (William Morrow & Co.: New York, 1969).
29. Lee, *Public Personnel Systems*, 174.
30. "Union Membership Edges up, but Share Continues to Fall," *Monthly Labor Review*, January (1999):1–2.
31. Brian Friel, "At DHS, the Bush Team and Unions are Actually Getting Along," *Govexec.com* (2003), http://www.govexec.com/dailyfed/0703/070103b1.htm.
32. Jonathan Walters, "Civil Service Tsunami" *Governing* 16 (May 2003): 34–40.
33. Charles W. Gossett, "Civil Service Reform," *Review of Public Personnel Administration* 22 (2002):94–113.
34. J. Edward Kellough and Sally Coleman Selden, "The Reinvention of Public Personnel Administration: An Analysis of the Diffusion of Personnel Management Reforms in the States," *Public Administration Review* 63 (2003):165–175.

Chapter 10

1. Minnesota Department of Transportation road construction and maintenance webpage, http://www.dot.state.mn.us/construction.html.
2. Thomas Birkland, *An Introduction to the Policy Process* (M.E. Sharpe: Armonk, NY, 2001), 178.
3. David Spence, "The Benefits of Agency Policymaking: Perspectives From Positive Theory," in *Politics, Policy, and Organizations: Frontiers in the Scientific Study of Bureaucracy*, eds. George Krause and Kenneth J. Meier (University of Michigan Press: Ann Arbor, MI, 2003).

4. Terry Moe, "The New Economics of Organization," *American Journal of Political Science* 28 (1984):739–777.

5. Daniel Mazmanian and Paul A. Sabatier, *Implementation and Public Policy* (University Press of America: Lanham, MD, 1989), 25–26.

6. U.S. Department of Health and Human Services, *Reducing Tobacco Use: A Report of the Surgeon General* (U.S. Department of Health and Human Services, Centers for Disease Control and Prevention: Atlanta, 2000).

7. Joel H. Brown, Marianne D'Emidio-Caston, and John A. Pollard, "Students and Substances: Social Power in Drug Education," *Educational Evaluation and Policy Analysis* 19 (1) (Spring 1997):65–82.

8. Kevin B. Smith, "Data Don't Matter? Academic Research and School Choice," *Perspectives on Politics* 3 (2005):285–299.

9. James Gosling, *Understanding, Informing, and Appraising Public Policy* (Longman: New York, 2004).

10. Ibid., 107.

11. James Anderson, *Public Policymaking*, 5th ed. (Houghton Mifflin: Boston, 2003).

12. Ibid., 223.

13. John Scholz and Neil Pinney, "Duty, Fear, and Tax Compliance: The Heuristic Basis of Citizenship Behavior," *American Journal of Political Science* 39 (1995):490–512.

14. Peter Jacobson and Jeffrey Wasserman, *Tobacco Control Laws: Implementation and Enforcement* (RAND Corporation: Santa Monica, CA, 1997); Michael J. Licari, "Bureaucratic Discretion and Regulatory Success Without Enforcement," in *Politics, Policy, and Organizations: Frontiers in the Scientific Study of Bureaucracy*, eds. George Krause and Kenneth J. Meier (University of Michigan Press: Ann Arbor, MI, 2003).

15. Anderson, *Public Policymaking*.

16. Anne Schneider and Helen Ingram, "Behavioral Assumptions of Policy Tools," *Journal of Politics* 52 (1990):510–529.

17. *New York Times*, "NASA Plans to Cut Aviation Research 20% Dismays Experts," March 17, 2005; *New York Times*, "Scientific Group Criticized NASA Budget Cuts," June 8, 2005.

18. Daniel Mazmanian and Paul A. Sabatier, *Implementation and Public Policy* (University Press of America: Lanham, MD, 1989).

19. Ibid.

20. Anne Schneider and Helen Ingram, "Social Constructions of Target Populations: Implications for Politics and Policy," *American Political Science Review* 87 (1993):334–347.

21. The following discussion is based on Anne Schneider and Helen Ingram, *Policy Design for Democracy* (University Press of Kansas: Lawrence, 1997).

22. Mazmanian and Sabatier, *Implementation and Public Policy*.

23. U.S. Census Bureau, *Historical Poverty Tables*, http://www.census.gov/hhes/income/histinc/histpovtb.html.

24. Kenneth J. Meier, "Bureaucracy and Democracy: The Case for More Bureaucracy and Less Democracy," *Public Administration Review* 57 (1997):193–199.

25. Mazmanian and Sabatier, *Implementation and Public Policy*.

26. Meier, "Bureaucracy and Democracy."

27. Theodore Lowi, *The End of Liberalism,* 2nd ed. (Norton: New York, 1979).
28. Purpose statement from the Cedar Falls, Iowa, police department.
29. Gosling, *Understanding, Informing, and Appraising Public Policy.*
30. Ibid., 107.
31. Pressman and Wildavsky call these decisions "clearance points;" Jeffrey Pressman and Aaron Wildavsky, *Implementation* (University of California Press: Berkeley, 1973).
32. "Florida's Legislature Redoubles Its Effort to Restrict Rulemaking Authority," *Administrative and Regulatory Law News* 25 (1) (1999): News from the States section.
33. Equal Employment Opportunity Commission website, "1965–1971: A 'Toothless Tiger' Helps Shape the Law and Educate the Public," http://www.eeoc.gov/abouteeoc/35th/1965-71/index.html.
34. Christopher Hood, *The Limits of Administration* (John Wiley: New York, 1976).
35. James Q. Wilson, *Bureaucracy* (Basic Books: New York, 1989).
36. Michael Lipsky, "Street Level Bureaucracy and the Analysis of Urban Reform," *Urban Affairs Quarterly* 6 (1971):391–409.
37. Ibid., 36.
38. Lowi, *The End of Liberalism.*
39. Wilson, *Bureaucracy,* 83–89.
40. Barry Bozeman, *Bureaucracy and Red Tape* (Prentice Hall: Upper Saddle River, NJ, 1999).
41. Graham Allison, *Essence of Decision Making* (Addison-Wesley: Boston, 1972).
42. Christopher Hood, *The Limits of Administration* (John Wiley: New York, 1976).
43. Pressman and Wildavsky, *Implementation.*

Chapter 11

1. D.M. West, "Assessing E-Government: The Internet, Democracy and Service Delivery by State and Federal Governments" (World Bank, 2000), http://www1.worldbank.org/publicsector/egov/EgovReportUs00.htm.
2. Ellen Perlman, "eGovernment Special Report," *Governing Magazine* (2002), http://www.governing.com/archive/2002/sep/eg2c.txt.
3. M. Moon Jae, "The Evolution of E-Government Among Muncipalities: Rhetoric or Reality?" *Public Administration Review* 62 (2002):424–434; Darrell West, "E-Government and the Transformation of Service Delivery and Citizen Attitudes," *Public Administration Review* 64 (2004):15–27.
4. H. George Frederickson and Kevin B. Smith, *The Public Administration Theory Primer* (Westview Press: Boulder, CO, 2003) 215.
5. Ibid., 222.
6. Christopher Lee, "For Homeland Agency, Transition Just Starting," *Washington Post,* March 4, 2003.
7. Philip Shenon, "Establishing New Agency is Expected to Take Years and Could Divert it From Mission," *New York Times,* November 19, 2003.

8. Charles Pope, "War on Terrorism: Security Costs Weigh Heavily at Local Level," *Seattle Post-Intelligencer,* Feb. 10, 2003, http://seattlepi.nwsource.com/local/107967/homeland10.shtml.

9. Ibid.

10. Gregory Lewis and Sue Frank, "Who Wants to Work for the Government?," *Public Administration Review* 62(4) (2002): 395–404.

11. Ibid.

12. Dwight Waldo, *The Administrative State* (Chandler: San Francisco, 1948).

13. For an example of these differences see Robert D. Behn, "The Big Questions of Public Management," *Public Administration Review* 55 (1995):313–325; John J. Kirlin, "The Big Questions of Public Administration in a Democracy," *Public Administration Review* 56 (1996): 416–423.

14. Frederickson and Smith, *The Public Administration Theory Primer,* 246. ◆

Photo Credits

Chapter 1

Page 6—iStock; page 15—iStock.

Chapter 2

Page 32—Library of Congress, Prints and Photographs Division, FSA-OWI Collection, LC-USF34-100602-D; page 33—Library of Congress, Prints & Photographs Division, FSA/OWI Collection, LC-USF34-009098.

Chapter 3

Page 49—United States Army, photo by Spc. Jeffery Sanstrum; page 56—iStock.

Chapter 4

Page 77—Library of Congress, Prints and Photographs Division LC-USZ62-13028; page 83—iStock.

Chapter 5

Page 109—National Archives and Records Administration; page 118—© John Nordell/The Image Works.

Chapter 6

Page 126—United States Army, photo by Spc. Bill Putnam; page 129—Library of Congress.

Chapter 7

Page 157—Courtesy of the Agricultural Research Service, photo by Bruce Fritz.

Chapter 8
Page 193—U.S. Air Force, photo by John Rossino; page 197—www.governor.state.mn.us.

Chapter 9
Page 216—Nast, Thomas, artist. "Tweed-le-dee and Tilden-dum." *Harper's Weekly,* July 1, 1876. Prints and Photographs Division, Library of Congress, LC-USZ62-117137; page 219—Library of Congress.

Chapter 10
Page 250—iStock; page 255—Photo by Mark Ide; page 263—U.S. Air Force.

Chapter 11
Page 281—Department of Defense; page 286—Library of Congress.

Author Index

Subject Index

311

CPSIA information can be obtained
at www.ICGtesting.com
Printed in the USA
BVOW07s2335070816

458088BV00009B/9/P